BARRON'S

WRITING WORKBOOK
for the
NEW SAT*

4TH EDITION

George Ehrenhaft, Ed.D.
Former Chairman of the English Department
Mamaroneck High School, Mamaroneck, NY

BARRON'S

*SAT is a registered trademark of the College Board, which was not involved in the production of, and does not endorse, this product.

All inquiries should be addressed to:
Barron's Educational Series, Inc.
250 Wireless Boulevard
Hauppauge, New York 11788
www.barronseduc.com

Library of Congress Catalog Card No. 2015949750

ISBN: 978-1-4380-0623-9

PRINTED IN THE UNITED STATES OF AMERICA

9 8 7 6 5 4 3 2 1

10%
POST-CONSUMER
WASTE
Paper contains a minimum
of 10% post-consumer
waste (PCW). Paper used
in this book was derived
from certified, sustainable
forestlands.

Contents

Greetings from the Author v

SAT Writing Overview vii

SECTION ONE: THE WRITING AND LANGUAGE TEST

1 Overview 3

Answering the Questions 4

Sample Questions 5

Questions on Organization 6

Questions on Style and Expression 24

Questions on Sentences 33

Questions on Standard English Usage 66

Answer Key to Mini-Workouts 92

2 Writing and Language Practice Tests 103

Practice Writing and Language Test A 107

Answer Key 117

Answer Explanations 117

Practice Writing and Language Test B 135

Answer Key 145

Answer Explanations 145

Practice Writing and Language Test C 163

Answer Key 174

Answer Explanations 174

SECTION TWO: THE SAT ESSAY

3 Getting Acquainted with the SAT Essay 193

Overview of the "Optional" Essay 193

What to Expect on Test Day 193

The Essay Topic: What You'll Write About 194

The Essay "Prompt" 196

How the Essay Is Scored 197

Use of Your Essay Score 199

4 Getting Prepped to Write 201

Reading the Source 201

Finding the Evidence 204

Screening the Evidence 222

Annotating: The Gold Standard of Source Analysis 228

Practice in Annotation 233

Answer Key to Mini-Workouts 247

5   How to Write an Analytical Essay in 3,000 Seconds 257

Tactics for Writing a 4/4/4 Essay 258

Planning Your Essay.. 261

SAT Essays: What to Say and How to Say It 279

Answer Key to Mini-Workouts 299

6   You Be the Ump: Essays for Evaluation 305

SAT Essay Readers: What They Do and How They Do It...................... 305

Essay Scoring Guide 306

Essays for Evaluation 307

7   Practice, Practice, Practice 341

Practice Essay #1 342

Practice Essay #2 348

Practice Essay #3 354

Practice Essay #4 360

Practice Essay #5 366

Index 373

Greetings from the Author

Hello, and welcome to the world of the SAT, in particular, to the two parts of the SAT that relate specifically to writing:

1. The Writing and Language Test
2. The SAT Essay

Your performance on the **Writing and Language Test**, along with your performance on the reading section of the SAT, will determine your overall **verbal** score on the SAT. (As you probably know, you'll also get a **math** score.) The Writing and Language Test asks you to read short passages of nonfiction and answer multiple-choice questions about them. Its main purpose is not to assess your comprehension of the passage—as on the Reading Test—but rather to see how well you can identify and analyze, among other things, effectiveness of expression, paragraph development, matters of sentence structure, word choice, and the use of standard written English.

As for the optional SAT Essay, it's possible that you've never before been asked to write anything exactly like it. You'll be given a prose passage to read. Instead of writing about what the passage says, you'll be asked to analyze how the author wrote it—that is, you are to discuss the writing techniques the author used to make a case in behalf of a particular point of view.

Does all this sound daunting? If so, not to worry, for you're holding in your hands a book that will give you everything you need to do well on the SAT.... Well, almost everything. The time, a writing implement, and the determination to perform splendidly on the exam—those things are up you.

If the SAT is weeks or months away, let this book work for you. Use it regularly and often. Let it acquaint you with the format of the Writing and Language Test. Take the practice tests provided. Let it also accustom you to writing clear, coherent, and purposeful analytical essays in 50 minutes. Read and evaluate actual essays composed by high school juniors and seniors as they prepared themselves for the SAT Essay.

Much of the book consists of a handy guide to writing. It contains thumbnail reviews of English grammar, writing exercises called Mini-Workouts, and several prompts to give you practice in writing SAT-type essays.

I've done a mountain of work to write this book for you. Now it's time for you to shake a leg and get started.

Best of luck! I'll be rooting for you every step of the way.

George Ehrenhaft

SAT Writing Overview

The new SAT is a three-hour multiple-choice exam that covers math and verbal skills. Eighty minutes are devoted to math, 65 minutes to reading, and the remaining 35 minutes to the Writing and Language Test.

In addition, the SAT offers an optional essay to be written during a 50-minute block of time following the scheduled three-hour testing period.

Format of the New SAT

Reading	52 multiple-choice questions	65 minutes
Writing and Language*	44 multiple-choice questions	35 minutes
Math	58 multiple-choice questions	80 minutes
SAT Essay (Optional)*	1 Essay	50 minutes

*This book is a complete guide to prepare you for the Writing and Language section and for the optional SAT Essay.

Both the Writing and Language section and the SAT Essay give you an opportunity to show that you're ready to deal successfully with college-level work.

Questions in the Writing and Language Test pertain to revising and editing the text of four reading passages, one each drawn from the fields of history/social studies, the humanities, science, and careers. Accompanying each multiparagraph passage, you'll find 11 multiple-choice questions that will ask you, among other things, to identify the best way to revise sentences that need some sort of help. They might, for example, be irrelevant to the topic of the passage or be awkwardly expressed or poorly structured. Or they might contain errors in standard English usage. Some sentences may be misplaced within the passage or paragraph or incorrectly state information drawn from data presented in a chart or graph related to the topic of the passage.

The SAT Essay, as its name suggests, asks you to write an essay that analyzes the writing in a nonfiction prose passage. The passage will be one in which the writer takes a stand on an issue and tries to persuade readers that his position is valid. In other words, the passage is written as an argument in behalf of particular point of view. Your job is not to comment on the validity of the writer's position but to analyze how the writer uses evidence to build an argument. You might, for instance, discuss the facts and examples the writer uses to back up particular claims or show how the writer uses logic to build a persuasive case or pick out individual words and phrases chosen to appeal to readers' emotions.

Writing the essay is an option, but some students must write it anyway in order to apply to colleges that require it for admission. Turn to Section 2 of this book for more detailed information on exercising the option.

TEST SCORES

Your performance on the Writing and Language section of the SAT, along with your performance on the reading section of the SAT, will determine your overall verbal SAT score.

Test results are reported in a number of different ways, probably too complicated to worry about at this point in your preparation for the SAT. Let it suffice to say that everybody gets two Section scores, one in Evidenced-Based Reading and Writing the other in Math. Each score is reported on a scale of 200 to 800. If you write the essay, the results are reported in a separate score.

You'll also receive three Test scores in Reading, in Writing and Language, and in Math. Add to them several "Cross-Test," scores on a 10 to 40 scale, as well as "subscores" ranging from 1 to 15. All these numbers are meant to give you a multidimensional picture of your performance in reading, writing, science, history/social studies, standard English usage, the expression of ideas, and various aspects of math.

USING THIS BOOK

Chapter 1 of this book explains what the SAT Writing and Language Test is all about. Be sure to study these pages and complete the Mini-Workouts exercises to tune you up for a high score.

Chapter 2 consists of three full-length practice tests, with all the answers fully explained. Allow 35 minutes for each test.

Chapter 3 describes the SAT Essay and details the assignment, or prompt. You'll also find an explanation of what you are expected to write and how the essay is scored.

Chapter 4 is about reading and annotating passages, or "sources," in order to write about them. Sample passages are included for practice.

Chapter 5 takes you through the process of writing a clear, insightful, and correct analytical essay. It includes guidelines for what to do and what to avoid.

Chapter 6 puts you to work evaluating a collection of good, medium, and poor SAT-type essays. Compare your assessments with those of experienced SAT Essay readers.

Chapter 7 is for practice, practice, practice. Five sources are waiting to have you write essays about them. A Self-Scoring Guide will help you grade your essays.

Throughout the book you'll find numerous samples of essay excerpts and complete essays, some good and some not so good. Let them serve as models of what to do and what to avoid when you write your own essay.

SECTION ONE
The Writing and Language Test

Overview

1

→ **ANSWERING THE QUESTIONS**
→ **SAMPLE QUESTIONS**
→ **QUESTIONS ON ORGANIZATION**
→ **QUESTIONS ON STYLE AND EXPRESSION**
→ **QUESTIONS ON SENTENCES**
→ **QUESTIONS ON STANDARD ENGLISH USAGE**

Twenty percent of the SAT is devoted to the Writing and Language Test. During the 35 minutes it takes to complete, you won't actually write anything. Instead, you'll answer 44 multiple-choice questions about revising, editing, and improving the text of four nonfiction prose passages, each about 450 words long.

Each passage comes with 11 questions about such matters as the choice of words, sentence structure, and use of standard English. Most questions, however, pertain to effective English expression, the organization and development of paragraphs, and other elements of style and usage.

At least one of the passages will include a graph or a chart—along with a question that asks about how accurately the passage interprets the visual presentation of data. One of the four passages comes from a scientific field such as biology, earth science, and oceanography. A second passage relates to one of the social sciences, including history, economics, the law, and psychology. A third passage will pertain to an area of the humanities—art, music, literature, and so forth—and the fourth one will discuss trends, issues, and other matters related to careers and the world of work.

In addition to being drawn from separate fields of study, the passages represent three different genres. One of them will be a nonfiction narrative—an account of an event or set of circumstances related to science, history, or one of the other fields. In addition, one passage—or sometimes two—will be in the form of an argument, in which the writer espouses a certain point of view on an issue. If two of the passages are arguments, the remaining passage will be informative or explanatory—in other words, it is meant to acquaint readers with facts and ideas about a particular topic. Similarly, if only one passage is argumentative, the other two will be informative or explanatory.

Four Passages on the Test

1 non-fiction narrative

1 or 2 argumentative

1 or 2 informative/explanatory

ANSWERING THE QUESTIONS

Each question focuses on a writing weakness or error that needs revision or correction. Because the sum of potential writing problems dwarfs the number of questions on the exam, you'll need to know far more about writing than you'll use on the test. To prepare, therefore, you should familiarize yourself with the range of writing problems that might show up. And here's some good news: That's what the pages ahead will help you do.

Whatever you learn, whether or not it shows up on the test, is bound to reward you in the future. First, the odds are that your own writing will improve, and what's more, you're bound to become a more adept and alert writer, thereby avoiding the pitfalls that beset less able writers.

Each multiple-choice question on the test comes with four possible answers: A, B, C, or D. Before deciding on the best answer, be sure to read all the choices. Try to articulate why you reject each incorrect choice. Once you've eliminated even one choice the chances of hitting the jackpot are one in three. By eliminating two wrong answers, they jump to 50-50—very decent odds in any circumstances.

TIP

Answer every question. You won't be penalized for wrong answers.

If a question stumps you, don't panic, and don't let it slow you down. Mark it with your pencil and go on to questions that you can answer more easily. Later, come back to it. If you still can't come up with a decent answer, guess. Be sure to answer every question. You won't lose credit for a wrong answer, but it's guaranteed that you won't earn any credit by leaving a blank space on your answer sheet.

Because there's no predicting which writing issues you'll encounter, it pays to know the possibilities. What follows is a menu of topics you may be questioned about. Study them all, and if in doubt about any of them, study them again. Then check your mastery of topics by completing the "Mini-Workouts" scattered throughout this chapter

QUESTIONS ON ORGANIZATION

1. Purpose/main idea, p. 6
2. Sequence/coherence, p. 9
3. Evidence to support claims, p. 12
4. Transitions, p. 21
5. Interpretation of data from a graph, chart, or table, p. 23

QUESTIONS ON STYLE AND EXPRESSION

6. Words in context, p. 24
7. Standard idiom, p. 25
8. Wordiness, p. 28
9. Awkwardness, p. 30
10. Redundancy and repetition, p. 31

QUESTIONS ON SENTENCES

11. Sentences, p. 33
    11A. Subjects and predicates, p. 33
    11B. Clauses, p. 34
12. Combining and augmenting sentences, p. 41

13. Mixed construction, p. 44

14. Coordination and subordination, p. 47

15. Parallel structure, p. 50

16. Active and passive construction, p. 54

17. Misplaced and dangling modifiers, p. 56

18. Punctuation, p. 59

QUESTIONS ON STANDARD ENGLISH USAGE

19. Noun–verb agreement, p. 66

20. Verbs, p. 72

    20A. Verb tenses, p. 72

    20B. Verb forms, p. 75

21. Pronouns, p. 77

    21A. Pronoun choice, p. 77

    21B. Pronoun agreement with antecedent, p. 82

    21C. Pronoun reference, p. 84

22. Comparisons, p. 87

A WORD OF ENCOURAGEMENT ABOUT GRAMMAR

If your sense of English grammar is rusty, or even if grammar is a complete mystery, take heart. This book covers *virtually* all you need to know for the test and is meant to help you earn a score to make you proud.

Virtually is the key word, however, because a complete guide to English grammar lies beyond the scope of these pages. If you're even a little bit inclined to master the ever-challenging but fascinating nitty-gritty of grammar, however, look online, where you'll find literally dozens of grammar sites with names such as *Grammarbook.com*, *EnglishGrammar.org*, and *UsingEnglish.com*. Or check the catalog of the publisher of this book, Barron's, for a selection of popular grammar books. In a pinch, take yourself to the library or ask your English teacher to lend you a grammar book until the SAT is behind you.

SAMPLE QUESTIONS

Most questions on the Writing and Language Test consist of a sentence or more that includes an underscored word or group of words. Your job is to decide which of four alternatives (A, B, C, or D) best conforms to the conventions of standard written English. Choice A is often "NO CHANGE," meaning, of course, that the underlined words should remain as they are.

Note: For clarity and brevity, each sample question that follows is based on the text of a single sentence or a short excerpt from a passage. During the actual Writing and Language Test, though, as you decide how to revise and edit text, you'll have to keep in mind the meaning, style, and other characteristics of individual paragraphs or in some cases, the entire passage.

QUESTIONS ON ORGANIZATION

1. Purpose/Main Idea

Almost any topic is fair game for passages used on the Writing and Language Test. More important than the topic itself, however, is what the writer has to say about the topic. In other words, the passage must have a point—a main idea. A passage may be written with beautiful words, contain profound thoughts, make readers laugh or weep. But without a unifying central idea it remains a void, befuddling readers who've arrived at the end only to scratch their heads and ask "Huh? What's the point?"

On the test, main-idea questions ask test-takers to identify the idea that best articulates the point of the passage or paragraph. If you decide that the underlined sentence is the best answer, choose A. NO CHANGE. Otherwise choose B, C, or D.

➡ SAMPLE QUESTION #1 _____

For those who favor a rural lifestyle, Llewelyn County is a kind of paradise. The population of Llewelyn County in its southeastern quadrant was 19,788, according to the last census. The county's eastern half is fertile. On both sides of the nonnavigable river that runs east to west across the county are miles and miles of soybean and cotton fields. In the hills are farms raising livestock and poultry. Family farms employ more than 80 percent of the county's work force. A board of supervisors, consisting of 17 representatives elected to two-year terms, governs the county. Two are general farmers, one a rice grower, one a poultry producer. In addition, there are six bankers and three industrial workers. The remainder are local business owners and homemakers.

Which choice best conveys the central idea of the passage?

A. NO CHANGE
B. A diverse population imposes real challenge on the governing board of Llewelyn County.
C. Representative government is hardly more than illusion in Llewelyn County.
D. In spite of its rural lifestyle, representative democracy is alive and well in Llewelyn County.

Answer Explanation

Choice C is the best answer because the writer emphasizes that, although the vast majority of the county's population works in agriculture, the county board of supervisors consists largely of non-farming representatives.

Choice A is not the best answer. Although it may be an accurate statement, the writer says almost nothing about the county being an ideal place to live.

Choice B is not the best answer because it consists of a claim about Llewelyn County cannot be supported by evidence in the passage.

Choice D is not the best answer. In fact, it seems to contradict the paragraph's main idea.

Questions on the central idea of a passage or paragraph have several purposes, among them to test your ability to determine whether a writer has used sound evidence to support a claim. Central idea questions also relate to paragraph development, coherence, and unity. To determine the best answer to a central idea question, you'll need a firm grip of the content of the passage or paragraph.

➡ SAMPLE QUESTION #2

Though the ancestry of the poet Robert Frost was New England, he was born in California. The most American of poets, he was first recognized in England and not in the United States. Not believing in competitions, he never entered them. Yet, he won the Pulitzer Prize in poetry four times. The rough conversational tones of his verse are remarkable for their lyrical music. Though he chose one part of the country on which to focus his work, no poetry has ever been so universal.

Which choice most accurately captures the main idea of the paragraph?

A. Robert Frost is considered the "most American of poets" because his verses are often patriotic.

B. A distinctive characteristic of Robert Frost's poetry is its association with one section of the country.

C. There are curious contradictions in the life and work of Robert Frost.

D. The author believes that Robert Frost's life was typical of a poet's life.

Answer Explanation

This question, based on an excerpt from a humanities passage, tests your grasp of the paragraph's central point. Each choice may correspond to information or a specific idea found in the paragraph, but your task is to choose the answer that applies more generally to the entire excerpt. Sometimes a main idea remains unstated but may nevertheless be implied by an accumulation of certain details or even the writer's choice of words, images, or tone.

Choice C is the best answer because the passage consists entirely of a series of incongruities, or paradoxical pieces of information.

Choice A is not the best answer because Frost's patriotic verse is not mentioned in the paragraph.

Choice B is not the best answer because it refers to an idea discussed only briefly in the paragraph and, therefore, doesn't warrant being its central idea.

Choice D is not the best answer because it brings up an idea unrelated to the content of the paragraph.

Mini-Workout in Choosing a Main Idea

> **Directions:** Respond to each of the following prompts by writing three or more sentences that could serve as main ideas for an essay.

1. "Whether you think you can, or that you can't, you are usually right."

   Henry Ford, 1863–1947

   Assignment: Does attitude determine success and failure in an endeavor?

   A. _____

   B. _____

   C. _____

2. There's an old proverb, "Spare the rod and spoil the child."

   Assignment: Which is a more effective way to teach children to behave—to promise rewards or to instill a fear of punishment?

   A. _____

   B. _____

   C. _____

3. Advertisements for the New York State Lottery say "All you need is a dollar and a dream," a slogan that encourages the fantasy that a big win will solve all of life's problems. Yet, many lottery winners have suffered unexpected negative consequences. Their dreams have often turned into nightmares, and their lives are worse than they were before.

   Assignment: Should state and local governments sponsor lotteries that can leave both winners and losers worse off than before?

   A. _____

   B. _____

   C. _____

4. "There is nothing like returning to a place that remains unchanged to find the ways in which you yourself have altered."

   Nelson Mandela, *A Long Walk to Freedom*

   Assignment: Do we need to understand our past in order to understand ourselves?

   A. _____

   B. _____

   C. _____

5. "Destiny is not a matter of chance. It is a matter of choice. It is not a thing to be waited for, it is a thing to be achieved."

William Jennings Bryan (1860–1925)

Assignment: Do you think that a destiny achieved by the decisions and choices you have made is preferable to a destiny that comes from chance or luck?

A. _____

B. _____

C. _____

Suggested answers are on page 92.

2. Sequence/Coherence

When a passage or paragraph discusses more than one main idea, it lacks unity. When its sentences skip from topic to topic, it lacks coherence, or cohesion. On the Writing and Language Test, you're apt to find questions about alien sentences—sentences that are out of place and, therefore, undermine a paragraph's unity or weaken its coherence. In the following paragraph, for instance, pay close attention to sentence 4. Explain why it shouldn't be hanging out between sentences 3 and 5.

[1] Like many other leaders throughout history, George Washington established his authority through the force of his personality. [2] Almost everyone who met him thought that he was charming, dignified, charismatic. [3] Some people of the time referred to him as a "superior being." [4] Yet the Father of Our Country had been soundly defeated in 1755, when he first sought elective office. [5] At six-feet two-inches in his stockings, he was taller and more impressive than most men of his time. [6] His frame was padded with well-developed muscles, indicating great strength, and his blue-grey eyes could sparkle with humor at one moment and grow hard and determined at the next. [7] John Adams described him as a "gentleman whose great talents and excellent universal character...would command the respect of all the Colonies."

The paragraph's purpose is to describe the power of Washington's personality. Because sentence 4 fails to contribute to this laudatory portrait of our first president, it should be deleted.

➡ SAMPLE QUESTION _____

[1] In wartime, the military develops a way of speaking that disguises meaning and makes the horrors of battle less dirty and gruesome. [2] In Vietnam, when our own troops were shelled by mistake, the event was called "an accidental delivery of ordnance equipment." [3] The use of euphemisms enables both soldiers and civilians to keep a psychological distance and turn war into an antiseptic, clinical abstraction. [4] In the Gulf War, as well as during the Iraq and Afghanistan conflicts, "friendly fire" became the phrase of choice. [5] When wayward bombs killed innocent civilians, "incontinent ordnance" was responsible for causing "collateral damage." [6] Arms and legs were not blown off in combat; they were severed in a "traumatic amputation." [7] Such euphemisms, according to language experts, can be

protective, but at the same time, they put us in danger of losing the real sense of war's ghastliness.

For the sake of cohesion in this paragraph, sentence 3 should be placed

    A. where it is now.

    B. before sentence 1.

    C. after sentence 1.

    D. after sentence 7.

Answer Explanation

Choice C is the best answer because locating sentence 3 after sentence 1 enables the writer to cite *euphemisms* as an example of a "way of speaking" mentioned in sentence 1. Moreover, in its new location, sentence 3 develops the claim made in sentence 1 that the military's way of speaking reduces the horrors of battle. Altogether, then, the new location of sentence 3 enhances the coherence of the paragraph.

Choice A is not the best answer because sentence 1 introduces the idea of a special wartime "way of speaking" that lessens the horrors of battle. Because that kind of speech—*euphemisms*—is identified in sentence 3, leaving sentence 2 in place interrupts the flow of ideas and weakens the overall coherence of the paragraph.

Choice B is not the best answer because sentence 1 in its present position serves as the topic sentence of the paragraph, conveying the general idea that language has an effect on how we deal with wartime horrors. If sentence 3 were to become sentence 1, readers would come away with the impression that the paragraph's purpose is far narrower.

Choice D is not the best answer because the content of sentence 3 needs to be revealed early in the passage. As the last sentence in the paragraph, it would be anticlimactic, redundant, and largely irrelevant.

Mini-Workout in Sequencing Sentences

> **Directions:** The sentences in each group make up a paragraph. But they are not in the proper order. In the blank spaces write the number that represents the proper place of each sentence in the paragraph.

1. ____ a. In the end, morale got so low that members started quitting the team.

    ____ b. Whether you were a polevaulter, a sprinter, or a distance runner, practices were the same for everyone.

    ____ c. He was forcing the team to work out the same way every day.

    ____ d. Mr. Reese, the track coach, had been acting like a tyrant.

2. ____ a. First, put in the large, firm, and heavy items that won't be crushed or damaged by putting something on top of them.

____ b. Meanwhile, think of all the items that can be easily bruised, crushed, or broken, such as eggs, packages of bread, fruit, and light bulbs.

____ c. To fill up a paper bag with groceries usually takes about fifteen seconds if you do it right.

____ d. Immediately after that, put in light but firm items such as crackers, cereal, and butter.

____ e. Canned goods and bottles fit the bill perfectly.

____ f. Those should be saved for last.

3. ____ a. Then, too, I started feeling comfortable talking with adults.

____ b. Most people think of "maturity" in terms of responsibility, but I think it has more to do with learning to control one's actions.

____ c. I could actually talk to them instead of shutting up like a clam and just standing there like a dummy.

____ d. For example, I knew that I was more mature than others when I didn't laugh out loud in science class when the teacher talked about reproduction.

4. ____ a. As blood circulates, it cleans out body waste, like the collector who cruises the neighborhood picking up trash.

____ b. In return, it deposits oxygen and food in every body part, from the top of the head to the little toe.

____ c. Yet human life depends on those four quarts of blood that are pumped from the heart, flow to every cell in the body, and return to the heart to be pumped again.

____ d. If you drained the blood from the body of a girl weighing about 125 pounds, you would fill little more than a gallon milk container.

5. ____ a. The essay was to be handed in on Monday morning.

____ b. The first part of the exam was a take-home essay in which we were to answer one of three questions.

____ c. On Friday night I settled myself down with my textbook and took exceptionally detailed notes.

____ d. Four weeks ago, I, like many other eleventh graders, worked hard to prepare for an American History midterm exam.

____ e. The next day, determined to have more information than I could use when I began to write the essay, I went to the public library to do further research.

6. ____ a. His mistake was corrected fifty years later by Carl Blegen of the University of Chicago.

____ b. He figured out that every few centuries a new city had been built upon the ruins of the old.

____ c. In the 1870s, the archeologist Heinrich Schliemann dug in the correct spot and discovered nine ancient cities of Troy, one lying on top of the other.

____ d. But without realizing it, Schliemann had dug right past the layer he had been seeking, the layer containing the ruins of the famous city of the Trojan Horse.

____ e. By then, it was too late for Schliemann, who had been dead for fifty years.

7. ____ a. For months at a time Jerry's fans would devotedly follow his group around the country wherever it played in concert.

____ b. Just two years after its debut, Jerry and his band left an indelible mark on millions of young fans.

____ c. In spite of his family, who told him that he would never be a successful professional singer, Jerry decided to take up guitar and form a musical group.

____ d. He not only created a whole new subculture but developed a following.

8. ____ a. He felt terribly anxious about his wounded leg.

____ b. The slightest movement of his knee caused a sudden and intense pain, unlike anything he had ever felt before.

____ c. He could not sleep, in spite of the sedative administered to him by the British nurse.

____ d. In Milan, the lieutenant lay in a hospital bed.

____ e. It was even worse than the pain he recalled when, as a child, he had pulled a pot of steaming water over on himself.

9. ____ a. Each layer is another page that tells the story of volcanic eruptions, massive floods, and the advance and retreat of the Ice Age.

____ b. Unfortunately, it also tells of the present day's pollution of the earth's air and lands.

____ c. If you can read its language, the sediments contain a record of all the dramatic and catastrophic events that have occurred through the earth's history.

____ d. The ocean floor is a diary of the earth.

10. ____ a. He became blind in 1652 and used his daughter as an instrument to write some of his finest poems.

____ b. His daughter, with her quill pen in hand, sat with her father to record his thoughts, to read them back, to make revisions in whatever way Milton wanted.

____ c. The first poet to use a word processor was John Milton.

____ d. The actual processing of words went on in Milton's head.

11. ____ a. After winning two Critics' Circle awards and the Pulitzer Prize for drama, Tennessee Williams earned fame and lots of money.

____ b. Usually, he's named with Eugene O'Neill and Arthur Miller as one of the leading American dramatists of the twentieth century.

____ c. They flocked to Broadway to see his plays and later swarmed to the movies to see filmed versions of his works.

____ d. All of a sudden, the public began to view him as one of the best of the modern playwrights.

Answers are on page 93.

3. Evidence to Support Claims

Most paragraphs are made up of two kinds of sentences: **Topic sentences**, which tell readers generally what the paragraph is about, and **supporting sentences** that provide evidence to back up the claim made by the topic sentence. Supporting sentences themselves occasionally need support that is provided by minor, or secondary, supporting sentences. The paragraph that follows contains examples of each kind of sentence:

[1] Children with IQs well below average represent an almost insoluble problem for educators. [2] Such children often feel inadequate, rejected by teachers and peers in a school environment that values and rewards academic success. [3] Failure in school is the number one cause of poor behavior in school and of juvenile delinquency in general. [4] The best that schools can do for children with low IQs is to teach them how to get by in the world and to teach them a vocation. [5] But vocational training is very limited in many schools. [6] Those that provide such training usually do so only for older adolescents.

Sentence 1 is the topic sentence of the paragraph. To be convincing, it needs the support of sentences 2–5. Each supporting sentence adds a piece of evidence to prove the point of the paragraph—that children with low IQs create a problem for schools. Sentence 5 is a supporting sentence that requires additional support, provided by sentence 6.

Location of Topic Sentences. Although a topic sentence may be anywhere in a paragraph, it usually appears at or close to the beginning. It isn't always a separate and independent sentence; it may be woven into a supporting sentence as a clause or phrase. (In the paragraph you are now reading, for example, the main idea is stated in the second clause of the initial sentence.) Writers vary the location of topic sentences to avoid monotony. They could, for example, save the topic sentence for the end, letting it stand out boldly as the climax of the paragraph. Or they might omit the topic sentence, letting an accumulation of telling details imply the paragraph's main idea.

Note the location of the topic sentence in each of the following paragraphs:

[1] It is pitch dark and very chilly. [2] No one in his right mind wants to pry open their eyes and leave the cozy warmth of bed and blanket. [3] No one wants to walk in bare feet across the frigid floor to peer out the window at the icy rain slanting down in the early morning gloom. [4] The thought of damp clothes and cold feet keeps you where you are, at least for a few more minutes. [5] **It's torture to get up on dark winter mornings.**

The supporting details in sentences 1–4 lead inevitably to sentence 5, the topic sentence, which summarizes the point of the paragraph.

On the Writing and Language Test you may be asked to identify the topic sentence of the passage itself or, if not that, the topic sentence of one of its paragraphs. In addition, a follow-up question may ask you to choose a quotation or other piece of evidence in the text that led you to your answer to the first question. In other words, you're being asked to demonstrate your awareness of how writers use evidence to build a case for the claims they make.

Let's say, for example, that you've identified sentence 3 as the topic sentence of the following paragraph:

[1] For a long time about 50,000 people were killed annually in automobile accidents on the nation's roads. [2] Reduced speed limits, seatbelt requirements, and increased police patrols had almost no effect on changing the number of fatalities. [3] **The most promising way to reduce fatalities, however, proved to be making cars safer.** [4] In addition to front and side

airbags, stronger steel frames enabled people to survive crashes that would certainly have killed them before. [5] Electronic devices warn drivers of approaching dangers in blind spots and alert them to road hazards, such as stopped traffic and bicycles ahead.

By placing the topic sentence in the middle of the paragraph, the author uses it as a pivot point between sentences 1 and 2, which describe the problem of automobile fatalities and list some ineffectual solutions, and sentences 4 and 5, which specify a handful of life-saving innovations.

A follow-up question might ask you to choose which sentence most effectively supports the claim made by the topic sentence.

A. Sentence 1
B. Sentence 2
C. Sentence 4
D. Sentence 5

Answer Explanation

Choice C is the best answer because sentence 4 states that improvements saved the lives of people who would have been killed without them. The other choices may have contributed to your selection of sentence 3 as the topic sentence, but it is not as compelling as sentence 4.

The key to unlocking a paragraph's purpose lies in the topic sentence, and the effectiveness of the paragraph depends on how tightly the topic sentence is linked to its supporting details. On the Writing and Language Test, you may be asked to improve a paragraph by tightening that link.

➡ SAMPLE QUESTION

Designers of book covers work for publishing companies to convert hundreds of pages of words into a modest rectangle of color, shape, and pattern that for most readers will be their first impression of a book (and for many others their last). Their tools are manifold but finite. Greenfield, a methodical thinker, lists the possible subjects of a book's cover art: character, object, event, place, time, text samples, tone, plot, theme, and parallel imagery. Of course, these are not equal choices. Pictures of people should generally be avoided, because they can "rob readers of their satisfying acts of imagination." Objects work better, because they are "saturate with metaphoric potential." The worst cover Greenfield labels "The Tell-All": it is crammed with illustrations of plot events. "Only one part of the author's output is being addressed here—the most mundane part, namely: 'what happens during the course of a given tale.'" Greenfield writes. "I detest this kind of book jacket."

(Adapted from Joshua J. Friedman, "Reviews: Full Mental Jacket," *Columbia Magazine*, Fall, 2014, pp. 56–7.)

Which of the following choices most accurately states the main topic of the paragraph?

A. Greenfield believes that human faces should not be put on book covers.
B. Fictional books' jackets must convey key moments in the plot of the book.

C. Booksellers believe that a book's design is no less important than its contents.

D. Book designers like Greenfield translate words into a visual medium that will attract buyers.

Answer Explanation

Choice D is the best answer because the paragraph discusses several ways in which the contents of books can be artistically represented on a book jacket.

Choice A is not the best answer because it is only one of several incidental statements in the paragraph.

Choice B is not the best answer because it misstates what book designers such as Greenfield believe.

Choice C is not the best answer. It may be a conclusion inferred from the paragraph, but it is not the writer's main concern.

Mini-Workout in Developing Topic Sentences

PART A

> **Directions:** The following paragraphs have been taken from longer passages. Underline the topic sentence in each. Some paragraphs may have an implied topic sentence.

1. [1] My family has moved so often I sometimes feel like a gypsy. [2] The first time we moved I was only four years old, and it didn't bother me. [3] It seemed as though we just got settled, though, when my father announced a new transfer—to California, where I got to start school and where we stayed for three years. [4] But then we heard it was time to move on, and we settled in Minnesota. [5] Just as I began to make friends and get used to the Midwest, the company sent us to Georgia. [6] From there it was two years in England and a year in Washington, D.C. [7] We've been in Massachusetts for almost six months now, and my main problem is answering *that* question, "Where are you from?"

2. [1] Another difficulty is that a person with a police record may have a hard time getting or renewing a driver's license. [2] A conviction for a felony can prevent a person from being able to enter a profession such as medicine, law, or teaching. [3] It can also make it difficult to get a responsible position in business or industry. [4] Special hearings are required before an ex-convict can hold a government job.

3. [1] Music blasts from twenty boom boxes. [2] Children screech while splashing their friends at the edge of the sea. [3] Teenagers throw frisbees at each other. [4] The waves rush up the sand, gurgle a bit, stop, and retreat. [5] A single-engine plane, trailing a long sign—EAT PIZZA AT SAL'S—buzzes overhead. [6] A vendor shouts, "Hey, cold drinks here, getcha cold drinks." [7] During the summer the beach is a noisy place.

4. [1] Clothing designers create new styles every year. [2] Therefore, consumers rush out and buy the new styles and cast away last year's designs even before the clothes are worn out. [3] Forgotten styles hang in closets gathering dust. [4] They'll never be worn again. [5] People fall in love with new cars and sell their old models long before they are obsolete. [6] Just for the sake of flashy style and shiny good looks, they scrimp and save their money or go deeply into debt. [7] And for what? [8] Just to look good. [9] All the money goes into the pockets of the manufacturers. [10] If people would get in the habit of buying goods only when they need replacement, waste would become an exception in America instead of a way of life.

5. [1] Perhaps it's true that "all the world's a stage," as Shakespeare said, because I have noticed that I act one way with one group of people and another way with a different group. [2] With one person I may act like a little kid. [3] I may act very shy or silly. [4] It's as though I can't control what I'm doing. [5] The circumstances just make me act that way. [6] Then, at another time with different people, I am the life of the party. [7] I won't stop talking, and people think I am about 20 years old. [8] I feel that I can pretend so realistically that I sometimes convince myself that I really am what I'm pretending to be. [9] That's a very scary thought.

6. [1] To date, the Damon family has had about sixty foster children come into their house to live. [2] They have had children from all backgrounds, races, and religions. [3] Each child brought to their door brings a different tale of misfortune. [4] These stories have gradually grown worse over the years. [5] When they first started, the parents of the child usually wanted to keep him or her but were temporarily unable or unprepared to care for their son or daughter. [6] Now, it is not unusual for the mother to be sixteen years old, a drug addict, or a convict. [7] Most of the time the mother is a combination of those. [8] Right now, the Damons have two children living with them. [9] Three of their four parents are in jail, and one of the fathers is unknown. [10] Truly, as time goes on, caring for foster children has become more challenging.

7. [1] True totalitarianism champions the idea that everyone should be subservient to the state. [2] All personal goals and desires should be thrown aside unless they coincide with the common good of society. [3] Freedom for the individual is sacrificed so that the level of freedom for all can be raised. [4] With this philosophy, drastic improvements may be made in a relatively short time. [5] Almost by edict from the head of the society, education and literacy rates can be improved, and unemployment and crime rates may decrease.

8. [1] During adolescence the most obvious change that occurs is physical. [2] Childlike boys and girls suddenly blossom into young men and women. [3] Besides undergoing physical changes, though, this period is usually the time when personal values are explored and molded. [4] Decisions need to be made about what is important and what is not. [5] A struggle takes place within the mind of every adolescent to form a moral and intellectual code that determines the quality of the lives they will have in both the immediate and long-range future.

9. [1] The story by Stephen Crane raises the question whether a soldier who runs away from inevitable death in battle must be considered less of a man than one who stays and dies. [2] To answer the question, one must first define "man." [3] Consider the stereotypical options. [4] There is the Arnold Schwarzenegger type who solves all of life's problems with physical strength and advanced weapons. [5] Then there is the Howard Roark type, a character from *The Fountainhead*, who climbs to the top by using his brilliant mind and integrity. [6] Finally, there is the Willy Loman type, a character in *Death of a Salesman*, who struggles his whole life pursuing an illusion. [7] At the end, he realizes that he has fought a hopeless battle, but at least he has fought.

10. [1] In World War II, the United States dropped two atomic bombs, one on Hiroshima and one on Nagasaki, in order to defeat the Japanese. [2] American history textbooks justify the bombings as something that needed to be done in order to prevent even more deaths during a longer war. [3] Our history books also say that the death toll was about 50,000, while the Japanese claim the bombs took almost twice that many lives. [4] If the United States had lost the war, then the bombings would have been thought to be criminal actions. [5] But since we won, the judgment of history is that the end justifies the means. [6] In fact, throughout history, the war crimes of the victors have repeatedly been justified.

Answers are on page 93.

PART B

> **Directions:** Topic sentences have been deleted from the following paragraphs. After reading each paragraph, write an appropriate topic sentence in the space provided. Omit a topic sentence if none is needed.

1. _____

_____

One example of a self-destructive monopoly was the auto industry in the twentieth century. In order to maintain their grip on the domestic market, Chrysler, General Motors, and Ford squelched the competition. Inventions that might have helped them in the long run were ignored. Automobiles were changed very little from year to year. Millions of dollars more were budgeted for advertising than for improving either the cars themselves or the process of building them.

2. _____

_____

This was especially true in track and field. As other countries learned American techniques of training, however, their runners improved. Now athletes from all over the world win as many as or even more medals than American track and field athletes.

3. _____

_____

My mother's nature is very outgoing, emotional, and impulsive. She enjoys dancing, going to parties, being with lots of people, and spending money freely. My father, on the other hand, is quiet, reserved, and controlled. He looks at things logically and practically, not giving in to his emotions. He feels more comfortable with only one or two friends, if any, and is content reading a book or going on a solitary walk for recreation.

4. _____

_____

An angry crowd thrust its way into the palace courtyard. Hundreds of people wielding sticks and knives and pastry rollers screamed at the figure who emerged on the balcony. "We need bread," they shouted, "we need bread!" The aristocratic figure above straightened her perfumed hair, wrapped her ermine shawl more tightly around her shoulders, and with a lift of her chin, turned and muttered to one of her ladies in waiting, "Let them eat cake."

5. _____

_____

From the first page to the last, I couldn't put it down. The author must have lived with the family in the book because she describes the members in lifelike detail. She tells what they ate, how they felt about religion, housing, politics, and sex. By the end, you know them as though they were your own brothers and sisters.

6. _____

_____

They did not have written language, but by 1000 A.D., they had built preplanned apartment houses four and five stories high. The foot-thick walls of oven-baked adobe brick, plastered over smoothly with clay, kept the occupants warm in winter and cool in summer. But by far their greatest architectural achievement was the intricate system of canals and reservoirs that irrigated their fields and brought water for miles across the desert directly into their homes.

7. _____

Probably the most important part of this new life is learning to get along with your roommates, the people you see most often. Finding the perfect roommate may be impossible. The person should be a nonsmoker and have similar interests to mine. She (it must be a *she*) should be considerate, courteous, generous, thoughtful, studious when I want to study, fun-loving when I want to party, respectful of privacy and personal property, and finally, she should have a great sense of humor. In a nutshell, she should be like me.

8. _____

In childhood I never hesitated to take chances, to jump over wide cracks in the rocks. Sometimes I made it across with no problems; at other times I was not so lucky. I scraped my knees, bled a little, but came back daring to try again. But now that I'm older, I increasingly find myself shying away, afraid to fail, fearful of getting hurt. I live a style of life in which being in control and on top of things is paramount, where being the best and being perfect is what I yearn for. I am afraid to make mistakes, afraid to bleed, and afraid of being powerless. I take fewer chances.

9. _____

The patient was aware that he grew irritable more frequently. Why shouldn't he, when nurses spoke to him as though he was seven years old, pronouncing their words deliberately and slowly. They must have thought he was hard of hearing or didn't understand. They constantly forced medicine on him and did everything for him as though he were incapable of helping himself. Sometimes he grew angry about the way he was ignored after he asked for something. His words were nothing to them, just as he was nothing.

10. _____

One day Ethan was smoking in the boys' bathroom when a teacher walked in. He took Ethan down to the principal's office, where he was given a three-day suspension. Ethan's mother grounded him for a month, and he didn't get the loan his dad had promised him to buy his friend's used car.

Suggested answers are on page 93.

> **Directions:** What follows is a three-paragraph excerpt from the journal of a visitor to the South Pole. In the blank spaces, write a topic sentence that is suitable for each paragraph.

Antarctic Adventure

a. _____

_____

Bellies flattened on the snow, they pant and claw their way across miles and miles of frozen landscape. On downhills, they have to be braked and kept under control by winding ropes around the runners of the sleds. After a day's run, the dogs eat supper and sleep soundly. The next morning, they bark and yip cheerfully, as though to shame their weary masters.

b. _____

_____

The scale is unreal, almost as if it were a landscape from another planet. Away from the coast, no life exists, and therefore, no bacteria, no disease, no pests, no human interference. It is antiseptic and can only be compared with life under the ocean or in space.

c. _____

_____

Although snow offers shelter, insulation, drink, building material, and a highway, its friendliness is a dangerous illusion. Ice blocks and sinister piles of snow tell a tale of avalanches tumbling regularly from the mountains all around. A person on skis could suddenly disappear in a cavern of deep, glistening powder. On foot, sunk to the hips in snow, you might cover less than a mile before dropping from exhaustion. Sudden snow squalls will blind you, cause you to lose your bearings and balance, trapping you hopelessly inside a drift that may ultimately be your burial mound.

Suggested answers are on page 94.

TIP

Develop your ideas with more than one sentence or single example.

In general, a paragraph of only one or two sentences may be too scanty. Most of the time, thorough development of an idea calls for several sentences. Journalists, however, often write paragraphs consisting of one or two sentences. But the bulk of contemporary nonfiction consists of paragraphs of four to eight sentences.

In a coherent paragraph each sentence has its place and purpose. Disjointed paragraphs, on the other hand, consist of sentences arranged in random order. Or they contain ideas vaguely related or irrelevant to the main idea. Meaning serves as the primary glue that holds a coherent paragraph together, but transitional words and phrases such as *for example, also, but,* and *on the other hand* also help. In the following paragraph, notice how the italicized words and phrases tie sentences to each other.

4. Transitions

Considerate writers treat their readers as tourists in a foreign land. To show them the way, they lead them from place to place and remind them now and then of where they've been.

In long pieces of work, readers need more reminders than in short ones. To keep readers from going astray, a writer often chooses words that set up relationships between one thought and the next. This can be done with such words as *this*, which actually ties the sentence you are now reading with the previous one. Fortunately, the English language is brimming with transitional words and phrases that tie ideas together and keep readers from getting lost.

What follows is a collection of common transitional words and phrases grouped according to their customary use. With a bit of thought, you could probably add to the list.

When you **ADD** ideas: *moreover, in addition, further, besides, also, and then, then too, again, next, secondly, equally important*

When you make a **CONTRAST**: *however, conversely, in contrast, on the other hand, on the contrary, but, nevertheless, and yet, still, even so*

When you **COMPARE** or draw a **PARALLEL**: *similarly, likewise, in comparison, in like manner, at the same time, in the same vein*

When you cite an **EXAMPLE**: *for example, for instance, as when, as illustrated by*

When you show **RESULTS**: *as a result, in consequence, consequently, accordingly, therefore, thus, hence*

When you **REINFORCE** an idea: *indeed, in fact, as a matter of fact, to be sure, of course, in any event, by all means*

When you express **SEQUENCE** or the passing of **TIME**: *soon after, then, previously, not long after, meanwhile, in the meantime, later, simultaneously, at the same time, immediately, next, at length, thereafter*

When you show **PLACES**: *here, nearby, at this spot, near at hand, in proximity, on the opposite side, across from, adjacent to, underneath*

When you **CONCLUDE**: *finally, in short, in other words, in a word, to sum up, in conclusion, in the end, when all is said and done*

You don't need a specific transitional word or phrase to bind every sentence to another. Ideas themselves can create strong links. Notice in the following paired sentences that underlined words in the second sentences echo an idea expressed in the first.

[1] As a kind of universal language, music unites people from age eight to eighty. [2] No matter how old they are, people can lose themselves in melodies, rhythms, tempos, and endless varieties of sound.

[1] At the heart of *Romeo and Juliet* is a long-standing feud between the Capulets and the Montagues. [2] As enemies, the two families always fight in the streets of Verona.

[1] To drive nails into very hard wood without bending them, first dip the points into grease or soap. [2] <u>You can accomplish the same end</u> by moistening the points of the nails in your mouth or in a can of water.

➡ **SAMPLE QUESTION**_____

The artist Ed Ruscha was fascinated by words, and so they formed the principal subject of his paintings starting in the 1960s. <u>On the other hand</u>, in some works the words appear in isolation floating against backgrounds of beautifully graded colors that give the illusion of infinite space.

    A. NO CHANGE
    B. For instance
    C. However
    D. Likewise

To answer this question, you must choose the transitional word or phrase that best fits the context.

Answer Explanation

Choice B is the best answer because the transitional phrase *for instance* logically follows the statement in the previous sentence that the artist used words as the principal subject of his paintings. The transition indicates that the writer will cite an example of just such a painting, and that is precisely what he does.

Choice A is not the best answer because the phrase *On the other hand* indicates that the next sentence will contrast with or contradict the previous sentence. But instead, the writer describes an example of the artist's work.

Choice C is not the best answer because *However* suggests that the next sentence will contradict or in some way contrast with the previous sentence. Instead, the writer provides a specific example of a Ruscha painting.

Choice D is not the best answer because the transitional word *Likewise* indicates that the writer is about to move on to a new subject, but one that resembles the old one in some way. Instead, however, what follows is a more detailed description of Ruscha's paintings.

Mini-Workout in Using Transitions

> **Directions:** Use as many transitions as you can while writing paragraphs on the following suggested topics.

    1. Write a paragraph on how to do something—drive a car from home to school, pull a practical joke, avoid doing homework, burn a CD, get on the good side of a teacher, give your cat/dog a bath. Use as many SEQUENCE/TIME transitions as possible, but don't overdo it.

2. Write a paragraph detailing a cause and its effect: the cause and effect of good teaching, of a new fad, of stress in high school students, of taking risks, of lying, of a close friendship. Use as many RESULT transitions as you can, but don't go overboard.

3. Write a paragraph that compares and contrasts one of the following: the way people respond to pressure, groups in your school, two athletes, then and now, boredom and laziness, two books, a friend who turned into an enemy, an enemy who became a friend. Use as many COMPARISON/CONTRAST transitions as you can, but don't get carried away.

4. Write a paragraph in which you argue for or against an issue—electronic eavesdropping, school dress codes, educational vouchers, privileges for senior citizens, censoring the Internet, dieting, restrictions on smoking. Use as many ADDITION transitions as you can, but only where they make sense.

Sample answers are on page 94.

5. Interpretation of Data from a Graph, Chart, or Table

The Writing and Language Test includes at least one question that requires you to consider information related to data drawn from a visual display such as a graph, chart, or table. Your task is to determine whether the passage accurately describes the data presented visually.

➡ SAMPLE QUESTION _____

Although relatively few people in the U.S. commute to work by walking, non-motorized travel modes play an increasingly important role in many of the nation's transportation systems. In fact, the number of American workers who travel to work on foot increased by a larger percentage between 2010 and 2015 than did those who use any other commuting mode, including bicycles. Research findings show that <u>the greatest increases in walking to work took place in large cities.</u> Studies also show that people who walk to work experience improved mental health. They report feeling less stress and improving their sense of well being.

Which choice most accurately conveys information based on the graph?

A. NO CHANGE
B. Workers in the South have fewer opportunities to walk to work than those in other regions of the country.
C. Walking to work is more common in large cities than in small or medium-size cities.
D. Residents of rural and suburban areas do not walk to work.

Walking to Work by Region and City Size: 2008–2015

(Data based on sample.)

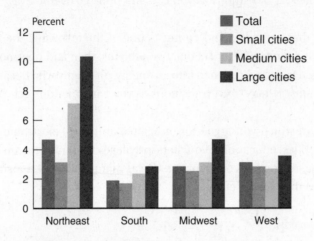

Source: U.S. Census Bureau

Answer Explanation

Choice C is the best answer. The graph shows that the highest percentage of commuting on foot takes place in large cities.

Choice A is not the best answer because the graph does not show data about changes in modes of commuting but rather percentages of commuters who walk to work.

Choice B is not the best answer because the graph contains no information about opportunities to walk to work.

Choice D is not the best answer. Although the statement may be true, it is not supported by data in the graph.

QUESTIONS ON STYLE AND EXPRESSION

6. Words in Context

The primary purpose of words-in-context questions is to check your understanding of how words and phrases fit the context of a given sentence, paragraph, or sometimes a whole passage. To answer the question, you must take into account not just the definition of the word or phrase but also its connotations and its compatibility with the purpose and tone of the passage.

➡ SAMPLE QUESTION _____

Frogs are a sentinel species, like the canary that tells miners when their air is poisoned. The death and deformity of so many frogs is telling us that our environment is <u>polluted</u>.

A. NO CHANGE
B. ruined
C. destroyed
D. mistreated

Answer Explanation

The writer of this science-based excerpt points out the similarity between canaries and frogs. Both species warn us of danger. Canaries die when the air in a mine is "poisoned." Frogs suffer the same fate from polluted environment. The writer uses the adjective *polluted* as the equivalent of *poisoned*. The question, therefore, is which of the choices best captures the sense of toxic danger.

Choice A is the best answer. In the context, *polluted* comes closest in meaning to *poisoned*.

Choice B is not the best answer because *ruined* describes the deteriorated state of the environment but does not suggest danger.

Choice C is not the best answer. Although *destroyed* is related to the decline of the environment, its meaning is less specific and, therefore, less effective than *polluted*.

Choice D is not the best answer. Although *mistreated* may explain in general the reason for the environment's condition, its tone is less ominous than *polluted*.

7. Standard Idiom

An idiom usually consists of a group of words that seems absurd if taken literally. When you "have a ball," the experience has nothing to do with a spherical object used on the basketball court or soccer field. The expression "that's cool" is not related to temperature, and so on. Such idioms often puzzle speakers of other languages, but to native speakers of English, they are as natural as breathing.

On the SAT, the word *idiom* refers not only to such expressions but also to idiomatic usage—that is, to the selection and sequence of words used to convey a meaning. The italicized words in the following sentences are examples of faulty idiom:

> The general was unwilling to pay the *price for victory*.
> Nancy has a negative *opinion towards* me.
> *As regards* to her future, Tina said she'd go to college.

The meaning of each sentence is clear, but the italicized sections don't conform to standard English idiom. Revised, the sentences would read:

> The general was unwilling to pay the *price of victory*.
> Nancy has a negative *opinion of* me.
> *With regard* to her future, Tina said she'd go to college.

➥ SAMPLE QUESTION _____

Employment of firefighters is projected to grow 7 percent from 2016 to 2024, slower than the average for all occupations. Competition for jobs will likely be intense because firefighters are well-respected, important members of a community. They often have a flexible work schedule and a good salary, and like soldiers, they often bond like brothers and sisters. Still another quality common to firefighters is their reliability on their fellow firefighters in emergency situations.

A. NO CHANGE
B. to firefighters is they must rely on
C. to firefighters is their reliance on
D. of firefighters is to depend on

Answer Explanation

Choice C is the best answer because it correctly conveys the writer's intended meaning.

Choice A is not the best answer because it uses *reliability* instead of *reliance*, an example of faulty word choice.

Choice B is not the best answer because it uses mismatched sentence parts: in standard usage, a noun (*quality*) may not be defined by a clause (*they must rely*) but only with another noun.

Choice D is not the best answer because it uses nonstandard English idiom. In the context of the sentence, the phrase *common of firefighters* should be *common to firefighters*.

Mini-Workout on Word Choice and Standard Idiom

Directions: Many of the following sentences contain word-choice or idiom problems. Use the spaces provided to write in the correct word or phrase. Not all sentences contain errors.

1. To stop at a dime is what the engineers were after when they designed brakes for the high-speed train.

   _____

2. In those days, it was an honor to die at battle for their religion.

   _____

3. At this year's conference, no new plans were proposed in respect to the environment.

   _____

4. Einstein's theory of relativity is, for most of us, one that is understood only with difficulty.

   _____

5. Della hopes that the college admissions office will comply to her request to extend the application deadline.

_____

6. Bronze was manufactured by primitive people long before either iron and tin.

_____

7. Preparing to parachute from the airplane, Cameron received verbal instructions instead of written ones.

_____

8. After decades of living alone in Alaska's wilderness, the old man gazed with childish wonder at his first iPhone.

_____

9. Because of his preoccupation in classical music, Justin bought a season's subscription to Symphony Hall concerts.

_____

10. Griffith's new novel tells the tale of a posse that went in pursuit after horse thieves.

_____

11. Our office building's new security system uses digital eye scans to identify employees.

_____

12. Because the boat's engine had failed, the sailor was never far away from harm during the storm.

_____

13. Signs have been posted that proscribe hanging out in the parking lot during the school day.

_____

14. The program is being run for schoolteachers which need to stay current on educational technology.

_____

15. Columbus sailed west in search for a way to the Indies.

_____

16. During the last ten days, at least seven visitors flouted the prohibition against flying drones in the park.

   _____

17. Billy Collins is regarded to be one of the most popular contemporary American poets.

   _____

18. More travelers during the Thanksgiving weekend prefer driving more than flying.

   _____

19. Generic drugs are not nearly as expensive than brand-name medications.

   _____

20. Artists must often choose between teaching or devoting their time to creating art.

   _____

Answers are on page 95.

8. Wordiness

Good writers never use two words when one will do. They tell readers quickly and directly what they have to say because brevity works best. They cut out needless words because readers value economy.

Stop! Have you noticed that the previous sentences ignore the very principles they discuss? Do you see the excess verbiage? Couldn't the point have been made more briefly and succinctly?

Hold it, again! Look at that phrase, *briefly and succinctly*. Aha! Another instance of wordiness: Two adverbs where one is enough.

➡ SAMPLE QUESTION _____

Millions of middle-school-age children now carry smart phones, and parents find themselves facing <u>a brand new challenge of today's modern life</u>—setting guidelines for where, when, and how the device may be used.

   A. NO CHANGE
   B. a challenge of current modern life
   C. today's new challenge
   D. a new challenge

Answer Explanation

This question is about concise expression. Your task is to decide which version of the text conveys the idea most economically without changing the meaning of the sentence.

Choice D is the best answer. It uses the fewest words to express the writer's idea.

Choice A is not the best answer because it contains redundancies. The phrase *today's modern life* is unnecessarily repetitive. In addition, the word *brand* is superfluous in the context.

Choice B is not the best answer because the words *current* and *modern* mean essentially the same thing. What's more, the word *now* in the first clause of the sentence has already indicated that the challenge is a current phenomenon.

Choice C is a redundant phrase. A challenge that arrives today must, by definition, be *new*. Besides, the word *now* in the first clause of the sentence has already informed the reader when the challenge came into being.

Mini-Workout in Wordiness

Directions: Trim the following sentences without changing their basic meaning. Write your answers in the spaces provided, or cross out all needless words.

1. You should work through every sentence you write by examining each word and crossing out all the words that you don't definitely need.

   _____

2. When Maria was sixteen years of age she accepted a position at Wilkens' Fabrics, a position in which she learned about fabrics and about how to handle customers.

   _____

3. Thomas Edison was a man who was obsessed by the wonders of electricity.

   _____

4. What the ambassador most wanted was that the terrorists would release the hostages.

   _____

5. Hamlet returned home as a result of his father's death.

   _____

6. The troops were in danger due to the fact that mines had been planted in the field.

   _____

7. Among the many numerous threats in the contemporary world in which we live are both the threat of climate change and the shortage of clean, potable drinking water.

_____

8. Because of her gender was the reason why Emma felt she was deprived of a place playing on the varsity football team.

_____

9. As a result of the country's shortage of energy sources, the nation's government spends literally millions of dollars in money each and every year to make energy-conserving improvements that can result in huge money savings on its gas and electric bills.

_____

10. While she was inspecting her newly purchased house, which is in the suburbs, Ms. Draeger stumbled over a loose piece of flooring board and fell down the steps leading to the basement.

_____

Answers are on page 95.

9. Awkwardness

Awkward and _clumsy_ are vague words that cover a great many writing weaknesses, including poor grammar and flawed sentence structure. Most often, though, awkwardness occurs when the words sound peculiar, jarring, or out of tune. Awkwardness is difficult to define, but you know it when you hear it. Much of the time you must rely on your ear to detect odd and clumsily worded sentences because there are no specific rules that can explain their defects except that they fail to conform to standard English idiom.

➡ SAMPLE QUESTION

Vertical take-off and landing aircraft get their fixed-wing capability from high-speed air pumped from slots in the trailing edges of their rotors, in which it increases the airflow over them to create lift.

    A. NO CHANGE
    B. which increases the airflow
    C. the end result being it increases airflow
    D. consequently which increases the airflow

Answer Explanation

Choice B is the best answer because it is both concise and free of awkward expression.

Choice A is not the best answer because it is awkwardly worded, in part because the pronoun _it_ doesn't refer to a specific noun or other pronoun.

Choice C is not the best answer because it contains the redundancy *end result* and leaves the pronoun *it* without a specific antecedent.

Choice D is not the best answer because the words *consequently which* do not conform to standard English idiom.

10. Redundancy and Repetition

Sentences need revision when they include words and phrases that either fail to add meaning or repeat what has already been stated. For example:

> A necessary requirement for applying to most colleges is the SAT.
> An important essential ingredient of a hamburger is meat.
> You should read *Lust for Life*, the biography of the life of Vincent van Gogh.

All three sentences contain a needless word or phrase. In the first sentence, omit *necessary* because *necessary* by definition implies *requirement*. Therefore, *necessary requirement* is redundant. In the next sentence, an ingredient described as *essential* must by definition be *important*, so delete the word *important*. And in the last sentence, the phrase *of the life* should be removed because a biography cannot be anything other than the story of someone's life.

➡ SAMPLE QUESTION _____

When we listen to a musical work we are somewhat in the position of travelers on a train who watch the landscape speed by their windows. They carry away only a general impression. With each additional trip through the same territory, the details emerge from the mass and engrave themselves upon their minds—a house here, a clump of trees there—until the terrain has become a clear and familiar pattern.

As we become familiar with the piece, we grow increasingly aware of what is in it. However, upon our initial hearing for the first time the work is apt to leave us with a hazy image. On the other hand, the melody—the notes we sing or hum or whistle—may leave a clearer impression.

   A. NO CHANGE
   B. listening to a work for the first time, the initial hearing is apt to leave a hazy image on us.
   C. our first hearing of a work is apt to leave us with a hazy image.
   D. a hazy image is apt to be left on us from the first time a work is heard.

Answer Explanation

This question asks you to decide which choice expresses the idea most clearly, concisely, and correctly.

Choice C is the best answer because it is free of needless words.

Choice A is not the best answer because it contains the redundancy *initial hearing* and *for the first time*.

Choice B is not the best answer because it contains the redundancy *first time* and *initial*. (Incidentally, it also contains a dangling modifier. The construction beginning with *listening* should modify the person or thing doing the listening, such as, e.g., *a person, the audience* or *one*, but not *the initial hearing*. More about dangling modifiers later. Can you bear to wait?)

Choice D is not the best answer. Although it is relatively concise and clear, it is constructed in the passive voice, which always uses more words than necessary. (More about that later, too.)

Mini-Workout in Redundancy and Repetition

> **Directions:** Revise the following sentences for economy of expression.

1. She constantly irritates and bothers me all the time.

_____

_____

2. He spoke to me concerning the matter of my future.

_____

_____

3. Is it a true fact that the ozone layer is being depleted?

_____

_____

4. I thought that if I didn't take chemistry that I couldn't go to a good college.

_____

_____

5. Consequently, as a result of the election, the state will have its first female governor.

_____

_____

6. My father's habitual custom is to watch the sun set in the West.

_____

_____

7. Harold picked up a brush at the age of ten years old and hasn't stopped painting since.

_____

_____

8. Research shows that avid sports fans not only suffer fewer depressions, but they are also generally healthier, too, than those not interested in sports.

_____

_____

9. His field of work is that of a chemist.

_____

_____

10. For the second time, the cough recurred again.

_____

_____

Answers are on pages 95–96.

QUESTIONS ON SENTENCES

11. Sentences

A sentence is a group of words that begins with a capital letter and ends with a mark of punctuation, usually a period. Most of the time, a sentence conveys a more or less complete thought.

That's a handy description of a sentence, but it doesn't tell the whole story. There's much more to know about a creature that takes innumerable forms and shapes and can perform an endless variety of functions. A simple definition just won't do.

With that in mind, here's a fact that may surprise you: The longest sentence in the world will never be written. That's because a sentence can go on indefinitely. The shortest sentence, on the other hand, is probably a single letter—the answer to a question such as, "Is your name spelled with a *J* or a *G*?" Some might argue that a letter of the alphabet doesn't qualify as a sentence because sentences consist of two parts—a *subject* and a *predicate*. We'll take a closer look at subjects and predicates in Section 11A.

The reason you need to be up on subjects and predicates is that some questions on the Writing and Language Test ask you to recognize common sentence errors such as ***fragments*** (grammatically incomplete sentences), ***run-on sentences*** (two or more sentences that are written as though they were one), and ***comma splices*** (sentences with commas between them instead of period and a capitalized word signifying the start of a new sentence).

More about those juicy writing problems coming up soon, but try to contain your excitement for the moment—if possible.

11A. Subjects and Predicates

The simplest subject of a sentence is a noun or pronoun, and the simplest predicate is a verb:

> Ophelia (*subject*) wept (*verb*).
> She (*subject*) wailed (*verb*).

Push! (*verb*) (In this sentence the subject *you* is implied. Spelled out, the sentence is *You push!*)

It goes without saying that sentences are rarely as short and simple as these examples. In fact, a sentence subject can contain any number of words that modify, or describe, the noun or pronoun, as, for example, in *poor, broken-hearted, miserable, pitiful, pathetic Ophelia.*

Furthermore, a subject can be made up of a string of nouns or pronouns as in

Snow, sleet, and freezing rain (*subject*) poured down on the city.
He and she (*subject*) plan to be married.

Phrases that contain neither nouns nor pronouns can also be the subject of a sentence. A verb, for example, when it functions as a noun, as in

To eat (*subject consisting of the infinitive form of a verb*) like a pig is the sole purpose of Matt's existence.

To identify the grammatical subject of a sentence, look first for the verb. Then ask who or what is performing the action described by the verb, and chances are you'll have found the subject.

Jack ran away with Jill. Who ran? Jack did. Therefore, *Jack* is the subject.
The *mail* arrived late this afternoon. What arrived late? The *mail.*
There were *cars* parked illegally. What was parked? *Cars.*

Subjects usually precede verbs, but not always, as in *There in the middle of the room stood the angry ghost.* Who stood? The *ghost.*

Although this method of finding the subject works much of the time, some sentences refuse to yield their subjects so readily. Then you need to employ additional steps, detailed in "Finding the 'bare bones' of a sentence" on page 36.

Predicates, on the other hand, are easy to find because they consist of everything in a sentence that isn't the subject. They can be just a single verb or a verb accompanied by strings of additional words (italicized in the following sentence) that tell you something about the subject.

Ophelia (*subject*) wept (*verb*) *without stopping for two hours this afternoon, then all through dinner and into the evening until her boyfriend Hamlet sent her a text to apologize for thoughtlessly calling her a moron.*

11B. Clauses

TIP

Some clauses are complete sentences, others are not.

A clause is part of a sentence that contains a subject and a verb. By that definition, a clause sounds strangely like a sentence, and to a point, it *is* a sentence—but even though some clauses are complete sentences, others are not. Those that are full-fledged sentences go by the name of independent or main clauses. The others are called dependent clauses because they depend for their meaning and grammatical validity on independent clauses.

Without an independent clause they would be *sentence fragments*—that is, incomplete sentences.

To illustrate, here is a complete, independent sentence with its subject and verb italicized:

Ikuku drives slowly.

Now let's add a dependent clause:

Because she is prudent, Ikuku drives slowly.

The new clause contains a subject (*she*) and a verb (*is*), but by themselves that subject and that verb don't make a sentence. The clause *Because she is prudent* is a fragment, a piece of a sentence. On its own, it lacks grammatical status, which can be achieved only by attaching it to an independent clause.

Dependent clauses serve various functions—They can act as nouns, as adjectives, and even as adverbs. Naturally, therefore, they are called noun clauses, adjective clauses…and you can probably guess the other one.

Noun clauses often begin with words such as *that, which, who, whom, when, whoever,* and *whatever.* They can be, among other things, the subject of a sentence, the object of a preposition, or the object of a verb.

Whoever fears spiders should stay out of the cellar (*Whoever fears spiders* is the subject).

Over the years Ikuku realized *that she was a certifiable arachnophobe* (the words *that she was a certifiable arachnophobe* are the object of the verb *realized*).

Adjective clauses often begin with the relative pronoun*s who, whom, whose, which,* or *that.* Like single-word adjectives, they modify nouns and pronouns.

The spider web *that spanned the doorway* **caught her by surprise.**

(The clause *that spanned the doorway* modifies the noun *web.*)

Adverbial clauses start with such words as *although, because, while, since, as, as though, unless, so that,* and many other subordinating conjunctions. They modify verbs, adjectives, and adverbs.

She screamed *as though she'd been stung* **by a bee.**

(The clause *as though she'd been stung* modifies the verb *screamed.*)

> **Note:** Take comfort from knowing to know that the SAT Writing and Language Test won't ask you about clauses *per se*. But you can count on questions that test your proficiency in spotting sentence fragments, run-ons, and comma splices. That's why it helps to know about clauses. If you can tell at a glance whether a group of words is, say, a dependent or an independent clause, you'll never again have to puzzle long and hard over fragments, run-ons, and comma splices. You'll recognize them immediately.

Sentence Fragments

Sentence fragments usually occur when writers fail to distinguish between dependent and independent clauses, when they confuse phrases and clauses, or when they attempt to use verbals as verbs. To determine whether a sentence is complete, uncover its bare bones. That is, deconstruct the sentence by eliminating dependent clauses, phrases, and verbals. If what remains does not have a subject and a verb, it's probably a fragment.

To identify the subject of long sentences may take some doing, but the "bare bones" strategy usually works. Using this approach, you'll strip away everything in a sentence but its subject and verb, a task that may be easier said than done. It's not very formidable, though, if you remember that the grammatical subject can never be in (1) a prepositional phrase, (2) a dependent clause, or (3) a phrase that interrupts the flow of the sentence.

Frankly, identifying the bare bones of a sentence is often a more complex process than that suggested in the examples that follow. Sometimes the bare bones are buried deep within long and complicated sentences. But by carefully peeling away sentence parts that cannot contain the subject or verb, you'll eventually find them.

Finding the "bare bones" of a sentence:

(STEP 1) Look for prepositional phrases, such as *up the wall, around the corner, to the beach, over the counter,* and cross them out. For example, if you were to eliminate all the prepositional phrases in these sentences, only the subject and the verb—the "bare bones"—will remain.

Complete sentence:	In the middle of the night, Pricilla slept.
Bare bones:	Pricilla slept
Complete sentence:	Several of the sentences are in the book.
Bare bones:	Several are
Complete sentence:	One of Frida's friends is in need of help.
Bare bones:	One is

(STEP 2) Locate all the dependent clauses—those parts of sentences containing a noun and a verb but that don't qualify as complete sentences because they begin with words and phrases like *although, as, as though, because, before, even though, if, in spite of, regardless of, since, so that, unless, whenever, whether,* and *while.* Another group of dependent clauses are statements (not questions) that start with *when, where, which, who,* and *what.*

After deleting the dependent clauses in the following sentences, only the main clause will remain. That's where to find the bare bones of each sentence.

Complete sentence:	Because she missed the bus, Marnie wept.
Bare bones:	Marnie wept
Complete sentence:	While Willie waited for the bus, he studied vocabulary.
Bare bones:	he studied
Complete sentence:	Andy helps out whenever he has the time.
Bare bones:	Andy helps out

(STEP 3) Look for and delete interrupters—those parts of sentences that impede the smooth flow of the main idea. Interrupters may be just one word, such as *however* or *nevertheless,* or dozens. They're often set off by commas.

Complete sentence:	Ellen, regardless of the look on her face, rejoiced.
Bare bones:	Ellen rejoiced
Complete sentence:	The boat, a sleek white catamaran, sank.
Bare bones:	boat sank
Complete sentence:	Marty, who got ticketed for doing 60 in a 30 MPH zone, paid the fine.
Bare bones:	Marty paid

Foods containing any poisonous or hazardous substances are defined as adulterated and prohibited by the Food and Drug Act. <u>However, foods that naturally contain harmful substances. These may be permitted</u> if the amount of the substance does not ordinarily injure health. Thus, foods containing caffeine, like coffee and tea, are approved despite caffeine's adverse health effects at high levels.

   A. NO CHANGE
   B. Which naturally contain harmful substances. These may be permitted
   C. However, foods that naturally contain harmful substances may be permitted
   D. Foods that naturally contain harmful substances, however, these may be permitted

Answer Explanation

This question focuses on grammatically correct sentences.

Choice C is the best answer because the sentence contains a subject, a compatible verb, and a grammatically correct dependent clause.

Choice A is not the best answer because it includes a sentence fragment consisting solely of the dependent clause, *However, foods that naturally contain harmful substances.*

Choice B is not the best answer because it includes the sentence fragment, *Which naturally contain harmful substances.*

Choice D is not the best answer because the dependent clause *Foods that naturally contain harmful substances* is not grammatically compatible with the independent clause beginning with *these may….*

Run-on Sentences

A run-on sentence consists of two independent clauses separated by neither a conjunction (*and, but, or, nor, yet,* or *so*) nor an appropriate mark of punctuation, as in

   Birthstones are supposed to bring good luck mine has never brought me any.

A conjunction or a mark of punctuation is needed between *luck* and *mine*.

   Birthstones are supposed to bring good luck, *but* mine has never brought me any.

Adding *but* solves the problem. A comma has also been added because sentences made up of two or more independent clauses joined by a conjunction usually require a comma. Another possibility is writing two separate sentences:

   Birthstones are supposed to bring good luck. Mine has never brought me any.

Separating the sentences with a semicolon is also an acceptable alternative. In effect, the semicolon functions like a period. Note, however, that the initial letter of the second sentence is not capitalized:

   Birthstones are supposed to bring good luck; mine has never brought me any.

➡ SAMPLE QUESTION _____

As a food additive, caffeine is regulated as a "generally recognized as safe" (GRAS) substance. Because of this regulatory status, food processors are not required to prove caffeine's safety before adding it to their products. Instead, caffeine's long and widespread history of use is <u>considered sufficient proof of safety when used as directed</u> caffeine presents no health risks to the vast majority of consumers. The FDA has published rules that limit the amount that can be added to foods, however.

    A. NO CHANGE
    B. considered sufficient proof of safety. When used as directed
    C. considered sufficient proof of safety when they are used as directed
    D. sufficiently considered proof of safety, when used as directed

Answer Explanation

Choice B is the best answer because it properly divides two separate and independent sentences.

Choice A is not the best answer because two grammatically sound sentences run together with no punctuation between them.

Choice C is not the best answer because the pronoun *they* lacks a grammatically valid antecedent.

Choice D is not the best answer because two independent sentences are spliced with a comma instead of a period.

Comma Splices

A comma splice is a form of a run-on sentence. It is a construction in which a comma is used between two independent sentences instead of a period or a semicolon. Remember that a semicolon is a substitute for a period, NOT for a comma. Correctly used, a semicolon must lie between two independent sentences.

➡ SAMPLE QUESTION #1 _____

Toni Morrison is one of America's outstanding <u>authors, she is known</u> for her critical essays, her novels, and her frequent appearances on television.

    A. NO CHANGE
    B. authors; she is known
    C. authors famous
    D. authors. Known

Answer Explanation

Choice B is the best answer because a semicolon is used to separate two independent clauses.

Choice A is not the best answer because it contains a comma splice.

Choice C is not the best answer because it needs a comma at the start of the dependent clause, which starts with the word *known*.

Choice D is not the best answer because the clause beginning with *Known* is a sentence fragment.

➥ SAMPLE QUESTION #2 _____

Mending a fracture takes from four weeks to a <u>year; depending</u> on the size of the bone, the location, and the age of the person.

    A. NO CHANGE
    B. year depending
    C. year, it depends
    D. year, depending

Answer Explanation

Choice D is the best answer because it properly uses a comma to separate the two parts of the sentence. The first part is an independent clause; the second is a participial phrase.

Choice A is not the best answer because a semicolon is used to separate an independent clause and a sentence fragment, which in this case is a participial phrase.

Choice B is not the best answer because a comma is needed between the two parts of the sentence.

Choice C is not the best answer because it contains a comma splice. Either a period or semicolon is needed to separate two independent sentences.

Mini-Workout in Writing Correct Sentences

> **Directions:** Some of the following are sentence fragments, others are run-ons, and still others contain comma splices. Use the spaces provided to write complete and correct sentences.

1. Although Elizabeth is stressed out about the SAT.

    _____

    _____

2. She asked the teacher for an extension on the assignment, the teacher agreed.

    _____

    _____

3. My grandmother is eighty-six years old therefore she walks very slowly.

    _____

    _____

4. Many other examples that I could choose to show who I am, many of them not vivid images of memorable moments, but everyday aspects of my life.

_____

_____

5. I woke up, having slept for the four shortest hours of my life, I force open my eyes and I crawl to the shower then my brain begins to function.

_____

_____

6. For me to believe that the crucial time has arrived when I will leave the protective world of high school and enter the world of college.

_____

_____

7. The large brown garage door creaks open slowly, out into the morning sunshine a rider on a road bike emerges.

_____

_____

8. What are the rules which we all must follow what might happen if we break them.

_____

_____

9. A biologist working in the field of genetic engineering and involved in the controversy surrounding cloning.

_____

_____

10. Using the space below, telling one story about yourself to provide the admissions committee, either directly or indirectly, with an insight into the kind of person you are.

_____

_____

Answers are on page 96.

12. Combining and Augmenting Sentences

For the sake of paragraph coherence, or cohesion, you may be asked to improve a paragraph by choosing a revision that effectively combines two or more short or disconnected or repetitive sentences.

As you weigh the four answer choices, keep in mind that the most concise and most clever revision may not always be the best one. Instead, the best revision is likely to be the one that fits most logically and stylistically into the context of the paragraph

➡ SAMPLE QUESTION

Together with freedom of the press, the right to keep and bear arms became one of the individual rights most prized by the colonists. When British troops seized a militia arsenal in September 1774, and incorrect rumors that colonists had been killed spread through Massachusetts, 60,000 citizens took up arms. A few months later Patrick Henry delivered his "Give me liberty or give me death" speech. He gained long lasting fame. Over time, his words came to support the proposition "that a well regulated militia…is the natural strength and only security of a free government."

The underscored section marks a sentence break. Which choice most effectively combines the two sentences?

A. NO CHANGE
B. speech; from it gaining
C. speech but gained
D. speech, gaining

Answer Explanation

This question tests your understanding of how sentences can be effectively combined.

Choice D is the best answer because it combines two sentences smoothly and logically, thereby strengthening the connection between the speech and its effect on Henry's fame.

Choice A is not the best answer. Although it is grammatically correct, the logical cause-and-effect relationship between the two sentences is weakened by the sentence break.

Choice B is not the best answer because of the clumsy usage *from it*. In addition, the semi-colon turns the second clause into a sentence fragment.

Choice C is not the best answer because it is illogical. The word *but* suggests that the two ideas are contradictory.

Mini-Workout in Combining and Augmenting Sentences

Directions: Use the spaces provided to combine the sentences in each of the following groups. Because any group can be combined in numerous ways, write at least two versions. If necessary, add, delete, and/or alter words. Try alternatives; that's the best way to discover the possibilities and to improve your skill.

1. She is only thirteen. She is an expert gymnast. She has won recognition.

_____

_____

_____

2. An accident occurred. The accident was a hit and run. Broken glass lay on the street.

_____

_____

_____

3. Aunt Ellen went to the grocery store. She bought tomato juice. The tomato juice was in a glass bottle. The bottle was in the grocery bag. Aunt Ellen dropped the grocery bag. The bottle broke. Aunt Ellen had a mess. The mess was on her hands.

_____

_____

_____

4. The baseball hit the picture window. The picture window belonged to Mr. Strickman. The glass shattered. The glass shattered in a thousand pieces.

_____

_____

_____

5. There was a storm. The snow fell. Snow fell on the roads. It was two feet deep. I could not go out. I had nothing to do. I watched TV. I worked on a jigsaw puzzle. Time passed slowly.

_____

_____

_____

6. The Earth revolves around the sun. It takes about 365 days for a revolution. The Earth rotates on its axis. One rotation occurs every 24 hours. The revolution determines the length of the year. The rotation determines the duration of a day.

_____

_____

_____

7. Euripides lived more than 2,000 years ago. He lived in ancient Greece. He wrote plays. The plays were tragedies. The plays are still performed.

_____

_____

_____

8. Music has a unique power. Music often transports people's minds. People dream and think while listening to music. People often feel refreshed after listening to music.

_____

_____

_____

9. Human beings have skulls. Skulls are made up of bones. The skull has twenty-two bones. Eight bones make up the cranium. The cranium protects the brain. Fourteen bones are used to form the face and jaw.

_____

_____

_____

10. The Hopi Indians value peace and contentment. The word *Hopi* means peaceful and happy. The name reflects the culture. The culture lacks tension. The people lack competitiveness. Material possessions are unimportant. Self-discipline is important. So is restraint. So is concern for the welfare of others. The family is the highest value. The family is the whole Hopi tribe.

Answers are on pages 96–97.

Augmenting Sentences

In the same vein, you may encounter a question about augmenting an existing paragraph or sentence with details or additional evidence to support a claim. Such a question asks you to choose a sentence, a clause, a phrase, or in some cases a single word that somehow adds to the effectiveness of the text. As you decide on the best answer, take into account the meaning, grammar, style, tone, and overall purpose of the passage or paragraph, then pick the answer that is the most compatible with the existing text.

Beginnings are delicate moments, the beginning of constructing a house no less than the beginning of a friendship, the inception of a years-long stint in college, or the start of a marriage. And how do these things begin? With a glance, a word, a phrase. Intuition, not reason, guides us, which is why the moment of beginning has often been the occasion for magic. The origin of the handshake, the high-five, or more recently, the fist bump, is almost certainly magical, especially when it is used to signify the closing of an agreement—that is, the beginning of a contract. It is a wonderfully potent moment: the touching of palms, fingers, or fists, the mutual tensing of muscles, the momentary sensation of defenselessness, and. . . .There are many such practices associated with beginnings. The bride carries flowers that represent hoped-for fruitfulness, and she is dressed in white, signifying virginity. A meal is begun with a prayer, an examination like the SAT with a ritual of tension, hope, anticipation, and relief that test day has finally come round.

The writer wants to finish the underlined sentence with an additional example of feelings that accompany the beginning of an agreement or contract. Which choice best accomplishes this goal?

A. above all, other impressions that something noteworthy has happened
B. above all, the confidence and trust demonstrated by the extended hand
C. more than anything, a strong handshake symbolizes trust and confidence
D. even better, you're on a roll, it's too late to turn back, the die has been cast

Answer Explanation

Choice B is the best answer because the phrase "confidence and trust" effectively continues the sentence's series of potent physical and emotional feelings: "tensing of muscles," "sensation of defenselessness," conveying the magical effects evoked by momentous beginnings.

Choice A is not the best answer because the phrase "other impressions that something noteworthy has happened" is too vague and general to constitute an effective example of magical effects that the writer claims accompany significant beginnings.

Choice C is not the best answer because the words "a strong handshake symbolizes trust and confidence" does not convey a sense of magic that comes with an important beginning. Also, this choice breaks the structural pattern of phrases used earlier in the sentence. Instead of a noun followed by a prepositional phrase ("the touching of open palms, the mutual tensing of muscles"), it introduces—inappropriately—an independent clause.

Choice D is not the best answer because it fails to convey the sense of magic created by significant beginnings. Rather, it consists of trite expressions that seem almost irrelevant to the context and, incidentally, contain a comma splice.

13. Mixed Construction

Mixed construction occurs when different parts of a sentence don't fit grammatically or logically with each other. Mixed sentence parts suggest that the writer lost track of where the sentence was going or, in finishing a sentence, ignored how it had begun, as in

Maggie's goal is to apply to nursing school and is hoping to be one after graduation.

The grammatical subject *goal* appears to have been forgotten in the second half of the sentence because the verb *is hoping* lacks an appropriate subject.

> Maggie aspires to be a nurse, and she is hoping to go to nursing school after graduation.

With a compound sentence containing two subjects and two verbs, the problem is solved. But subordinating one of the clauses is an even better solution to the problem:

> Maggie, who aspires to be a nurse, hopes to go to nursing school after graduation.

Another example:

> When Lana came to school with a black eye was a signal that she is an abused child.

The verb *was* needs a subject.

> Lana's coming to school with a black eye was a signal that she is an abused child.

The problem has been solved by using *coming* as the grammatical subject.

Still another type of faulty parallelism occurs when the grammatical subject of a sentence is changed from one clause to another. For example:

> To fix a flat tire, I jack up the car, and then the damaged tire is removed.

The subject of the first clause is *I*. In the second clause the subject is *tire*, a shift to the passive voice that weakens the effectiveness of the whole sentence.

> To fix a flat tire, I jack up the car and then remove the damaged tire.

When the grammatical subject is maintained, parallelism is restored, and the sentence is active and concise.

➡ SAMPLE QUESTION

The next morning, after Larry Hayden's car was found abandoned, <u>a nationwide search for the missing actor began.</u>

    A. NO CHANGE
    B. there was a nationwide search for the missing actor had started.
    C. there was the beginning of a nationwide search for the missing actor
    D. a nationwide search for the missing actor will have began

Answer Explanation
Choice A is the best answer because it consists of a clause that grammatically and logically fits the previous part of the sentence.

Choice B is incorrect because its subject, *search*, has two different verbs in two different tenses.

Choice C is wrong because it changes the grammatical subject from *search* to *beginning*, a stylistic change that weakens the sentence.

Choice D contains an error is verb form—*will have began* instead of *will have begun*.

Mini-Workout in Mixed Construction

> **Directions:** Some of the sentences below contain (1) shifts in verb tense, (2) shifts in sentence subject, (3) shifts from active to passive voice, and (4) shifts of another kind. Use the spaces provided to identify the problem or problems. Then write a correct version of each sentence.

1. Jay had been working out in the weight room for months when the wrestling coach invites him to try out for the team.

   _____

2. For Thanksgiving, Julie went to Richmond; however, for Christmas a trip to Syracuse was made by her.

   _____

3. The movie is about how loyalty to a friend can create a moral crisis, whereas conventional values are challenged.

   _____

4. The board recognizes the school's troubles, and now a giant fundraising drive was being undertaken by them.

   _____

5. The report said that years ago city planners had envisioned building a facility that turns salt water into fresh water, and financial woes make that impossible.

   _____

6. Students lacking financial resources can still go to college because they can borrow money from banks, hold part-time jobs, and scholarships are available.

   _____

7. When a woman comes home after a full day of problems in the office, you don't want to face additional problems.

   _____

8. Jocko left for the university as soon as his breakfast had been eaten.

_____

9. You turn your iPhone off; then the phone is put into your backpack until the end of the school day.

_____

10. When the CEO announced her resignation, the workers have a meeting and decided to postpone their strike.

_____

Answers on page 97.

14. Coordination and Subordination

One variety of mismatched sentence parts is evident when clauses are somehow incompatible, illogical, or otherwise at odds with each other. Still another problem—more of style than of grammar—occurs when coordinate clauses are overused.

Faulty Coordination

In everyday conversation people often use lengthy compound sentences made up of several short sentences joined by *and, so,* or other conjunctions:

> In school on Tuesday the lights went out, *and* we were in the dark for more than an hour, *and* the electricity was off, *so* we couldn't use the computers, *and* we heard that a car had hit a utility pole, *and* the driver was killed, *and* they let us go home early.

This sentence tells a story without breaking a single rule of usage or grammar. Yet, it is stylistically flawed, not because it's monotonous but because each idea appears in an independent clause, suggesting that all the ideas are equally important. Clauses of equal rank in a sentence are called coordinate clauses and are usually joined by the conjunctions *and, but, or, nor, yet,* or *so.* Faulty coordination occurs (1) when it is illogical or inappropriate to assign equal importance to two or more coordinate clauses, or (2) when the connecting word fails to create a reasonable relationship between the clauses.

> Tom was away at summer camp, and his parents decided to split up after twenty years of marriage.

The two coordinate clauses state seemingly unrelated ideas, obviously of unequal importance. In the following sentence, as well as in most other complex sentences, the contents of the independent clause are assumed to contain more important information than the contents of other clauses. In other words, making clauses dependent reduces the significance of the information they contain, thereby changing the effect of the sentence:

> While Tom was away at summer camp, his parents decided to split up after twenty years of marriage.

What follows is a sentence in which the conjunction *and* fails to convey a meaningful relationship between the ideas in the two clauses.

> **Ms. Sheridan has become the new assistant principal, and she has never been a classroom teacher.**

Making the second clause dependent by using *although* creates a more sensible connection between the ideas:

> **Ms. Sheridan has become the new assistant principal, although she has never been a classroom teacher.**

For the sake of unity and coherence, it is usually better not to shift from one grammatical subject to another between clauses. Maintaining the subject helps readers glide easily from one clause to the next without realigning their focus.

Faulty: The plan will be a great success, or great failure will be the result.

Plan is the subject of the first clause; *failure* is the subject of the second.

Unified: The plan will be a great success, or it will be a great failure.

The pronoun *it* keeps the subject in focus from one clause to the next.

➡ SAMPLE QUESTION #1

Elizabeth hopes to attend Ohio Wesleyan University, <u>and she has not yet sent in her application.</u>

    A. NO CHANGE
    B. and she hasn't sent her application in yet.
    C. but her application hasn't as yet been sent in by her.
    D. but she hasn't yet sent in her application.

Answer Explanation

Choice D is the best answer because it contains a main clause and the subordinate clause that are logically related to each other.

Choice A is not the best answer because the conjunction *and* fails to express a reasonable relationship between the two coordinate clauses.

Choice B is not the best answer because the conjunction *and* fails to create a reasonable relationship between the two coordinate clauses.

Choice C is not the best answer. Although it contains two clauses joined by the conjunction *but*, a new subject is introduced in the second clause resulting in a switch from active to passive construction.

Faulty Subordination

By means of subordination, writers are able to convey not only the interrelationship of ideas but also the relative importance of one idea to another. Here, for instance, are two statements:

Joe rushed to school. He ate a tuna sandwich.

The relationship between the two ideas is not altogether transparent, but it can be clarified by subordinating one of the ideas.

While he rushed to school, Joe ate a tuna sandwich.
or
While he ate a tuna sandwich, Joe rushed to school.

In each sentence, the more important idea appears in the main clause instead of in the subordinate clause. The subordinate clause in both sentences begins with *while*, one of many common subordinating conjunctions. Others include *after, although, as if, as though, because, before, if, in order to, since, so that, that, though, unless, until, when, whenever, where, whereas, wherever,* and *whether*. The presence of one of these conjunctions in a sentence-improvement question should alert you to the possibility of faulty subordination. The sentences that follow illustrate typical problems:

While she is a mature young woman, she is afraid of the dark.

The subordinating conjunction *while* usually refers to time, as in *while he was away in Boston*. Here, however, *while* obscures both the meaning of the sentence and the relationship between the two statements.

Although she is a mature young woman, she is afraid of the dark.

A new subordinating conjunction clarifies the meaning.

I read in the paper *where* the fleet is coming back to Norfolk.

The meaning may be clear, but in this context *where* is not standard usage.

I read in the paper *that* the fleet is coming back to Norfolk.

Another problem concerns the placement of emphasis. The conjunction *and* in the following sentence gives equal emphasis to unequal ideas.

I arrived home from school *and* I received my acceptance letter from Ohio State.

Stating the more significant event in the main clause places the emphasis where it belongs:

When I arrived home from school, I received my acceptance letter from Ohio State.

When he suddenly started to grin like an imbecile, I was walking with Dirk in the park.

    A. NO CHANGE

    B. While I walked with him in the park, Dirk suddenly started to grin like an imbecile.

    C. Suddenly starting to grin like an imbecile, he was walking in the park with me.

    D. Dirk, walking in the park with me and suddenly grinning like an imbecile.

Answer Explanation

Choice B is the best answer because it places the main idea in the main clause.

Choice A is not the best answer because it places the more important idea in the subordinate clause.

Choice C is not the best answer because it puts the major idea into a phrase.

Choice D is not the best answer because it is a sentence fragment.

15. Parallel Structure

Orderly construction of a sentence keeps parallel ideas in the same grammatical form. For example, a sentence describing the contents of a school locker might read this way:

> The locker held a down jacket, aromatic sweatpants, three sneakers, two left-handed gloves, an unused tuna sandwich, a broken ski pole, a hockey puck, six overdue library books, a disposable camera, and a hiking boot.

Every item listed is an object, each expressed in the same grammatical form: a noun preceded by one or two adjectives. When the owner of the locker wrote a list of favorite pastimes, though, the sentence lost its balance:

> I like skiing, hiking, to take pictures, and running.

The message is clear, but the phrase "to take pictures" is not parallel with the other phrases. To revise it, write "taking pictures."

To recognize faulty parallelism in SAT sentences, you should know that:

1. Ideas in a series should be in the same grammatical form, even when the series consists of only two items:

> The neighbors objected to the noisy parties on Friday nights and to the trash on the lawn on Saturday mornings.

The parallel ideas are expressed as prepositional phrases, *to the noisy parties* and *to the trash*.

> After graduation, Nan promised to turn the volume down and to come home earlier.

Each parallel idea consists of an infinitive followed by a noun and an adverb.

2. In comparisons, parallel ideas should be in the same grammatical form.

Going out to eat no longer thrills me as much as to cook at home.

The gerund *going* may not be paired with the infinitive *to cook*.

Going out to eat no longer thrills me as much as *cooking* at home.

The ideas are now stated in parallel form.

3. Parallel ideas are often signaled by pairs of words like *either/or, neither/nor, whether/or, both/and,* and *not only/but also.* A usage error to watch out for is the misuse of one word in the pair, as in:

Alice will attend *neither* NYU *or* Columbia.

Revise by changing *neither* to *either*, or changing *or* to *nor*.

    Still another error occurs when one of the words in the pair is situated too far from the parallel ideas, as in:

Jake *both* started on the basketball and the volleyball teams.

The signal word *both* is too far removed from the parallel phrase, *basketball and volleyball teams*. Its placement misleads the reader into thinking that the verb *started* is one of the parallel ideas. Correctly worded, the sentence reads:

Jake started on *both* the basketball and the volleyball teams.

➡ SAMPLE QUESTION

The community park was transformed into a showpiece brought about by the hiring of Lucy Collins as town planner, engaging the services of Whitney's Nursery, and <u>we convinced</u> the Chamber of Commerce to raise funds.

   A. NO CHANGE
   B. to convince
   C. convince
   D. convincing

Answer Explanation

This question asks you to revise a sentence with phrases in a series that are not grammatically parallel to each other.

Choice D is the best answer because the verb *convincing* is grammatically parallel to *hiring* and *engaging*.

Choice A is not the best answer because the verb *convinced* is not parallel in tense or structure to *hiring* and *engaging*. All three verbs should be in parallel form.

Choice B is not the best answer because of faulty parallelism. The verb *to convince* is not parallel in form or structure to *hiring* and *engaging*.

Choice C is not the best answer because of faulty parallelism. The verb *convince* is not parallel in form or structure to *hiring* and *engaging*. (It's also in the wrong tense, but we'll get to that topic later.)

Mini-Workout in Parallel Structure

> **Directions:** Look for faulty parallelism in the following sentences. Write a correct version of the offending word or phrase in the space provided. Some sentences may be correct.

1. Mr. Phillips is funny, interesting, and inspires his classes to learn history.

   _____

2. The talk-show host not only was accused of being a bigot but also too stupid to continue working at the station.

   _____

3. Since Jenny started taking AP Math, she has worked harder and fewer parties.

   _____

4. Her job consisted mostly of writing and typing letters, reports, and various types of telephone calls.

   _____

5. Mike likes to go to bed early and getting up early to do his work.

   _____

6. Our cat Sylvia was short-haired, affectionate, intelligent, and disappeared for days at a time.

   _____

7. Maggie hasn't yet decided whether to be an art historian or commercial art.

   _____

8. The audience at the graduation ceremony both felt pride and satisfaction when the announcement was made.

   _____

9. The police officer walked into the courtyard, got caught in a crossfire, and was shot in the chest.

   _____

10. Either way, Nat expects to move to the country because he loves nature and live simply because he has little money.

_____

11. The kids had not only scattered their books all over the bus but also the sidewalk.

_____

12. His ideal house would be in a good location, with land around it, and with a view.

_____

13. Joan's pencil was broken, yellow, and came from this box.

_____

14. His training in design would help him to know how to furnish the house simply and decorating would be simple, too.

_____

15. The landlady told him that he could not have a microwave in his room and showers after 11:00 o'clock.

_____

16. Hearing no car horns and buses and to be miles from friends may cause him to become bored and restless.

_____

17. Either the mouse will find a quick way into the attic or will gnaw at the siding for days.

_____

18. City living is exciting, convenient, and provides plenty of entertainment.

_____

19. After winning the lottery, he'll have an apartment in town, a house in the country, and find a job in the suburbs.

_____

20. I think that Adam has the ability to win his match, defeat Tom in the sectionals, and he'll emerge eventually as the best high school wrestler in the state.

_____

Answers are on pages 97–98.

16. Active and Passive Construction

Active sentences strengthen prose; passive sentences weaken it. In an **active sentence** the person or thing performing an action is usually mentioned early so that readers know right away who or what you are talking about. In some contexts, though, the actor is unknown or irrelevant. That's when a **passive sentence**—a sentence structured in the *passive voice*—is more appropriate. For example:

Passive: The curtain was raised at 8:30 sharp.

Active: At 8:30 sharp, a stagehand (or Maryanne, the production assistant) raised the curtain.

In the passive version, curtain time is the important fact. Who pulled the rope or pushed the button is beside the point.

Other occasions when a passive-voice sentence may be appropriate, or even preferable, include:

- When the point of the sentence is to reveal the identity of the actor:

  Active: Tommy, an eight-year-old boy, hacked into the agency's computer system.

  Passive: The agency's computer system was hacked into by Tommy, an eight-year-old boy.

- When you want to conceal the actor.

  Active: Sorry, I lost the library book.

  Passive: Sorry, the library book has been lost.

- When you want to avoid using gender-based pronouns.

  Active: Every member of the marching band must return his or her uniform.

  Passive: Uniforms must be returned by every member of the marching band.

Transforming a passive sentence to an active one may take a bit of doing:

Six weeks were spent preparing for the voter registration drive.

This sentence needs revision because it fails to tell who performed the action. That is, who prepared for the campaign to register voters?

Six weeks were spent preparing for the voter registration drive by the Young Republican Club.

This version contains more information than the original, but it still emphasizes the action instead of who performed the action. Complete the transformation from a passive to an active sentence by saying something like

The Young Republican Club prepared for the voter registration drive for six weeks.

Why is the active voice preferable to the passive voice? Usually passive verbs are less emphatic than active verbs, and they often lead to dull, involved, wordy, or vague sentences. What's more, most events in life don't just occur by themselves. Somebody—a person or thing—acts. Burgers, for instance, don't just get eaten; people cook and devour them. Marriages don't just happen; couples deliberately go out and wed. Goals don't score, salmon don't get caught, and wallets don't get lost all by themselves. People do these things.

Good writers, taking advantage of readers' innate curiosity about others, strengthen their prose by making performers the grammatical subject of their sentences.

➥ SAMPLE QUESTION

Growing up in San Diego, Doreen Davis was never far from the sea or from the U.S. Navy. At an early age, she set her sights on enrolling in the U.S. Naval Academy in Annapolis, Maryland. Her appetite for hard work and discipline fueled her desire to become a commissioned naval officer. She might say, in fact, that Navy blood runs in her veins. Annapolis was attended by her brother, her cousin, and three of her uncles, and she is determined to keep the family tradition alive.

   A. NO CHANGE
   B. Annapolis had been attended by her brother, cousin, and three uncles,
   C. Her brother, cousin, and three of her uncles went to Annapolis,
   D. Her brother, her cousin, and three uncles will have attended Annapolis,

Answer Explanation

Choice C is the best answer because it is written in the active voice and follows logically from the idea in the previous sentence.

Choice A is not the best answer because it is written in the passive voice and shifts the focus of the passage to Annapolis instead of keeping it on the idea that "Navy blood runs in her veins."

Choice B is not the best answer because, as a passive sentence, it needlessly shifts the subject to Annapolis. In addition, the verb *had been attended*, while not incorrect, is awkward in the context.

Choice D is not the best answer because the future perfect tense of the verb *will have attended* is inappropriate in the context.

Mini-Workout in Revising Passive Sentences

> **Directions:** Please rewrite the following sentences, putting each in the active voice.

1. Statistics from the Census Bureau were cited by the author.

_____

2. The crisis in the Middle East was discussed by us.

_____

3. Friday's quiz was failed because I had been at a play rehearsal instead of studying every night that week.

_____

4. Portland was driven to at the start of our week-long college tour.

_____

5. The great white whale was pursued by Captain Ahab and his crew.

_____

6. The news of the day is checked online by Carrie every morning.

_____

7. The decision to go to war was made by the president and his advisors.

_____

8. Dinner was taken out by more than twenty customers on Friday night.

_____

9. Five of Shakespeare's plays were seen by our group in three days.

_____

10. Normally, the brain is called on by the body before you do something physical.

_____

Answers are on page 98.

17. Misplaced and Dangling Modifiers

MISPLACED MODIFIERS

Modifiers are words, phrases, and clauses that tell something about or limit the meaning of a particular word or statement. For example:

Every house on the block had *broken* windows.

The adjective *broken* is a modifier because it tells something about the condition of the *windows*. In other words, *broken* "modifies" *windows*.

Jessie ordered a mouse online *that was guaranteed to work with her computer*.

The clause *that was guaranteed to work with her computer* is a modifier because it tells something about the mouse. Therefore, it "modifies" the noun *mouse*.

Modifiers must be placed so that they modify the correct words:

> Mike only loves Sharon.

Here *only* modifies the verb *loves*. The modifier is appropriate if Mike feels nothing but love for Sharon—no admiration, no awe, no respect, nor any other emotion. If, however, Mike has but one love, and she is Sharon, then *only* is misplaced. Properly placed, *only* should come either before or after *Sharon*:

> Mike loves *only* Sharon. or Mike loves Sharon *only*.

Another example:

> Naomi decided *when she had finished the essay* to watch TV.

In this sentence, *when she had finished the essay* is the modifier. But it is hard to tell whether it modifies *decided* or *watch*. If it modifies *decided*, Naomi finished her essay and then made a decision to watch TV. If it modifies *watch*, Naomi worked on her essay and decided at some point that she would watch TV when she had completed the work.

> When she had finished the essay, Naomi decided to watch TV.
> While writing an essay Naomi decided to watch TV when she had finished.

Now the meaning of both sentences is unambiguous.

Obviously, misplaced modifiers can cloud a writer's intentions. To avoid the problem, place modifiers as close as possible to the words they modify:

> **Misplaced:** Juan donated his old car to a charity *that no longer ran well*.

The modifier *that no longer ran well* is too far from *car*, the word it modifies.

> **Clear:** Juan donated to a charity his old car that *no longer ran well*.

> **Misplaced:** The bowling alley lends out shoes to its customers *of all sizes*.

The modifier *of all sizes* should be closer to *shoes*, the word it modifies.

> **Clear:** The bowling alley lends out shoes *of all sizes* to its customers.

DANGLING MODIFIERS

In a sentence, words must fit together like pieces of a jigsaw puzzle. Sometimes, a misplaced word looks as though it fits, but it fails to say what the writer intended.

> (1) While running to English class, the bell rang.
> (2) Working full time, the summer passed quickly.
> (3) When only eight years old, my father warned me about smoking.

The ludicrous meaning of these sentences may not strike you immediately, but look again. Do you see that these sentences describe a surreal world in which bells run to class, summers hold full-time jobs, and youthful fathers dispense advice? The problem is that these sentences try to mate two groups of words that can't go together. The parts are mismatched. After the comma in sentence 1, you expect to find out who is running, but you are not told. Likewise, after the commas in sentences 2 and 3, you are not told who was working and who is only eight years old. In short, you're left dangling. Hence, the label **dangling modifier** has been given to this type of construction. To correct the error, add the noun or pronoun to be modified, as in:

While the boys were running to English class, the bell rang.
Because Charlotte worked full-time, her summer flew by.
When I was eight, my father warned me about smoking.

Re-writing the whole sentence is often the best cure for a dangling modifier, as in:

Dangling:	Still sound asleep at noon, my mother thought I might be sick.
Clear:	My mother thought I might be sick because I was still sound asleep at noon.
Dangling:	While texting Juliet, the stew burned in the pot.
Clear:	While I texted Juliet, the stew burned in the pot.

Mini-Workout in Misplaced and Dangling Modifiers

Directions: Revise any of the sentences that contain misplaced or dangling modifiers. Some sentences may be correct. To correct a faulty sentence, shift the placement of one or more words. Some sentences may need more substantial revisions.

1. After completing that chemistry homework, that pizza tasted great.

   _____

2. Sound asleep in the hammock, Denise discovered her boyfriend.

   _____

3. Used all night to illuminate the steps, Cora needed new batteries for her flashlight.

   _____

4. Driving down the mountain road, the brakes failed.

   _____

5. Stopping to rest after a long hike, a grizzly bear stood in front of me.

   _____

6. After a quick breakfast, the school bus picked me up.

_____

7. A report was submitted about the bank robbery by the police.

_____

8. At the age of ten, Sasha's family emigrated from Russia.

_____

9. The bone was chewed by the dog we threw in the trash after last night's dinner.

_____

10. Left alone in the house, every sound terrified the child.

_____

Answers on page 98.

18. Punctuation

A few basic rules cover 90 percent of everyday punctuation. The hardest thing about the rules is knowing where and when to apply them.

Apostrophes. Apostrophes are used in only three places:

1. In **contractions** such as *won't, it's, could've*, and *where's*. Apostrophes mark places where letters have been omitted.
2. In **plurals** of letters, signs, or numbers, as in *A's* and *B's*, the *1960's*, and *10's* and *20's*, *although* many experts simplify matters by writing *1960s, Ps* and *Qs*, and so forth.
3. In **possessive nouns** such as the *student's class* and *women's room* and in indefinite pronouns such as *anybody's guess*. When the noun is plural and ends in *s*, put the apostrophe after the *s*, as in *leaves' color* and *horses' stable*. Some possessive forms use both an apostrophe and *of*, as in *a friend of the family's*; some others that specify time, space, value, or quantity also require apostrophes, as in *an hour's time, a dollar's worth, at my wit's end*.

Commas. Commas divide sentences into parts, clarify meaning, and prevent confusion.

1. Use a comma to signal a **pause**, as in

No pause: After brushing his teeth gleamed.
Pause: After brushing, his teeth gleamed.

Commas are needed after some introductory words and in forms of address:

Well, you can open it whenever it's convenient.
The letter will be waiting for you at home, *Jimmy*.

2. Commas set off words that **interrupt the flow** of a sentence, as in

Carolyn, *regrettably*, was omitted from the roster.
Jennie, *on the other hand*, was included.

The hikers, who had come from New Jersey, found shelter in a cave.

This sentence conveys the basic information that the hikers found shelter in a cave. The fact that they came from New Jersey may be interesting but it's more like a piece of trivia than a crucial bit of information.

On the other hand, these very same words can be written without commas:

The hikers who had come from New Jersey found shelter in a cave.

Do you see how the absence of commas has changed the meaning? As noted, in the first sentence (with commas) the origin of the hikers is incidental to the crucial point—that they found shelter. In the second sentence (without commas) the hikers' home state is essential because it specifically identifies which hikers found shelter. They're not the hikers from Delaware, Maryland, or anywhere else. They're the New Jersey hikers.

Grammarians have given the name *nonrestrictive* clause or *nonrestrictive* phrase to the words that fall between the commas. And they use the name *restrictive* to describe the clause or phrase that is written without commas.

Got it? If not, here's a quick review:

Nonrestrictive applies to a clause or phrase that does <u>not</u> identify the noun. It needs commas.

Restrictive applies to a clause or phrase that <u>does</u> identify the noun. It does not need commas.

➡ SAMPLE QUESTION

<u>Diabetic patients who are extremely overweight or obese</u> are required to adhere to a carbohydrate-free diet.

A. NO CHANGE
B. Diabetic patients, who are extremely overweight or obese,
C. Diabetic patients who are extremely overweight, or obese,
D. Diabetic patients who are extremely, overweight or obese,

Answer Explanation

This question relates to the use of commas in sentences that contain restrictive and/or non-restrictive clauses.

Choice A is the best answer because a restrictive clause (i.e., the underlined portion of the text) should not be punctuated. The clause *Diabetic patients who are extremely overweight or obese* is restrictive because the information it contains is essential to the meaning of the sentence. In other words, it specifies the people who require the carb-free diet.

Choice B is not the best answer because it contains the punctuation needed by a nonrestrictive clause. Using commas to set off the words *who are extremely overweight or obese* turns that description of the patients into an nonessential element in the sentence.

Choice C is not the best answer because it improperly uses a comma to separate the two adjectives, *overweight* and *obese*, that define the patients. Nor is a comma needed after *obese*.

Choice D is not the best answer because it contains two unnecessary commas. Their placement improperly separates the sentence subject (*Diabetic patients who are extremely overweight or obese*) from the predicate (*are required to adhere to a carbohydrate-free diet*).

3. Commas set off **appositives:**

   Samantha, *the defense counsel*, entered the courtroom.
   The judge, *Mr. Peterson*, presided at the trial.

4. Commas separate the clauses of a **compound sentence:**

   The competition is stiff, but it won't keep Miriam from winning.
   Pete had better call my mother, or I'll be in big trouble.

5. Commas separate items in a **series:**

   Rosie's car needs *new tires, a battery, a muffler, and an oil change.*
   It was a wonder that Marv could sit through the *long, boring, infantile, and ridiculous* lecture.

   Some writers prefer to skip the comma before the conjunction that precedes the last element in a series of three of more. Enlightened writers generally refuse to do that, however. You should, too. In other words, use the so-called *Serial comma*—a.k.a. the *Oxford comma* and the *Harvard comma.*

6. Commas separate parts of **addresses, dates, and place names:**

   Who lives at 627 West 115th Street, New York, NY?
   Richard was born on May 27, 1996, the same day as Irene.
   Dave has lived in Madison, Wisconsin; Seattle, Washington; and Eugene, Oregon.

   Note that, because each item in the last example already contains a comma, semicolons help to avoid confusion.

7. Commas separate quotations from attributions in **dialogue:**

   John said, "Close the window."
   "I want it open," protested Ben.

Semicolons. Semicolons may be used between closely related sentences, in effect shortening the pause that would naturally occur between two separate sentences:

   Mother is worried; her daughters never stay out this late.
   The momentum was building; she couldn't be stopped now.

   A caution: Because semicolons function like periods, use them only between independent clauses or in a series in which one or more items contains a comma, as in:

   On his trek, Norwood met Allen, a carpenter from Maine; Dr. Jones, a pediatrician from St. Louis; Jonathan, an airline pilot; and me, of course.

Finally, quotation marks may enclose words that express the silent thoughts of a character, as in:

Carlos glanced at his watch. "I'm going to be late," he thought.

Periods and commas are placed inside close-quotation marks. Question marks and exclamation points go outside the quotation mark unless they are part of the quote itself.

"When will the seminar start?" asked Regis.
Do you understand the meaning of the concept "The end justifies the means"?

Mini-Workout in Punctuation

PART A. POSSESSIVES

Directions: Check your mastery of possessives by writing the correct possessive form of the italicized word in the space provided. Some items may be correct.

1. *Pauls* reason was personal.

   _____

2. The future of *Americas* foreign policy is being debated.

   _____

3. *Teams* from all over the county have gathered at the stadium.

   _____

4. Luis isn't at all interested in *womens* issues.

   _____

5. The *girls* locker room is downstairs, but the *boys* is upstairs.

   _____

6. We are invited to the *Andersons* house for New *Years* Eve.

   _____

7. All of the *Rosses* are going out to eat.

   _____

8. Have you seen *Morris* iPod, which he left here yesterday?

   _____

9. Both of the *computers* keyboards need repair.

   _____

10. He'll be back in two *months* time.

   _____

Answers are on pages 98–99.

PART B. COMMAS AND SEMICOLONS

Directions: In the following sentences, insert or remove commas and semicolons as necessary. Some sentences may be correct.

1. While Bill was riding his bike got a flat tire.

2. The mail carrier did not leave the package for Valerie was not at home.

3. After doing his homework Mikey as you might expect talked on his cell phone for an hour.

4. His work criticized many commonly held beliefs however and it was strictly censored.

5. The car, that ran into mine at the intersection, was an SUV.

6. Dad went to the airport to pick up Dave Ellie went to the train station to meet Debbie.

7. The people who live by the water must be prepared for occasional flooding.

8. The boat, was seventy-five feet long and eighteen feet wide, its mast was about eighty feet tall.

9. To anyone interested in flying planes hold endless fascination.

10. Jeff and Steve left alone for the weekend invited all their friends to a party.

11. I need street maps of Boston; and Portland, Maine.

12. Some of the theories dealt with the political social and religious ideas of the time.

13. Students, who want to try out for the chorus, have been asked to report to room 330.

14. Doug for example is both a scholar and an athlete.

15. Monica refused to go, unless Phil went with her.

16. The hero of the book John Coffey rode his bike across the United States.

17. After all she did for him what she could.

18. Starting in Minnesota the Mississippi runs all the way to the Gulf of Mexico.

19. Harold Watkins who comes from Chicago won a full tuition scholarship to Duke.

20. Although the characters are stereotypes they were interesting to read about.

21. Yo-Yo Ma the famous cellist will perform a recital on Saturday night.

22. This test covers Spanish literature culture and history; and it lasts for three hours.

23. Michelle is pretty tall and dark but her older sister Norma is pretty short and light.

24. Sean the twin brother of Ian was struck by a falling tree limb.

25. The window washer dropped by last evening but he didn't bring his squeegee.

Answers are on page 99.

Capitalization

Capitalization isn't totally standardized, but it's not a free-for-all either. You won't go wrong following these guidelines:

1. Capitalize the first words of sentences, direct quotations, and lines of poetry (most of the time). This includes sentences that follow colons, as in

   He had all the symptoms of love: He could think of nothing but Cheryl all day long.

2. Capitalize proper nouns and adjectives derived from proper nouns: *Victoria, Victorian; Shakespeare, Shakespearean; France, French dressing* (but not *french fries*, which has become a generic term).

3. Capitalize place names: *North America, Lake Moosilauke, Yosemite National Park, Gobi Desert, Mount Rushmore, Panama Canal, the Arctic Ocean, Times Square, Route 66.* Don't capitalize north, east, south, and west unless you are referring to a particular region of the country, as in

   They went camping in the *West*.

   Nor should you capitalize the common noun that is not part of the actual place name: the *canal across Panama,* the *city of Moline,* and the *plains of the Midwest.*

   Answer to math problem on page 306: 64.

4. Capitalize languages, races, nationalities, and religions: *the Hungarian language, Inuit, Argentinian, Hispanic, Muslim.*

5. Capitalize organizations, institutions, and brand names: *United Nations, Pittsburgh Pirates, Library of Congress, Automobile Club of America, Amtrak, Southwest Airlines, the Internet, Toyota.* Don't, however, capitalize the common noun associated with the brand name, as in *Crest toothpaste or Starbuck's coffee.*

6. Capitalize titles of persons that indicate rank, office, profession, when they are used with the person's name: *Congressman Kelly, Doctor Dolittle, Coach McConnell, Judge Judy, Lieutenant Lawlor.* Also, the titles of high officials when they are used in place of the official's name, as in *the Secretary General, the Prime Minister, the Secretary of the Treasury.* Don't capitalize titles when referring generically to the position: *the superintendent of schools, the assistant librarian, the clerk of the highway department.*

7. Capitalize family relationships, but only when they are used with a person's name: *Uncle Wesley, Grandma Jones, Cousin Dave.*

8. Capitalize titles of books, plays, stories, articles, poems, songs, and other creative works: *The Grapes of Wrath, Hamlet, "An Occurrence at Owl Creek Bridge," "Ode to a Grecian Urn," "Box of Rain."* Note that articles, conjunctions, and prepositions of less than five letters are not capitalized unless they appear as the last or the first words in the title.

9. Capitalize references to the Deity and religious tracts: *God, the Gospel, the Torah, the Koran, the Lord, the Prophet.* Also capitalize pronouns referring to *Him* or *Her.*

10. Capitalize historical names, events, documents, and periods: *Battle of Gettysburg, Alien and Sedition Acts, War of 1812, Bill of Rights, Middle Ages.*

11. Capitalize days of the week, months, holidays: *Monday, May, Mother's Day.* The seasons are not capitalized unless given an identity such as *Old Man Winter.*

12. Capitalize the names of specific courses and schools: *History 101, Forensic Science, Brookvale High School, Columbia College.* While course names are capitalized, subjects are not. Therefore, you study *history* in *American History 101* and learn *forensics* in *Forensic Science.* Similarly, you attend *high school* at *Brookvale High School* and go to *college* at *Columbia.*

Mini-Workout in Capitalization

Directions: Add capital letters where they are needed in the following sentences.

1. on labor day bennington county's fire department plans to hold a turkey shoot on the field at miller's pond.

2. the judge gave district attorney lipman a book entitled *the rules of evidence* and instructed her to read it before she ever dared set foot in the court of appeals of the ninth circuit again.

3. the secretary of state greeted the president of austria at the ronald reagan airport in washington, d.c.

4. the shackleton expedition nearly met its doom on georgia island in antarctica.

5. for christmas he got a black & decker table saw from the sears store next to the old bedford courthouse.

6. according to georgetown's high school principal, eugene griffiths, georgetown high school attracts students from the whole west coast. at georgetown students may major in drawing and painting, design, graphics, or sculpture. mr. griffiths said, "i attended a similar high school in new england just after the vietnam war."

7. we expect to celebrate new year's eve again this year by ordering a movie of an old broadway musical from netflix and settling down in front of the dvd player with some pepsi and a box of oreos.

8. after traveling all the way to the pacific, the corps of discovery rode down the missouri river going east on their way back to st. louis.

9. This irish linen tablecloth was bought at k-mart in the emeryville mall off powell street.

10. yellowstone national park is located in the northwestern corner of the state of wyoming.

Answers are on pages 99–100.

QUESTIONS ON STANDARD ENGLISH USAGE

19. Noun-Verb Agreement

Sentence subjects and verbs must agree in number. A singular subject must be paired with a singular verb, and a plural subject with a plural verb. That's simple enough to remember but in some circumstances not so easy to apply.

1. When intervening words obscure the relationship between the subject and verb, as in:

Delivery (singular subject) of today's newspapers and magazines *have been* (plural verb) delayed.

The prepositional phrase *of today's newspapers and magazines* blurs the relationship between subject and verb. The plural noun *magazines* can mislead the writer into using a plural verb. With a singular subject and verb properly matched, the sentence reads:

Delivery of today's newspapers and magazines *has been* delayed.

Or with matched plural subject and verb:

Deliveries of today's newspapers and magazines *have been* delayed.

A writer can also err when words and phrases such as *including, in addition to, along with,* and *as well as* come between the subject and verb.

> *One* of his paintings, in addition to several photos, *is* on display at the library.
> The *bulk* of English poetry, including the plays of Shakespeare, *is written* in iambic pentameter.

2. When subjects are composed of more than one noun or pronoun. For example,
   a. Nouns, both singular and plural, when joined by *and,* are called compound subjects, which need plural verbs.

   > The *picture and the text* (compound subject) *fit* (plural verb) inside this box.
   > Several *locust trees and a green mailbox stand* outside the house.

   b. Compound subjects thought of as a unit need singular verbs.

   > Green *eggs and ham* (compound subject as a unit) *is* (singular verb) Sam's favorite breakfast.
   > The parents' *pride and joy* over the birth of their baby *is* self-evident.

   c. Singular nouns joined by *or* or *nor* need singular verbs.

   > A Coke *or* a Pepsi (two nouns joined by *or*) *is* (singular verb) what I thirst for.
   > *Neither* my history teacher *nor* my economics teacher *plans* to discuss the crisis.

   d. When a subject consists of a singular noun and a plural noun joined by *or* or *nor,* the number of the verb is determined by the noun closer to the verb.

   > *Either one pineapple or a few oranges were* on the table.
   > *Neither the linemen nor the quarterback was* aware of the tricky play.

   e. When a subject contains a pronoun that differs in person from a noun or another pronoun, the verb must agree with the closer subject word.

   > Neither Meredith nor *you are* expected to finish the work today.
   > Either he or *I am* planning to work late on Saturday.

   f. When the subject is singular and the predicate noun is plural, or vice-versa, the number of the verb is determined by the subject.

   > The *extent* of Wilkinson's work *is* two novels and a collection of stories.
   > Two *novels and a story are* the extent of Wilkinson's work.

3. When singular subjects contain words that sound plural, use singular verbs. The names of books, countries, organizations, certain diseases, course titles, and other singular nouns may sound like plurals because they end in –*s,* but most of the time—although not always—they require a singular verb.

> The *news is* good.
> *Measles is* going around the school.

4. When the subject is sometimes singular and sometimes plural, the number of the verb depends on the context. Collective nouns sound singular but may be plural. A family, for example, is singular. But if you are referring to separate individuals, *family* takes a plural verb.

The *family* (members) *are* arriving for the wedding at different times.

Other collective nouns include *group, crowd, team, jury, audience, herd, public, dozen, class, band, flock, majority, committee, heap,* and *lot.* Other words and expressions governed by the same rule are units of time, money, weight, measurement, and all fractions.

The *jury is* going to decide today.
The *jury are* returning to their homes tomorrow.

5. When the subject word is an indefinite pronoun, such as *everyone, both,* and *any,* choosing the correct verb poses a special problem. Some indefinite pronouns must be matched with singular verbs, some with plural verbs, and some with one or the other, depending on the sense of the sentence. There's no getting around the fact that you need to know which number applies to which pronoun.

a. These words, although they sound plural, get singular verbs: *each, either, neither,* the "ones" (*anyone, no one, everyone, someone*), and the "bodies" (*anybody, everybody, nobody, somebody*).

Each man and woman in the room *gets* only one vote.
Everyone who works hard *is* going to earn an "A."

b. These words get plural verbs: *both, many, few, several.*

In spite of rumors to the contrary, *both are* on the verge of a nervous breakdown.
Several in the band *are* not going on the trip to Boston.

c. The following words get singular verbs when they refer to singular nouns and plural verbs when they refer to plural nouns: *any, none, some, all, most.*

Some of the collection is valuable.

In this sentence, *some* is singular because it refers to *collection*, a singular noun.

Some of the bracelets are fake.

Here *some* is plural because it refers to *bracelets*, a plural noun.

6. When the subject comes after the verb. When the subject of a sentence follows the verb, the verb takes its number from the subject, as usual.

Behind the building *was* an *alley* (singular subject).
Behind the building *were* an *alley and a vacant lot* (compound subject).

At some big state universities the <u>problem of giving scholarships, as well as other perks, to good athletes have gotten</u> out of hand.

    A. NO CHANGE
    B. problem of giving a scholarship as well as other perks, to good athletes have gotten
    C. problems of giving a scholarship and other perks to a good athlete has gotten
    D. problem of giving scholarships as well as other perks to good athletes has gotten

Answer Explanation

Choice D is the best answer because the singular subject of the sentence *problem* and the verb *has gotten* agree in number.

Choice A is not the best answer because the singular sentence subject, *problem*, fails to agree in number with the plural verb *have gotten*.

Choice B is not the best answer because the sentence subject, *problem*, is singular and does not agree in number with the plural verb *have gotten*.

Choice C is not the best answer because the subject *problems* is plural and fails to agree in number with the singular verb *has gotten*.

Mini-Workout in Establishing Noun–Verb Agreement

> **Directions:** In some of the following sentences, nouns and verbs do not agree. Locate the error and write the corrected version in the space provided. Some sentences may be correct.

1. Tucker's talent in chess and weight lifting, two of our school's most popular teams, prove his mental and physical strength.

_____

_____

2. The book told stories of thirteen young heroes, each a member of a firefighting team, who dies fighting forest fires.

_____

_____

3. At the end of the season, the team, regardless of whether they win the championship, are splitting up.

_____

_____

4. Either Don or you is going to lead the class discussion on Tuesday.

_____

_____

5. Jane and Mark, who began their yard cleanup business last spring, have decided to hire two new helpers.

_____

_____

6. There is many levels on which a reader will be able to enjoy this book.

_____

_____

7. Admission proceeds from the concert is going toward rebuilding the gazebo, burned down by vandals during the summer.

_____

_____

8. The newspaper reports that a rescue team experienced in climbing rugged mountains are expected to arrive at the site of the crash tomorrow morning.

_____

_____

9. Before they were laid off by the company, neither the assistant managers nor Mr. McCallum were told that their jobs were in danger.

_____

_____

10. Many Democratic senators contend that reforms in the tax system has not brought about the economic growth that had been predicted.

_____

_____

11. Learning to read the daily box scores printed in the newspaper is a desirable thing to do by any fan who expect to develop a deep understanding of baseball.

_____

_____

12. Politics on both the national and local level have always been one of Dave's passions.

_____

_____

13. Charles Darwin, along with his contemporary, Abraham Lincoln, are among the most impressive figures in nineteenth-century history.

_____

_____

14. Katie Green, one of the hottest jazz pianists in town and known for something she calls "3-D playing," and her accompanist Lenny is planning to tour the South in May.

_____

_____

15. Nancy, along with her friend Sluggo, appear to be coming down the escalator.

_____

_____

16. The sale of computers in a market that has nearly a billion potential customers have created enormous hope for the company's future.

_____

_____

17. Here's the two statutes to which the defense lawyer referred during the trial.

_____

_____

18. The commissioner's insistence on high ethical standards are transforming the city's police force.

_____

_____

19. No one in the drum corps, in spite of how they all feel about the issue, want to participate in the rally.

_____

_____

20. According to school policy, there is to be two security guards stationed in the playground during recess to protect the children.

_____

_____

Answers are on page 100.

20. Verbs

Verbs serve as the backbone of written and spoken language. Every sentence needs one. Many writers assert that no other part of speech carries as much power as verbs.

20A. Verb Tenses

The tense of all verbs—both action and state-of-being verbs—tells you approximately when an action occurred. Past action, for example, is usually indicated by adding *–ed* to the basic form of the verb, as in *walk/walked* and *paint/painted*. Each tense is indicated by a slight alteration of the basic verb, often by tacking on a certain ending or with the addition of a so-called helping verb, as in *will graduate* (future), *has graduated* (present perfect), and *had graduated* (past perfect).

Passages on the SAT Writing and Language Test may contain errors in verb tense. Sometimes the wrong tense is used or an inappropriate shift from one tense to another occurs, either between sentences or within a single sentence, as in

Before it went out of business, the video store puts its flat-screen TVs on sale.

The sentence begins in the past tense and then shifts to the present. When cast in the past tense from start to finish, the sentence reads:

Before it went out of business, the video store put its flat-screen TVs on sale.

The English language offers six basic tenses that convey information about the time of an action or event:

Present:	The judge *hears* cases daily.
Past:	She *heard* cases daily.
Future:	Her colleague *will hear* cases every day from now on.
Present Perfect:	Their new associate *has heard* cases for years.
Past Perfect:	He *had heard* most of the case before it was settled out of court.
Future Perfect:	They all *will have heard* hundreds of cases by year's end.

All verbs also have a progressive form, created by adding *–ing*, so that you can say things like:

They are swimming. (Present Progressive)
Rose was swimming. (Past Progressive)
The dog will be swimming. (Future Progressive)
I have been swimming. (Present Perfect Progressive)

Charles had been swimming. (Past Perfect Progressive)
They will have been swimming. (Future Perfect Progressive)

Each of these tenses permits you to indicate time sequence very precisely. Someone not attuned to the different meaning that each tense conveys may say something like this:

When her little brother was born, Sarah was toilet trained for six months.

Perhaps the writer's intent is clear enough, but because precision is important, the sentence should read:

When her little brother was born, Sarah *had been* toilet trained for six months.

The revised version, using the past perfect progressive verb *had been*, indicates that the action (Sarah's toilet training) had taken place prior to her brother's birth. The original sentence actually says that her brother's birth and Sarah's toilet training took place at the same time—a physical impossibility, since potty training usually takes weeks or even months.

Notice also the difference in meaning between these two sentences:

There was a condo where the park was.
There was a condo where the park had been.

The meaning of the first sentence may be clear, but it says that the condo and the park were in the same place at the same time. The revision more accurately conveys the idea that the condo replaced the park.

➡ SAMPLE QUESTION

Janine had been working as an intern in the bank's loan department for months before the manager <u>invites her</u> to work as his executive assistant.

    A. NO CHANGE
    B. will invite her
    C. invited her
    D. has invited her

Answer Explanation

Choice C is the best answer because it accurately conveys the sequence of events. The use of the past tense (*invited*) indicates that Janine's work as an intern occurred not only prior to the manager's invitation but that it was in progress at the time the manager asked her to accept another job.

Choice A is not the best answer because the present tense verb *invites* is inconsistent with the past perfect tense of the verb *had been working*.

Choice B is not the best answer. In the context, the use of a verb in the future tense is illogical and confusing.

Choice D is not the best answer because the present perfect tense cannot be used to express past action.

Mini-Workout in Verb Tenses

Directions: In these sentences, many of the underlined verbs are in the wrong tense. Write the revised verbs in the spaces provided. Some sentences contain no error.

1. They biked to the top of the mountain and then <u>come</u> back down in time to eat lunch.

   _____

2. The garage mechanic thinks that Mrs. Murphy <u>has brought</u> her car in last night.

   _____

3. For anyone with enough brains to have thought about the problem, now <u>is</u> the time to work out a solution.

   _____

4. When Washington was sworn in as president, he <u>rode</u> to New York from his home in Virginia.

   _____

5. If the wagon train <u>would have reached</u> Salt Creek in time, the massacre would have been prevented.

   _____

6. The aircraft controller <u>expects</u> to have spotted the plane on radar before dusk last night.

   _____

7. The family already <u>finished</u> dinner when the doorbell rang.

   _____

8. First he built a fire, then dragged a log over to use as a seat, and finally <u>collected</u> enough wood to keep the fire going all night.

   _____

9. Rose kept the promise she <u>has given</u> to Charles last year in India.

   _____

10. When he talks with Horatio, Hamlet <u>began</u> to suspect foul play in the kingdom.

   _____

11. As they drove to Vermont, they <u>had stopped</u> for lunch at Bucky's Bagel Shop.

_____

12. On Route 684, a trooper pulls him over and <u>gave</u> him a speeding ticket.

_____

13. <u>Working</u> all year to improve her writing, Debbie got a story published in the newspaper.

_____

14. That night at the show we met many people that we <u>saw</u> that afternoon.

_____

15. Once the drought had hit eastern Africa, the Somalis <u>have suffered</u> terribly.

_____

Answers are on pages 100–101.

20B. Verb Forms

Most verbs follow a prescribed formula for changing tenses. A problem arises, however, with so-called irregular verbs—those verbs that don't follow the usual pattern. The verb *to choose*, for instance, is *choose* in the present tense, *chose* in the past, and *chosen* in its participle, or "perfect," form. Other common examples of irregular verbs include *break, broke, has broken*; *begin, began, has begun*; and *rise, rose, has risen*. Sentence errors occur when the wrong form is used.

Another kind of error—usually a sentence fragment—occurs when the writer tries to use the *–ing* form of a verb as the main verb in a sentence, as in

The researcher in the greenhouse measuring plant growth after applying fertilizer.

The problem is that the *–ing* form cannot be used as the main verb unless accompanied by a helping verb, as in

The researcher in the greenhouse *was measuring* plant growth after she applied the fertilizer.

The addition of the helping verb *was* corrects the error. Other helping verbs include *is, will be, has been*, and other forms of the verb *to be*.

In spite of the cold and discomfort of the journey, Max and his fellow students were thrilled to have underwent the experience of studying the northern lights in person.

    A. NO CHANGE
    B. to have undergone the experience of studying
    C. to have undertook the experience to study
    D. undergoing the experience of studying

Answer Explanation

Choice B is the best answer because it uses the verb in its proper form.

Choice A is not the best answer because it uses *have underwent,* a nonstandard form of the verb *to undergo.*

Choice C is not the best answer because it uses *have undertook* a nonstandard form of the verb *to undertake.* It also contains the unidiomatic phrase *experience to study.*

Choice D is not the best answer because it improperly uses the *–ing* form of a verb without a helping verb.

Mini-Workout in Verb Forms

> **Directions:** In these sentences, the underlined verbs may not be in the correct form. Write the standard form of the verb in the spaces provided. Some verbs may be correct.

1. The company's security assistant was fired because he use to arrive late almost every day.

    _____

2. Conflicts between the salesmen and the office staff have regularly arose under the pressure of the holiday season.

    _____

3. Given the choice of Monday, Wednesday, or Friday for her talk, the attorney demanded to speak on Thursday.

    _____

4. During her audition for the part of Laura in *The Glass Menagerie,* Sarah cleared the table and blowed out the candles.

    _____

5. They had begun the simulation on their own before the technical personnel arrived.

_____

6. When the new mechanic revved the engine, the radiator hose had bursted.

_____

7. To get a seat at the conference table, you should have went to the meeting earlier than you did.

_____

8. The chorus messed up that song because they had never sang it before.

_____

9. Halfway to the office I realized that my front tire had sprang a leak.

_____

10. The novels of John Greene have managed attracting millions of adolescent readers.

_____

Answers are on page 101.

21. Pronouns

It can't be proved, but adult writers of English probably use the correct pronoun 99 out of a 100 times. Total compliance with the rules of pronoun usage may be out of reach, but knowing how to choose the right pronoun at the right time will help you avoid pitfalls that may show up on the Writing and Language Test, such as

- A pronoun in the wrong "case" or "person"
- A pronoun that fails to agree in number or gender with its antecedents (i.e., the nouns for which the pronoun is a substitute)
- A pronoun reference that is unclear or ambiguous

21A. Pronoun Choice

A dozen common English pronouns—*I, me, he, she, him, her, it, they, them, we, us,* and *you*—cause more trouble than almost any other words in the language. Almost as troublesome—but not quite—are the possessive pronouns *my, mine, his, her, hers, your, yours, our, ours, their,* and *theirs.*

PRONOUN CASE

Most of the time you can probably depend on your ear to tell you what's right and wrong. For example, you'd never say to the bus driver, "Let *I* off at the corner." But when you can't depend on the sound of the words, it helps to know that those twelve pronouns fall into two groups.

Group 1	Group 2
I	me
he	him
she	her
it	it
they	them
we	us
you	you

In grammatical terms, the pronouns in Group 1 are in the **nominative case** (sometimes called *subjective case*); pronouns in Group 2 are in the **objective case**. (FYI, a third case consists of **possessive** pronouns, such as *my, mine, your, yours, hers, his, our, ours, their,* and *theirs,* but they're rarely used incorrectly by native speakers of English.)

Remember that you mustn't mix pronouns from different cases in the same phrase. You may not, for example, use such pairs as *she and them* or *they and us.* Any time you need a pair of pronouns and you know that one of them is correct, you can easily pick the other from the same group. If you're not sure of either pronoun, though, substitute *I* or *me* for one of the pronouns. If *I* seems to fit, you're in Group 1; if *me* fits better, use Group 2.

Elvis asked that (he, him) and (she, her) practice handstands.

If you insert *me* in place of one of the pronouns, you'll get:

Elvis asked that *me* practice handstands.

Because no one would say that seriously, *I* must be the word that fits. So the pronouns you need come from Group 1, and the sentence should read:

Elvis asked that *he* and *she* practice handstands.

Now, if you can remember a few more rules, you'll be well prepared to deal with pronoun errors on the SAT.

1. Use nominative case pronouns for the subject of sentences and for predicate nominatives.
The term *predicate nominative* refers to words not in the subject of the sentence that identify, define, or mean the same as the subject.

Then he and I went home. (*he and I* = subject)

The instructors in the computer coding course were Donald and he. (*instructors* = subject; *Donald and he* = predicate nominative)

Yes, it may sound strange, or even wrong, to say "It was *I* (not *me*) who sent the e-mail" or "It is *I*" in response to the question "Who's there?" but those are instances of formal

English usage—the usage appropriate for the SAT. Of course, when you're hanging out with friends, you won't impress them very much by saying "It was I...," etc., but as you know, on the SAT your friends' opinions don't count.

2. Use objective case pronouns in phrases that begin with prepositions, as in

<u>between</u> *you* and *me*
<u>to</u> Sherry and *her*
<u>among</u> *us* women
<u>at</u> *us*
<u>from</u> *her* and *him*
<u>with</u> *me* and *you*

3. Use objective case pronouns when the pronoun refers to a person to whom something is being done:

The personnel office invited *him* back for a second job interview.
The waiter handed *her* and *me* the wrong menu.

4. To find the correct pronoun in a comparison, complete the comparison using the verb that would follow naturally:

Jacqueline texts faster than *she* (texts).
My brother has a bigger ego than *I* (do).
Carol is as tough-minded as *he* (is).
No one such as *I* (am) could solve that problem.

5. When a pronoun appears side by side with a noun (*we* boys, *us* women), deleting the noun will help you pick the correct pronoun:

(*We, Us*) seniors decided to take a day off from school in late May. (Deleting *seniors* leaves <u>We</u> *decided to*...).
This award was presented to (*we, us*) students by the faculty. (Deleting *students* leaves *award was presented to* <u>us</u> *by the*...).

6. Use possessive pronouns (*my, our, your, his, her, their*) before a *gerund*, a noun that looks like a verb because of its *–ing* ending.

Her asking the question shows that she is alert. (*Asking* is a gerund.)
Mother was upset about *your* opening the presents too soon. (*Opening* is a gerund.)

Not every noun with an *–ing* ending is a gerund. Sometimes it's just a noun, as in *thing, ring, spring*. At other times, *-ing* words are verbs, in particular, they're participles that modify pronouns in the objective case.

I hope you don't mind *my* intruding on your conversation. (Here *intruding* is a gerund.)
I hope you don't mind *me* intruding on your conversation. (Here *intruding* is a participle.)

> ## WHAT IS A GERUND?
>
> A gerund is a verb form that ends in *-ing* and is used as a noun.
>
> *Fishing* is my grandpa's favorite pastime.
> He started *fishing* as a boy in North Carolina.
> As a result of all that *fishing*, he hates to eat fish.
>
> In all three sentences the gerund is derived from the verb to *fish*. Don't confuse gerunds with the participle form of verbs, as in:
>
> Participle: *Fishing* from the bank of the river, my Grandpa caught a catfish.
>
> Gerund: *Fishing* from the bank of a river is my Grandpa's greatest pleasure.

➡️ SAMPLE QUESTION

The newspaper column was written to help students like <u>he and I</u> to write more interesting college application essays.

    A. NO ERROR

    B. him and me

    C. he and me

    D. him and I

Answer Explanation

Choice B is the best answer because the pronouns *him* and *me* are objects of the preposition *like* ("like him and me" is a prepositional phrase) and, therefore, must be in the objective case.

Choice A is not the best answer because both *he* and *I* are nominative case pronouns and, therefore, may not be objects of the preposition *like*.

Choice C is not the best answer because the nominative case pronoun *he* may not be the object of the preposition *like*.

Choice D is not the best answer because the nominative case pronoun *I* may not be the object of the preposition *like*.

Mini-Workout in Pronoun Case

> **Directions:** Circle the correct pronoun in each of the following sentences.

1. Judith took my sister and (I, me) to the magic show last night.

2. We thought that Matilda and Jorge would be there, and sure enough, we saw (she, her) and (he, him) sitting in the front row.

3. During the intermission, Jorge came over and asked my sister and (I, me) to go out after the show.

4. Between you and (I, me) the magician was terrible.

5. It must also have been a bad evening for (he, him) and his assistant, Roxanne.

6. Trying to pull a rabbit out of a hat, Roxanne and (he, him) knocked over the table.

7. When he asked for audience participation, my sister and (I, me) volunteered to go on stage.

8. He said that in my pocket I would find $10 in change to split between (I, me) and my sister.

9. When the coins fell out of his sleeve, the audience laughed even harder than (we, us).

10. If I were (he, him), I'd practice for a long time before the next performance.

Answers are on page 101.

SHIFT IN PRONOUN PERSON

Pronouns are categorized by person:

First-person pronouns:	*I, we, me, us, mine, our, ours*
Second-person pronouns:	*you, your, yours*
Third-person pronouns:	*she, he, it, one, they, him, her, them, his, hers, its, their, theirs, ours*

Indefinite pronouns such as *all, any, anyone, each, none, nothing, one, several,* and *many* are also considered to be in the third person.

Pronouns must be in the same person as their **antecedents**—the words they refer to. When a sentence is cast in, say, the first person, it should stay in the first person throughout. Consistency is the key.

Inconsistent:	When you (second person) walk your (second person) dog in that park, I (first person) must carry a pooper-scooper.
Consistent:	When you (second person) walk your (second person) dog in that park, you (second person) must carry a pooper-scooper.

The need to be consistent applies also to the use of indefinite pronouns, particularly when a writer switches from singular to plural pronouns in mid-sentence:

Inconsistent:	If *someone* tries to write a persuasive essay, *they* should at least include a convincing argument.
Consistent:	If *one* tries to write a persuasive essay, *one* should at least include a convincing argument.

➡ SAMPLE QUESTION

The more you travel around the world, the more our outlook and horizons expand.

A. NO CHANGE
B. The more we travel
C. The more one travels
D. As they travel more

Answer Explanation

Choice B is the best answer because plural pronouns in the first person (*we* and *our*) are used in both clauses of the sentence.

Choice A is not the best answer because of a shift in pronoun person between the clauses. The first clause uses the second-person pronoun *you*; the second uses the first-person pronoun *our*.

Choice C is not the best answer because a shift in pronouns from singular to plural takes place between the first and second clauses.

Choice D is not the best answer because it improperly uses the third-person pronoun *they* to refer to the first-person pronoun *our*.

21B. Pronoun Agreement with Antecedent

Singular pronouns must have singular antecedents; plural pronouns, plural antecedents. Errors sometimes occur when antecedents are indefinite, as in *each, neither, everyone* (also *no one, someone, anyone*), and *everybody* (also *nobody, somebody,* and *anybody*). Note the problem of pronoun–antecedent agreement in these sentences:

> Everybody is sticking to *their* side of the story.
> Anybody can vote if *they* have registered.
> Neither professor plans to change *their* policy regarding attendance in class.

Correctly stated, the sentences should read

> Everybody is sticking to *his* side of the story.
> Anybody can vote if *he* has registered.
> Neither professor plans to change *his* policy regarding attendance in class.

Objecting to the use of specific gender pronouns, some people prefer the phrase "he or she," but most good writers avoid using it.

Still other words may sound singular but are plural in certain contexts:

> The audience showed *its* respect for the queen by withholding applause until the end of her speech.
> The audience was asked to turn off *their* smart phones during the performance.
> The senior class posed for *its* picture.
> The senior class had *their* portraits taken for the yearbook.

➡ SAMPLE QUESTION

When any one of those collisions <u>happen, it is</u> probably caused by faulty design of the intersection.

    A. NO CHANGE
    B. happen, they are
    C. happens, it is
    D. happens, they are

Answer Explanation

Choice C is the best answer because it maintains agreement between the sentence's singular subject *one* and the singular verb *happens*.

Choice A is not the best answer because the plural verb *happen* does not agree in number with the sentence's singular subject *one*.

Choice B is not the best answer because the plural verb *happen* does not agree in number with the sentence's singular subject *one* and the plural pronoun *they* fails to agree with the singular antecedent *any one*.

Choice D is incorrect because the plural pronoun *they* fails to agree in number with the singular antecedent *any one*.

Mini-Workout in Pronoun Shift and Pronoun Agreement

Directions: Some of the following sentences contain shifts in pronoun person or errors in agreement between pronouns and antecedents. Make all appropriate corrections in the spaces provided. Alter only those sentences that contain errors.

1. The English teacher announced that everyone in the class must turn in their term papers no later than Friday.

   _____

   _____

2. When you are fired from a job, a person collects unemployment.

   _____

   _____

3. The library put their collection of rare books on display.

   _____

   _____

4. Each of my sisters own their own car.

   _____

   _____

5. In that class, our teacher held conferences with us once a week.

   _____

   _____

6. In order to keep yourself in shape, one should work out every day.

_____

_____

7. The teacher dictates a sentence in French, and each of the students write it down in English and hand it in.

_____

_____

8. Each horse in the procession followed their riders down to the creek.

_____

_____

9. The school's chess team has just won their first match.

_____

_____

10. When one is visiting the park and you can't find a restroom, they should ask a park ranger.

_____

_____

Answers are on page 101.

21C. Pronoun Reference

Sentences in which a pronoun fails to refer specifically to another noun or pronoun (its antecedent) can cause confusion. Some references are ambiguous because the pronoun seems to refer to one or more antecedents.

The teacher, Ms. Taylor, told Karen that it was *her* responsibility to hand out composition paper.

Who is responsible? The teacher or Karen? It's impossible to tell because the pronoun *her* may refer to either of them. Revised, the sentence might read:

Ms. Taylor told Karen that it was *her* responsibility as the teacher to hand out composition paper.

A sentence containing two or more pronouns with ambiguous references can be especially troublesome and unclear:

Mike became a good friend of Mark's after *he* helped *him* repair *his* car.

Whose car needed fixing? Who helped whom? To answer these questions, the sentence needs to be rewritten:

Mike and Mark became good friends after Mark helped Mike repair *his* car.

This version is better, but it's still uncertain who owned the car. One way to set the meaning straight is to use more than one sentence:

When Mark needed to repair his car, Mike helped him do the job. Afterwards, Mike and Mark became good friends.

To be correct, a pronoun should refer directly and clearly to a specific noun or another pronoun, or it should refer by implication to an idea. Such implied references frequently involve the pronouns *it*, *they*, and *you*, and the relative pronouns *which*, *that*, and *this*, and cause trouble mostly when the pronoun is used to refer to rather general or ambiguous ideas, as in:

Homeless people allege that the mayor is indifferent to their plight, *which* has been disproved.

What has been disproved? That an allegation was made? That the mayor is indifferent? The intended meaning is unclear because *which* has no distinct antecedent. To clear up the uncertainty, the sentence might read:

Homeless people allege that the mayor is indifferent to their plight, but the allegation has been disproved.

➡ SAMPLE QUESTION

Rick, Mike, and Alberto were driving a fully loaded moving van from Boston to Indianapolis when, falling asleep behind the wheel, he hit a guard rail on the Interstate.

  A. NO CHANGE
  B. and then he hit a guard rail after falling asleep behind the wheel
  C. when Rick fell asleep behind the wheel and hit a guard rail
  D. when Rick, falling asleep behind the wheel and hitting a guard rail

Answer Explanation

Choice C is the best answer because it avoids the pronoun reference problem by naming the person who hit the guardrail.

Choice A is not the best answer because the pronoun *he* fails to refer to a specific noun or pronoun.

Choice B is not the best answer because the pronoun *he* fails to refer to a specific noun or pronoun.

Choice D is not the best answer because it lacks a valid verb, thereby creating an incomplete sentence.

Mini-Workout in Pronoun Reference

Directions: Each of the following sentences suffers from a pronoun problem. Please eliminate the problem by revising each sentence. Use the blank spaces to write your answers.

1. When we teenagers loiter outside the theater on Friday night, they give you a hard time.

2. I answered the test questions, collected my pencils and pens, and handed them in.

3. Barbara told Ken that she wanted only a short wedding trip to Florida, which lies at the root of their problem.

4. His father let him know that he had only an hour to get to the airport.

5. During Dr. Rice's tenure in office, she traveled more than any other secretary of state.

6. Henry, an ambulance driver, disapproved of war but drove it to the front lines anyway.

7. After the campus tour, Mike told Todd that he thought he'd be happy going to Auburn.

_____

_____

8. Peggy's car hit a truck, but it wasn't even dented.

_____

_____

9. Within the last month, Andy's older brother Pete found a new job, broke his leg skiing, and got married to Felicia, which made their parents very happy.

_____

_____

10. Eddie grew fond of the novels of John Steinbeck because he had lived in California.

_____

_____

Answers are on page 102.

22. Comparisons

Comparisons are part of everyday speech and writing. No doubt you've heard people say such things as "strong as an ox" and "faster than lightning." These figures of speech are accurate sometimes but they are also clichés, used so often they have lost their punch.

In passages on the Writing and Language Test, you may run into literal comparisons clearly meant to compare one thing to another, as in

Yellowstone National Park is bigger than Yosemite.
In many businesses, men often make more money than women for equivalent work.

But what if the sentences had been worded this way:

Yellowstone National Park is more bigger than Yosemite.
In many businesses, men make as much if not more than women.

Each of these sentences contains an error. If you didn't spot the mistake, you should spend a little time reviewing the rules governing the use of comparisons. You need to know, for example, that comparisons (1) must be complete, (2) must be stated in parallel form, and (3) must pertain to things that can be logically compared.

Most comparisons are made by using different forms of adjectives or adverbs. The degree of comparison is indicated by the ending (usually *–er* and *–est*) or by the use of *more* or *most* (or *less* and *least*). The English language offers three degrees of comparison, called *positive*, *comparative*, and *superlative*.

Positive	Comparative	Superlative
tall	taller	tallest
dark	darker	darkest
handsome	handsomer *or* more handsome	handsomest *or* most handsome
graceful	more graceful	most graceful
prepared	less prepared	least prepared
happily	more happily	most happily
Some words deviate from the usual pattern. For example:		
good	better	best
well	better	best
bad	worse	worst
little	less	least
much	more	most
many	more	most

Use the following guidelines to hunt down errors in comparative degree:

1. To form the comparative and superlative degree of one-syllable words, add *–er* or *–est* to the positive form (*brave, braver, bravest; late, later, latest*).

2. To form the comparative and superlative degrees of most two-syllable words, use *more* or *most*, or *less* and *least* (*more famous, most nauseous, less skillful, least jagged*). Some two-syllable words follow the guidelines for words of one syllable (*pretty, prettier, prettiest*), although you wouldn't err by applying the rule for two-syllable words (*more pretty, most pretty*).

3. To form the comparative and superlative degree of three-syllable words and of all words ending in *–ly*, use *more* and *most*, or *less* and *least* (*beautiful, more beautiful, most beautiful; gladly, more gladly, most gladly*).

4. To compare two things use the comparative degree, but to compare three or more things use the superlative degree.

> My *younger* sister takes dancing lessons. (The writer has two sisters.)
> My *youngest* sister takes swimming lessons. (The writer has at least three sisters.)

5. Never create a double comparison by putting words like *more, most, less,* and *least* in the same phrase with words in the comparative or superlative degrees. For example, avoid *more friendlier, less prouder, most sweetest, least safest*. Such usages are both ungrammatical and redundant. Instead, use adjectives and adverbs in the positive degree: *more friendly, less proud, more sweet, least safe*.

INCOMPLETE COMPARISONS

In everyday speech, people give emphasis to their opinions by saying things like "We had the best time" and "That was the worst accident!" Neither statement is complete, however, because technically the "best" time must be compared to other times, and the "worst" accident must be compared to other accidents.

An incomplete comparison made colloquially may suffer no loss of meaning, but standard written usage calls for unmistakable clarity. On the SAT you may find sentences that omit some words needed to make a comparison clear:

Mimi visited her aged aunt longer than Kathy.

This could mean either that Mimi spent a longer time with her aunt than Kathy did, or that Mimi spent more time with her aunt than she spent with Kathy. To eliminate the ambiguity, simply complete the comparison:

Mimi visited her aged aunt longer than she visited Kathy.

A comparison using *as* usually requires a repetition of the word: as good *as* gold, as fast *as* a speeding bullet, as high *as* a kite.

| **Incomplete:** | On the exam, Nicole expects to do as well if not better than Nat. |
| **Complete:** | On the exam, Nicole expects to do as well *as*, if not better than, Nat. |

For the sake of completeness, when you compare one thing to a group of which it is a part, be sure to use *other* or *else*.

Lieutenant Henry was braver than any pilot in the squadron.

This suggests that Henry may not have been a member of the squadron. If he belonged to the squadron, however, add *other* to complete the comparison:

Lieutenant Henry was braver than any *other* pilot in the squadron.

Similarly, notice the difference between these two sentences:

Diana talks more nonsense than anyone in the class.
Diana talks more nonsense than anyone *else* in the class.

Only the second sentence makes clear that Diana is a member of the class.

ILLOGICAL COMPARISONS

Logic breaks down when two or more unlike things are compared.

Boston's harbor is reported to be more polluted than any city in the country.

This sentence is meant to compare pollution in the Boston harbor with pollution in the harbors of other cities. Instead, it compares Boston's harbor with a city, an illogical comparison. Properly expressed, it would read this way:

Boston's harbor is reported to be more polluted than the harbor of any other city in the country.

Similarly, note the difference between these two sentences.

> Unlike most cars on the block, Ellie has her Toyota washed almost every week.
> Ellie's Toyota, unlike most cars on the block, is washed almost every week.

The first sentence is intended to compare Ellie's car with the other cars on the block. But it nonsensically compares Ellie to the other cars.

➡ SAMPLE QUESTION #1

<u>A more easier and more direct route exists</u> between Mt. Kisco and Pleasantville than the one taken by the county bus service.

    A. NO CHANGE
    B. An easier and direct route exist
    C. An easier and more direct route exists
    D. A both more easy and a more direct route exists

Answer Explanation

Choice C is the best answer because it accurately and grammatically conveys the meaning of the sentence.

Choice A is not the best answer. The phrase *more easier* is a redundancy because each word is in the comparative degree. Delete *more*.

Choice B is not the best answer because it contains an error in parallelism. *Easier*, an adjective in the comparative degree, is not parallel in form to *direct*. Use *more direct*.

Choice D is not the best answer because it is wordy. Delete the word *both* and also each use of *more*.

➡ SAMPLE QUESTION #2

Elton John combines various techniques of singing and piano playing <u>as effortlessly as any pop star</u> ever has.

    A. NO CHANGE
    B. as effortlessly as any other pop star
    C. as effortlessly like any other pop star
    D. as effortlessly, if not more so, than any pop star

Answer Explanation

Choice B is the best answer because it follows the requirements for making a comparison in standard English.

Choice A is not the best answer because it omits *other*, a word that must be used when comparing one thing with a group of which it is a member. Use the phrase *as any other*.

Choice C is not the best answer because it uses *like* instead of *as*. Use *like*, a preposition, to introduce a phrase; use *as* to introduce a clause.

Choice D is not the best answer because it fails to complete the comparison. To complete the comparison use *as effortlessly as.*

Mini-Workout in Comparisons

Directions: Find the errors in comparative degree in the following sentences. Write the correct usage in the spaces provided. Some sentences may be correct.

1. Bill Gates of Microsoft is a lot more rich than Mark Zuckerberg of Facebook.

2. Although Stephen King and John Grisham write suspense-filled books, King is the best storyteller.

3. Of all the colleges Amanda applied to, Reed stood out as the most unique one.

4. Doritos are tastier than any snack.

5. Dr. Parker is about the most forgetfullest medical practitioner in the hospital.

6. Of all of Shakespeare's plays, *Hamlet* is the more popular.

7. It's difficult to decide who is the most liberal—Senator Mills or Governor Michaels.

8. Both crises were terrible, but the bureau first tried to deal with the worst of the two.

9. Unlike every other math teacher, watching cartoons is Dr. Rich's way of relaxing.

10. After weighing the three fish she had caught, Bitsy threw the lightest one back.

11. Cal's victory was more sweeter because Oregon had beaten them badly last year.

_____

12. Norton's idea was profounder than Vickie's.

_____

13. Both I-95 and the parkway will take you to New Haven, but the latter is the fastest route.

_____

14. In the autumn, the leaves in Vermont are prettier than other states.

_____

15. That was the most unkindest remark made during the entire hearing.

_____

Answers are on page 102.

ANSWER KEY TO MINI-WORKOUTS

Choosing a Main Idea, pages 7–9

These are suggestions only. Your answers may be equally or more effective.

1. **A.** Henry Ford knew more about cars than about people, because talent, ability, and a little bit of luck are the most important ingredients of success.
   B. If Henry Ford's statement is correct, the world is filled with self-deluded people.
   C. From spelling bees to Nobel Prizes, nobody with a negative attitude has ever been a winner.
2. **A.** While rats may learn to run through a maze for a food pellet, children are different.
   B. Political history shows that if a dictator wants to control his people, he should scare the living daylights out of them.
   C. Knowing that acceptance to a good college waits for them, most students willingly go through hell, including the SAT, to get there.
3. **A.** Those who say "Money is the root of all evil" know what they are talking about.
   B. Dreaming of wealth is as American as apple pie—part of the great American dream.
   C. Only a ding-a-ling, or someone named Jay Gatsby, would truly believe that money can buy happiness.
4. **A.** Mandela is partly right and partly wrong because everything keeps changing.
   B. Going back to old places that haven't changed tells you more about what you were than about what you've become.
   C. After a recent visit to my old elementary school, I could not agree more with Mandela's observation.

5. **A.** Bryan is definitely on the right track. Nothing is as personally satisfying as achieving a goal through hard work.

  B. Which kind of success do I prefer? Frankly, I'll take it either way.

  C. I've heard that people make their own good luck by their decisions and choices. Therefore, it's simplistic to think that your destiny can be achieved without it.

Sequencing Sentences, pages 10–12

1. a. 4 b. 3 c. 2 d. 1
2. a. 2 b. 5 c. 1 d. 4 e. 3 f. 6
3. a. 3 b. 1 c. 4 d. 2
4. a. 3 b. 4 c. 2 d. 1
5. a. 3 b. 2 c. 4 d. 1 e. 5
6. a. 4 b. 2 c. 1 d. 3 e. 5
7. a. 4 b. 2 c. 1 d. 3
8. a. 3 b. 4 c. 2 d. 1 e. 5
9. a. 3 b. 4 c. 2 d. 1
10. a. 2 b. 4 c. 1 d. 3
11. a. 1 b. 4 c. 3 d. 2

Developing Topic Sentences, pages 15–20

PART A

1. Sentence 7
2. None. Implied topic sentence
3. Sentence 1
4. Sentence 10
5. Sentence 1
6. Sentence 6
7. Sentence 1
8. Sentence 3
9. Sentence 2
10. Sentence 1

PART B

Answers may vary.

1. Monopolies often destroy not only themselves but the incentive of businesses to change and make progress.
2. In the past, U.S. athletes dominated the Olympic Games.
3. Mother and Father are very different from each other.
4. How little the aristocracy understood the needs of the masses.
5. Vera Simon wrote a gripping and realistic book.
6. Although backward in some respects, a so-called primitive culture can be technologically sophisticated.
7. But here are my requirements for the perfect roommate.
8. Age and experience have deprived me of courage and spirit.
9. No topic sentence is needed.
10. Smoking in school is just not worth the trouble it can lead to.

PART C

Answers will vary. The topic sentences you wrote may be as good as or even better than these examples.

a. Of all the equipment needed to traverse the inhuman land of Antarctica, nothing is more important than a team of well-trained sled dogs.

b. Antarctica takes your breath away.

c. This is not an idle comparison, because at every turn you are putting your health and safety in jeopardy.

Using Transitions, pages 22–23

These paragraphs only illustrate the use of transitions. Your answers will no doubt be different.

1. To get on the good side of a teacher takes practice, but the technique explained below almost never fails. First you must try to create the impression that you think, say, Ms. Douglas, is the best teacher in the world. You must immediately choose a seat that is near to her in the classroom. Then you must pretend to listen intently to her every word and nod your head as though you agree with everything she says. Next, smile at her, laugh at her jokes, and never leave the room right after class. Soon after the bell, ask her a question about the lesson and thank her profusely for taking the time to answer it. After a while, she'll think that you are an intelligent, highly motivated student and with luck will reward you handsomely on your report card.

2. Some people are bored with their lives. As a result, they seek out dangerous situations in order to get a thrill. Accordingly, many movie stuntmen ache to put their lives in jeopardy. As a result, they volunteer to crash through windows, fall down stairs, jump from high places, drive cars into walls and into each other. As a consequence, they often get hurt, but their work is more important to them than their safety and well-being. Hence, it takes a sort of masochist to be a stuntman.

3. Because my father is an optimist and my mother a pessimist, they respond to life in different ways. Unlike my mother, my father is always pretty upbeat, even when he's worried about his job, about money, and about me and my sister. On the other hand, Mom frets about every little thing, from the weather (it's never quite right) to dirt on the living room rug (there's too much of it). In spite of their differences, Dad and Mom get along just fine. Still, I prefer Dad's way because it resembles mine. Nevertheless, I can see where Mom is coming from and love her all the same.

4. It's time to reconsider how the United States squanders billions of dollars every year on probing Mars, Jupiter, and other remote places in outer space. Because money is also wasted on glitzy high-tech telescopes that can bring the edges of the universe into view, the government should reevaluate its entire space program. In addition to being a misuse of money that is sorely needed to solve problems here on the Earth, studying outer space has been less fruitful than predicted. Besides failing to live up to their promise, so-called successes have been either modest or totally irrelevant. What's more, the cost of developing technology required to make worthwhile journeys even to the closest planets or asteroids is, if you'll pardon the pun, "astronomical." Equally important is that, given the choice, the American people would prefer to see tax revenues used to improve their everyday lives.

Word Choice and Standard Idiom, pages 26–28

1. stop *on* a dime
2. die *in* battle
3. *with* respect to
4. No error
5. comply *with* her request
6. iron *or* tin
7. *oral* instructions
8. *childlike* wonder
9. preoccupation *with* classical music
10. pursuit *of* horse thieves
11. No error
12. far *from* harm
13. No error
14. *who* need
15. search *of* a way
16. No error
17. regarded *as* one
18. prefer driving *to* flying
19. expensive *as*
20. teaching *and* devoting

Wordiness, pages 29–30

Answers will vary. Some of your sentences may be more concise than these.

1. You should review your sentences and cross out any unecessary words.
2. Working at Wilkens' Fabrics at age sixteen, Maria learned to handle both fabrics and customers.
3. The wonders of electricity obsessed Thomas Edison.
4. The ambassador most wanted the terrorists to release the hostages.
5. Hamlet returned home because his father died.
6. The minefield endangered the troops.
7. Today's world faces, among many other threats, climate change and too little potable water.
8. Emma felt that her gender kept her from playing on the varsity football team.
9. To compensate for a shortage of energy sources and to reduce its utility bills, the federal government annually spends millions of dollars to conserve energy.
10. While inspecting her new suburban house, Ms. Draeger stumbled on a loose floorboard and fell down the basement steps.

Redundancy and Repetition, pages 32–33

Answers may vary.

1. She constantly bothers me.
2. He spoke to me about my future.
3. Is it true that the ozone layer is being depleted?

4. I thought that without chemistry I couldn't go to a good college.
5. As a result of the election, the state will have its first female governor.
6. My father habitually watches the sun set.
7. Harold hasn't stopped painting since picking up a brush at age ten.
8. Research shows that avid sports fans suffer fewer depressions and are generally healthier than those not interested in sports.
9. He is a chemist.
10. The cough recurred twice.

Writing Correct Sentences, pages 39–40

Answers will vary. No doubt some of your sentences will be better than these.

1. Although Elizabeth is stressed out about the SAT, she won't let it get her down.
2. The teacher agreed to her request for an extension on the assignment.
3. At eighty-six years old, my grandmother walks very slowly.
4. I could choose many other examples to show who I am, not all of them vivid images of memorable moments but rather everyday aspects of my life.
5. I woke up, having slept for the four shortest hours of my life. I force my eyes open and crawl to the shower. Only then my brain begins to function.
6. I can't believe that I'll soon leave the protective world of high school and enter the world of college.
7. The large brown garage door creaks open slowly. Out into the morning sunshine emerges a rider on a road bike.
8. What are the rules? What happens if we break them?
9. Phyllis, a biologist in the field of genetic engineering, is involved in the cloning controversy.
10. Use the space below to tell one personal story to provide the admissions committee, either directly or indirectly, an insight into the kind of person you are.

Combining and Augmenting Sentences, pages 41–43

Because many different answers are possible, these are suggestions only. As you compare your answers to these, be sure that you have included all the information from each group of sentences.

1. At thirteen, she has already won recognition as an expert gymnast.
2. After the hit-and-run accident, broken glass lay on the street.
3. Aunt Ellen had a mess on her hands after she dropped a bag containing a glass bottle of tomato juice that she had bought at the grocery store.
4. The baseball hit Mr. Strickman's picture window, shattering it into a thousand pieces.
5. Since the storm dumped two feet of snow on the roads, I could not go out. I had nothing to do but watch TV and assemble a jigsaw puzzle. The time passed slowly.
6. The Earth revolves around the sun every 365 days. At the same time, it rotates on its axis every twenty-four hours. The Earth's revolution around the sun determines the length of a year just as its rotation determines the duration of a day.
7. The 2,000-year-old tragedies of Euripides, an ancient Greek playwright, are still performed today.
8. Music has the unique power to transport people's minds. While listening, people often dream and think, and afterwards feel refreshed.

9. The skulls of humans consist of twenty-two bones: eight in the cranium, which protects the brain, and fourteen in the face and jaw.

10. The culture of the Hopi Indians, whose name means "peaceful and happy," exemplifies peace and contentment. Lacking competitiveness, Hopis rarely feel tense. What they value instead are self-discipline, restraint, and the welfare of others. But the highest value is the family, consisting of the entire Hopi tribe.

Mixed Construction, pages 46–47

Answers may vary.

1. Jay had been working out in the weight room for months before the wrestling coach invited him to try out for the team. (*Shift in verb tense*)

2. For Thanksgiving, Julie went to Richmond; however, for Christmas she traveled to Syracuse. (*Shift from active to passive*)

3. The movie is about how loyalty to a friend can create a moral crisis in which conventional values are challenged. (*Transitional word choice*)

4. The board recognized the school's troubles and undertook a giant fundraising drive. (*Shift from active to passive; shift in sentence subject*)

5. The report said that years ago city planners had envisioned building a facility that turns salt water into fresh water, but financial woes made that impossible. (*Shift in verb tense; transitional word choice*)

6. Students lacking financial resources can still go to college because they can borrow money from banks, hold part-time jobs, and apply for scholarships. (*Shift in subject; lack of parallelism*)

7. When a woman comes home after a full day of problems in the office, she doesn't want to face additional problems. (*Shift in pronoun person*)

8. Jocko left for the university as soon as he finished his breakfast. (*Shift in subject; switch from active to passive*)

9. You turn your iPhone off; then put it into your backpack until the end of the school day. (*Shift in sentence subject; shift from active to passive*)

10. When the CEO announced her resignation, the workers held a meeting and decided to postpone their strike. (*Shift in verb tense*)

Parallel Structure, pages 52–53

These are suggested answers. Other answers may also be correct.

1. and inspiring to his class
2. was accused not only of being a bigot but also of being too stupid
3. and gone to fewer parties
4. preparing letters and reports, and making various types of telephone calls
5. and to get up early
6. and she had a habit of disappearing
7. or a commercial artist
8. felt both pride and satisfaction
9. Correct
10. plans to live simply
11. The kids had scattered their books not only all over the bus but also all over the sidewalk.

12. have a good location, have land around it, and have a view
13. Joan's broken yellow pencil came from this box.
14. how to furnish and decorate the house simply
15. neither have a microwave in his room nor take a shower after 11:00 o'clock
16. and being miles from friends
17. The mouse will either find a quick way into the attic or gnaw at the siding for days.
18. and entertaining.
19. and a job in the suburbs
20. that he'll defeat Tom in the sectionals, and that he'll emerge

Revising Passive Sentences, pages 55–56

Your sentences may differ from these, but be sure you've used the active voice.

1. The author cited statistics from the Census Bureau.
2. We discussed the crisis in the Middle East.
3. I failed Friday's quiz because instead of studying I had rehearsed the play every night that week.
4. We began our week-long college tour by driving to Portland.
5. Captain Ahab and his crew pursued the great white whale.
6. Every moring Carrie checks the news of the day online.
7. The president and his advisors decided to go to war.
8. On Friday night, more than twenty customers took out dinners.
9. In three days, our group saw five Shakespearean plays.
10. Before you do something physical, the body normally calls on the brain.

Misplaced and Dangling Modifiers, pages 58–59

Your answers needn't be identical to these, but your sentences should be free of dangling and misplaced modifiers.

1 The pizza I ate after completing my chemistry homework tasted great.
2. Denise discovered her boyfriend sound asleep in the hammock.
3. Having been used all night to illuminate the steps, Cora's flashlight needed new batteries.
4. While I drove down the mountain road, the brakes failed.
5. When I stopped to rest after a long hike, a grizzly bear stood in front of me.
6. Before the school bus picked me up, I ate a quick breakfast.
7. The police submitted a report about the bank robbery.
8. His family emigrated from Russia when Sasha was ten.
9. The bone we threw in the trash after last night's dinner was chewed by the dog.
10. Left alone in the house, the child was terrified by every sound.

Punctuation, pages 62–64

PART A. POSSESSIVES

1. Paul's
2. America's
3. Correct

4. women's
5. girls', boys'
6. Andersons', Year's
7. Correct
8. Morris's
9. computers'
10. months'

PART B. COMMAS AND SEMICOLONS

1. While Bill was riding, his bike got a flat tire.
2. The mail carrier did not leave the package, for Valerie was not at home.
3. After doing his homework Mikey, as you might expect, talked on his cell phone for an hour.
4. His work criticized many commonly held beliefs, however, and it was strictly censored.
5. The car that ran into mine at the intersection was an SUV.
6. Dad went to the airport to pick up Dave; Ellie went to the train station to meet Debbie.
7. Correct
8. The boat was seventy-five feet long and eighteen feet wide; its mast was about eighty feet tall.
9. To anyone interested in flying, planes hold endless fascination.
10. Jeff and Steve, left alone for the weekend, invited all their friends to a party.
11. I need street maps of Boston and Portland, Maine.
12. Some of the theories dealt with the political, social, and religious ideas of the time.
13. Students who want to try out for the chorus have been asked to report to room 330.
14. Doug, for example, is both a scholar and an athlete.
15. Monica refused to go unless Phil went with her.
16. The hero of the book, John Coffey, rode his bike across the United States.
17. After all, she did for him what she could.
18. Starting in Minnesota, the Mississippi runs all the way to the Gulf of Mexico.
19. Harold Watkins, who comes from Chicago, won a full tuition scholarship to Duke.
20. Although the characters are stereotypes, they were interesting to read about.
21. Yo-Yo Ma, the famous cellist, will perform a recital on Saturday night.
22. This test covers Spanish literature, culture, and history, and it lasts for three hours.
23. Michelle is pretty, tall, and dark, but her older sister Norma is pretty, short, and light.
24. Sean, the twin brother of Ian, was struck by a falling tree limb.
25. The window washer dropped by last evening, but he didn't bring his squeegee.

Capitalization, pages 65–66

1. On Labor Day Bennington County's fire department plans to hold a turkey shoot on the field at Miller's Pond.
2. The judge gave District Attorney Lipman a book entitled *The Rules of Evidence* and instructed her to read it before she ever dared set foot in the Court of Appeals of the Ninth Circuit again.
3. The secretary of state greeted the president of Austria at the Ronald Reagan Airport in Washington, D.C.

4. The Shackleton expedition nearly met its doom on Georgia Island in Antarctica.
5. For Christmas he got a Black & Decker table saw from the Sears store next to the old Bedford Courthouse.
6. According to Georgetown's high school principal, Eugene Griffiths, Georgetown High School attracts students from the whole west coast. At Georgetown students may major in drawing and painting, design, graphics, or sculpture. Mr. Griffiths said, "I attended a similar high school in New England just after the Vietnam War."
7. We expect to celebrate New Year's Eve again this year by ordering a movie of an old Broadway musical from Netflix and settling down in front of the DVD player with some Pepsi and a box of Oreos.
8. After traveling all the way to the Pacific, the Corps of Discovery rode down the Missouri River going east on their way back to St. Louis.
9. This Irish linen tablecloth was bought at Kmart in the Emeryville Mall off Powell Street.
10. Yellowstone National Park is located in the northwest corner of Wyoming.

Noun-Verb Agreement, pages 69–72

1. talent…proves
2. heroes…die
3. team…is
4. Correct
5. Correct
6. are…levels
7. proceeds…are
8. team…is
9. neither…was
10. reforms…have
11. fan…expects
12. Politics…has
13. Darwin…is
14. Katie Green…and accompanist…are
15. Nancy…appears
16. sale…has
17. Here are…statutes
18. insistence…is
19. No one…wants
20. are…guards

Verb Tenses, pages 74–75

1. came
2. brought
3. No error
4. had ridden
5. had reached
6. expected
7. had finished
8. No error

9. gave
10. begins
11. stopped
12. gives
13. Having worked
14. had seen
15. suffered

Verb Forms, pages 76–77

1. used to arrive
2. have regularly arisen
3. Correct
4. blew
5. had begun
6. had burst
7. should have gone
8. had never sung
9. had sprung
10. have managed to attract

Pronouns Case, pages 80–81

1. me
2. her, him
3. me
4. me
5. him
6. he
7. I
8. me
9. we
10. he

Pronoun Shift and Pronoun Agreement, pages 83–84

Answers may vary.

1. The English teacher announced that everyone in the class must turn in his term paper no later than Friday.
2. When fired from a job, one collects unemployment.
3. The library put its collection of rare books on display.
4. Each of my sisters owns her own car.
5. Correct
6. In order to stay in shape, you should work out every day.
7. The teacher dictates a sentence in French. Then each student writes it down in English and hands it in.
8. Each horse in the procession followed its rider down to the creek.
9. The school's chess team has just won its first match.
10. When you visit the park, ask a park ranger if you can't find a rest room.

Pronoun Reference, pages 86–87

These are suggested answers. Yours may be different but equally valid.

1. When teenagers loiter outside the theater on Friday night, the police give them a hard time.
2. Before collecting my pencils and pens, I handed in the test questions I had answered.
3. At the root of Barbara and Ken's problem is that she wanted only a short wedding trip to Florida.
4. With only an hour to get to the airport, his father was in a rush and told him so.
5. During her tenure in office, Dr. Rice traveled more than any other secretary of state.
6. Although he disapproved of the war, Henry drove his ambulance to the front lines.
7. After the campus tour, Mike told Todd, "I'd be happy going to Auburn."
8. Peggy's car wasn't even dented after it hit a truck.
9. Within the last month, Andy's older brother Pete broke his leg skiing and got a new job. He also married Felicia, which made his parents very happy.
10. Because he had lived in California, Eddie grew fond of John Steinbeck's novels.

Comparisons, pages 91–92

1.	a lot richer	*More rich* may be acceptable in some contexts, but ordinarily *–er* should be added to one-syllable adjectives in the comparative degree.
2.	the better	Use adjectives in the comparative degree when comparing two things or people.
3.	unique	*Unique* is an absolute adjective that cannot be used in making comparisons.
4.	than any other	When comparing one thing to a group of which it is a part, use *other*.
5.	most forgetful	Use *more/most* with three-syllable adjectives.
6.	most popular	Use the superlative degree to compare more than two things.
7.	more liberal	Use adjectives in the comparative degree when comparing two things or people.
8.	the worse	Use adjectives in the comparative degree when comparing two things.
9.	Dr. Rich watches cartoons to relax	Re-structure the sentence to make the comparison logical.
10.	No error	
11.	was sweeter	Avoid making redundant double comparisons.
12.	more profound	Use *more/most* with many two-syllable adjectives.
13.	the faster	Use adjectives in the comparative degree when comparing two things.
14.	than those in	Use *those in* to avoid an illogical comparison.
15.	unkindest	Avoid making redundant double comparisons.

Writing and Language Practice Tests

2

By taking practice tests, you'll quickly become familiar with the length and format of the exam. You'll not only begin to identify your strengths and weaknesses in analyzing and correcting prose passages, you'll also figure out what and how much to study in order to boost your test score.

Try to simulate actual test conditions as you test yourself. Here's how:

→ **SET ASIDE AN UNINTERRUPTED 35-MINUTE TESTING PERIOD.**

→ **USE A TIMER, A WATCH, OR A CLOCK.**

→ **FEEL FREE TO MARK UP EACH PASSAGE BY UNDERLINING, DRAWING CIRCLES AROUND KEY IDEAS, JOTTING NOTES IN THE MARGIN—ANYTHING, REALLY, TO FIND ANSWERS TO THE QUESTIONS.**

→ **MARK YOUR ANSWERS ON THE ANSWER SHEET PROVIDED FOR EACH TEST.**

When you've completed each test, check your answers with the Answer Key. Even if you've answered the question correctly, read the answer explanation. You're sure to find nuggets of valuable information and advice about writing and language that you haven't seen before and they will almost certainly help you sail with confidence through the SAT.

ANSWER SHEET
Writing and Language Test A

Passage 1

1. Ⓐ Ⓑ Ⓒ Ⓓ
2. Ⓐ Ⓑ Ⓒ Ⓓ
3. Ⓐ Ⓑ Ⓒ Ⓓ
4. Ⓐ Ⓑ Ⓒ Ⓓ

5. Ⓐ Ⓑ Ⓒ Ⓓ
6. Ⓐ Ⓑ Ⓒ Ⓓ
7. Ⓐ Ⓑ Ⓒ Ⓓ
8. Ⓐ Ⓑ Ⓒ Ⓓ

9. Ⓐ Ⓑ Ⓒ Ⓓ
10. Ⓐ Ⓑ Ⓒ Ⓓ
11. Ⓐ Ⓑ Ⓒ Ⓓ

Passage 2

12. Ⓐ Ⓑ Ⓒ Ⓓ
13. Ⓐ Ⓑ Ⓒ Ⓓ
14. Ⓐ Ⓑ Ⓒ Ⓓ
15. Ⓐ Ⓑ Ⓒ Ⓓ

16. Ⓐ Ⓑ Ⓒ Ⓓ
17. Ⓐ Ⓑ Ⓒ Ⓓ
18. Ⓐ Ⓑ Ⓒ Ⓓ
19. Ⓐ Ⓑ Ⓒ Ⓓ

20. Ⓐ Ⓑ Ⓒ Ⓓ
21. Ⓐ Ⓑ Ⓒ Ⓓ
22. Ⓐ Ⓑ Ⓒ Ⓓ

Passage 3

23. Ⓐ Ⓑ Ⓒ Ⓓ
24. Ⓐ Ⓑ Ⓒ Ⓓ
25. Ⓐ Ⓑ Ⓒ Ⓓ
26. Ⓐ Ⓑ Ⓒ Ⓓ

27. Ⓐ Ⓑ Ⓒ Ⓓ
28. Ⓐ Ⓑ Ⓒ Ⓓ
29. Ⓐ Ⓑ Ⓒ Ⓓ
30. Ⓐ Ⓑ Ⓒ Ⓓ

31. Ⓐ Ⓑ Ⓒ Ⓓ
32. Ⓐ Ⓑ Ⓒ Ⓓ
33. Ⓐ Ⓑ Ⓒ Ⓓ

Passage 4

34. Ⓐ Ⓑ Ⓒ Ⓓ
35. Ⓐ Ⓑ Ⓒ Ⓓ
36. Ⓐ Ⓑ Ⓒ Ⓓ
37. Ⓐ Ⓑ Ⓒ Ⓓ

38. Ⓐ Ⓑ Ⓒ Ⓓ
39. Ⓐ Ⓑ Ⓒ Ⓓ
40. Ⓐ Ⓑ Ⓒ Ⓓ
41. Ⓐ Ⓑ Ⓒ Ⓓ

42. Ⓐ Ⓑ Ⓒ Ⓓ
43. Ⓐ Ⓑ Ⓒ Ⓓ
44. Ⓐ Ⓑ Ⓒ Ⓓ

PRACTICE WRITING AND LANGUAGE TEST A

TIME: 35 MINUTES

Directions: The underlined sentences and sentence parts in the passages below may contain errors in standard English, including awkward or ambiguous expression, poor word choice, incorrect sentence structure, or faulty grammar, usage, and punctuation.

Read each passage carefully and identify which of the four alternative versions most effectively and correctly expresses the meaning of the underlined material. Indicate your choice by filling in the corresponding space on the answer sheet. Choice A on most questions is "NO CHANGE." If none of the choices improves the underlined text, pick Choice A as your answer.

EXAMPLE

Some economists point out that the income gap in cities like San Francisco and the rising cost of housing is an issue for a long time before the tech industry or its workers showed up.

A. NO CHANGE

B. are

C. were

D. was

ANSWER: A   B   Ⓒ   D

Passage A1

The precise causes of stuttering are not understood. Recent research indicates that genetic components play a part. Some theorists propose that many stutterers have inherited certain traits that increase the likelihood that they will develop this disorder in their speech. The exact nature of these traits is presently unclear, [1] except that stuttering is more common among males than females. What is known, of course, is that stuttering is the repetition of sounds, prolonged vowels, and complete stops—verbal blocks. A stutterer's speech is often uncontrollable. Compared [2] to nonstutterers, it is sometimes faster than average but usually more slower. Sometimes, too, the voice changes in pitch, loudness, and inflection.

[3] Observation of young children during the early stages of stuttering have led to a list of warning signs that can help identify a child who is developing a speech problem. Most children use "um's" and "ah's," and will repeat words or syllables as they learn to speak. It is not a serious concern if a child says, "I like to go and and and play games," unless such repetitions occur often, more than once every twenty words or so.

Repeating whole words is not necessarily a sign of stuttering; however, repeating speech sounds or syllables such as in the song "K-K-K-Katy" is.

Sometimes a stutterer will exhibit tension while prolonging a sound [4]—meanwhile, the 8-year-old who says "Annnnnnd—and th-th-th-then I-I drank it" with lips trembling at the same time. Children who experience such a stuttering tremor usually become frightened, angry, and [5] feeling frustration from the inability to speak. A further danger sign is a rise in pitch as the child draws out the syllable.

The appearance of people experiencing the most severe signs of stuttering is dramatic. As they struggle to get a word out, their whole face may contort and the jaw may jerk the mouth [6] open. Tension can spread through the whole body. A moment of overwhelming struggle occurs during the speech blockage.

[1] A. NO CHANGE
B. in part, because not everyone predisposed to stutter will develop the disorder.
C. because some people who have stuttered for many years suddenly stop stuttering.
D. since those who have experienced unfavorable responses from listeners may develop emotional problems that worsen their conditions.

[2] A. NO CHANGE
B. to nonstutterers' speech, if not faster sometimes, then usually slower.
C. to that of nonstutterers, it is as fast, but usually slower.
D. to the speech of nonstutterers, it is sometimes faster but usually slower.

[3] A. NO CHANGE
B. Observations of young children during the early stages of stuttering
C. Observations of young children, which during the early stages of stuttering
D. Observation of young children, during the early stages of stuttering

[4] A NO CHANGE
B. —consequently
C. —for example
D. —to sum up

[5] A. NO CHANGE
B. frustrated from the
C. frustrated by their
D. a frustrating feeling because of the

[6] The writer wants to add examples of stutterers' physical reactions. Which choice most effectively accomplishes this goal?
A. open, the tongue protrudes, and an eyeroll takes place.
B. open, along with a protruding tongue and rolling eyes.
C. open; their tongues may protrude and their eyes may roll.
D. open; tongue protrudes, eyes roll.

While the symptoms of stuttering are easy to recognize, [7] it's underlying causes remains [8] a mystery. Hippocrates thought that stuttering was due to a dry tongue, and he prescribed blistering substances to drain away the black bile responsible. [9] The brilliant English scientist Sir Isaac Newton, who developed the law of gravity, also suffered a lifelong stuttering condition. A Roman physician recommended gargling and massages to strengthen a weak tongue. Seventeenth-century scientist Francis Bacon suggested hot wine to thaw a "refrigerated" tongue. Too large a tongue was the fault, according to a 19th-century Prussian physician, so he snipped pieces off stutterers' tongues. Alexander Melville Bell, father of the telephone inventor, insisted stuttering was simply a bad habit that [10] could be remedied, overcome, and eliminated by reeducation.

Some theorists today attribute stuttering to problems in the control of the muscles of speech. Decades ago, however, [11] stuttering was thought to arise from deep-rooted personality problems and recommended psychotherapy.

[7] A. NO CHANGE
B. its underlying cause
C. the underlying causes
D. their underlying cause

[8] A. NO CHANGE
B. a riddle
C. in the closet
D. a dilemma

[9] The writer is considering deleting the underlined sentence. Should it be kept or deleted?
A. Kept, because it adds evidence to the claim that stuttering has long been a subject of study and research.
B. Kept, because it provides still another example of a historical figure concerned about stuttering.
C. Deleted, because it blurs the paragraph's focus on various theories about how stuttering can be cured.
D. Deleted, because it fails to provide a specific example of a widely known symptom of stuttering and a possible cure.

[10] A. NO CHANGE
B. reeducation was needed to overcome it.
C. could be overcome by reeducation.
D. the elimination of which is being by reeducation.

[11] A. NO CHANGE
B. experts believed that stuttering arose from
C. theories insist that stuttering came from
D. claims were made that stuttering's origins were

Passage A2

One of the most significant art discoveries of all time began in 1940, when a group of five teenagers and their dog [12] walk to a nearby hill in southern France, looking for hidden treasure. They definitely found [13] some, they discovered the Cave of Lascaux, home of the famous Lascaux prehistoric cave paintings.

[14] At around 15,000 BC, the climate on earth had warmed and the glaciers had receded. Rising sea levels were causing more rainfall that supported vegetation and small game animals. Groups of prehistoric people took advantage of these improved conditions and migrated to the Pyrenees of France. Among them were the artists of the Lascaux cave.

[15] The fact that many of the paintings are located more than a mile from the mouth of the cave has led us to believe that the paintings were part of "ritual" activities and the cave was a type of sanctuary. To reach the painting site the artists had to go on an [16] expedition. Since it took days, provisions were needed. Lamps made of limestone or sandstone that burned animal fat, and torches made from wood coated with fat had to be brought along. The artists were not deterred by darkness, the lakes that had to be crossed, or the stalagmites that had to be removed to reach their destination.

The paintings are predominantly depictions of animals—almost 600 in all. The horse is the most popular animal. Others include aurochs, stags, ibex and bison and more rarely, bears and felines. There is only one human representation at the site, not unusual among paintings of this time period.

(#1) The images at Lascaux were created using primitive paints with pigments. (#2) The pigments at Lascaux include ochre, charcoal, iron oxide, hematite, manganese and other minerals that produced the browns, blacks, reds and grays in the paintings. (#3) A binder stabilized the paint and many have [17] forestalled permanent adhesion to the stone surface. (#4) No trace is left of the binder but possibilities are water, fat, saliva,

[12] A. NO CHANGE
B. walked
C. walks
D. had walked

[13] A. NO CHANGE
B. some, having discovered
C. some they discovered
D. some; discovering

[14] A. NO CHANGE
B. During approximately 15,000
C. Around roughly 15,000
D. By 15,000

[15] Which of the following sentences most effectively and accurately expresses the main topic of this paragraph?
A. The cave could not have been used for everyday activities.
B. Cave artists were likely a select group of talented people.
C. To protect the paintings from vandalism, they were created as far as possible from the cave entrance.
D. The Lascaux paintings are religious in nature.

[16] Which choice best combines the sentences where the segment of the passage is underlined?
A. expedition that since it took days it needed provisions.
B. expedition that took days and required provisions.
C. expedition, and since it took days, requiring artists to bring all the necessary provisions.
D. expedition, and provisions were needed, which took days.

[17] A. NO CHANGE
B. proposed
C. promoted
D. prompted

blood or urine. (#5) These minerals were most likely ground into a powder using stone mortars and pestles. (#6) A vehicle liquefied the paint and allowed it to be applied to the surface. (#7) Water or oil are typical vehicles that might have been used. **[18]**

The artists may have applied the paint with brushes and **[19]** underline(fingers or paint was blown through a straw.) Some of the paintings seem to have been created by using a crayon to draw an outline of the **[20]** underline(figures. And then filling) it in with a brush. Crayons were produced by mixing pigment with a binder, molding it into the desired shape and letting it dry. **[21]** underline(Brushes that may have been made from leaves with shredded ends) enabled the artists to leave both wide and narrow strokes of paint on the cave's walls. Moreover, bits of evidence indicate that the stone surface suggested shapes of animals and objects to **[22]** underline(the artist that they could then perfect) by applying paint.

[18] For the sake of cohesion in this paragraph, sentence #5 should be placed
A. where it is now.
B. after sentence #1.
C. after sentence #2.
D. after sentence #6.

[19] A. NO CHANGE
B. fingers, or blowing through straws
C. fingers and with straws through which they blew paint
D. fingers and with paint blown through a straw

[20] A. NO CHANGE
B. figures. Then filling
C. figures, and then they filled
D. figures, then filling

[21] A. NO CHANGE
B. Brushes, that may have been made from various leaves, with shredded ends,
C. Brushes that may have been made from various leaves, with shredded ends,
D. Brushes that may have been made from various leaves with shredded ends,

[22] A. NO CHANGE
B. the artists that they could then perfect
C. the artist that he or she could then perfect
D. artists, who then could perfect shapes

Passage A3

Home schoolers are now a **[23]** <u>divisive, multidimensional, heterogeneous</u> population. No longer the preserve of left wing unschoolers and right wing fundamentalists, the great range of people make it very difficult to draw even broad generalizations about the phenomenon. **[24]** <u>In addition</u>, one article of faith unites all home schoolers: that home schooling should be unregulated. Home schoolers of all stripes believe that they alone should decide how their children are educated, and they unite in order to press for the absence of regulations or the most permissive regulation possible.

[25] Flexibility in laws governing mandatory schooling for all children between certain ages opened the door to educational options. Matters of conscience, convenience, and custom led some parents to have their children schooled at home, or at least, away from traditional educational institutions. In no other educational setting are parents so fully responsible for determining what children are **[26]** <u>taught.</u> Unregulated home schooling is nothing less than total and complete parental authority over schooling with minimal regard for the quality and content of instruction. Home schooling, therefore, represents the ultimate parenting authority over schooling. The theoretical arguments **[27]** <u>for regulating</u> home schooling begin from this point. If compulsory education is the law of the land, the question must be asked whether the schooling of children should ever be under the total and complete control of parents.

[23] Which choice results in the most effective opening sentence of this paragraph?
A. NO CHANGE
B. multiethnic and heterogeneous
C. diversified and homogeneous
D. diverse

[24] A. NO CHANGE
B. Accordingly
C. Nevertheless
D. To be sure

[25] Which choice best describes the central idea of this paragraph?
A. Educational goals are uncertain when schooling is left completely to parents.
B. Home schooling should be a permissible educational option, of course, but strict regulations are needed to assure a reasonable level of quality.
C. The citizens of a free country can be free only up to a point.
D. In a free society, the requirement that all children to be schooled has served as an incentive to develop alternative means of education.

[26] The writer is thinking about listing additional responsibilities of parents who are home schooling their children. Which choice would best accomplish this goal?
A. taught and they must make decisions about the implementation of certain lessons.
B. taught, but also when, how, and with whom they are taught.
C. taught. Lessons must also be planned and they must supervise homework.
D. taught, as well as lessons and tests and homework.

[27] A. NO CHANGE
B. as pertaining to the regulation of
C. in behalf of the full regulation of
D. regulating

[28] Kathleen Lyons, a spokesperson for the National Education Association the largest and most powerful teachers' union in America believes that home schooling cannot provide students with a comprehensive education experience. Regardless, home schooling parents claim that they are, and always will be, the appropriate authority over their children, and that what needs to be changed is the state's authority over the upbringing of children. So let us ask two separate, but related, questions: What justifies, if anything, government authority over the education of children? and what justifies parental authority over the education of their own children?

Recognizing that parents ought indeed to possess wide ranging authority to raise their children as they see fit, [29] questions of the government's role need to be answered, especially where and when its stewardship of children's education starts and stops.

[30] This is so for many reasons, chief among them that parents are responsible for the care of their children, and [31] their knowledge of their children is better than any school teacher.

Let us take it as given, therefore, that parental authority over their children is legitimate and desirable. What reason is there, in that case, to accept sovereignty over the education of children by the government, an authority that could in certain circumstances curtail the authority of parents? The answer should lie in the quality of education that students receive. While critics insist that the government should regulate home schooling in order to ensure the quality of education, recent studies have shown that the degree to which home schooling is regulated by state governments has no bearing on student test

[28] A. NO CHANGE
B. Kathleen Lyons a spokesperson for the National Education Association the largest and most powerful teachers' union in America. States,
C. Kathleen Lyons, a spokesperson for the National Education Association, the largest and most powerful teachers' union in America,
D. Kathleen Lyons, a spokesperson for the National Education Association the largest, and most powerful teachers' union in America,

[29] A. NO CHANGE
B. questions about the role of government must be asked and answered
C. the government needs to answer questions about its role
D. the role of government is to answer crucial questions

[30] A. NO CHANGE
B. This guideline
C. This puzzle
D. Just such a controversy

[31] A. NO CHANGE
B. they know their children better than school teachers.
C. they know their children as well if not better than school teachers.
D. they know their children better than anyone else, including school teachers.

scores. In fact, **[32]** <u>on major achievement tests, almost a third of home schooled students earn scores in the highest decile</u> (i.e., the top 10 percent). With that level of performance, the

Standardized tests translate home school achievement into public-school-achievement terms

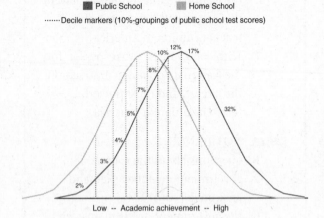

Low -- Academic achievement -- High

[32] Which choice most accurately reports data shown on the graph?
A. NO CHANGE
B. The number of public school students exceeds the number of home schooled students.
C. From 10 percent to 17 percent of home schooled students perform at the highest levels on standardized tests.
D. Ten percent of both public school and home schooled students achieve at the same level.

[33] A. NO CHANGE
B. avoids
C. to avoid
D. avoiding

so-called "citizenship argument" against unregulated home schooling, which seeks to justify providing children with a civic education, is highly questionable.

Advocates of another proposition, known as the "freedom argument," seek to justify providing children with an education that cultivates their freedom and thereby **[33]** <u>avoid</u> the development of what may be called "ethically servile" adults. Together, the two arguments justify some state authority over the education of children and rule out total parental control of education.

Passage A4

One of middle-school teacher Debbie Vasquez's [34] passions have long been to expose underprivileged students to robotics, biochemistry and biophysics, genetics, and marine aquatic biology, topics that schools like Debbie's, in Washington D.C.'s South East neighborhood rarely teach. [35] Many of Debbie's colleagues, who envy her energy and commitment, wish that they possessed as much enthusiasm for teaching [36] as her. Counting on the support of every faculty member, then, [37] Debbie's plans for awakening kids' interest in science consumes every day.

She aims to make science not just another subject that kids take in school but something that gets them out of bed in the morning and may someday lead to a career. "I never had the opportunity at that age," Debbie recalls. "The schools I went to weren't that great. Furthermore, in middle school I never did a single lab, ever. I never once met a scientist or an engineer until college."

Thanks to Debbie, her kids won't suffer the same fate. "Not as long as I'm their teacher," she vows. Now in her fourth year, Debbie teaches STEM-related topics—Science, Technology, Engineering and [38] Math. They hold the promise of a wide range of enticing careers in the decades ahead. As they look to the future, U.S. businesses frequently voice concerns over the supply and availability of STEM workers. There are now 26 million STEM-related jobs, and the number is rapidly growing. The U.S. Labor Department [39] anticipates a need for only 9.8 million non-STEM workers in 2018.

Recent and Projected Growth in STEM and Non-STEM Employment

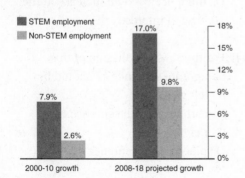

Source: U.S. Bureau of Labor Statistics

[34] A. NO CHANGE
B. passions for a lengthy and extended period of time has been to expose
C. passions has long been to expose her
D. longtime passions are to expose

[35] A. NO CHANGE
B. colleagues who envy Debbie's energy and commitment
C. colleagues who envy Debbie's energy and commitment,
D. colleagues, envying Debbie's energy and commitment

[36] A. NO CHANGE
B. like her
C. as she
D. as she possesses

[37] A. NO CHANGE
B. every day she is consumed by daily plans for waking up kids' interest in science
C. Debbie's plans for the waking up of kids' interest in science consumes every day
D. she is consumed every day by plans for awakening kids' interest in science

[38] Which choice most effectively combines the sentences at the underlined text?
A. Math, which holds the promise
B. Math because they hold the promise
C. Math, holding the promises
D. Math, and they hold the promise

[39] Which choice most accurately conveys data based on the graph?
A. NO CHANGE
B. reports that between 2000 and 2018 STEM workers will constitute 24.9 percent (i.e., 7.9% + 17% = 24.9%) of America's work force
C. projects a 17.0 percent growth of STEM occupations between 2008 and 2018
D. estimates that the growth rate of non-STEM employees will double between 2010 and 2018

[40] (#1) According to Debbie's account of her employment, the idea of teaching middle school kids [41] simultaneously frightened her. (#2) She wondered what she could teach them that would make a difference in their lives. (#3) Shocked by her students' attitudes and frustrated by their lack of skills, more often than not during her first months of teaching, she went home in tears. [42] (#4) Teachers who feel discouraged often seek help from colleagues or administrators, and as she brought STEM-related lessons to her [43] kids it raised the level of interest increased, not only because of numerous hands-on activities but because of who she herself was. (#5) "I represented new, tangible options," she says. (#6) "I was a role model. (#7) I even looked like my students and had a similar background. (#8) Because of me, what hadn't been on the kids' radars before was now becoming accessible in a very real way." (#9) She raised kids' sights and made them realize that the growth of STEM jobs with higher salaries than they ever imagined was the means to one day lifting themselves out of the ranks of the impoverished and into the middle class and beyond. [44]

[40] Which choice serves most effectively as the main topic of this paragraph?

A. Students thrive and learn more when they are given meaningful, hands-on work to do in the classroom.

B. Students benefited not only from Debbie's lessons but also from her background and experience.

C. For low-income students, STEM offers untold opportunities to succeed in the future.

D. The promise of high salaries motivates impoverished students to raise their aspirations and work harder.

[41] A. NO CHANGE
B. initially
C. originally, at the start
D. as it turns out

[42] Which version of the underlined section of sentence #4 maintains the sentence pattern established by the paragraph?
A. NO CHANGE
B. It sometimes takes superhuman effort to turn failure into success.
C. But gradually, she began to perceive new possibilities.
D. It is more important to explain new material to a class than to berate them for their behavior.

[43] A. NO CHANGE
B. it raised their level of interest
C. their interest grew
D. there occurred an increase in the level of interest

[44] For the sake of cohesion of this paragraph, sentence #7 should be
A. left as it is.
B. combined with sentence #6.
C. deleted.
D. placed after sentence #9.

END OF PRACTICE TEST A

ANSWER KEY

1. **B**	12. **B**	23. **D**	34. **C**
2. **D**	13. **B**	24. **C**	35. **A**
3. **B**	14. **D**	25. **B**	36. **C**
4. **C**	15. **A**	26. **B**	37. **D**
5. **C**	16. **B**	27. **A**	38. **B**
6. **C**	17. **C**	28. **C**	39. **C**
7. **D**	18. **C**	29. **C**	40. **B**
8. **A**	19. **C**	30. **A**	41. **B**
9. **C**	20. **D**	31. **D**	42. **C**
10. **C**	21. **A**	32. **A**	43. **C**
11. **B**	22. **D**	33. **B**	44. **A**

Number of Correct Answers _____

How did you do? The number of correct answers will determine your score, calculated on a scale of 10 (low) to 40 (high). For the actual Writing and Language Test, you'll also receive two subscores based on your answers to questions the College Board designates "Expression of Ideas" and "Standard English Conventions."

Although each Writing and Language Test is different, the following chart will give you a general idea of your performance.

Number of Correct Answers	Range of Scores
34–44	33–40
23–33	26–32
12–22	18–25
1–11	10–17

ANSWER EXPLANATIONS

Note: Although some choices contain multiple errors, only one or two major errors are explained for each incorrect choice. All questions are rated by level of difficulty.

Key to Levels of Difficulty

Rating	Percentage of Students Likely to Answer Correctly
EASY	>80%
MEDIUM	>65%
HARD	<65%

Passage A1

1. **(B)** Choice B is the best answer because it helps to develop the paragraph's main topic—the puzzling characteristics of stuttering.

   Choice A is not the best answer because it diverges from the main idea of the sentence—namely, that traits that appear to cause stuttering remain unclear.

   Choice C is not the best answer because it presents a fact that is irrelevant in the discussion of traits that cause stuttering.

   Choice D is not the best answer because it wanders from the focus of the paragraph—the possible causes, not the effects, of stuttering.

   EASY

2. **(D)** Choice D is the best answer because it creates a comparison between like terms: the speed of spoken language by stutterers and by nonstutterers.

   Choice A is not the best answer because it creates a comparison between unlike things: *speech* and *nonstutterers*.

   Choice B is not the best answer because the construction lacks a verb and, therefore, is a sentence fragment.

   Choice C is not the best answer because the comparison is incomplete. In standard English, the word *fast* should be followed by *as* (i.e., *as fast as*).

   MEDIUM

3. **(B)** Choice B is the best answer because *Observations*, the plural subject of the sentence agrees in number with the verb *have*, and it contains no needless punctuation.

   Choice A is not the best answer because *Observation*, the singular subject of the sentence, fails to agree with the plural verb *have led*.

   Choice C is not the best answer because it lacks a verb and, therefore, is a sentence fragment.

   Choice D is not the best answer because it contains an unnecessary comma, and the singular noun *Observation* fails to agree in number with the plural verb *have led*.

   MEDIUM

4. **(C)** Choice C is the best answer because the transitional phrase *for example* logically introduces a relevant example of a stutterer with the characteristics described by the first part of the sentence.

Choice A is not the best answer because the transitional word *meanwhile* is not logical in the context. It also creates a run-on sentence, in this case, two independent sentences separated by a dash.

Choice B is not the best answer because, among other things, the word *consequently* indicates a cause-and-effect relationship that is not present in the context.

Choice D is not the best answer because the phrase *to sum up* is ordinarily used before a review or recapitulation of some kind and, therefore, is neither appropriate nor possible in the context.

EASY

5. **(C)** Choice C is the best answer because the adjective *frustrated* is structurally parallel to the two preceding adjectives, *frightened* and *angry*.

Choice A is incorrect because it is not structurally parallel to the preceding adjectives, *frightened* and *angry*.

Choice B is not a good answer because the phrase *frustrated from* fails to conform to standard English idiom.

Choice D is not the best answer because it is neither structurally nor grammatically parallel to the preceding adjectives, *frightened* and *angry*.

MEDIUM

6. **(C)** Choice C is the best answer. The original sentence ends with the word *open*. What follows is new wording that lists additional physical reactions, each one named in a clause parallel in form to those in the original sentence.

Choice A is not the best answer because the phrases naming stutterers' reactions are not parallel in structure to those in the original sentence.

Choice B is not the best answer because the added phrases are structured differently—with one adjective and a noun—from those in the original sentence.

Choice D is not the best answer because it contains a sentence fragment.

HARD

7. **(D)** Choice D is the best answer because the plural pronoun *their* agrees in number with *symptoms*, its antecedent.

Choice A is not the best answer because the word *it's*, a contraction of *it is*, does not fit the context of the passage.

Choice B is incorrect because the singular pronoun *its* fails to agree in number with its plural antecedent *symptoms*.

Choice C is not the best answer because the plural noun *causes* fails to agree with the singular verb *remains*.

MEDIUM

8. **(A)** Choice A is the best answer because the word *mystery* aptly characterizes the question of what causes stuttering.

Choice B is not a good answer because *riddle* suggests a problem with a predetermined solution—which stuttering definitely is not.

Choice C is incorrect because the phrase *in the closet* implies a secret deliberately hidden from view. Also, its informality is inconsistent with the tone of the passage and has connotations unrelated to stuttering.

Choice D is not the right answer because *a dilemma* is a kind problem often solved by deciding between two equally compelling alternatives, such as "To be, or not to be," and, therefore, is inappropriate in the context.

EASY

9. **(C)** Choice C is the best answer because the sentence blurs the paragraph's focus on historical proposals for treating stutterers.

Choice A is not the best answer because the new sentence would detract from the purpose of the paragraph—to cite historical examples of proposals for the treatment of stutterers.

Choice B is not the best answer. Although it adds another famous name to the list of people concerned about stuttering, it fails to mention another proposal for a cure.

Choice D is not the best answer because it is irrelevant to the main purpose of the paragraph—to cite historical examples of proposals for treating stutterers.

HARD

10. **(C)** Choice C is the best answer because it succinctly and correctly states Bell's beliefs about overcoming stuttering problems.

Choice A is not the best answer because it contains three largely redundant verbs.

Choice B is not the best answer because of mixed sentence construction. An extra sentence subject and verb (*reeducation was needed*) has been added to a sentence that already has a subject and a verb.

Choice D is not the best answer because its wording fails to adhere to standard English idiom.

MEDIUM

11. **(B)** Choice B is the best answer. The sentence, in providing an alternate theory about the cause of stuttering maintains paragraph cohesion by using *experts* as the subject of the sentence, thereby echoing the subject of the prior sentence—*theorists*.

Choice A is not the best answer because of mixed sentence construction. The verb *recommended* is not grammatically or logically related to the subject *stuttering*.

Choice C is not the best answer because of an improper shift in verb tense from past to present.

Choice D is not the best answer because the noun *claims* cannot logically be the subject of the verb *recommended*.

HARD

Passage A2

12. **(B)** Choice B is the best answer because the sentence calls for a verb in the past tense.

Choice A is not the best answer because *walk* is a plural verb that fails to agree with its singular subject, *group*.

Choice C is not the best answer because the present-tense verb *walks* may not be used in a passage cast in the past tense.

Choice D is not the best answer because of an inappropriate shift from the past tense of the verb to the past perfect.

EASY

13. **(B)** Choice B is the best answer because the subject of the sentence *They* is correctly modified by the participial phrase that starts with *having discovered*.

Choice A is not the best answer because it uses a comma to connect, or splice, two independent sentences.

Choice C is not the best answer because it creates a run-on sentence.

Choice D is not the best answer because it uses a semicolon instead of a comma to separate a complete sentence, or independent clause, from a phrase.

MEDIUM

14. **(D)** Choice D is the best answer because it uses succinct standard English to identify the time of the Earth's warming.

Choice A is not the best answer because of faulty idiom. *At around* is not standard English usage.

Choice B is not the best answer because the meaning of the phrase *During approximately* is confusing. The phrase also fails to conform to standard English idiom.

Choice C is not the best answer because it contains a redundancy. The words *around* and *roughly* mean essentially the same thing.

MEDIUM

15. **(A)** Choice A is the best answer because most sentences in the paragraph allude to difficulties faced by the artists—or at least the steps they were forced to take—in order to reach the area of the cave where they created their paintings.

Choice B is not the best answer because the paragraph emphasizes the artists' determination, not their talent.

Choice C is not the best answer because while the artists may have purposefully chosen a secure site for their paintings, the paragraph doesn't say so.

Choice D is not the best answer because the paragraph says nothing about the paintings' religiosity.

HARD

16. **(B)** Choice B is the best answer because it eliminates needless words and accurately conveys meaning by subordinating one clause to another.

Choice A is not the best answer because it lacks the punctuation needed to separate the clauses of a complex sentence, and it needlessly repeats the pronoun *it*.

Choice C is not the best answer because the verb *requiring* may not serve as the main verb of an independent clause or a sentence.

Choice D is not the best answer because of a misplaced modification. The clause *which took days* is meant to modify *expedition* but seems to modify *provisions*.

HARD

17. **(C)** Choice C is the best answer because the word *promoted* suggests that the binder probably helped the paint adhere to the walls, a possibility borne out by the continued existence of the paintings.

Choice A is not the best answer because it fully contradicts the fact that the paintings exist to this day.

Choice B is not the best answer because the word *proposed* makes little sense in the context of the passage.

Choice D is not the best answer because while the word *prompted* is used in terms of help or encouragement, the word does not apply to inanimate objects such as paint.

EASY

18. **(C)** Choice C is the best answer because the phrase *These minerals* refers directly to the substances—*ochre*, *charcoal*, etc.—listed in sentence 2.

Choice A is not the best answer because in its current location sentence 5 intrudes upon the description of ingredients in the paint.

Choice B is not the best answer because sentence 5 makes reference to minerals that have not been mentioned in sentence 1.

Choice D is not the best answer because it would turn sentence 5 into an irrelevant afterthought.

HARD

19. **(C)** Choice C is the best answer because it maintains parallelism while listing the various means the artists used to apply paint.

Choice A is not the best answer because of the shift from active to passive voice part way through the sentence.

Choice B is not the best answer because the *blowing through straws* is not structurally parallel to the phrase *with brushes and fingers*.

Choice D is not the best answer because of the awkward redundancy of "applied the *paint* with … *paint* blown through.…"

MEDIUM

20. **(D)** Choice D is the best answer because it explains the artists' process in clear, grammatically correct language.

    Choice A is not the best answer because the construction beginning with *And then* is a sentence fragment.

    Choice B is not the best answer because the segment beginning with *Then filling* is a sentence fragment.

    Choice C is not the best answer because the pronoun *they* lacks a specific antecedent.

    MEDIUM

21. **(A)** Choice A is the best answer because *that may have been made from leaves with shredded ends* is, in the context, a restrictive clause that should not be set off with punctuation. *That may have been made from leaves with shredded ends* is essential information that explains the width of the artists' brush strokes.

    Choice B is not the best answer because it incorrectly sets off the restrictive clause *that may have been made from leaves* with commas as though the clause were nonrestrictive—that is not essential to the meaning of the sentence.

    Choice C is not the best answer because it incorrectly sets off the essential element *with shredded ends* with commas as though the phrase were not essential to the meaning of the sentence. *With shredded ends* is essential information that helps to explain the width of the artists' brush strokes.

    Choice D is not the best answer because it inserts an unnecessary comma after the word *ends*, incorrectly separating the subject of the sentence (*brushes that may have been made from various leaves with shredded ends*) from the predicate ("enabled the artists...").

    HARD

22. **(D)** Choice D is the best answer, in part because it is grammatically and stylistically sound and avoids the weaknesses of the other choices.

    Choice A is not the best answer because the plural pronoun *they* disagrees with its singular antecedent "artist."

    Choice B is not the best answer because the pronoun *they* refers ambiguously to both the phrase "animals and objects" and to the word "artists."

    Choice C is not the best answer because while not grammatically incorrect, it uses the awkward phrase *he or she*.

    MEDIUM

Passage A3

23. **(D)** Choice D is the best answer because it accurately conveys an idea consistent with the writer's point that a "range of people" makes up the home schooling population.

    Choice A is not the best answer because it contains redundant adjectives and characterizes home schoolers as divisive—a claim not at all supported by the paragraph.

    Choice B is not the best answer because no evidence in the paragraph supports the claim that home schoolers are multiethnic.

    Choice C is not the best answer because it is self-contradictory.

    HARD

24. **(C)** Choice C is the best answer because *Nevertheless* introduces a sentence that offers a description of home schoolers that differs from that in the previous sentence

    Choice A is not the best answer because the statement following the transitional phrase *In addition* fails to add evidence that supports any ideas in the previous sentence.

    Choice B is not the best answer because the statement following the transitional word *Accordingly* is not at all in accord with the previously stated idea.

    Choice D is not the best answer because the statement following the transitional phrase *To be sure* fails to reinforce the previously stated idea.

    EASY

25. **(B)** Choice B is the best answer because the paragraph cites the need for some regulation of home schooling.

    Choice A is not the best answer because educational goals are not discussed to any great extent in the paragraph.

    Choice C is not the best answer because it states a general rule that looms in the background of the home schooling movement but is not by any means the focus of the paragraph.

    Choice D is not the best answer. Although it probably is a valid observation, it is not discussed in the paragraph.

    HARD

26. **(B)** Choice B is the best answer because it maintains the style and structure of the phrase *what children are taught*.

Choice A is not the best answer because it introduces a coordinate clause that, while grammatically correct, is stylistically weak. In the context a subordinate clause would be preferable. Also, the pronoun *they* lacks a specific antecedent.

Choice C is not the best answer because the new sentence weakens the cohesion of the paragraph. Also, the sentence itself is flawed because it consists of two clauses, one active and one passive. Finally, the pronoun *they* lacks a clear antecedent.

Choice D is not the best answer because of mixed construction. That is, it is not grammatically related to the first clause of the sentence.

HARD

27. **(A)** Choice A is the best answer. The phrase is succinct and expressed in standard English.

Choice B is a not the best answer because of awkward, unidiomatic wording.

Choice C is not the best answer because it is needlessly wordy.

Choice D is not the best answer because it is ambiguous. It leaves the reader guessing whether the arguments are in favor of or against home schooling.

EASY

28. **(C)** Choice C is the best answer. It correctly punctuates the sentence, which contains two appositives, each one defining or describing proper nouns ("Kathleen Lyons" and "National Education Association.") In each case, the appositives are correctly set off with commas.

Choice A is not the best answer because it lacks a comma that is needed to set off the appositive describing the National Education Association.

Choice B is not the best answer because it lacks commas needed to set off the two appositives in the sentence.

Choice D is not the best answer because it includes a misplaced comma after *largest*.

MEDIUM

29. **(C)** Choice C is the best answer. The construction beginning with *Recognizing that parents …* correctly modifies *the government.*

Choice A is not the best answer because it contains a dangling modifier. The construction beginning with *Recognizing that parents …* should modify *government*, not *questions.*

Choice B is not the best answer because it contains a dangling modifier. The construction beginning with *Recognizing that parents …* should modify *government*, not *questions.*

Choice D is not the best answer because it contains a dangling modifier. The construction beginning with *Recognizing that parents …* should modify *government*, not *the role.*

HARD

30. **(A)** Choice A is the best answer because the demonstrative pronoun *This* refers generally to the question raised in the previous sentence about both the parental and the governmental role in educating children.

Choice B is not the best answer because the previous sentence contains nothing that could be deemed a guideline.

Choice C is not the best answer because the previous sentence makes no reference to any sort of puzzle.

Choice D is not the best answer because the previous sentence makes no reference to a controversy of any kind.

EASY

31. **(D)** Choice D is the best answer. It clearly states that parents' knowledge of their children is superior to that of any school teachers' knowledge.

Choice A is not the best answer because it illogically compares *knowledge* and *any school teacher.*

Choice B is not the best answer because it misstates the author's intent by saying that parents know their children better than they know school teachers.

Choice C is not the best answer because it is an incomplete comparison. To make the comparison whole, use the phrase *as well as.*

MEDIUM

32. **(A)** Choice A is the best answer because the graph shows that 32 percent of home schooled students performed in the highest decile.

Choice B is not the best answer because the graph does not show the number of students in either educational setting but only the percentages of home schooled students performing at various levels.

Choice C is not the best answer because the figures 10 percent and 17 percent on the graph refer to the percentage of home schooled students whose achievement places them in specific deciles.

Choice D is not the best answer because the percentages on the chart refer only to home schooled students.

HARD

33. **(B)** Choice B is the best answer because the singular verb *avoids* agrees in number with the singular noun *education*.

Choice A is not the best answer because the plural verb *avoid* fails to agree in number with the singular noun *education*.

Choice C is not the best answer because an infinitive form of a verb is not grammatical in a context that calls for a singular verb in the present tense.

Choice D is not the best answer because the progressive form of a verb is not grammatical in a context that calls for a singular verb in the present tense.

MEDIUM

Passage A4

34. **(C)** Choice C is the best answer because the singular verb *has … been* agrees in number with the sentence's singular subject, *One*.

Choice A is not the best answer because the plural verb *have … been* does not agree in number with the singular subject of the sentence, *One*.

Choice B is not the best answer because it consists of too many words, including the redundancy *lengthy and extended*.

Choice D is not the best answer because the plural verb *are* does not agree in number with the singular subject of the sentence, *One*.

EASY

35. **(A)** Choice A is the best answer because *who envy her (Debbie's) energy and commitment* is a nonrestrictive clause, meaning that every one of Debbie's fellow teachers envies her. That information is essential to the meaning of the sentence and, therefore, must be set off with a comma at both ends.

Choice B is not the best answer because it lacks the punctuation needed for a nonrestrictive clause. The words *envious of energy and commitment* are essential to the meaning of the sentence and, therefore, should be set off by commas.

Choice C is not the best answer because it has a superfluous comma tacked onto the end.

Choice D is not the best answer because it contains two commas that have no function or purpose.

HARD

36. **(C)** Choice C is the best answer because the comparison requires a pronoun in the nominative case. The word *as* is usually a conjunction and introduces a subordinate clause—in this case, *as she* (*does*). [*Hint*: When in doubt, add the appropriate verb after the pronoun.]

Choice A is not the best answer because a pronoun in the nominative case is needed to complete a comparison correctly. The word *as* is usually a conjunction and introduces a subordinate clause—in this case, *as she* (*does*). [*Hint*: When in doubt, add the appropriate verb after the pronoun.]

Choice B is not the best answer because a pronoun in the nominative case (*she*) is needed to complete the comparison. *Like* is a preposition and should not be used as a substitute for *as*, which is a conjunction used to introduce a clause such as *as if* or *as though*.

Choice D is not the best answer. Although grammatically correct, it contains needless repetition—*possessed/possesses*—a stylistic flaw.

MEDIUM

37. **(D)** Choice D is the best answer because the phrase that begins *Counting on the support*... correctly modifies the pronoun *she*.

Choice A is not the best answer because it contains a dangling participle. The phrase that begins *Counting on the support* should modify *Debbie* instead of *Debbie's plans*.

Choice B is not the best answer because of the redundancy, *every day* and *daily*.

Choice C is not the best answer because it contains a dangling participle. The phrase that begins *Counting on the support* ... should modify *Debbie* instead of *Debbie's plans*. Also, the phrase *the waking up of kids' interest* is awkwardly worded.

MEDIUM

38. **(B)** Choice B is the best answer because it seamlessly combines the two sentences and explains why Debbie teaches STEM topics.

Choice A is not the best answer because the singular verb *holds* fails to agree in number with the four STEM-related topics.

Choice C is not the best answer because the connection between the two parts of the sentence although grammatically correct, is ambiguous. Is it only math, or is it all four topics that hold career promises?

Choice D is not the best answer because the connection between the sentences, although grammatically correct, abruptly and awkwardly shifts the focus away from Debbie's teaching to careers of the future.

EASY

39. **(C)** Choice C is the best answer because the graph, which shows recent and anticipated growth in STEM employment, establishes that a 17.0 percent increase is expected during the decade 2008–2018.

Choice A is not the best answer because it misstates the basic purpose of the data shown on the graph—data related to projected growth, not the anticipated need for more workers.

Choice B is not the best answer because it misstates the basic purpose of the data. The graph is meant to show projected growth of STEM and non-STEM employment, not the percentage of the work force engaged in such jobs.

Choice D is not the best answer because it cites erroneous statistics. Data on the graph show that the growth rate of non-STEM employment—2.6 percent in 2008—will increase to 9.8 percent by 2018, a rate more than three times higher.

HARD

40. **(B)** Choice B is the best answer because it clearly states the main idea of the paragraph: How Debbie helped her students.

Choice A is not the best answer because it mentions only one of Debbie's teaching techniques.

Choice C is not the best answer. Although it may be a valid statement, it far exceeds the scope of the paragraph.

Choice D is not the best answer. While the paragraph asserts that STEM raised the aspirations of Debbie's students, the statement refers to only one idea in the paragraph.

MEDIUM

41. **(B)** Choice B is the best answer because, following a paragraph full of facts about STEM, it quickly brings the narrative back to the main focus of the passage— Debbie's experience as a teacher.

Choice A is not the best answer because *simultaneously* has no apparent relationship to the previous paragraph. Nor does the passage contain a reference to any simultaneous occurrences.

Choice C is not the best answer. Although it refers to the start of Debbie's teaching career, its redundancy disqualifies it as a viable answer.

Choice D is not the best answer because the phrase is misleading. Rather than discuss Debbie's long lasting fear of teaching middle schoolers, the writer details Debbie's success as a teacher.

EASY

42. **(C)** Choice C is the best answer because it most closely maintains the sentence pattern established by the two preceding sentences, each of which uses *she* as the subject and includes a verb that describes her actions (*wondered, went home*).

Choice A is not the best answer because it fails to maintain the sentence pattern established by the two preceding sentences, each of which uses *she* as the subject and includes a verb that describes her actions (*wondered, went home*). Rather, it shifts focus to teachers in general before returning in the second clause of the sentence to discuss Debbie again.

Choice B is not the best answer because it fails to maintain the sentence pattern established by the two preceding sentences, each of which uses *she* as the subject and includes a verb that describes her actions (*wondered, went home*). Rather, it generalizes about turning failure into success before returning to Debbie's teaching again.

Choice D is not the best answer because it fails to maintain the sentence pattern established by the two preceding sentences, each of which uses *she* as the subject and includes a verb that describes her actions (*wondered, went home*). Rather it makes an irrelevant statement about teaching methods before focusing on Debbie once again.

HARD

43. **(C)** Choice C is the best answer because it succinctly and clearly reports the effect of Debbie's lessons on her students.

Choice A is not the best answer because of wordy and awkward construction and the inclusion of a redundancy (*raised, increased*).

Choice B is not the best answer because the singular pronoun *it* fails to agree in number with its plural antecedent *lessons*.

Choice D is not the best answer. Although grammatically correct, it is excessively wordy.

EASY

44. **(A)** Choice A is the best answer because the sentence effectively supports Debbie's claim made in the previous sentence that she was a role model.

Choice B is not the best answer because combining the sentences would dilute the effect of Debbie's claim that she was a role model and would also take away from her assertion that she looked like her students and came from a similar background.

Choice C is not the best answer. The sentence should remain in the text because it cites two important reasons for Debbie's success as a teacher.

Choice D is not the best answer because placing the sentence last would create the impression that it was an afterthought instead of an integral part of the paragraph.

MEDIUM

ANSWER SHEET
Writing and Language Test B

Passage 1

1. Ⓐ Ⓑ Ⓒ Ⓓ
2. Ⓐ Ⓑ Ⓒ Ⓓ
3. Ⓐ Ⓑ Ⓒ Ⓓ
4. Ⓐ Ⓑ Ⓒ Ⓓ

5. Ⓐ Ⓑ Ⓒ Ⓓ
6. Ⓐ Ⓑ Ⓒ Ⓓ
7. Ⓐ Ⓑ Ⓒ Ⓓ
8. Ⓐ Ⓑ Ⓒ Ⓓ

9. Ⓐ Ⓑ Ⓒ Ⓓ
10. Ⓐ Ⓑ Ⓒ Ⓓ
11. Ⓐ Ⓑ Ⓒ Ⓓ

Passage 2

12. Ⓐ Ⓑ Ⓒ Ⓓ
13. Ⓐ Ⓑ Ⓒ Ⓓ
14. Ⓐ Ⓑ Ⓒ Ⓓ
15. Ⓐ Ⓑ Ⓒ Ⓓ

16. Ⓐ Ⓑ Ⓒ Ⓓ
17. Ⓐ Ⓑ Ⓒ Ⓓ
18. Ⓐ Ⓑ Ⓒ Ⓓ
19. Ⓐ Ⓑ Ⓒ Ⓓ

20. Ⓐ Ⓑ Ⓒ Ⓓ
21. Ⓐ Ⓑ Ⓒ Ⓓ
22. Ⓐ Ⓑ Ⓒ Ⓓ

Passage 3

23. Ⓐ Ⓑ Ⓒ Ⓓ
24. Ⓐ Ⓑ Ⓒ Ⓓ
25. Ⓐ Ⓑ Ⓒ Ⓓ
26. Ⓐ Ⓑ Ⓒ Ⓓ

27. Ⓐ Ⓑ Ⓒ Ⓓ
28. Ⓐ Ⓑ Ⓒ Ⓓ
29. Ⓐ Ⓑ Ⓒ Ⓓ
30. Ⓐ Ⓑ Ⓒ Ⓓ

31. Ⓐ Ⓑ Ⓒ Ⓓ
32. Ⓐ Ⓑ Ⓒ Ⓓ
33. Ⓐ Ⓑ Ⓒ Ⓓ

Passage 4

34. Ⓐ Ⓑ Ⓒ Ⓓ
35. Ⓐ Ⓑ Ⓒ Ⓓ
36. Ⓐ Ⓑ Ⓒ Ⓓ
37. Ⓐ Ⓑ Ⓒ Ⓓ

38. Ⓐ Ⓑ Ⓒ Ⓓ
39. Ⓐ Ⓑ Ⓒ Ⓓ
40. Ⓐ Ⓑ Ⓒ Ⓓ
41. Ⓐ Ⓑ Ⓒ Ⓓ

42. Ⓐ Ⓑ Ⓒ Ⓓ
43. Ⓐ Ⓑ Ⓒ Ⓓ
44. Ⓐ Ⓑ Ⓒ Ⓓ

PRACTICE WRITING AND LANGUAGE TEST B

TIME: 35 MINUTES

Directions: The underlined sentences and sentence parts in the passages below may contain errors in standard English, including awkward or ambiguous expression, poor word choice, incorrect sentence structure, or faulty grammar, usage, and punctuation.

Read each passage carefully and identify which of the four alternative versions most effectively and correctly expresses the meaning of the underlined material. Indicate your choice by filling in the corresponding space on the answer sheet. Choice A on most questions is "NO CHANGE." If none of the choices improves the underlined text, pick Choice A as your answer.

EXAMPLE

When someone works as a ranger in a national park, <u>you will be employed by</u> the U.S. Department of the Interior.

A. NO CHANGE

B. you would be an employee of

C. the employment would be by

D. he or she is employed by

ANSWER: A   B   C   Ⓓ

Passage B1

As Mars-bound rockets are still being tested, NASA, along with the space agencies of other countries, [1] have continued to evaluate risks of manned missions to the Red Planet, including radiation exposure and the effects of microgravity, [2] the risks of which we don't yet fully understand, although [3] it's a slam dunk that when left untreated they can adversely affect health. [4] To be sure, harmful radiation from galactic cosmic rays and solar energetic particles can easily penetrate typical shielding. With regard to gravity, we don't know precisely how much gravity is needed to avoid the potential problem of too little. However, of the two planets, Mars and the Earth, the latter has [5] the strongest gravity by far—66 percent to be exact—and six times stronger than the Moon. Mars also has readily available resources such as water and its roughly 24-hour day/night cycle is closer to the Earth's

[1] A. NO CHANGE
B. continued
C. continues
D. will continue

[2] A. NO CHANGE
B. that we don't yet fully understand the risk of
C. a risk not yet fully understood by us
D. risks we don't yet fully understand,

[3] A. NO CHANGE
B. it is a near certainty
C. it's a veracity
D. you can depend on it

[4] The writer wants to develop the paragraph with evidence about the risk to health posed by radiation. Which choice best accomplishes this goal?
A. NO CHANGE
B. Recently, in fact, space researchers, using a Cosmic Ray Telescope, have documented, quantified, and correlated the impact of radiation on human health.
C. Clearly, the environment of space poses significant risks to both humans and satellites.
D. Indeed, the relationship between exposure to radiation and the menace of cancer has long been known.

[5] A. NO CHANGE
B. the stronger gravity by far—66 percent higher to be exact—and six times stronger than the Moon
C. the stronger gravity by far—66 percent stronger to be exact—and six times stronger than that of the Moon
D. the strongest gravity by far—66 percent higher to be exact—and six times stronger than the Moon's

than that of any other planet or moon. [6] The risk from radiation is visualized more easily when compared to other risks.

The world's space agencies have put in place radiation exposure limits for astronauts over their careers. [7] At Mars, the risk can be managed by monitoring each crew member's radiation exposure and limiting the surface exploration time of those most at risk. The limits depend on the sex and the age of the astronaut, and are designed to keep the risk of radiation-induced fatal cancer below 3 percent. Based on a report by the National Council on Radiation Protections, [8] for females under 30, the threat of radiation exposure virtually exceeds the maximum allowable for their lifetime.

[6] For the sake of paragraph cohesion, what is the best thing to do with this sentence?
A. NO CHANGE
B. Change it from passive to active voice and leave it where it is.
C. Delete it.
D. Delete as many words as possible and combine it with the next sentence.

[7] A. NO CHANGE
B. In Mars risks are managed
C. The risks on Mars can be managed
D. Managing risks on Mars is

[8] Which choice completes the sentence with accurate data drawn from the graph?
A. NO CHANGE
B. limits of allowable exposure for females between 35 and 45, increase at approximately the same rate as the limits for men of the same age.
C. limits of cumulative exposure for men age 45 and older increase at a rate that is slower than that for women age 45 and older.
D. all other conditions being equal, it is more harmful for men than it is for women to be exposed to radiation.

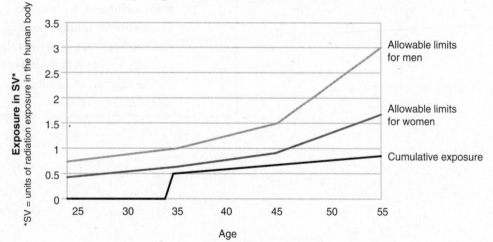

Comparing the Risks of Radiation on Mars

Current Exposure Limits, Depending on Age
Lines show resulting exposure for crew members arriving on Mars at age 35 and spending an average of two hours per day outside a habitat built on the planet.

But in the end, why are we even considering such a journey? In a word: life. [9] To go there to see if we can find evidence of life, a second genesis, and if we don't find it, we want to establish new life on Mars—[10] our own. But here is the thing: for the first time in history a species on Earth has the knowledge and technology to ensure its own survival on new worlds. For many enthusiasts it is an escape, a chance for a new start and the challenge of a lifetime. This is the broad-brush view of why we need to go to Mars, but on a more personal level, what is it that drives people to want to go to such places, so far away, so hostile to life? [11]

[9] A. NO CHANGE
B. We want to go there
C. Going there
D. It is to go there

[10] A. NO CHANGE
B. our own. And here is the clincher: for the first time in history a species on Earth has
C. our own, and furthermore, for the very first time in the history of our species on Earth, we have
D. our own, and for the first time in history our species on Earth have

[11] The writer wants to conclude the passage by answering the question with a sentence that emphasizes the romantic lure of space travel and settling on Mars in spite of the risks involved. Which choice would best accomplish that goal?
A. The answer is that Mars is a new frontier.
B. The answer is that, while Mars is not for everyone, our planet is teeming with men and women who burn with desire to take chances in the interest of science.
C. The answer is that humans like challenges that test their knowledge, resourcefulness, and abilities.
D. The answer is that the risks of radiation are no worse than the everyday risks we face here on earth—such as smoke that causes lung cancer.

Passage B2

[12] How to explain the popularity of the Beatles, a group that broke up officially in 1970 in the 21st century? The Beatles break up was marked with rancor and resentment between Paul McCartney and [13] John Lennon. Lawsuits were filed and legal matters dragged out for years, during which time the principals hardly communicated.

(#1) This sour end to the most popular music group of all time has not cooled the ardor of their fans. (#2) Beatle fanatics continue to make pilgrimages to iconic Liverpool and London locations to experience the landmarks of Beatles history. (#3) Go to any Paul McCartney or Ringo concert and you'll see fans of all generations, not just aging baby boomers. (#4) Many of these fans continue to gather at annual Beatles fests in America and Liverpool to pay [14] loyalty to their favorite band. (#5) This is the most powerful testament to the enduring legacy of the Beatles. (#6) As the magical melodies travel from generation to generation, you can be assured that the Beatles will remain as relevant today as they were in those halcyon days of 1963–70. [15]

Although the group's musical innovations are often cited to account for [16] their continued popularity, inventiveness alone cannot be the whole story. Some observers insist they gain their importance in the history of music because of their refreshing humor. Of the popular rock artists [17] prior to the Beatles; they came across as dull, including the Beach Boys, and the Four Seasons. Even Elvis Presley and the Rolling Stones, when compared to the Beatles, lacked humor and insightfulness.

So where did their humor come from? One theory says that it was a natural coping mechanism of residents who used to rely on humor to relieve the hardships they experienced in Liverpool, England, their post-World War II blue-collar hometown. Liverpudlians, as the

[12] A. NO CHANGE
B. When they officially broke up in 1970, can the popularity of the Beatles be explained in the 21st century?
C. Although they broke up in 1970 officially, in the 21st century can the Beatles' popularity be explained?
D. Can the popularity of the Beatles, a group that broke up officially in 1970, be explained in the 21st century?

[13] A. NO CHANGE
B. John Lennon. They filed lawsuits and legal matters were dragged out
C. John Lennon and lawsuits were filed and legal matters dragged out
D. John Lennon, who filed lawsuits and their legal matters dragged out

[14] A. NO CHANGE
B. homage
C. kudos
D. servility

[15] For the sake of the cohesion of this paragraph, sentence 5 should be placed
A. where it is now.
B. before sentence 1.
C. after sentence 3.
D. after sentence 6.

[16] A. NO CHANGE
B. its enduring notoriety
C. its uninterrupted popularity
D. their interminable popularity

[17] A. NO CHANGE
B. prior to the Beatles, the Beach Boys and the Four Seasons came across as dull.
C. prior to the Beatles, they came across as dull, including the Beach Boys and the Four Seasons.
D. prior to the Beatles, like the Beach Boys, and the Four Seasons, they all came across as dull.

natives are called, **[18]** <u>even make jokes about their city!</u>

    Why does the River Mersey run through Liverpool? Because it doesn't want to get mugged. Their wit got a boost, too, from the screenwriter of their first movie, *A Hard Day's Night*, who, in crafting the movie script, drew upon their sense of humor, their manner of talking, and **[19]** <u>they had like a natural bond between them</u>. Humorous quips, especially cutting ones from John Lennon, became their standard manner of speaking in public.

    When the Beatles were about to debut on American television in 1964, "I Want to Hold Your Hand" had already sold a million copies **[20]** <u>a larger number than any group.</u> **[21]** <u>Consequently,</u> arriving at the airport in New York, **[22]** <u>an avalanche of reporters greeted the group.</u> That there were many reporters there to skewer these longhaired interlopers was not a delusion. As one CBS News commentator said, "They symbolize the 20th century non-hero as they make non-music, wearing non-haircuts, give non-mercy." Luckily for the Beatles, their wit won over the American media—and helped ensure that we'd still be celebrating them more than a half century later.

[18] A. NO CHANGE
    B. regularly made jokes about their city:
    C. are accustomed to making jokes about the city.
    D. got into the regular habit of joking about their city;

[19] A. NO CHANGE
    B. they had a natural bond between them
    C. their bond being natural between them
    D. the natural bond between them

[20] A. NO CHANGE
    B. a higher amount than any song
    C. more than the sales of any other song
    D. the highest number of any group

[21] A. NO CHANGE
    B. In comparison
    C. At the same time
    D. As a matter of fact

[22] A. NO CHANGE
    B. a large amount of reporters greeted the group
    C. the group was greeted by an avalanche of reporters
    D. reporters in great numbers greeted the group

Passage B3

At approximately 2:00 A.M. on August 6, 1945, a modified American B-29 Superfortress bomber named the *Enola Gay* left the island of Tinian for Hiroshima, Japan. Piloted by Colonel Paul Tibbets, commanding officer of the 509th Composite Group, who named the bomber after his mother, [23] flew the four-engine plane followed by two observation planes carrying cameras and scientific instruments. One of seven aircraft making the trip to Hiroshima, only the *Enola Gay* carried a bomb nicknamed "Little Boy"—a bomb that was expected to [24] lay waste to almost everything within a 3 square-mile area of the city. Measuring over 10 feet long and almost 30 inches across, it weighed close to 5 tons and had the explosive force of 20,000 tons of TNT.

(#1)The *Enola Gay's* weaponeer, Navy Captain Deak Parsons, was concerned about taking off with the bomb fully assembled and live. (#2) Some heavily loaded B-29s had crashed on takeoff from Tinian. (#3) If that happened to the *Enola Gay*, the bomb might explode and wipe out half the island. (#4) Thus, Parsons, assisted by Lt. Morris Jeppson, finished the assembly and armed the bomb after takeoff. (#5) Carrying an atomic bomb for the first time, the crew had to be careful. [25]

[26] Four hours into the flight, it was 6:00 A.M., and that was when the bomb was fully armed, and then Tibbets announced to the crew that the plane was carrying the world's first atomic bomb. Close to 7:00 A.M., the Japanese radar net detected aircraft heading toward Japan, and an alert [27] is broadcasted throughout the Hiroshima area. Soon afterward, a weather plane circled over the city but found no sign of bombers. The citizenry of Hiroshima, [28] consequently, began their daily routine and thought the danger had passed. At 7:25, the *Enola Gay* approached Hiroshima at 26,000 feet. By 8:00, Japanese radar again detected B-29s heading toward the city. Although radio stations broadcast additional warnings for people to take shelter, [29] but many ignored it and continue as before to carry out business as usual. At 8:09, the crew of the *Enola Gay* could see the city appear below and received a message

[23] A. NO CHANGE
B. the four-engine plane was followed by
C. flew the four-engine plane. It was followed by
D. the four-engine plane and he was followed

[24] A. NO CHANGE
B. decompose
C. cripple
D. trash

[25] Which choice describes the most effective placement in the paragraph of sentence #5, the paragraph's topic sentence?
A. After sentence 2
B. After sentence 3
C. After sentence 4
D. None of the above; delete it

[26] A. NO CHANGE
B. Four hours after take-off at 6:00 A.M., the bomb was fully armed and Tibbets
C. At 6:00 A.M., four hours into the flight, and the bomb was fully armed and that was when Tibbets
D. By 6:00 A.M. the bomb was fully armed, and Tibbets

[27] A. NO CHANGE
B. was broadcast
C. has been broadcast
D. had been broadcasted

[28] A. NO CHANGE
B. in consequence, therefore, began its daily routine
C. therefore, began its daily routine
D. began their daily routine

[29] A. NO CHANGE
B. but many citizens ignored the warnings and continued to carry out their
C. many ignored them and continued to carry out their
D. many of them were ignored and they conducted

indicating that the weather was good over Hiroshima.

A T-shaped bridge at the junction of the Honkawa and Motoyasu rivers near downtown Hiroshima was the target. **[30]** The aircraft arrived over the target area at 8:15 A.M. Upon seeing the target in the bomb sight, Little Boy was dropped. It exploded, instantly killing 80,000 to 140,000 people and seriously injuring 100,000 more. The bomb exploded some 1,900 feet above the center of the city, over Shima Surgical Hospital, some 70 yards southeast of the Industrial Promotional Hall (now known as the Atomic Bomb Dome). Crew members of the aircraft saw a column of smoke rising fast, observed intense fires springing up, **[31]** and a mushroom cloud, which almost enveloped the observation planes, was noticed, too. The burst temperature, estimated to reach over a million degrees Celsius, ignited the surrounding air, forming a fireball some 840 feet in diameter. Eyewitnesses more than 5 miles away said **[32]** its brightness exceeded the sun's ten times over. In less than one second, the fireball had expanded to 900 feet. The blast wave shattered windows for a distance of ten miles and was felt as far away as 37 miles. Over two-thirds of Hiroshima's buildings were demolished. **[33]** Huge fires by the hundreds, ignited by the thermal pulse, produced a firestorm that incinerated everything within 4.4 miles of ground zero.

To the crew of the *Enola Gay*, Hiroshima had disappeared under a thick, churning foam of flames and smoke. The co-pilot, Captain Robert Lewis, commented, "My God, what have we done?"

[30] In the context, which choice is the best way to combine the two underlined sentences into one?
A. The aircraft arrived over the target area at 8:15 A.M., and upon seeing the target in the bomb sight, Little Boy was dropped.
B. Overhead at 8:15 A.M., the bridge was seen through in the aircraft's bomb sight and Little Boy was dropped.
C. At 8:15 A.M., viewing the bridge through the aircraft's bomb sight, Little Boy was dropped.
D. Arriving over the bridge and seeing the target in the bomb sight at 8:15 A.M., the crew dropped Little Boy.

[31] A. NO CHANGE
B. and noticed a mushroom cloud almost enveloping the observation planes
C. and along with a mushroom cloud which almost enveloped the observation planes was noticed
D. noticing, too, that the observation planes were being almost enveloped in a mushroom cloud

[32] A. NO CHANGE
B. the brightness exceeded the sun tenfold
C. it was over ten times more brighter than the sun
D. the brightness of it exceeded the sun ten times over

[33] A. NO CHANGE
B. Huge fires by the hundreds ignited by the thermal pulse produced a firestorm, it incinerated
C. Huge fires by the hundreds, ignited by the thermal pulse; and produced a firestorm that incinerated
D. Huge fires, by the hundreds, and ignited by the thermal pulse, produced a firestorm that incinerated

Passage B4

Although history and the outdoors, including hiking in the mountains and deserts, [34] is Ari Drummond's greatest joy, he hadn't realized he wanted to be an archaeologist until he was 23 and was nearly finished with a totally unrelated college degree. He pinpoints his decision to be an archaeologist to a single day: Having been traveling overseas for a while and wandering around Izmir, Turkey, [35] a museum of archaeology caught his eye. The halls of the museum contained an impressive collection of ancient Greek artifacts, ancient statues, vases, stone carvings, and even long-buried sarcophaguses (coffins). The archaeologist's job would be [36] to pull centuries-old objects like those out of the ground, and seemed like something he might like to try. By chance, he struck up a conversation with a Mr. Yilmaz, an archaeologist and one of the museum's curators. They got along [37] very good; so good in fact that Mr. Yilmaz invited him to lunch next day. [38] He suggested that he study archaeology during lunch.

Ari followed through. It happens that Indiana Jones movies were the rage at the time. To Ari, Indiana Jones was a role model. The films portrayed the archaeologist's routine with surprising accuracy. [39] Ari was an avid fan of Indiana Jones' movies. Snakes, especially rattlers,

[34] A. NO CHANGE
B. was Ari Drummond's greatest joy
C. have been what have given Ari Drummond his greatest joy
D. were Ari Drummond's greatest joy

[35] A. NO CHANGE
B. his eye caught a museum of archaeology
C. he came across a museum of archaeology
D. an archaeological museum caught his eye

[36] A. NO CHANGE
B. having the experience of pulling centuries-old objects like these ones
C. experiencing the pulling of ancient, centuries-old objects like those
D. to pull those ancient, centuries-old objects

[37] A. NO CHANGE
B. very well, so well in fact that
C. very well. So well that
D. very good, so good that

[38] A. NO CHANGE
B. He suggested to Ari that he study archaeology at lunch
C. As they ate, Mr. Yilmaz suggested that Ari study archaeology
D. Mr. Yilmaz made the suggestion to Ari that he should study archaeology at lunch

[39] For the sake of paragraph cohesion, which choice is the most effective substitute for the underlined sentence?
A. No substitute; delete the sentence from the passage.
B. Ari's hat is never far from his head, and khaki pants are part of his standard uniform.
C. The work entails travel to many remote places on the map.
D. Despite their education and training, archaeologists usually don't get rich.

are often an issue in wilderness areas where Ari works. Other dangers include spiders, bears, and stumbling upon back country drug-growing **[40]** areas while he is out on a survey perils such as those don't deter him. The search for evidence of ancient humans totally **[41]** will totally devour his entire mind and body. Managing an active dig site, he says, is like keeping multiple plates spinning all at once. (#11) He spends most of the time tirelessly digging into the earth and getting completely **[42]** filthy, but there are not frequent discoveries of arrowheads or other objects.

For Ari, there's nothing so thrilling as reaching into the dirt and picking up varieties of stone tools or weapons that human hands have not touched for 800 years or **[43]** more. Such artifacts link him instantly to those ancient people who left them there so long ago. In fact, finding an arrowhead once led Ari to discover a previously unknown Shoshone Indian village in Utah.

Archaeologists dig excruciatingly **[44]** slowly. They engage in a methodical process of shaving the ground just a few centimeters at a time so the soil and the artifacts can tell us the story of the past. It's a destructive science, really, because once the earth is disturbed, it can never be returned exactly as it had been.

[40] A. NO CHANGE
B. areas. While he is out on a survey,
C. areas while he is out on a survey,
D. areas, while he is out on a survey

[41] A. NO CHANGE
B. has devoured his entire mind and body
C. devours his mind and body
D. will totally devour his mind and body

[42] A. NO CHANGE
B. filthy, but he discovers arrowheads and other objects fairly infrequently.
C. filthy, and infrequently are arrowheads and other objects discovered.
D. filthy, but a discovery of arrowheads or other objects are not frequent.

[43] A. NO CHANGE
B. more; artifacts that link him instantly to the ancient people who left them
C. more. Such artifacts, they are an instant link to the people which left them
D. more. These artifacts create an instant link-up with ancient people who have left them

[44] For the sake of cohesion, which choice most effectively combines the sentences in the underlined portions?
A. slowly, and they engage
B. slowly; while digging, they engage
C. slowly, but they engage
D. slowly, engaging

END OF PRACTICE TEST B

ANSWER KEY

1. **C**	12. **D**	23. **B**	34. **D**
2. **D**	13. **A**	24. **A**	35. **C**
3. **B**	14. **B**	25. **D**	36. **A**
4. **D**	15. **A**	26. **D**	37. **B**
5. **C**	16. **C**	27. **B**	38. **C**
6. **C**	17. **B**	28. **C**	39. **C**
7. **C**	18. **B**	29. **C**	40. **B**
8. **B**	19. **D**	30. **D**	41. **C**
9. **B**	20. **C**	31. **B**	42. **B**
10. **B**	21. **A**	32. **A**	43. **A**
11. **A**	22. **C**	33. **A**	44. **D**

Number of Correct Answers _____

How did you do? The number of correct answers will determine your score, calculated on a scale of 10 (low) to 40 (high). For the actual Writing and Language Test, you'll also receive two subscores based on your answers to questions the College Board designates "Expression of Ideas" and "Standard English Conventions."

Although each Writing and Language Test is different, the following chart will give you a general idea of your performance

Number of Correct Answers	Range of Scores
34–44	33–40
23–33	26–32
12–22	18–25
1–11	10–17

ANSWER EXPLANATIONS

Note: Although some choices contain multiple errors, only one or two major errors are explained for each incorrect choice. All questions are rated by level of difficulty

Key to Levels of Difficulty

Rating	Percentage of Students Likely to Answer Correctly
EASY	>80%
MEDIUM	>65%
HARD	<65%

Passage B1

1. **(C)** Choice C is the best answer because *continues*, a singular verb agrees in number with the singular subject *NASA*.

   Choice A is not the best answer because it is a plural verb that fails to agree in number with the singular subject *NASA*.

   Choice B is not the best answer because it causes an inappropriate shift in the passage from the present to the past tense.

   Choice D is not the best answer because it causes an inappropriate shift in the passage from the present to the future tense.

   EASY

2. **(D)** Choice D is the best answer because the plural *risks* refers unambiguously to both *radiation exposure* and *effects of microgravity*.

   Choice A is not the best answer because it is unclear whether the relative pronoun *which* refers to one or to both of the phrases *radiation exposure* and *effects of microgravity*.

   Choice B is not the best answer because *risk* is singular and could refer to either *radiation exposure* or *microgravity*.

   Choice C is not the best answer because it switches the text from active to passive voice, resulting in an awkwardly worded sentence.

   MEDIUM

3. **(B)** Choice B is the best answer because the idea is expressed in standard English.

   Choice A is not the best answer because the trite, colloquial phrase *slam dunk* is not appropriate to the serious tone of the passage.

   Choice C is not the best answer because it fails to adhere to the conventions of standard English idiom.

   Choice D is not the best answer because of the inappropriate shift from third person (*we*) to second person (*you*).

   MEDIUM

4. **(D)** Choice D is the best answer because the sentence effectively cites a specific effect of radiation on human health.

Choice A is not the best answer because it fails to develop the idea of radiation's effect on human health.

Choice B is not the best answer because it merely reiterates the idea that radiation can adversely affect health.

Choice C is not the best answer because it adds nothing to what has already been stated and, therefore, fails to achieve the writer's goal.

EASY

5. **(C)** Choice C is the best answer because in making a comparison between two things: the gravity on Mars and the gravity on Earth, it uses the correct adjectives in the comparative degree. It also correctly compares the gravity on Earth with the gravity on the Moon.

Choice A is not the best answer because it incorrectly uses the superlative degree (strongest) to compare two things: the gravity on Mars and the gravity on Earth.

Choice B is not the best answer because it compares to unlike things: *gravity* and *the Moon*.

Choice D is not the best answer because it incorrectly uses the superlative degree (strongest) to compare the gravity on Mars and the gravity on Earth.

MEDIUM

6. **(C)** Choice C is the best answer because the sentence in question is irrelevant in the content of the paragraph.

Choice A is not the best answer because the sentence in question is irrelevant in the content of the paragraph.

Choice B is not the best answer because changing the sentence from passive to active fails to make it more relevant to the paragraph.

Choice D is not the best answer because reducing the number of words and combining the remaining words with the next sentence fails to strengthen the cohesiveness of the paragraph.

HARD

7. **(C)** Choice C is the best answer because it uses standard English idiom.

Choice A is not the best answer because *At Mars* is nonstandard English idiom.

Choice B is not the best answer because the phrase *In Mars* is nonstandard English idiom.

Choice D is not the best answer because the text following the verb *is* creates an unidiomatic sentence. Standard English calls for a verb such as *done, achieved,* or *accomplished*—instead of *be managed.*

EASY

8. **(B)** Choice B is the best answer because in the section of the graph showing limits of allowable radiation between ages 35 and 45, the lines for both men and women are virtually parallel, indicating the same rate of increase over that ten-year period.

Choice A is not the best answer because the graph shows that the limits of radiation exposure for women under 35 average roughly 0.5 SV exposure, while lifetime limits are far higher.

Choice C is not the best answer because the line representing the allowable limits of radiation exposure for men swerves sharply upward at age 45, indicating a faster growth rate than that for women.

Choice D is not the best answer because the line representing allowable limits for women is closer to the line that represents the cumulative allowable limits than the line for men. Therefore, women are more susceptible than men to radiation poisoning.

HARD

9. **(B)** Choice B is the best answer because it correctly expresses the idea in standard English idiom.

Choice A is not the best answer because it leads to an incomplete sentence.

Choice C is not the best answer because it leads to an incomplete sentence.

Choice D is not the best answer because the pronoun *It* has no clear antecedent and the idea is awkwardly expressed.

MEDIUM

10. **(B)** Choice B is the best answer because it expresses the author's view most forcefully.

Choice A is not the best answer because the word *But* suggests that what follows will be contrary to the previously stated idea, but it isn't, and the word *thing* is less precise than *clincher*, used in choice B.

Choice C is not the best answer because it is needlessly wordy. It also implies that our species may have occupied a place in the universe other than Earth.

Choice D is not the best answer because the plural verb *have* fails to agree in number with the singular noun *species*.

HARD

11. **(A)** Choice A is the best answer because with one powerful word—*frontier*—the writer captures the essence of people's aspirations to go to Mars.

Choice B is not the best answer. It fails to achieve the writer's purpose because it emphasizes a practical rather than a romantic or existential reason for a Martian expedition.

Choice C is not the best answer. Although it may be an astute observation, it ignores altogether any element of danger and excitement associated with adventure in outer space.

Choice D is not the best answer because, while it may be true, it doesn't meet the goal of explaining why some humans are willing to risk everything for a Martian adventure.

HARD

Passage B2

12. **(D)** Choice D is the best answer because it clearly and grammatically asks the question the author intends to discuss in the rest of the passage.

Choice A is not the best answer because of ambiguity of meaning created by the misplaced modifier *in the 21st century*, a phrase meant to modify the verb *explain*. Also, the construction, which lacks a subject and verb, is not a complete sentence, although the context—(i.e., introducing the subject of the passage) may not necessarily require the use of a grammatical sentence.

Choice B is not the best answer because the sentence consists of two unrelated parts. The use of *When* in the first clause suggests that the sentence will discuss events of 1970, but the second clause switches focus to the 21st century.

Choice C is not the best answer because the word *officially* is misplaced. It should modify *broke up* but instead modifies *1970*.

HARD

13. **(A)** Choice A is the best answer because it is a correctly constructed sentence that clearly describes what occurred after the break up of the Beatles.

Choice B is not the best answer because the sentence suddenly shifts from active (*They filed*) to passive (*were dragged*) construction.

Choice C is not the best answer because the sentence structure, consisting of a series of independent clauses connected by the conjunction *and,* is stylistically weak and awkward.

Choice D is not the best answer because a structural shift that occurs after the phrase *who filed lawsuits* results in faulty parallelism.

MEDIUM

14. **(B)** Choice B is the best answer because *homage* is the most contextually appropriate way to capture the sense of the fan's continued awe and admiration of the Beatles.

Choice A is not the best answer. Although *loyalty* relates to a sense of attachment to the Beatles, it does not convey the intensity of the fans' emotional fervor portrayed throughout the passage.

Choice C is not the best answer because *kudos* fails to capture the emotional qualities of the fans' attachment to the Beatles. Also the phrase *to pay kudos* is not standard English idiom.

Choice D is not the best answer because *servility* suggests a kind of meek deference that is inappropriate in the context of the passage.

EASY

15. **(A)** Choice A is the best answer because it maintains the cohesion of the paragraph. The transitional word *This* refers to the loyalty of Beatles fans described in sentence 4.

Choice B is not the best answer because it weakens the cohesion of the passage by removing a clear antecedent of the pronoun *This*.

Choice C is not the best answer because in that location the sentence would intrude on the discussion of fans' continued loyalty to the Beatles created by sentences 3 and 4.

Choice D is not the best answer because it would be anticlimactic, weakening the idea stated in sentence 6 that the Beatles are still relevant.

HARD

16. **(C)** Choice C is the best answer because its word choice is effective and it uses the singular pronoun *its* to refer to its singular antecedent *group*.

Choice A is not the best answer because the plural pronoun *their* fails to agree in number with its singular antecedent *group*.

Choice B is not the best answer because of its inappropriate choice of *notoriety*, a word related to the concept of fame, but fame with a negative connotation—certainly not what the author intended in a passage that virtually glorifies the Beatles.

Choice D is not the best answer because of its inappropriate choice of *interminable*, a word related to the concepts of time and distance, but only in a negative sense—such as a long and boring answer explanation to a test question.

MEDIUM

17. **(B)** Choice B is the best answer because it is a complete and grammatically correct sentence.

Choice A is not the best answer because the construction before the semicolon is a sentence fragment.

Choice C is not the best answer because of confusing syntax in the structure of the sentence. The names of the groups (*the Beach Boys and the Four Seasons*) should appear in place of the pronoun *they* immediately after the word *Beatles*.

Choice D is not the best answer because of mismatched sentence parts. The clause beginning with *they all came . . .* is not grammatically related to the preceding part of the sentence. Also, a superfluous comma is inserted after the word *Boys*.

EASY

18. **(B)** Choice B is the best answer because like the rest of the paragraph it is written in the past tense, and the colon properly introduces an example of Liverpudlian humor.

Choice A is not the best answer because of a shift in verb tense from the past to the present and the inappropriate use of an exclamation point.

Choice C is not the best answer because of a shift in verb tense from the past to the present.

Choice D is not the best answer because of redundant language. A *habit* by definition is *regular*. Also, in the context, a semicolon is an inappropriate mark of punctuation.

EASY

19. **(D)** Choice D is the best answer because the phrase is parallel in structure to the other phrases that identify the group's characteristics

Choice A is not the best answer because it includes the common but nevertheless nonstandard usage "like," a word that is incongruent with the tone and style of the passage.

Choice B is not the best answer because it is not parallel in structure to the other phrases meant to identify the characteristics of the group.

Choice C is not the best answer because it is awkwardly expressed.

MEDIUM

20. **(C)** Choice C is the best answer because it properly compares the sales of "I Want to Hold Your Hand" with the sales of any other song.

Choice A is not the best answer because it tries to compare two unlike things: a *number* and a *group*—an illogical comparison.

Choice B is not the best answer because the word *amount* may not be used to refer to plural nouns (copies) but only to singular nouns.

Choice D is not the best answer because it tries to compare two unlike things, *copies* and *number*—an illogical comparison.

HARD

21. **(A)** Choice A is the best answer because it provides a logical cause-and-effect transition between the sales record of a Beatles song and the reception the group received in New York.

Choice B is not the best answer because no comparison is made between facts about the sales of "I Want to Hold Your Hand" and the group's arrival in New York.

Choice C is not the best answer because the sales performance of the Beatles' song took place before the group arrived in New York.

Choice D is not the best answer because it fails to provide a logical transition between the facts regarding sales of "I Want to Hold Your Hand" and the group's arrival in New York.

MEDIUM

22. **(C)** Choice C is the best answer because the phrase *arriving at the airport* correctly modifies *the group*.

Choice A is not the best answer because of a dangling modifier. The phrase *arriving at the airport* should modify *group*, not *avalanche*.

Choice B is not the best answer because the word *amount* may not be used to refer to plural nouns (reporters) but only to singular nouns.

Choice D is not the best answer because of a dangling modifier. The phrase that begins with *arriving at the airport* should modify *group*, not *reporters*.

MEDIUM

Passage B3

23. **(B)** Choice B is the best answer because the noun *plane* is correctly modified by the phrase *Piloted by Colonel Paul Tibbets*.

Choice A is not the best answer because of mixed sentence construction. The phrase *flew the four-engine plane …* has no grammatical relationship with the earlier part of the sentence.

Choice C is not the best answer. Faulty sentence construction has left the verb *flew* without a subject.

Choice D is not the best answer because of mixed sentence construction. The first part of the sentence, ending with *mother*, lacks a grammatical relationship with the rest of the sentence.

MEDIUM

24. **(A)** Choice A is the best answer because it is the most contextually appropriate way to indicate that the bomb was meant to completely destroy a large part of the city of Hiroshima.

Choice B is not the best answer. Although *decompose* is related to destruction, it ordinarily refers to a gradual process of deterioration, not the instant annihilation caused by an atomic bomb.

Choice C is not the best answer. Although *cripple* conveys a sense of causing damage, it relates more closely to injury or disability than to the scale of destruction wrought by an atomic bomb.

Choice D is not the best answer because it is a slang term that is inconsistent with the overall tone and style of the passage.

EASY

25. **(D)** Choice D is the best answer. Because the entire paragraph is devoted to a description of the crew's precautions in dealing with the bomb, sentence 5 is superfluous.

Choice A is not the best answer because it would interrupt the train of thought between sentences 2 and 3.

Choice B is not the best answer because it would interfere with the flow of ideas from sentence 3 to 4.

Choice C is not the best answer because placing it after sentence 4 reiterates an idea developed through the entire paragraph. To restate it is unnecessary and redundant.

MEDIUM

26. **(D)** Choice D is the best answer because it conveys the author's intention more economically than any of the other choices.

Choice A is not the best answer. Although grammatically correct, its use of a series of short sentences connected with the conjunction *and* is stylistically awkward.

Choice B is not the best answer. Although grammatically correct, its wording suggests that the plane took off at 6:00 A.M. Inserting a comma after *take-off* would clarify the meaning.

Choice C is not the best answer. Although it is grammatically correct, a succession of clauses beginning with *and* make for a stylistically awkward and wordy sentence.

HARD

27. **(B)** Choice B is the best answer because it correctly uses a verb in the past tense, the tense in which the entire passage is written.

Choice A is not the best answer because of an improper shift in verb tense from past to present.

Choice C is not the best answer because of an inappropriate shift in verb tense from past to present perfect.

Choice D is not the best answer because of an inappropriate shift in verb tense from past to past perfect.

EASY

28. **(C)** Choice C is the best answer because it succinctly and correctly expresses the author's intended meaning.

Choice A is not the best answer because the plural pronoun *their* fails to agree in number with its singular antecedent *citizenry.*

Choice B is not the best answer because it contains redundant transitional words.

Choice D is not the best answer because the plural pronoun *their* fails to agree in number with its singular antecedent *citizenry.*

HARD

29. **(C)** Choice C is the best answer because it provides a grammatical and logical main clause to the sentence.

Choice A is not the best answer because the pronoun *it* does not agree in number with its antecedent *warnings,* and because of the shift in verb tenses from past (*ignored*) to present (*continue*).

Choice B is not the best answer because the use of *but* illogically makes the meaning of the two clauses in the sentence seem at odds with each other.

Choice D is not the best answer because of the uncertainty to which the pronouns *they* and *them* are meant to refer.

HARD

30. **(D)** Choice D is the best answer because it uses proper modification and economically combines the two sentences.

Choice A is not the best answer because it is excessively wordy and repetitive. It also contains a dangling participle. The phrase *upon seeing the target* should modify a noun such as "the crew" or "the bombadier," not *Little Boy.*

Choice B is not the best answer because of a misplaced modifier. The phrase *Overhead at 8:15 A.M.* should modify a noun such as "the plane" or "the aircraft," not *the bridge.* It is written in the passive voice.

Choice C is not the best answer because of a dangling participle. The phrase *viewing the bridge* should modify a noun such as "the crew" or "the bombadier," not *Little Boy.*

MEDIUM

31. **(B)** Choice B is the best answer because it is structurally parallel to the other phrases in the sentence that describe what the crew members saw.

Choice A is not the best answer because it fails to follow the parallel structure of the series of phrases that describe what the crew members saw.

Choice C is not the best answer because of the awkward redundancy of the phrase *and along with*. It also fails to follow the parallel structure of the series of phrases that describes what the crew saw.

Choice D is not the best answer because of the stylistically awkward use of the verb *were being almost enveloped*. Also, it fails to follow the parallel structure of the series of phrases that describe what the crew members saw.

EASY

32. **(A)** Choice A is the best answer because it properly compares the brightness of the fireball with the brightness of the sun.

Choice B is not the best answer because it attempts to compare *brightness* with *the sun*, an illogical comparison.

Choice C is not the best answer because the words *more* and *brighter* are both in the comparative degree and therefore are redundant.

Choice D is not the best answer because it attempts to compare *brightness* with *the sun*, an illogical comparison.

EASY

33. **(A)** Choice A is the best answer because it provides correct punctuation to set off the parenthetical, or nonrestrictive, element in the sentence: *ignited by the thermal pulse*.

Choice B is not the best answer because it lacks the correct punctuation to set off the parenthetical, or nonrestrictive, element (*ignited by the thermal pulse*) from the rest of the sentence.

Choice C is not the best answer because the text on both sides of the semicolon is an incomplete sentence.

Choice D is not the best answer because it contains punctuation and text that serve no purpose other than to obscure meaning and confuse the reader.

MEDIUM

Passage B4

34. **(D)** Choice D is the best answer because the plural verb *were* agrees in number with the plural subject *history and the outdoors.*

    Choice A is not the best answer because the singular verb *is* fails to agree in number with the plural subject *history and the outdoors.*

    Choice B is not the best answer because the singular verb *was* fails to agree in number with the plural subject *history and the outdoors.*

    Choice C is not the best answer because it is awkwardly expressed and excessively wordy.

    MEDIUM

35. **(C)** Choice C is the best answer because it accurately and grammatically expresses the author's idea and avoids the modification error made in the other choices.

    Choice A is not the best answer because of a misplaced, or dangling, modifier. The construction beginning *Having been traveling* should modify *he*, not *a museum.*

    Choice B is not the best answer because of a misplaced, or dangling, modifier. The construction beginning *Having been traveling* should modify *he*, not *his eye.*

    Choice D is not the best answer because of a misplaced, or dangling, modifier. The construction beginning *Having been traveling* should modify *he*, not *an archaeological museum.*

    HARD

36. **(A)** Choice A is the best answer because it expresses the idea clearly and concisely.

    Choice B is not the best answer because it is excessively wordy and awkwardly expressed.

    Choice C is not the best answer because it is excessively wordy and contains the redundancy *ancient, centuries-old objects*

    Choice D is not the best answer because the pronoun *those* refers illogically to the objects in the museum and contains the redundancy *ancient, centuries-old objects.*

    MEDIUM

37. **(B)** Choice B is the best answer because it uses an adverb *well* to modify the verb *got*, thereby clearly and grammatically expressing the idea.

Choice A is not the best answer because an adverb is needed to modify the verb *got*. Instead of *good*, use *well*. Also, the construction after the semicolon is a sentence fragment.

Choice C is not the best answer because the construction after the period is a sentence fragment.

Choice D is not the best answer because an adverb is needed to modify the verb *got*. Instead of *good*, use *well*.

EASY

38. **(C)** Choice C is the best answer because it expresses the idea clearly and grammatically.

Choice A is not the best answer because of a misplaced modifier. The phrase *during lunch* should modify *suggested* instead of *study*.

Choice B is not the best answer because of a misplaced modifier. The phrase *at lunch* should modify *suggested* instead of *study*.

Choice D is not the best answer because of an ambiguous pronoun reference. The pronoun *he* could refer either to Mr. Yilmaz or to Ari. Also, the phrase *during lunch* is misplaced. Its proper location is directly after the verb *suggested*.

MEDIUM

39. **(C)** Choice C is the best answer because it seamlessly follows sentence 4 by specifying one of the routines of an archaeologist's work.

Choice A is not the best answer because the omission of sentence 5 leaves no connection in meaning between sentences 4 and 6.

Choice B is not the best answer because it adds an irrelevant idea to the discussion of the archaeologist's routine.

Choice D is not the best answer because it interrupts the flow of ideas in the paragraph with an irrelevant detail.

EASY

40. **(B)** Choice B is the best answer because it provides punctuation that creates two grammatically complete and standard sentences.

Choice A is not the best answer because it results in a run-on sentence as well as some confusion about whether the clause *while he is out on a survey* refers to specific situations when Ari faces dangers or to Ari's overall fearlessness when out on a survey.

Choice C is not the best answer because it results in a comma splice.

Choice D is not the best answer because it results in a comma splice.

MEDIUM

41. **(C)** Choice C is the best answer because the verb *devours* is consistent with the tense in which the paragraph is written

Choice A is not the best answer because it uses the future tense and contains the redundant words *totally* and *entire.*

Choice B is not the best answer because its verb *has devoured* is not consistent with the tense of the paragraph.

Choice D is not the best answer because *totally devour* is a redundancy. The word *devour* implies total consumption.

MEDIUM

42. **(B)** Choice B is the best answer because the meaning is clearly and grammatically expressed, and parallel structure is maintained from the first to the second clause of the sentence.

Choice A is not the best answer because the second clause shifts awkwardly and inexplicably from active to passive voice.

Choice C is not the best answer because the second clause, beginning with *and*, shifts the sentence from the active to the passive voice.

Choice D is not the best answer because the plural verb *are* fails to agree in number with the singular subject *discovery.*

MEDIUM

43. **(A)** Choice A is the best answer because it conveys the writer's intended meaning with two closely related sentences, the link between them strengthened by the phrase *Such artifacts*.

Choice B is not the best answer because the material after the semicolon is a sentence fragment.

Choice C is not the best answer because of an abrupt switch of sentence subject from *artifacts* to *they*. Also, the relative pronoun *which* should not used to refer to humans.

Choice D is not the best answer because of the use of the present perfect verb *have left* in a context that calls for a verb in the past tense.

HARD

44. **(D)** Choice D is the best answer. Subordinating one clause to the other effectively tightens the relationship between the two original sentences.

Choice A is not the best answer. Although grammatical, the compound sentence joined by the conjunction *and* is not significantly more cohesive than the original sentences.

Choice B is not the best answer because the addition of the phrase *while digging* adds nothing appreciable to the cohesion of the text.

Choice C is not the best answer because the use of the conjunction *but* creates a contradiction in meaning between the two clauses of the sentence.

HARD

ANSWER SHEET
Writing and Language Test C

Passage 1

1. Ⓐ Ⓑ Ⓒ Ⓓ
2. Ⓐ Ⓑ Ⓒ Ⓓ
3. Ⓐ Ⓑ Ⓒ Ⓓ
4. Ⓐ Ⓑ Ⓒ Ⓓ

5. Ⓐ Ⓑ Ⓒ Ⓓ
6. Ⓐ Ⓑ Ⓒ Ⓓ
7. Ⓐ Ⓑ Ⓒ Ⓓ
8. Ⓐ Ⓑ Ⓒ Ⓓ

9. Ⓐ Ⓑ Ⓒ Ⓓ
10. Ⓐ Ⓑ Ⓒ Ⓓ
11. Ⓐ Ⓑ Ⓒ Ⓓ

Passage 2

12. Ⓐ Ⓑ Ⓒ Ⓓ
13. Ⓐ Ⓑ Ⓒ Ⓓ
14. Ⓐ Ⓑ Ⓒ Ⓓ
15. Ⓐ Ⓑ Ⓒ Ⓓ

16. Ⓐ Ⓑ Ⓒ Ⓓ
17. Ⓐ Ⓑ Ⓒ Ⓓ
18. Ⓐ Ⓑ Ⓒ Ⓓ
19. Ⓐ Ⓑ Ⓒ Ⓓ

20. Ⓐ Ⓑ Ⓒ Ⓓ
21. Ⓐ Ⓑ Ⓒ Ⓓ
22. Ⓐ Ⓑ Ⓒ Ⓓ

Passage 3

23. Ⓐ Ⓑ Ⓒ Ⓓ
24. Ⓐ Ⓑ Ⓒ Ⓓ
25. Ⓐ Ⓑ Ⓒ Ⓓ
26. Ⓐ Ⓑ Ⓒ Ⓓ

27. Ⓐ Ⓑ Ⓒ Ⓓ
28. Ⓐ Ⓑ Ⓒ Ⓓ
29. Ⓐ Ⓑ Ⓒ Ⓓ
30. Ⓐ Ⓑ Ⓒ Ⓓ

31. Ⓐ Ⓑ Ⓒ Ⓓ
32. Ⓐ Ⓑ Ⓒ Ⓓ
33. Ⓐ Ⓑ Ⓒ Ⓓ

Passage 4

34. Ⓐ Ⓑ Ⓒ Ⓓ
35. Ⓐ Ⓑ Ⓒ Ⓓ
36. Ⓐ Ⓑ Ⓒ Ⓓ
37. Ⓐ Ⓑ Ⓒ Ⓓ

38. Ⓐ Ⓑ Ⓒ Ⓓ
39. Ⓐ Ⓑ Ⓒ Ⓓ
40. Ⓐ Ⓑ Ⓒ Ⓓ
41. Ⓐ Ⓑ Ⓒ Ⓓ

42. Ⓐ Ⓑ Ⓒ Ⓓ
43. Ⓐ Ⓑ Ⓒ Ⓓ
44. Ⓐ Ⓑ Ⓒ Ⓓ

PRACTICE WRITING AND LANGUAGE TEST C

TIME: 35 MINUTES

Directions: The underlined sentences and sentence parts in the passages below may contain errors in standard English, including awkward or ambiguous expression, poor word choice, incorrect sentence structure, or faulty grammar, usage, and punctuation.

Read each passage carefully and identify which of the four alternative versions most effectively and correctly expresses the meaning of the underlined material. Indicate your choice by filling in the corresponding space on the answer sheet. Choice A on most questions is "NO CHANGE." If none of the choices improves the underlined text, pick Choice A as your answer.

EXAMPLE

The acclaimed French chef Henri Lagarde, who once thought he would grow up to become a stone mason, now loves to cook, and eating also.

A. NO CHANGE

B. to cook and to eat

C. cooking, and also to eat

D. to cook and, in addition, eating

ANSWER: A Ⓑ C D

Passage C1

The gap between science and public understanding [1] prevent action on global warming. This is disheartening news in many ways because it makes the prospect of change seem incredibly [2] difficult to some the movement needs a more scientific consensus as well as a human heart.

Matthew Spiegel, an associate professor of communications at St. Mary's University, has thought a great deal about ways [3] to inform the public as well as talking about global warming in a way that will persuade and convince people that it is a serious problem. He believes that the means of telling people about our rapidly warming planet need improvement. Polls say that 55 percent of America's adults use television news for information on current events. Knowing that fact, the movement to stop global warming [4] must rely more heavily on Fox News, CNN and other broadcasters to persuade the public that the perils of climate change have two main [5] characteristics: they are real should be feared, with the emphasis on their reality.

[1] A. NO CHANGE
B. prevents action on global warming
C. preclude actions on global warming
D. blocks preventative action in behalf of global warming

[2] A. NO CHANGE
B. difficult. To some, the movement needs
C. difficult to some. The movement needs
D. difficult to some, the movement needs

[3] A. NO CHANGE
B. that persuasively informs the public as to the effects of global warming
C. to use information about global warming to persuade
D. to keep the public informed about global warming

[4] Which choice most accurately states a conclusion that can be drawn from the data shown by the graph on page 165?
A. NO CHANGE
B. Anti-global warming forces can rest assured that organizations devoted to the perils of environmental causes are having great success in convincing the public about global warming.
C. Anti-global warming forces should push for more science programs on the subject to be shown on television.
D. Anti-global warming forces must train more teachers to incorporate lessons in global warming in their classes.

[5] A. NO CHANGE
B. characteristics: they are real and they should be feared; with
C. characteristics. They are real and they should be feared; with
D. characteristics: they are real and they should be feared. With

The Public's Trust in Sources of Information About Global Warming

How much do you trust or distrust the following as a source of information about global warming? (*order of items randomized*)

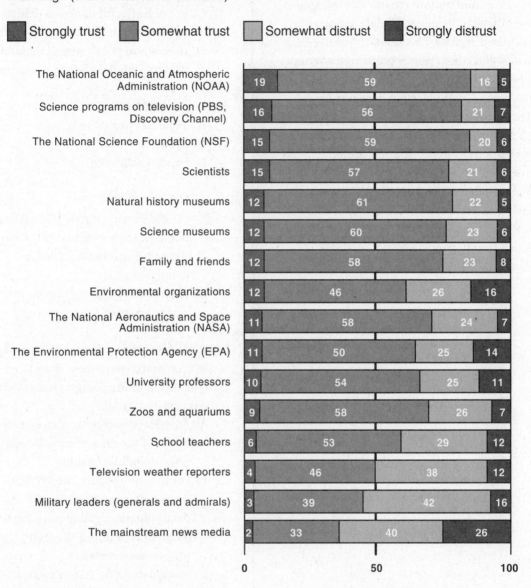

■ Strongly trust ■ Somewhat trust □ Somewhat distrust ■ Strongly distrust

Source	Strongly trust	Somewhat trust	Somewhat distrust	Strongly distrust
The National Oceanic and Atmospheric Administration (NOAA)	19	59	16	5
Science programs on television (PBS, Discovery Channel)	16	56	21	7
The National Science Foundation (NSF)	15	59	20	6
Scientists	15	57	21	6
Natural history museums	12	61	22	5
Science museums	12	60	23	6
Family and friends	12	58	23	8
Environmental organizations	12	46	26	16
The National Aeronautics and Space Administration (NASA)	11	58	24	7
The Environmental Protection Agency (EPA)	11	50	25	14
University professors	10	54	25	11
Zoos and aquariums	9	58	26	7
School teachers	6	53	29	12
Television weather reporters	4	46	38	12
Military leaders (generals and admirals)	3	39	42	16
The mainstream news media	2	33	40	26

Percent of Respondents

Spiegel, in order to identify the most effective method to alert the people to the hazards of global warming, has built three different arguments: (1) the customary environmental argument, (2) the national security argument, and (3) the public health argument. Having found **[6]** <u>indifference</u> in people's reactions to the environmental consequences, **[7]** <u>threatening effects of global warming were described</u> in terms

[6] A. NO CHANGE
   B. irrelevancy
   C. mediocrity
   D. indecency

[7] A. NO CHANGE
   B. global warming's long-term effects were described
   C. he stressed the effects of global warming
   D. he emphasized the threatening long-term effects

of calamitous events eventually striking both national security and public health. Hypothesizing that these arguments would help sway both conservatives and minorities—the demographics most apathetic or hostile to climate change—he was surprised at first by his research results. Both minorities and conservatives paid more attention [8] to public health than national security issues and concerns. Upon reflection, however he recalled that the public health [9] angle had earlier been a useful tool for environmentalists before and was especially effective when combined with tangible events that illustrate the insidious nature of climate change. Back in 1948, in Donora, Pennsylvania, an industrial town, [10] demonstrated the dangers when smog blanketed it. It killed twenty people and sickened six-thousand more. [11]

[8] A. NO CHANGE
B. to public health issues than national security
C. to public health than was paid to national security issues and concerns
D. to issues of public health than they paid to national security concerns

[9] A. NO CHANGE
B. angle has proved to be
C. debate is
D. conflict was once

[10] A. NO CHANGE
B. the dangers of climate change were put on display by a blanket of smog
C. a blanket of smog heralded its dangers
D. provided evidence of the dangers of climate change

[11] If placed at the end of the paragraph, which choice would best serve as a conclusion to the paragraph and to the passage as a whole?
A. America is becoming increasingly aware of the danger air pollution poses to public health.
B. For minority groups, which face unemployment, crime, and discrimination, global warming is not going to be a top-of-the-mind risk unless disaster strikes,
C. Spiegel explains, "Once you start telling people with problems that climate change is going to make things in their communities even worse, and the communicators are not environmentalists or scientists but public health officials—now you've got a story and a messenger that connects."
D. Such events have spurred passage of legislation like the Clear Air Act, which has played a large part in the reduction of six major air pollutants by 72 percent since its passage.

Passage C2

Harriet Beecher Stowe's [12] unique novel, *Uncle Tom's Cabin*, was unprecedented for a reading and publishing phenomenon. Soon after it was published in the 1850s the book became a [13] sensation, the work became the second best-selling book in America during the nineteenth century. [14] It sold the greatest amount of copies except the Bible. In a statement nearly as famous as the one Lincoln is [15] supposed to have made about the novel—that it started the Civil War—Stowe claimed providential inspiration as the source of *Uncle Tom's Cabin:* "I did not write it. God wrote it. I merely recorded His dictation."

Readers throughout the nation, north and south, found themselves [16] deepened by the book in ways they had never before experienced. Charles Holbrook, a North Carolina teacher, described his reading experience by confessing in his journal that "the tears rushed into my eyes" when Little Eva died. "I believe it to be the most soul-stirring book I ever read." [17] Characters took on a life of their own. Plot and narrative blossomed with almost uncontrollable vitality.

It was, in fact, the uncanny ability of *Uncle Tom's Cabin* to ensnare readers in the most intimate and compelling concerns of its characters that made Stowe's book so overwhelmingly popular. Southern editors decried

[12] A. NO CHANGE
B. *Uncle Tom's Cabin*, a unique novel for a reading
C. novel *Uncle Tom's Cabin* evolved uniquely into an unprecedented reading
D. novel *Uncle Tom's Cabin* was unprecedented as a reading

[13] A. NO CHANGE
B. sensation; the work became
C. sensation the work became
D. sensation, the work had become

[14] A. NO CHANGE
B. Except for the Bible, it sold the greatest amount of copies
C. Only the Bible sold more copies
D. The Bible only sold more copies

[15] A. NO CHANGE
B. suppose to have said
C. reportedly to have been made
D. allegedly made

[16] A. NO CHANGE
B. engrossed in the book
C. moved by
D. enhanced in

[17] Which choice combines and improves the underlined sentences most effectively?
A. Characters took on a life of their own, and the plot and narrative blossomed with almost uncontrollable vitality.
B. As plot and narrative blossomed with almost uncontrollable vitality, the characters took on a life of their own.
C. Although the plot and narrative blossomed with almost uncontrollable vitality, the characters took on a life of their own.
D. While the characters took on a life of their own, and as plot and narrative blossomed with almost uncontrollable vitality.

the book, however, for one main **[18]** reason: its unscrupulous depiction of slave life enlisted sympathies on behalf of slaves through imaginative identification—an unfair tactic, it seemed to them, in the polemical war over abolition.

[19] At the height of segregation, the novel helped provide a literary and social history for the still recent slave past, enduring as a touchstone reading experience for African Americans well into the twentieth century. But one place the novel did not endure was the academy. For much of the twentieth century, *Uncle Tom's Cabin* was seen by most literary professionals as a cultural embarrassment. The literary critic, J. W. Ward, wrote "The problem with *Uncle Tom's Cabin* is how a book so seemingly artless, so lacking in literary talent, was not only an immediate success but has endured among common readers."

This attitude would not begin to change until **[20]** the 1980s. During that decade feminist critics resurrected many overlooked masterpieces of sentimental fiction, hoping to discover an alternative tradition to the male-dominated "American Renaissance."

Ultimately, the novel remains elusive, uncategorizable. Not entirely representative of any particular mode or genre, **[21]** Stowe wrote a novel that was the rarest of literary phenomena: a cultural sensation. Striking a responsive chord in innumerable readers at a flashpoint in history, the novel's career in the social realm was **[22]** equally unpredictable as it was profound. If Stowe's remarkable book set unrealistic expectations for subsequent generations about the extent to which fiction might effect social change, it also illustrates the latent, marvelous power of the novel.

[18] A. NO CHANGE
B. reason; its unscrupulous depiction of slave life, which enlisted
C. reason, which was its unscrupulous depiction of slave life, which enlisted
D. reason. That being its unscrupulous depiction of slave life, which enlisted

[19] Which choice most effectively establishes the main topic of this paragraph?
A. Critics had little use for a book made odious by false emotion and old-fashioned piety.
B. The overall meaning of the book changed for U.S. culture as the abolition movement and the Civil War became memories.
C. One of the book's major accomplishments was to encourage empathetic rapport between whites and African Americans.
D. *Uncle Tom's Cabin* has an ambiguous role in America's social and literary history.

[20] A. NO CHANGE
B. the 1980s. It was during that ten-year decade that
C. the 1980s. Simultaneously,
D. the 1980s, when

[21] A. NO CHANGE
B. a rare phenomenon of literature was the result of Stowe's novel writing:
C. the novel *Uncle Tom's Cabin* was the rarest of literary phenomena:
D. the novel writing of a rare literary phenomenon is what Stowe accomplished,

[22] A. NO CHANGE
B. both equally unpredictable as well as profound.
C. as unpredictable as it was profound.
D. equally unpredictable as profound.

Passage C3

Censorship of books, along with a number of media rating systems, [23] have been used for years by individuals and groups to prevent and control the creation, access, and dissemination of ideas and information. In schools the issue of censorship is potentially [24] volatile because of the conflicting interests and responsibilities of [25] various stakeholders, school boards, librarians, teachers, parents, students, and the community at large may suddenly find themselves embroiled in heated disagreements. Statutes related to public education, however, grant to school boards the right [26] of ultimately making the final decisions about which materials may and may not be used in the classroom and which should be made available to students in the school library.

When materials are banned, appeals can be made, of course, leading to such legal wrangles as *Board of Education vs. Pico*, in which the Supreme Court declared unconstitutional the banning of books from school libraries because it limits [27] student's rights to explore and to learn, and their enjoyment of reading, too.

[28] Nevertheless, throughout the country, books are regularly being challenged. Individuals or groups deem material inappropriate for young people. Objectionable material is usually cited as the reason. At first, they may request that the material be removed from library shelves, or they insist that it be excised from school curricula. If their initial efforts fail, they may petition higher authorities or rally additional support from the larger community. As a last resort, they may turn to the legal system for help, filing a lawsuit to enjoin the availability of materials they find offensive. [29]

In one infamous case, titles in the Harry Potter series were banned from a school library because of allegations that they "promoted witchcraft and defiance of authority." Data compiled in recent years by the American Library Association keeps

[23] A. NO CHANGE
B. is a years-old method used by
C. are a method used for years by
D. for years have served both

[24] A. NO CHANGE
B. vociferous
C. varied
D. voluble

[25] A. NO CHANGE
B. various stakeholders: school boards
C. various stakeholders school boards
D. various stakeholders; school boards

[26] A. NO CHANGE
B. of ultimate decision making regarding
C. to finally make the decisions on
D. to make the final decisions about

[27] A. NO CHANGE
B. students rights to explore, to learn, and enjoyment of reading, too
C. a student's right to explore, to learn, and to enjoy reading
D. student's rights to explore, learn, and enjoy reading

[28] A. NO CHANGE
B. In that regard
C. Irregardless
D. In contrast

[29] Which choice most effectively establishes the main topic of this paragraph?
A. It is difficult to challenge the availability of books or other material because what is objectionable to some people may not be objectionable to others.
B. All citizens enjoy the right to challenge the use of objectionable material in the classrooms and libraries of public schools.
C. Those who want to keep certain books or other materials away from youngsters protest in a more or less predictable way.
D. Challenges to books and other objectionable materials are usually made with the well-being of young people in mind.

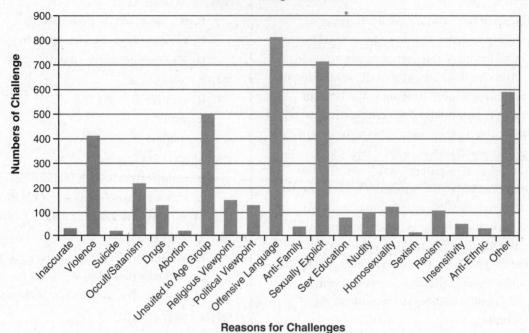

Book Challenges 2010–2014

track of the reasons behind challenges to books across the United States. [30]

While book challenges are a by-product of life in a free society, banning books, especially in public schools supported by taxpayers, often provokes rigorous objections. Opponents of book banning argue that not everyone on earth is the same, [31] and you do a disservice to young people when one prevents them from learning about the values and lifestyles of people other

[30] Which choice most accurately interprets data found on the graph?
A. Challenges on the basis of excessive violence are more likely to succeed than challenges based on racism.
B. Foul language has been the leading cause of book challenges, with sexually explicit content close behind.
C. A combination of reasons labeled "Other" and "Unsuited to Age Group" make up the third most common cause of book challenges.
D. Between 2010 and 2014, most issues failed to attract more than an average 100 challenges per year.

[31] A. NO CHANGE
B. by doing a disservice to young people you keep them away from learning
C. it is a disservice to young people to prevent or keep them from learning
D. and young people are hurt when they are kept from learning

than themselves. At the same time, [32] it's either naive and foolish to assume that school-age youngsters don't know very much about the world. After all, the vast majority of adolescents have access to digital media, [33] the content of which is as provocative than that in most library books. So indeed, young children should be granted the same rights as other citizens, especially because a deprivation of rights could mean diminished chances for them to question and learn.

[32] A. NO CHANGE
B. it is either naive or foolish
C. its both naive and foolish
D. it is neither naive or foolish

[33] A. NO CHANGE
B. whose content is as provocative as most library books
C. with more provocative contents than is found within most library books
D. the content of which can be more provocative than most library books

Passage C4

Of course [34] a good teacher should know their subject and, within limits, they should know their students. [35] But, also there is another necessary qualification. Good teachers are men and women of exceptionally wide and lively intellectual interests. It is useless to think of teaching as a business, like banking or insurance: to learn the necessary [36] quota of rules and facts, to apply them day by day as the bank manager applies them, [37] going home in the evening and sinking into a routine of reality TV and Spotify, to take pride in being an average citizen, indistinguishable from the dentist and the superintendent of the gas-works—and then hope to stimulate young and active minds. Teachers in schools and colleges must [38] see, think, and understand more better that the average man and woman of today's society.

(#1) This doesn't mean that they must have a better command of language and know special [39] subjects, such as Spanish literature is one of them and marine biology would be another. (#2) It means that they must become intimately acquainted with the world and the human condition. (#3) Much of their careers should be spent widening the horizons of their spirit. (#4) And they should also have an enthusism for delving into the problems of the mind. (#5) And yes, this too—they must even have a keen taste for some of the superficial enjoyments of life—from baseball to blogging. (#6) They must partake of

[34] A. NO CHANGE
B. to be a good teacher, their subject should be known to them
C. their subject should be known by a good teacher
D. good teachers should know their subject

[35] A. NO CHANGE
B. But they need other qualifications, too
C. On the other hand, another qualification is necessary
D. But another qualification is needed

[36] A. NO CHANGE
B. amount
C. allotment
D. slew

[37] A. NO CHANGE
B. and in the evening going home to sink into a routine of reality
C. to go home in the evening and sink into a routine of reality
D. then go home for the evening routine sunk into reality

[38] A. NO CHANGE
B. see more, think more, and understand more than the average
C. see more, think more, understand as well or better than the average
D. see, think, and understand more compared to the average

[39] A. NO CHANGE
B. subjects. Spanish literature, for example. Marine biology being another.
C. subjects, such as Spanish literature and marine biology
D. subjects, and both Spanish literature and marine biology are respected fields of study.

the inexhaustible pleasures the sciences, the humanities, and history. [40]

[41] Most people stop growing between thirty and forty. They "settle down"—a phrase which implies stagnation—or at the utmost they "coast along," using their acquired momentum, applying no more energy, and gradually slowing down to a stop. No teachers should dream of doing this. Their job is understanding a large and important area of the world's activity and achievements and making it viable for the young. [42] Many teachers are apt to prepare work for the next day or for next week, having lost sight of the fact that they should plan their classes for a marking period, a semester, or even a whole year at a time. They should expect to understand more and more of it as the years go by.

Good teachers are interesting men and women. As such, they will make the work interesting for their students, in just the same way as they talk and write interestingly. Most teaching is done by talking. If a teacher's mind is full of lively awareness of the world, he'll never be at a loss for new points of view on matters related to the subject he teaches. Novel illustrations will constantly be suggested to such teachers and they will discard outworn types of argument and find fresh ones. Allusions and reminiscences will brighten their talk and keep their audience [43] from freaking out over the awful feeling that it knows ahead of time exactly what their teacher is going to say next. Teachers often explain the vague by the vivid, the unknown by the known, but even the known—sometimes called common knowledge—may challenge the intellect of some students and create a gap between the teachers and the taught. Indifferent students, therefore, sometimes allege that teachers are insensitive to them, [44] which is difficult to substantiate.

[40] For the sake of the paragraph's coherence, sentence #5 should be situated
A. where it is now.
B. after sentence #1.
C. after sentence # 3.
D. after sentence # 6.

[41] A. NO CHANGE
B. Besides, most people
C. Meanwhile, most people
D. Furthermore, most people

[42] In order to develop the paragraph effectively, what should be done with the underlined sentence?
A. Leave it as it is.
B. Break it into two or more short sentences.
C. Move it to the beginning of the paragraph.
D. Delete it.

[43] A. NO CHANGE
B. from freaking out over the awful feeling that they know exactly what their teacher is going to say next
C. from the awful feeling that it knows exactly what the teacher will say next
D. from suffering the awful feeling that they know exactly what their teacher is about to say

[44] A. NO CHANGE
B. which is difficult to prove
C. but they deny it
D. but the allegation is usually false

END OF PRACTICE TEST C

ANSWER KEY

1. **B**	12. **D**	23. **B**	34. **D**
2. **B**	13. **B**	24. **A**	35. **B**
3. **D**	14. **C**	25. **D**	36. **A**
4. **C**	15. **A**	26. **D**	37. **C**
5. **A**	16. **C**	27. **C**	38. **B**
6. **A**	17. **B**	28. **A**	39. **C**
7. **C**	18. **A**	29. **C**	40. **D**
8. **D**	19. **D**	30. **B**	41. **A**
9. **B**	20. **D**	31. **D**	42. **D**
10. **C**	21. **C**	32. **B**	43. **C**
11. **D**	22. **C**	33. **A**	44. **D**

Number of Correct Answers _____

How did you do? The number of correct answers will determine your score, calculated on a scale of 10 (low) to 40 (high). For the actual Writing and Language Test, you'll also receive two subscores based on your answers to questions that the College Board designates "Expression of Ideas" and "Standard English Conventions."

Although each Writing and Language Test is different, the following chart will give you a general idea of your performance.

Number of Correct Answers	Range of Scores
34–44	33–40
23–33	26–32
12–22	18–25
1–11	10–17

ANSWER EXPLANATIONS

Note: Although some choices contain multiple errors, only one or two major errors are explained for each incorrect choice. All questions are rated by level of difficulty.

Key to Levels of Difficulty

Rating	Percentage of Students Likely to Answer Correctly
EASY	>80%
MEDIUM	>65%
HARD	<65%

Passage C1

1. **(B)** Choice B is the best answer because the singular verb *prevents* agrees in number with the sentence subject *gap*.

   Choice A is not a good answer because the plural verb *prevent* fails to agree in number with the singular subject of the sentence—*gap*.

   Choice C is not the best answer because the plural verb *preclude* fails to agree in number with the singular subject of the sentence—*gap*.

   Choice D is not the right answer because it uses more words than are needed to express the idea stated by choice B.

   EASY

2. **(B)** Choice B is the best answer because it provides punctuation that creates two grammatically correct, related, and complete sentences.

   Choice A is not the best answer because the lack of punctuation results in a run-on sentence and some confusion about what the prepositional phrase *to some* modifies.

   Choice C is not the best answer because the sentence break creates two disjointed sentences seemingly unrelated to each other.

   Choice D is not the best answer because it is a comma splice. Also, the use of the phrase *to some* obscures meaning. Does the phrase mean *difficult to some*? Or does it mean *to some the movement needs ... etc.*?

   HARD

3. **(D)** Choice D is the best answer because it grammatically and economically conveys the writer's intended meaning.

   Choice A is not the best answer because the infinitive *to talk* should be used in place of *talking* in order to maintain parallelism in the sentence.

   Choice B is not the best answer because the singular verb *informs* fails to agree in number with the plural noun *ways*.

   Choice C is not the best answer because the phrase *persuade and convince* adds a redundancy to the sentence.

   MEDIUM

4. **(C)** Choice C is the best answer because the bar graph shows that people trust Fox- and CNN-type programs more than they trust almost any other sources.

Choice A is not the best answer because the bar graph shows that the fewest people trust the mainstream news media as a source of information on global warming.

Choice B is not the best answer because the bar graph shows that environmental organizations have won the strong trust of only 12 percent of those who responded to the poll.

Choice D is not the best answer because, according to the graph, school teachers are among the least persuasive sources of information about global warming.

HARD

5. **(A)** Choice A is the best answer because the colon after *characteristics* signals what follows—the naming of the two characteristics.

Choice B is not a good answer because a semicolon should not be used to separate a sentence from a sentence fragment.

Choice C is not the best answer because a semicolon should not be used to separate a sentence from a sentence fragment.

Choice D is not the right answer because the phrase beginning with *With* is a sentence fragment.

MEDIUM

6. **(A)** Choice A is the best answer because indifference, or apathy, is the most contextually appropriate way to describe people who, as the author notes subsequently, were "apathetic … to climate change."

Choice B is not the best answer. Although *irrelevancy* is related to a sense of being unconcerned, it would be awkward and unconventional in this context to say that people's reactions suffered from *irrelevancy*.

Choice C is not the best answer. Although *mediocrity* suggests something less than first-rate, it would be awkward and unconventional in this context to say that people's reactions suffered from *mediocrity*.

Choice D is not the best answer. Although *indecency* has unfavorable connotations, it would be awkward and unconventional in this context to say that people's reactions suffered from *indecency*.

MEDIUM

7. **(C)** Choice C is the best answer because it grammatically and economically conveys the writer's intent.

Choice A is not the best answer because it contains a dangling modifier. The construction beginning with *Having found* should modify *he* (Professor Speigel), not *threatening effects*.

Choice B is not the best answer because it contains a dangling modifier. The construction beginning with *Having found* should modify *he* (Professor Speigel), not *global warming's long-term effects*.

Choice D is not the best answer because of wordiness and redundancies. Because the sentence subsequently discusses *calamity eventually striking*, the reference to *threatening long-term effects* is unnecessary.

MEDIUM

8. **(D)** Choice D is the best answer because it creates a comparison between like, or at least, similar, terms: *issues of public health* and *national security concerns*.

Choice A is not the best answer because it creates a comparison between unlike terms: *public health* and *issues and concerns*.

Choice B is not the best answer because it creates a comparison between unlike terms: *issues* and *security*.

Choice C is not the best answer because in mid-sentence the verbs are switched from active to passive voice.

MEDIUM

9. **(B)** Choice B is the best answer because it clearly conveys the time sequence of the events being discussed.

Choice A is not the best answer. The past perfect tense is appropriate in the context, but the word *earlier* becomes redundant as the sentence continues to discuss events that took place in the past.

Choice C is not the best answer because it uses the present tense verb *is* in a sentence cast in the past.

Choice D is not the best answer because the word *once* creates a redundancy by expressing the same idea as the word *before*.

MEDIUM

10. **(C)** Choice C is the best answer because it provides the sentence with a grammatical subject and verb.

Choice A is not the best answer because of mixed sentence construction. The underlined words are not grammatically related to the early part of the sentence.

Choice B is not the best answer. Although it contains no grammatical errors, the phrase *put on display* inappropriately endows the smog blanket with human volition.

Choice D is not the best answer because it leaves the sentence without a grammatical subject.

EASY

11. **(D)** Choice D is the best answer because it refers to both the smog incident in Donora, Pennsylvania, and to one of its long-term effects—the passage of antipollution legislation.

Choice A is not the best answer because it is a broad statement about America's awakening to the dangers of air pollution that is not justified by the content of the paragraph or the passage.

Choice B is not the best answer because, while it may be a valid statement, it is only marginally relevant to the content of the paragraph and passage.

Choice C is not the best answer. Although it quotes an authority on educating the public about the dangers of pollution, it brings up a matter discussed early in the passage, not at the end.

MEDIUM

Passage C2

12. **(D)** Choice D is the best answer because it uses standard English idiom to convey the writer's meaning.

Choice A is not the best answer because of the redundancy *unique* and *unprecedented*.

Choice B is not the best answer because it lacks a verb and, therefore, is a sentence fragment.

Choice C is not the best answer because the use of both *unique* and *unprecedented* is a redundancy. Also, the word *evolved* suggests slow growth in the book's popularity, a claim contradicted in the next sentence, which says that the book became a sensation soon after publication.

MEDIUM

13. **(B)** Choice B is the best answer because the semicolon correctly separates two independent sentences.

Choice A is not the best answer because it contains a comma splice. That is, a comma may not be used to separate two independent clauses.

Choice C is not the best answer because it is run-on sentence. Punctuation is needed at the juncture of two independent sentences.

Choice D is not the best answer because it contains a comma splice. Also, the verb tense improperly shifts from past to past perfect.

EASY

14. **(C)** Choice C is the best answer because it uses standard and succinct English idiom to convey the writer's idea.

Choice A is not the best answer because it is awkwardly worded and incorrectly uses *amount*, a word reserved for singular words such as *money, wheat,* and *air.*

Choice B is not the best answer because it violates standard English usage by using *amount*—a word reserved for singular words such as *cheese, anxiety,* and *homework*—instead of *number.*

Choice D is not the best answer because of faulty modification. The word *only* should modify *Bible,* not *sold.*

HARD

15. **(A)** Choice A is the best answer because it uses standard English and maintains the verb tense in which the passage is written.

Choice B is not the best answer for two reasons: in the context, the word *suppose* is not standard English usage (use *supposed*), and in standard English, statements are *made,* not *said.*

Choice C is not the best answer because it is awkwardly worded and uses a verb tense that is inconsistent with the rest of the passage.

Choice D is not the best answer because the use of the verb *is* before *allegedly made* fails to conform to standard English usage.

MEDIUM

16. **(C)** Choice C is the best answer because of its appropriateness in view of the subsequent description of a reader's intense emotional reaction to the book.

Choice A is not the best answer because it is an ambiguous word that fails to capture the stunning emotional reactions felt by vast numbers of readers.

Choice B is not the best answer because it lacks the punch needed to capture readers' emotional reactions to the book.

Choice D is not the best answer because the phrase *enhanced in* fails to conform to standard English idiom. *Enhanced by* is the correct phrase.

MEDIUM

17. **(B)** Choice B is the best answer because the two sentences have been combined into a single complex sentence, with the second clause—its main clause—focusing on the characters. This revision leads gracefully into the next paragraph, which discusses the appeal of the book's characters.

Choice A is not the best answer because the two original sentences have become a single compound sentence in which the two independent clauses are joined by the conjunction *and*, in effect, making no discernible improvement.

Choice C is not the best answer because the subordinating conjunction *Although* suggests that the idea in the second clause will contrast or somehow be in conflict with that in the first clause. In fact, they should be in harmony, with the ideas in the second clause supporting those in the first.

Choice D is not the best answer because it is a sentence fragment, consisting of two dependent clauses.

HARD

18. **(A)** Choice A is the best answer because it clearly states the author's intended meaning and correctly uses a colon between independent clauses when the second clause is specifically meant to interpret or explain the first.

Choice B is not the best answer because the clause after the semicolon is an incomplete sentence.

Choice C is not the best answer because its repetitive use of relative clauses beginning with *which* is stylistically cumbersome and awkward.

Choice D is not the best answer because the construction beginning with *That being …* is a sentence fragment.

HARD

19. **(D)** Choice D is the best answer because it focuses on the divided opinions about the book's place in America's social and literary history.

Choice A is not the best answer because it refers only to matters discussed in the second half of the paragraph.

Choice B is not the best answer because it brings up a topic that may be implied by the paragraph but is not its major concern.

Choice C is not the best answer because the paragraph does not discuss white readers' responses to the book.

MEDIUM

20. **(D)** Choice D is the best answer because it economically combines sentences to improve the coherence of the expressed idea.

Choice A is not the best answer because it maintains an unnecessary gap between the sentences. The transitional phrase *During that decade* contributes nothing new to the discussion and redundantly defines the 1980s as a *decade*.

Choice B is not the best answer because it maintains an unnecessary gap between the sentences. The second sentence begins by redundantly defining the 1980s as *a ten-year decade*.

Choice C is not the best answer because it maintains an unnecessary gap between the sentences and includes the superfluous transitional word—*Simultaneously*.

EASY

21. **(C)** Choice C is the best answer because the sentence begins with an adjective clause that properly modifies the word *novel* and expresses the writer's idea in standard written English.

Choice A is not the best answer because the construction beginning with *Not entirely representative* ... must modify *novel* or *Uncle Tom's Cabin* (or an equivalent noun), but may not logically modify *Stowe*.

Choice B is not the best answer because of mixed sentence construction. The beginning with *Not entirely representative* ... is not grammatically related to the clause after the comma.

Choice D is not the best answer because the construction beginning with *Not entirely representative* ... must modify *novel* or *Uncle Tom's Cabin* (or an equivalent noun), but may not logically modify *writing*.

HARD

22. **(C)** Choice C is the best answer. Its use of the word *as* both before and after *unpredictable* casts the comparison in standard English.

Choice A is not the best answer because the construction fails to create a comparison in standard English idiom.

Choice B is not the best answer because the word *both* and the phase *as well as* are redundant.

Choice D is not the best answer because in standard English usage two adjectives—in this case *unpredictable* and *profound*, may not be joined by *as*. Use *and* instead.

EASY

Passage C3

23. **(B)** Choice B is the best answer because the singular verb *is* agrees in number with the sentence subject *Censorship*.

Choice A is not the best answer because the plural verb *have been* fails to agree in number with the singular subject *Censorship*.

Choice C is not the best answer because the plural verb *are* fails to agree in number with the singular subject *Censorship*.

Choice D is not the best answer because the plural verb *have served* fails to agree in number with the singular subject *Censorship*.

EASY

24. **(A)** Choice A is the best answer because it makes the most sense in the context of the passage, which discusses the potential for censorship decisions to generate discord between groups and individuals.

Choice B is not the best answer. Although *vociferous* relates to loud and forceful speech, the context of the passage requires a word suggesting the potential to quickly stir up controversy.

Choice C is not the best answer because, while it is appropriate to the passage, the context requires a word more highly charged than *varied*.

Choice D is not the best answer because *voluble*, a word related to long-windedness, is not altogether relevant to the context of the passage.

HARD

25. **(D)** Choice D is the best answer because it uses a semicolon to separate two grammatically complete and related sentences.

Choice A is not the best answer because the use of a comma after *stakeholders* leads to a comma splice.

Choice B is not the best answer because, while a colon appears to signal that what follows is a list of stakeholders, the sentence goes beyond the list, effectively turning the nouns—*school boards, librarians, … etc.*—into the subject of what becomes a sentence.

Choice C is not the best answer because the absence of punctuation after *stakeholders* creates a run-on sentence.

MEDIUM

26. **(D)** Choice D is the best answer because it clearly expresses the author's idea using standard English idiom.

Choice A is not the best answer because the phrase *the right of* is non-standard English. (The standard version would use *to*, not *of*.) Choice A also contains a redundancy created by using both *ultimately* and *final*.

Choice B is not the best answer because the phrase *the right of* is nonstandard English. (The standard version would use *to*, not *of*.)

Choice C is not the best answer because, by inserting *finally* between *to* and *make* changes the sense of the sentence—as if to say that the decisions were a long time in coming and—whew!—they were *finally* made.

HARD

27. **(C)** Choice C is the best answer because all the phrases in the series beginning with *to explore* are structured in parallel form.

Choice A is not the best answer because the phrase *enjoyment of reading* should be structurally parallel to the phrases *to explore* and *to learn*. Also, the sentence contains a misplaced apostrophe. Possession in a plural noun is indicated by an apostrophe after the *–s*, not before.

Choice B is not the best answer because of faulty parallel structure. The phrase *enjoyment of reading* should be structurally the same as *to explore* and *to learn*. Also, possession in a plural noun (*students*) should be indicated by an apostrophe after the *–s*.

Choice D is not the best answer because the possessive noun *student's* is plural and, therefore, should have an apostrophe after the final *–s*, not before it.

MEDIUM

28. **(A)** Choice A is the best answer because it signals a logical transition in the development of the passage between the conditions as they should be according to the law and what they actually are.

Choice B is not the best answer because it fails to provide a logical or meaningful link between ideas in the two contiguous sentences.

Choice C is not the best answer because the word *Irregardless*, although commonly used, is not standard English.

Choice D is not the best answer. Although it suggests that the discussion will make a distinction between ideas, it is less specific than *nevertheless* as a transitional word that introduces the idea that book censorship is practiced in spite of the law.

EASY

29. **(C)** Choice C is the best answer because the paragraph focuses mainly on the steps taken by individuals or groups intent on keeping certain books or other material away from children.

Choice A is not the best answer. Although the paragraph implies the difficulties involved in mounting a challenge, it fails to identify the central idea of the paragraph.

Choice B is not the best answer. The statement is relevant to the paragraph but serves only as background to the main discussion.

Choice D is not the best answer because the paragraph hardly touches on the motives of those who challenge books and other material.

MEDIUM

30. **(B)** Choice B is the best answer because the graph shows that "Offensive Language" and "Sexually Explicit" are the only categories that generated more than 500 challenges each.

Choice A is not the best answer because the graph does not include information about the success or failure of challenges.

Choice C is not the best answer because the sum of challenges labeled "Other" and "Unsuited to Age Group" is higher than the number of any other single category.

Choice D is not the best answer because the graph does not show the number of challenges per year but only the total numbers for the five-year period from 2010 to 2014.

MEDIUM

31. **(D)** Choice D is the best answer because it consists of a correctly written independent clause that develops the idea stated in the first clause of the sentence,

Choice A is not the best answer because of a sudden shift in pronoun person. The third person, used throughout the passage, is dropped in favor of the second person.

Choice B is not the best answer because of confusion created by reversing cause and effect.

Choice C is not the best answer because it creates a comma splice, *i.e.*, two independent sentences separated by a comma.

HARD

32. **(B)** Choice B is the best answer because it properly pairs the coordinating conjunctions *either* and *or*.

Choice A is not the best answer because in standard English the coordinating conjunction *either* may not be paired with *and*.

Choice C is not the best answer because *its* is a possessive pronoun, not a contraction meaning *it is*.

Choice D is not the best answer because in standard English the coordinating conjunction *neither* may not be paired with *or*.

EASY

33. **(A)** Choice A is the best answer because of wording that logically compares the content of digital media with the content of library books.

Choice B is not the best answer because it tries illogically to compare *content* with *library books*.

Choice C is not the best answer because it tries illogically to compare *contents* with *library books* and also uses the singular verb *is* with the plural noun *contents*.

Choice D is not the best answer because it illogically compares *contents* with *library books*.

MEDIUM

34. (D) Choice D is the best answer because its focus is on *teachers* (plural) rather than on a *teacher* (singular). This connects the opening sentence to the remainder of the paragraph, which also discusses *teachers* rather than a single teacher.

Choice A is not the best answer because the pronoun *their* does not agree in number with its antecedent *teacher*.

Choice B is not the best answer because the pronoun *their* does not agree in number with its antecedent *teacher*. In addition, its wording is awkward.

Choice C is not the best answer because the pronoun *their* has no apparent antecedent. Also, it is awkwardly constructed in the passive voice.

EASY

35. (B) Choice B is the best answer. By using *they* as the sentence subject, it follows the pattern set by the previous sentence and, thereby, helps to unify the paragraph. It also serves appropriately as an brief introduction to a list of the traits that good teachers should have.

Choice A is not the best answer because it contains a redundancy. Either *also* or *another* may be used, but not both.

Choice C is not the best answer because it includes a misleading transitional phrase—*On the other hand*—which suggests that the writer is about to contrast one idea to another. No such contrast is made, however.

Choice D is not the best answer because it sets up the expectation that the writer will add just one more qualification to the discussion. The rest of the paragraph, however, lists several additional qualifications of good teachers.

HARD

36. (A) Choice A is the best answer because the word *quota* works harmoniously with the writer's allusions to banking and insurance, businesses dominated by numbers.

Choice B is not the best answer because the word *amount* ordinarily applies only to singular nouns such as *sleep* and *chewing gum*.

Choice C is not the best answer because the word *allotment* usually refers to a quantifiable unit of some kind such as an allotment of space or drinking water.

Choice D is not the best answer because *slew* is a colloquial word bordering on slang that is out of place in the context of a passage like this one.

MEDIUM

37. **(C)** Choice C is the best answer because it maintains the parallel structure of the phrases, all of them beginning with infinitives (e.g., *to learn, to apply*) that both precede and follow it.

Choice A is not the best answer because *going home* fails to maintain the parallel structure of the phrases, all of them beginning with infinitives (e.g., *to learn, to apply*), that both precede and follow it.

Choice B is not the best answer because *going home* fails to maintain the parallel structure of the phrases, all of them beginning with infinitives (e.g., *to learn, to apply*), that both precede and follow it.

Choice D is not the best answer because *go home* fails to maintain the parallel structure of the phrases, all of them beginning with infinitives (e.g., *to learn, to apply*), that both precede and follow it.

HARD

38. **(B)** Choice B is the best answer because it makes a valid, accurately worded comparison. Some may claim that repetition disqualifies it as the best choice, but in this case the author uses repetition to reiterate the responsibility of teachers to rise above the average person in order to stimulate students' learning.

Choice A is not the best answer because it includes in the same phrase two words in the comparative degree: *more* and *better*. Use one or the other, not both.

Choice C is not the best answer because of an incomplete construction. In standard English, a comparison requires the inclusion of the word *as* to follow *as well*. In other words, use *as well as*.

Choice D is not the best answer because it contains a redundancy. The use of the word *more* indicates that a comparison is being made. To add the word *compared*, therefore, is superfluous.

HARD

39. **(C)** Choice C is the best answer. In a succinct, standard English sentence it cites examples of the *special subjects*.

Choice A is not the best answer because of mismatched sentence parts. The text before the comma fails to fit grammatically with the text that follows the comma.

Choice B is not the best answer because it consists of two sentence fragments.

Choice D is not the best answer because it is a compound sentence in which the coordinate clauses are neither equivalent nor logically related.

EASY

40. **(D)** Choice D is the best answer because the opening words of sentence #5 signal that the discussion is about to turn in a new direction. Indeed, the writer shifts the focus from lofty, intellectual pursuits to more mundane activities. The best location for the sentence, therefore, is the end of the paragraph.

Choice A is not the best answer because sentence #5 would detract from the discussion of intellectual matters.

Choice B is not the best answer because it would abruptly divert the discussion from the subject introduced in sentence #1.

Choice C is not the best answer because sentence #5 would interrupt the discussion of intellectual matters taking place in sentences #3 and #4.

MEDIUM

41. **(A)** Choice A is the best answer. No transition is needed because the writer is about to move the discussion in a totally new direction.

Choice B is not the best answer because the transitional word *Besides* suggests a nonexistent connection between the preceding paragraph and the material that follows.

Choice C is not the best answer because the word *Meanwhile* fails to provide an appropriate transition between the paragraphs..

Choice D is not the best answer because the transitional word *Furthermore*, which signals the writer's intent to add another idea to the discussion, fails to provide an appropriate link to the paragraph that follows.

MEDIUM

42. **(D)** Choice D is the best answer because the sentence is irrelevant to the paragraph's central topic, the unique qualities of experienced teachers.

Choice A is not the best answer because the content of the sentence is unrelated to the other sentences in the paragraph.

Choice B is not the best answer because the sentence, even if divided or shortened, would still be unrelated to the central idea of the paragraph.

Choice C is not the best answer because it would serve no useful purpose to place it at the beginning. Indeed, it could be mistaken for the paragraph's topic sentence, requiring the rest of the paragraph to be revised.

EASY

43. **(C)** Choice C is the best answer because the idea is expressed in standard grammatical English, including the singular pronoun *it* that agrees in number with its antecedent, *audience*.

Choice A is not the best answer because the semi-slang phrase "freaking out" is inconsistent with the style and tone of the passage.

Choice B is not the best answer, in part because the pronouns *they* and *their* fail to agree in number with the singular antecedent *audience*. In addition, the semi-slang phrase "freaking out" is inconsistent with the style and tone of the passage.

Choice D is not the best answer because the pronouns *they* and *their* fail to agree in number with the singular antecedent *audience*.

EASY

44. **(D)** Choice D is the best answer. Although the wordiest choice, its eliminates the ambiguity of the other choices.

Choice A is not the best answer because *which* lacks a clear antecedent. What is difficult to substantiate? That students sometimes make allegations or that some teachers are insensitive?

Choice B is not the best answer because the antecedent of *which* is ambiguous. What is difficult to prove? That some students make allegations or that some teachers are insensitive?

Choice C is not the best answer because the pronoun *they* has no specific antecedent. It could refer to either *students* or to *teachers*.

MEDIUM

SECTION TWO
The SAT Essay

Getting Acquainted with the SAT Essay

3

- → OVERVIEW OF THE "OPTIONAL" ESSAY
- → WHAT TO EXPECT ON TEST DAY
- → THE ESSAY TOPIC: WHAT YOU'LL WRITE ABOUT
- → THE ESSAY "PROMPT"
- → HOW THE ESSAY IS SCORED
- → USE OF YOUR ESSAY SCORE

OVERVIEW OF THE "OPTIONAL" ESSAY

The SAT is a requirement for admission to many colleges. To get in, you must sit for a three-hour examination consisting of multiple-choice questions in reading, writing, language, and math. Two scores, one for the verbal sections and one for the math sections of the exam, are reported on a scale of 200 to 800.

The SAT also includes an "optional" section that involves writing an essay. Although the essay is called optional, don't take the designation literally. It's not an option if you're applying to any of nearly three hundred colleges that require it. Many additional colleges "recommend" that their applicants write the essay.

Although a recommendation is not a requirement, it probably makes sense to register for and write the essay anyway. Voluntarily devoting less than an hour of your time to writing an essay of a few hundred words testifies to a high degree of self-motivation and initiative and sends a message to the college that says: "Hey, look at me. I'm dead serious about attending your institution." In the end, it could impress the college admissions officials and lift your application into the "admit" pile.

On the other hand, what if no college on your list of favorites either requires or recommends the SAT Essay? Can you still write it? Of course you can. Yes, you'll pay more to take the SAT, but there's an up side: Should you change your mind later and decide to apply to a college that wants the essay, you won't have retake the whole SAT just to write the essay.

WHAT TO EXPECT ON TEST DAY

After you've finished taking the three-hour SAT, you'll be given a short break. Then the materials for the SAT Essay will be distributed. You'll have 50 minutes to study the question, or "prompt," read a 650 to 700 word prose passage called the "source," and write your essay. Periodically, the proctor will announce how much time you have left. The number of words in your essay is up to you. No one will count the words. In fact, the length of your essay takes a back seat to its content. Basically, the essay will be judged according to how well you've understood the passage, analyzed the author's writing techniques, and written clear, interesting, and correct prose. So, is 250 words enough? Well … yes and no. It largely depends on

TIP

At many competitive colleges the "optional" essay isn't optional. It's required.

TIP

Q. How long should it be? (Is 250 words enough?)
A. Yes and no.

what the words say. You may have read claims that longer essays earn higher scores than shorter ones, but the definitive word on that subject is yet to be written.

A single paragraph consisting of, say, less than 200 words, most likely won't allow you to develop your idea sufficiently. Two paragraphs would be better, and three or more, better still. A multiple-paragraph essay 250 to 450 words long is most apt to produce the best results, although a top-notch essay may well fall outside that range. In the end, what matters most is that your essay reveals the breadth and depth of your thinking, and that you have what it takes to discuss a complex subject perceptively and logically.

THE ESSAY TOPIC: WHAT YOU'LL WRITE ABOUT

In a word, the topic of the SAT Essay is *rhetoric*.

"Great, but what is rhetoric?" you may be wondering. That's an excellent question.

Simply put, rhetoric is something people rely on when they communicate with one another in speech and writing.

Well, that's a pretty vague definition. Let's try again with a dictionary definition of rhetoric:

The art of expressive speech or discourse, originally of oratory, now especially of literary composition and the art of writing well in prose, as distinguished from versification and elocution.

Is that any clearer? It may be a little clearer, but not much.

Let's try another way—with a description of how rhetoric works: Whenever you write or speak, you consciously choose the words that will best convey your meaning and achieve your purpose. You also decide the order of your words. If you're using sentences, you determine which sentence goes first, second, third, and so on. The choices you make depend largely on who your audience is, but more importantly, *how* you want your audience to respond. You'll make one set of choices, for example, when texting your mom that you'll be home at five o'clock, another set to inform a good friend about a conversation you overheard at lunch in the cafeteria. You'll make different choices if you're telling a story to your little sister and still others when writing an e-mail to a college admissions office explaining why— God forbid—your application won't arrive on time.

TIP

Whenever you speak or write you make *rhetorical* decisions.

In short, your overall purpose influences the way you express yourself. To cite one more example, let's say you want your friend Lucy to go with you to the Apple store on Saturday. You're apt to choose the words you think will persuade Lucy to say yes. You might flatter her, for instance, or appeal to her sense of loyalty between friends or threaten dire consequences if she refuses. Whatever approach you use, your choices comprise what is called *rhetoric*. Whenever you speak or write you make *rhetorical* decisions and use what may be called *rhetorical strategies, rhetorical devices, rhetorical gimmicks, rhetorical tricks, rhetorical methods*, and more. The point is that, although we may not be aware of it, all of us use some degree of rhetoric whenever we speak and write.

It so happens that in everyday usage the word *rhetoric* has been given a bad rap. Many speeches and remarks of public figures—especially politicians—are perceived to be self-serving and pointless, full of hot air, half truths, and—believe it or not—downright lies. After hearing them speak, we shake our heads dismissively and say, "Oh, that's just rhetoric."

As it relates to the SAT Essay, however, the word is not "*just* rhetoric." Rather, it's a totally respectable term and is the very subject of the essay itself. To write the essay, you must analyze the rhetoric in what is called a *source*, a piece of nonfiction prose. In your analysis, you must identify and explain the rhetorical strategies or devices used by the author.

A source chosen for analysis on the SAT Essay expresses the writer's opinion on an issue. Its basic purpose is to convince readers to accept or even embrace the writer's point of view. Such a piece of persuasive writing is called an argument, although it doesn't in any way resemble a squabble between, say, two drivers arguing about whose fault it was that their cars hit each other at the intersection.

Rather, a source is a sober, high-quality, rational piece of writing that uses a variety of persuasive, or rhetorical, strategies to make a case in support of the author's beliefs. More than likely you yourself have written persuasive prose—perhaps as a class assignment or a text to a friend. Whatever the purpose, you presented your opinion and then mustered facts, details, and personal anecdotes as evidence to convince your reader that your point of view had merit.

Written for a wide audience, a source will have been previously published and will consist of 650 to 750 words—equivalent to about one-and-a-half pages of single-spaced type. It can be on virtually any subject: the arts, science, politics, social issues, or any other topic of interest and concern to a reasonably literate audience. Whatever the topic, the author of the source aims to sway readers to accept his or her opinion. Your job, however, is not to agree or disagree with the author. Instead, first and foremost—and this is the crux of the SAT Essay—you must explain, or analyze, exactly what the author did to build a persuasive argument. To put it another way, your essay should not be about *what* the writer says but rather about *how* the writer says it—that is, how rhetoric is used to help the writer achieve his or her purpose. You do that by breaking the passage into its component parts—for example, studying the kind of evidence the author uses to support the main idea or observing how emotional language is used to evoke a particular response.

To write a successful essay you must, of course, know what the passage says. But your primary goal is to pick out and describe those elements of language and thought that contribute most effectively to the persuasiveness of the author's argument. In short, you must analyze the writing in the passage.

TIP

In your essay, don't accept or reject the author's opinions—or even comment on them.

A WORD OF ENCOURAGEMENT

Maybe you've never before been asked to write an essay of this kind. If that describes you, please don't fret or freak out. First of all, you're not alone. But more importantly, you can count on the pages ahead to guide you every step of the way.

Make a pledge or take a vow to master the ins and outs of doing it. Sure, it may take a while to get there, but if you stick to it, you're bound to succeed.

The College Board, which administers the SAT, describes the purpose of the Essay this way:

> The basic aim of the Essay is to determine whether students can demonstrate college- and career-readiness proficiency in reading, writing, and analysis by comprehending a high-quality source text and producing a cogent and clear written analysis of that text supported by critical reasoning and evidence drawn from the source.

Whew! This high-flown sentence probably wasn't written for an audience of high school kids but for educators and writers like me whose job is to help prepare students for the SAT. Honestly, it took me a couple of readings to figure out the statement's full meaning. If you got it instantly, that's awesome. But if you didn't, allow this book to escort you from beginning to end through the world of the SAT Essay. Before long, every piece of the College Board's description will become transparent (guaranteed!) and you'll wonder why you didn't get it the first time.

THE ESSAY "PROMPT"

To write a successful essay, you should expect to do at least three things:

1. Comprehend the source.
2. Analyze how the writer uses rhetoric (evidence, reasoning, stylistic features) to support his or her point of view on the subject.
3. Present your ideas in a well-organized, interesting, and correctly written essay.

The first part of every official SAT Essay prompt reiterates these instructions, but it uses different words:

Read the following passage carefully. Consider how the author

- uses evidence such as examples and facts to back up claims
- provides reasoning to connect claims and evidence to develop ideas
- uses stylistic or persuasive elements, such as word choice or emotional appeals meant to add power to expressed ideas

---

It's vital that you follow this set of instructions to the letter. By referring to it again and again as you plan and write practice essays, you'll soon have it so firmly fixed in your memory that you won't need to read it again and will thereby save time on the actual exam. Each time the SAT is given, a different source is used. But the instructions recur again and again with not a syllable changed.

Part 2 of the prompt is printed in the test booklet after the text of the source. Its placement helps you focus on the main idea of the source as you begin to write. Moreover, this piece of the prompt includes a piece of information you can't do without—namely, a statement that clearly spells out the central idea of the source. Here, word for word, is how it begins:

Write an essay in which you explain how (name of author) builds an argument to persuade his/her audience that blah, blah, blah, etc.

No, it won't literally say "blah, blah, blah." Instead, you'll find a few words meant to define exactly what the focus of your essay should be, the point you should come back to again and again as you write your essay.

Now read a completed sample of the prompt's second section. It never varies except for the writer's name and a brief summary of the writer's main idea, highlighted below in italics:

> Write an essay in which you explain how Muriel Kemper builds an argument to persuade her audience that *declining literacy is a threat to the economy.* In your essay, analyze how Kemper uses one or more of the features listed in the set of instructions for this essay (or features of your own choice) to strengthen the logic and persuasiveness of her argument. Be sure that your analysis focuses on the most relevant features of the passage.
>
> Do not explain whether you agree or disagree with Kemper's views. Rather, explain how Kemper builds an argument to persuade her audience.

Other writers will build arguments to persuade readers that "*students should be paid as an encouragement to attend school*" or "*noise pollution is out of control*" or "*hospitals can be hazardous to health*" or any one of thousands of other issues that the College Board might pick.

Although the second section of the prompt is printed after the text of the source, study it *before* you begin reading the source. That's right: *Skip the source until you've read both parts of the prompt!* Why? By knowing beforehand what the source is all about, you can begin searching for its rhetorical features from its very first word.

TIP

Skip the source until you've read both parts of the prompt.

REVIEW

A Sample Prompt Showing Both the First and Second Parts

Read the following passage carefully. Consider how the author

- uses evidence such as examples and facts to back up claims
- provides reasoning to connect claims and evidence to develop ideas
- uses stylistic or persuasive elements, such as word choice or emotional appeals meant to add power to expressed ideas

[The source goes here.]

Write an essay in which you explain how Abigail Smith builds an argument to persuade her audience that grade inflation in high schools erodes the work ethic of students who experience it. In your essay, analyze how Smith uses one or more of the features listed in the set of instructions for this essay (or use features of your own choice) to strengthen the logic and persuasiveness of her argument. Be sure to focus your analysis on the most relevant features of the passage.

Do not explain whether you agree or disagree with Smith's views. Rather, explain how Smith builds an argument to persuade her audience.

HOW THE ESSAY IS SCORED

When it comes time to make judgments about writing, the word *effective* comes up repeatedly. It's a popular word—easy to use but oh, so hard to define. It means so much, and yet so little. You probably know "effective" writing when you see it, but what the SAT folks have in mind is the thoughtful analysis of a source, a mature writing style, clear organization of ideas, sensible paragraphing, coherent development, varied sentence structure, appropriate word choice, and correct grammar, spelling, and punctuation. (For details about these and other attributes of effective writing, turn to Section 1 of this book.) After each administration of the SAT Essay, large groups of qualified readers—mostly college and high school teachers—read and evaluate the essays. They are chosen for their experience and the ability to make sound judgments about student writing. Before their work begins, they are trained to use a common set of scoring standards and are given commonsense guidelines that stress the need to be both fair and objective. They are told things like

1. Read each essay once.
2. Read quickly and assign a grade immediately.
3. Read mainly for what has been done well.
4. Ignore poor handwriting as much as possible.
5. Don't penalize a well-developed but unfinished essay.
6. Don't use length as a criterion of evaluation.
7. Keep in mind that your assessment should be based on evidence in the essay that the student has understood the source, analyzed the author's rhetorical techniques, and demonstrated a command of essay writing skills, including organization, word choice, and the mechanics of writing.
8. Remember that each essay is a first draft written under pressure by a seventeen- or eighteen-year-old.

A NOTE ON HANDWRITING

As you see, handwriting is not supposed to count. But think about this scenario: Frustrated by their inability to decipher your words, essay readers may take a dim view of your work. If the letters are difficult to read, they may not give you the benefit of the doubt about spelling or grammar. Also, when a reader must stop regularly to puzzle out the words, the flow of your ideas will be interrupted—with adverse effects. And worst of all, an unreadable essay will be rejected altogether.

At this stage in life, you may find it hard to change your handwriting. But if you know that teachers and others have a problem interpreting your script, try to slow down as you form the letters, or as a last resort, print clearly. For most people printing is slower than cursive writing, but with practice you can increase your speed.

Your essay will be rated according to three analytic criteria: **(1) Reading, (2) Analysis,** and **(3) Writing,** and scored on a scale of 1 to 4 for each one. An essay score of 4/4/4 is top of the line. It means you did splendidly in all three domains. A score of 1/1/1 means … well, the exact opposite. An essay rated, say, 3/2/4 shows that your reading of the passage was rated 3 out of 4—good but not exceptional. The 2, for analysis, signifies that you did a mediocre job in analyzing the passage, and the 4 suggests that you've got what it takes to write first-rate prose.

Be confident that your scores will reflect how well you have followed the instructions given by the prompt and whether your essay shows evidence that you have (1) read the source with understanding, (2) analyzed the persuasive rhetoric used by the author of the source, and

(3) written a well-organized essay that contains a well-developed main idea, varied sentence structures, precise words, and an appropriate, consistent writing style. It helps a lot, too, if you follow all the conventions of standard written English.

If a reader can answer all the questions below with a resounding YES, you'll earn a high score. A bunch of NO's, on the other hand, will lower your score. (But that's not going to happen to you. This book, after all, has been expressly written to pave your way to essay heaven … more or less.)

1. **READING THE SOURCE**

Did you comprehend the source?

Did you recognize the source's main idea and its relation to important details in the text?

Did you make appropriate use of evidence from the source, such as quotes, paraphrases, brief summaries, statistics, and references to research reports?

2. **ANALYZING ITS RHETORIC**

Did you analyze the text?

Did you correctly identify evidence, reasoning, stylistic techniques, or other persuasive features used by the author to support a claim?

Did you focus on the most relevant features?

Did you explain how the rhetorical features contribute to the overall meaning and effect of the source?

Did you comment specifically on the effectiveness of each feature?

3. **WRITING EFFECTIVELY**

Did you include a precise main idea that serves as the focus of your essay?
Did you organize your ideas sensibly?

Did you vary your sentences?

Did you choose precise and appropriate words?

Did you use a consistent and appropriate style and tone?

Did you avoid making errors in standard written English?

Actually, SAT Essay readers don't use such checklists to see whether you've done everything right. Instead, they'll read your essay *holistically*, meaning that they'll read it quickly for an overall impression of your writing and then assign it a grade. With training and practice, essay readers develop the knack of scoring essays fairly and uniformly. In fact, two experienced readers reviewing an essay separately will give it the same scores 95 percent of the time.

For further information about scoring essays and for an opportunity to step into the shoes of an SAT Essay reader, turn to Chapter 6. There you'll find an essay scoring guide as well as a number of students' essays patiently waiting for your assessment.

USE OF YOUR ESSAY SCORE

How your essay score is used depends entirely on the college(s) to which you're applying. On some campuses, the essay functions solely as a criterion for admission. At others the score you've earned helps to determine your academic placement. A superb essay could entitle you to waive a basic composition course for freshmen. A low score could send you into a remedial writing course taken during the summer before classes start or during the first semester. To learn just how the essay score will affect you, consult college websites and catalogues, or raise the question during an interview with an admissions official.

Getting Prepped to Write

4

→ **READING THE SOURCE**
→ **FINDING THE EVIDENCE**
→ **SCREENING THE EVIDENCE**
→ **ANNOTATING: THE GOLD STANDARD OF SOURCE ANALYSIS**
→ **PRACTICE IN ANNOTATION**

Believe it or not, you began to prepare for the SAT Essay long before you even heard of the SAT—when you first scrawled words on paper or playfully poked keys on a computer keyboard. Or maybe it was when a string of school teachers began to bang the basics of English grammar into your head or someone told you to say *taught* instead of *teached*.

Well, that was years ago. Since then, you've come a long way, and now it's time to do some prep work specifically designed to get you ready for writing the SAT Essay.

Face it, writing an essay in less than an hour is a challenge. Even professional journalists, accustomed to working under the pressure of deadlines, would be hard-pressed to produce a good essay in that amount of time. But take heart! The essay score is just one piece of data on your college application, and no one taking the SAT will have a nanosecond more than you to complete the task. If you've been a reasonably successful essay writer in the past, be confident that you'll perform equally well on the SAT Essay. In fact, you may do even better than usual because you're likely to be pumped up to do your best work.

On test day, when you open your SAT Essay booklet, you'll be greeted by the first section of the prompt—dissected in Chapter 3 of this book. Next, you'll find a page or more of nonfiction prose—a reading passage called the "source." Ignore it for the time being. Instead, skip to the second portion of the prompt located just after the source. There you'll receive instructions to write an essay (as if you didn't already know), but more importantly, you'll also be given a thumbnail summary of the source's main idea, italicized in this example:

> Write an essay in which you explain how Josie Gregg builds an argument to persuade her audience that *federal funds would be more wisely spent on disaster preparedness than on disaster relief.*

Read those words once, twice, three times, if necessary—or until you know exactly what they say. With their meaning lodged firmly in your head, you'll know what to expect when you turn your attention to the passage itself.

 TIP

Don't read the source until you know its main idea—stated in the second section of the prompt.

READING THE SOURCE

Reading styles, like handwriting, vary from person to person. Some people read quickly and remember almost everything. Others labor over every word and remember next to nothing. Most people, though, fall somewhere between those extremes.

Increasing Your Reading Power

How you read the passage is up to you, of course, but to get the most out of your effort, it pays to know ahead of time the reading technique that produces the best results for you. That's why it's definitely worthwhile to try different methods as you prep for the SAT, not only while reading the sample passages in this book but whenever you read books, blogs, cereal boxes—anything. Over time, you'll discover a default method, the one with the biggest payoff for your efforts—increased understanding and retention of what you read. Once you've nailed down the method, stick with it. Force yourself to use it every time you read, or until it becomes second nature and you don't have to think about it any more. Here are some options.

Option	Technique
A	*Read the source carefully from start to finish.* Note where the writer makes claims and provides evidence of some kind that supports the claim. Remain on the lookout for secondary claims meant to support the main idea.
B	*Skim the source.* Read faster than you normally would. Stay alert for specific instances of rhetorical strategies—statistics, quotations, examples, appeals to emotion, and so forth. Then go back and find the claim or claims that each piece of evidence is meant to support.
C	*Skim the source for a general impression of the writer's argument.* Then go back and read it more carefully. During the second reading, concentrate on details the writer uses to make claims and how the claims are supported by evidence.

Give each of these options a chance to work for you. With practice, one of them could become routine. From then on, you'll turn to it automatically when you encounter a passage that needs analysis. Such habits rarely form overnight. But with patience and perseverance, you can count on developing a reading technique that gives you results not to die for but certainly to take you far.

Before reading the source you'll be writing about on the SAT, you'll encounter a kind of headline—a citation, really—that tells you the name and date of the source, who wrote it, and where it appeared in print or online. For example:

(Adapted from Karen V. Smith, "Sky High Grading: Why the Old 'C' Is the New 'A'," *Penpourri*, June 2015)

It pays to read the citation. The reason is that, although you may not recognize the author's name, you could use it in the essay. Instead of repeating such phrases as "the writer's use of facts …" and "the writer claims that …," you might, for variety's sake, occasionally plug in the writer's name, or even better—to save a few precious seconds—use only the writer's initials instead of phrases like "the writer" or "the author."

The title of the source may provide another clue to the contents of the passage—surely not a huge bonus, but better than nothing. Knowing the publication date of the passage might also be useful. A recent date may indicate that the passage discusses a current issue. A date from the distant past guarantees that the passage relates to an issue with a history but one that's probably still relevant. Such information, while not vital to writing a successful essay, sheds at least a sliver of light on the source and oughtn't be ignored.

TIP

Read the citation. It may contain information you can use.

Having read the prompt, you'll know what the author of the source intends to prove. From the very first word, then, you can put your favorite reading method to work and focus directly on how the writer goes about trying to persuade readers to accept, or at least to understand, his or her point of view on an issue.

To make the most of the time you spend reading the source, you're bound to deepen your understanding of the text if you do the following:

1. **READ THE SOURCE WITH PENCIL IN HAND.** Mark up the page with underscoring, asterisks, circles, arrows, or whatever wingdings help you highlight those parts of the passage that support the author's main idea, or claim—such things as statistics, an unusual use of language, a quotation from an authority on the subject of the passage. Jot down ideas that occur to you as you read. Your notes could eventually morph into an outline for your essay. An even faster alternative is to put a check in the margin next to anything you want to remember. However you highlight pieces of the passage, though, use your pencil selectively, or you may end up with huge gobs of the passage adorned with pencil markings, thereby defeating the purpose of highlighting in the first place.

    Another option, of course, is not to highlight anything. The time you spend underscoring or leaving marginal scribbles might better be spent rereading sections of the passage you didn't quite understand the first time around.

    Use whatever technique works best for you, although you won't know which one gets the results you want until you've practiced with the passages in this book.

2. **READ THE PASSAGE AT LEAST TWICE.** First, read for an overview of its point and purpose, and then read to track down examples of rhetorical devices. (More about that later.)

3. **CONCENTRATE ON PARAGRAPH OPENINGS AND CLOSINGS.** The passage will be written in standard English prose and will probably be constructed according to a common pattern. That is, it will consist of four, five, or more paragraphs, each with a topic sentence supported by specific details. More often than not, the topic sentence will be located near the beginning of the paragraph, although occasionally it won't show up until the end. Now and then, a writer, using just a phrase or two, might tuck the main idea deep into the interior of the paragraph or may even leave it out entirely if the paragraph's main idea is so obvious that it needn't be stated at all.

4. **LOCATE BOTH THE WRITER'S CLAIMS AND THE EVIDENCE USED TO SUPPORT THOSE CLAIMS.**

    Sometimes, writers state their claim early in the passage and then fill the remaining paragraphs with evidence to support it, often using secondary claims that require additional support. At other times, writers reverse the process, writing several paragraphs that lead inevitably to their main claim. Occasionally, however, the main claim may be inconspicuously ensconced somewhere in the vast middle of the passage. Still another possibility is that the writer chooses not to state the entire claim in any one place but to scatter segments of it throughout the source, leaving it for you, the reader, to piece together.

5. **SEARCH THE ENTIRE SOURCE FOR EVIDENCE THAT SUPPORTS THE CLAIM.** Keep in mind that supporting evidence may not necessarily appear in the same paragraph, or even in the same neighborhood where the claim is made. Some evidence may appear early in the passage, so early that you won't yet recognize it as evidence. Then, after the claim is made, the writer may provide additional evidence or allude to the evidence

Don't even think of reading the source without a pencil in your hand.

Knowing how paragraphs are constructed can speed up your reading and also guide your search for claims and supporting evidence.

stated earlier. What that means for you, the reader (and analyzer) of the passage, is that your search for evidence must be comprehensive—widespread enough to include the entire passage and not be limited to the proximity of the claim.

6. **SUSPEND YOUR PRIOR KNOWLEDGE.** A source may deal with a subject you know something about. That may help you to readily grasp its meaning. It may also tempt you to comment on the writer's viewpoint and judge the validity of the evidence used to support the claim. Don't do it. Cast aside your prior knowledge. Read the passage and write your analysis as objectively as you can.

FINDING THE EVIDENCE

Once again, take a look at the prompt, reprinted below. In this rendition, the most important words and phrases—those that name the types of evidence to look for and analyze in your essay—are numbered and underlined.

All these highlighted fragments are illustrated and explained in the pages ahead.

Read the following passage carefully. Consider how the author

- uses [1] evidence such as examples and facts to back up claims
- provides [2] reasoning to connect claims and [3] evidence to develop ideas
- uses stylistic or persuasive elements, such as [4] word choice or [5] emotional appeals meant to add power to expressed ideas

Write an essay in which you explain how Karen Smith builds an argument to persuade her audience that *grade inflation in high schools erodes the work ethic of students who experience it.* In your essay, analyze how Smith uses one or more of the features listed in the set of instructions for this essay (or use [6] features of your own choice) to strengthen the logic and persuasiveness of her argument. Be sure to focus your analysis on the most relevant features of the passage.

Do not explain whether you agree or disagree with Smith's views. Rather, explain how Smith builds an argument to persuade her audience.

---

1. Examples and Facts

To be persuasive, an argument needs strong supporting evidence. Facts, statistics, anecdotes, examples—this kind of evidence is the most common and also the easiest to find and explain. Because authors use it all the time to build an argument for their claims, it's almost certain to show up in the source you'll be analyzing.

WHAT IS A "CLAIM?"

Basically, it's another word for an assertion, an allegation, a pronouncement, or a conclusion, a statement that may have the ring of truth, but isn't unquestionably true. A claim may seem to be valid, but its validity ultimately depends on the type, quality, and amount of evidence the author has gathered to back it up.

Have you noticed that the foregoing definition of a claim also contains a claim—namely, that a claim can't be valid without evidence to support it? Well, to convince you, the reader, that that claim about claims is valid, your author has filled the next few pages with numerous examples of claims backed up by facts, statistics, quotes, and several other kinds of evidence.

For instance, the writer of the following excerpt builds an argument in behalf of a claim that America is currently doing its best to solve a longstanding problem—a shortage of intelligent, well-trained doctors. To uphold his view, the writer cites data from authoritative sources, including top-of-the-line university medical schools:

[Claim]: *America's medical education establishment is doing something to solve the problem of too few well-trained physicians.*

[Evidence]: In 2014 the number of applicants to medical schools surpassed 48,000, for 20,055 slots, according to the Association of American Medical Colleges. Both numbers were a record. And competition was intense. Harvard Medical School ultimately enrolled 2.3 percent of applicants. NYU took even fewer: 1.8 percent. The University of Buffalo enrolled 3.5 percent; the U of Pittsburgh, 3.2 percent.

Prospective applicants will need more stamina, too, to conquer the new version of the Medical College Admission Test. Next year the M.C.A.T. will be more than two hours longer, clocking in at 6 hours, 15 minutes and will cover three additional semesters' worth of material, in biochemistry, psychology and sociology, upping the number of prerequisite classes from 8 to 11.

The good news: The number of spots is growing. Eight years ago, the association called for 30 percent enrollment growth to offset a projected shortage of more than 90,000 doctors by 2020. Medical schools will come close to that goal by 2018–19, thanks to larger entering classes and new schools. Meanwhile, colleges of osteopathic medicine more than doubled their capacity form 2002 to 2013.

Many claims, of course, can't be supported by such cold, hard facts. The claim of a pop music critic, for instance, that Beyoncé's latest performance was a disaster can't be supported by facts. Instead, the writer must depend entirely on opinionated language to convince readers that Beyoncé's lip-synced rendition of "Drunk in Love" turned him off:

Knowing the tide against which I swim, I admit that Beyoncé once more left me cold and disappointed. Utterly baffled by the hoopla over this so-called entertainer, I see only hype and smoke and mirrors, not an ounce of talent in sight nor any skills of showmanship. Where in heaven's name is there any charm, magic or grace (much less a personal connection to the audience), in her tedious, repetitious strutting around a stage like a cheap nightclub stripper? Unbelievable!

Every claim need not be stated outright. Instead, it may be implied by the text:

What is truth? In the month of May you can go outdoors, out where there are trees and grass and open sky and wildflowers and wild birds, and know that you are in the midst of truth. You don't even have to define it, because it is there, obvious.

There is the truth of grass, growing, restoring itself year after year. There is the truth of a tree, which couldn't falsify a leaf or a nut or a winged seed if it tried, and which sets down the record of each year, exactly as it is, in its growth rings. There is the truth of water flowing downhill, a brook sweet to begin with and with the urgency to remain clean if given half a chance. There is the truth of sunrise and moonset, of the sky, the dew, the thunderstorm. There is the gleaming truth of the buttercup, the echoing truth of a robin singing.

May is a special kind of verity, a testament to the reality of a live and sentient world. Define it as you will, it is all around us now, a reality that needs no explanation.

You won't find literal "proof" in this answer to the question, "What is truth?" Rather, the writer provides a series of observations that more or less add up to a claim that *truth can be found outdoors during the month of May*. The writer doesn't set out to prove a theory. Nor is he trying to convince readers to take a walk in the park. Rather, he's written a lyrical passage meant to express his feelings about nature and at the same time suggest that *Truth* (with a capital T) may be too elusive to define precisely.

Another kind of evidence—namely, an anecdote or a brief story—can be a godsend for supporting a claim. Because virtually everybody loves a story, anecdotes can bolster an argument like almost nothing else. Not every anecdote is literally true, of course, but it can make its point by representing what could be true, and unless it's totally off the wall, leave a strong impression on a reader.

TIP

Be wary of conclusions drawn from limited evidence.

A savvy reader, however, ought to be wary of generalizing or drawing conclusions from a single account of, say, one person's experience. As a case in point, the following anecdote is meant to support a claim that the widespread use of mobile phones causes people to behave in unusual, even bizarre, ways:

The technology seems to trigger urges in addition to transmitting them, as though the city's inhabitants and its digital devices have merged into a single nervous system. A stranger once thrust his smartphone into a pretty woman's hands and ran off, hoping that she would feel obliged to track him down in order to return it.

Only the writer knows whether the event took place as described. Nevertheless, the story illustrates a single, quirky incident that could have happened in the society hooked on mobile phones. What it can't do, though, is serve as foolproof evidence for making a broad statement about life in the digital age.

In contrast, the author of the following paragraph depends on observations and incontestable facts to convince readers that the human foot is a far from simple appendage:

[Claim]: *The human foot is a complicated structure.* [Evidence]: It consists of twenty-six bones linked by many joints, attached to each other and to the leg bone by numerous ligaments, moved by muscles and tendons, nourished by blood vessels, controlled by nerves, and protected by a covering of skin. In a newborn infant, some of the bones are merely bone-shaped pieces of a gristle-like substance called cartilage. As a child grows, however, real bone appears within and gradually spreads throughout the cartilage form. The heel, the largest bone, is not completed until the age of about twenty years.

2. Reasoning to Connect Claims

By now it should be clear that the author of every source chosen for analysis intends to persuade readers to agree with his or her point of view on a specific subject. Typically, the writer will state a position and then make a case for it, using facts, details, personal anecdotes, opinions, and so forth, all meant to boost the persuasiveness of the argument. Some opinions may function as a subclaim, or *secondary* claim—that is, a claim that in some way serves as evidence to support a more important claim.

In the passage that follows, for instance, the author claims that politicians behave as though they can tell as many lies as they want without getting caught. In presenting his case, the author uses a number of subclaims:

> **[Main claim, part 1]:** *It's amazing how many politicians seem to believe that dishonesty is the best policy for getting elected. Why they think so is puzzling, but here are three reasons:*
>
> **[Subclaim #1]:** Many politicians are narcissists—arrogant and self-important. They see themselves as special. They require excessive admiration and have a sense of entitlement. **[Evidence to support subclaim #1]:** A case in point: As John Edwards, the former senator and vice-presidential nominee, noted, "My experiences fed a self-focus, an egotism, a narcissism that leads you to believe you can do whatever you want."
>
> **[Subclaim #2]:** Politicians know their followers will believe them, even in the face of irrefutable evidence to the countrary. **[Evidence to support subclaim #2 consisting of additional minor claims]:** Politicians and their adherents live in an echo chamber in which everyone watches the same news channel, listens to the same talk radio, reads the same newspapers and web sites, and hangs out with the same like-minded people. People don't want to hear the truth. Truth, as the saying goes, hurts, and no one wants to hear things that threaten their beliefs or make them uncomfortable. It is decidedly better for politicians to tell people what makes them feel good. Why should they be purveyors of bad news (and decrease the likelihood of getting people's votes) when they can tell fairy tales with happy endings and come out the victor?
>
> **[Subclaim #3]:** If a lie is told enough times, people will assume it is true. It is not a stretch to understand why people would believe something if they hear it enough. **[Evidence to support subclaim #3 consisting of additional minor claims]:** People expect that lies will be disproved and fade away. So, if the lies continue to be heard, people assume they must be true.
>
> **[Main claim, part 2]:** *Ultimately, politicians are not delusional. They've thought out the costs of lying versus the benefits they derive and found that lying works in their favor.*

(Adapted from Jim Taylor, "Six Reasons Why Politicians Believe They Can Lie (And Not Get Caught)," Huffington Post Blog, Posted 9/25/2012)

No doubt other reasons might be added to the list, such as the theory that politicians assume that audiences believe "facts" that confirm their own biases and prejudices. Even without this and other reasons, however, the writer builds a persuasive argument to support the main claim by using subclaims presented in an easy-to-follow format, and each subclaim is supported by additional, minor, subclaims.

Now let's turn to a claim made by a writer who argues that adults should not be prevented from participating in dangerous sports, particularly professional football, if it's their choice to do so. He reasons that if an informed individual craves the rewards of playing more than he fears the possibility of serious injury, so be it.

[Claim]: *Everyone retains the right to pursue potentially dangerous activities, as long as it's their own informed choice.*

[Evidence]: Any adult involved with football knows it's a brutal activity and is aware of the risks associated with playing a collision sport. It is suspected and widely reported that every head-to-head collision generates imperceptible "sub-concussions," slowly damaging the brain without the victim suffering the symptoms of an acute trauma. This means that many players are being injured on almost every play they are involved with (in every single game and in every full-contact practice). Professional athletes accept this risk in exchange for the chance at large financial reward and the right to pursue a rarefied livelihood they love and desire. (College and high-school students willingly do the same thing but without the benefit of a salary.)

(Adapted from Chuck Klosterman, "Hating the Game," *New York Times Magazine*, 9/7/14, p. 24)

Incidentally, have you noticed that writers often state their claims before presenting their evidence?

Here is a paragraph that starts with the claim that the origin of jazz can be traced to 19th-century New Orleans. Historical evidence is used to vouch for the validity of the claim:

[Claim]: *Historically the journey that jazz has taken can be traced with reasonable accuracy to New Orleans.* [Evidence]: Around 1895 the almost legendary Buddy Bolden and Bunk Johnson were blowing their cornets in the streets of the city for funeral parades which have always enlivened the social life of that uncommonly vital metropolis. Obviously, the need for jazz in New Orleans was coupled with the talent to produce it and a favorable audience to receive it. During those early years the local urge for musical expression was so powerful that anything that could be twanged, strummed, beaten, blown, or stroked was likely to be exploited for its musical usefulness.

In contrast, the authors of the following paragraphs cite their evidence first and then draw conclusions:

[Evidence]: This year's Los Angeles Dodgers have won more games than any other. Their team batting average (.304) exceeds that of any other team by twenty percentage points. They lead both leagues in fielding and have hit more home runs than the next two teams combined. [Claim]: *Without a doubt the Dodgers are currently the best team in baseball.*

[Evidence]: People who know nothing about rap music claim that it is just about sex and violence, but it is important to take the time to listen to a range of different rap artists. Kendrick Lamar raps about gang activity because that's what he lived through. His music allows listeners to look into the life of someone they don't know. [Claim]: *Any art form that gets a person thinking about events that they know nothing about is worthwhile.*

Neither approach is necessarily superior to the other. Both kinds of reasoning can make equally strong arguments.

For that matter, writers also support some claims by deploying reasoning structured in less clear-cut ways. Evidence, for instance, can be scattered throughout a passage, both before and after the claim. A claim itself can be spread over two or more sentences, sometimes back to back but at other times separated by any amount of discussion. Now and then, a sentence may be half claim and half evidence. Unfortunately, there is no single, surefire method for digging claims out of a passage. Consequently, source analysis—the art of discerning subtle links and interrelationships among ideas dispersed throughout a passage—takes practice.

The number of possible configurations and relationships between claims and evidence can't be calculated, but here are several common types to be aware of:

A. **A claim divided into two parts with the evidence inserted between them:**

> **[Claim, part 1]:** *Understanding the movement characteristics of groundwater could be an important step in solving the worldwide water crisis.* **[Evidence]:** Most groundwater originates as precipitation, percolates into the soil much as water fills a sponge, and moves from place to place along fractures in rock, through sand and gravel, or through channels in formations such as cavernous limestone. Constantly encountering resistance from surrounding material, groundwater moves in a manner considerably different from that of surface water. Varying with the time of formation, its flow ranges from a fraction of an inch to a few feet per day. **[Claim, part 2]:** *To improve their lives, two billion of the world's people currently deprived of clean water, need information about how to tap into the resource flowing right beneath their feet.*

B. **Factual information followed by a claim and additional facts:**

> **[Evidence, part 1]:** Nine out of ten doctors assume that being fat decreases longevity and that losing weight will increase it. But several recent studies conducted by exercise physiologists have found that, if fat people remain active and head off further weight gains, there is no correlation between being fat and dying early. **[Claim]:** *But Western medicine, being part of Western culture, has taken on prejudice against body fat.* **[Evidence, part 2]:** This bias has led to countless diet fads, shelves of books on how to lose weight, scores of pills and dietary supplements—in fact, a multi-billion dollar industry that promotes weight loss as a desirable goal.

C. **A mix of claims and counterclaims.** Writers can't always argue only one side of an issue. Finding some issues more gray than black and white, they may favor a balanced approach, recognizing that opposing claims each have merit. By acknowledging that their thinking is still in flux, they encourage readers, too, to keep an open mind on a particular issue. The author of an article on the effects of salt on health, for example, begins with this personal anecdote followed by a contradictory claim:

> Sports nutritionists know what they are talking about when they recommend that we should replenish salt in our bodies when we sweat it out in physical activity. ... I played high school football in suburban Maryland, sweating profusely through double sessions in the swamplike 90-degree days of August. Without salt pills, I couldn't make it through a two-hour practice; I couldn't walk across the parking lot afterward without cramping.
>
> Yet, the message that we should avoid salt at all other times remains strong.

By stating the two sides of controversy, the writer prepares the reader for a look at both the pros and the cons of salt intake. Indeed, the next paragraph discusses evidence in favor of limiting our salt consumption:

> Why have we been told that salt is so deadly? ... Eat more salt and your body retains water to maintain a stable concentration of sodium in your blood. This is why eating salty food tends to make us thirsty: we drink more; we retain water. The result can be a temporary increase in blood pressure, which will persist until our kidneys eliminate both salt and water.

Further along, the writer switches gears and cites the findings of a research study:

> Restricting how much salt we eat can increase our likelihood of dying prematurely.

Then, in an effort to strike a balance between pro- and anti-salt advocates, the writer observes:

> This attitude that studies that go against prevailing beliefs should be ignored on the basis that, well, they go against prevailing beliefs, has been the norm for the anti-salt campaign for decades. Maybe now the prevailing beliefs should be questioned.

(Adapted from Gary Taubes, *New York Times*, June 2, 2012)

Clearly, the writer hasn't yet made up his mind about salt. He claims that the definitive word on human salt consumption is yet to be written and, until it is, we'd best keep an open mind on the issue.

D. **Passages with no claim at all.** A writer may avoid making a claim because the accumulated evidence so strongly suggests a claim that to spell it out would be superfluous.

> Whales have often exceeded one hundred feet in length, and George Brown Goode, in his report on the United States fisheries, mentions a finback having been killed that was one hundred and twenty feet long. A whale's head is sometimes thirty-five feet in circumference, weighs thirty tons, and has jaws twenty feet long, fifteen feet high, nine feet wide at the bottom, and two feet wide at the top. A score of Jonahs standing upright would not have been unduly crowded in such a chamber.

Such a paragraph achieves a high degree of persuasiveness by the very absence of a claim. When readers have weighed all the evidence and then drawn their own conclusions—rather than having it handed to them—they're likely to cling more firmly to their beliefs.

3. Evidence to Develop Ideas

It would be rare indeed for a writer to construct an argument consisting solely of claim after claim, each one followed by a specific piece of supporting evidence. Such a passage would be a bore to read as well as to write. Writers, therefore, often comment on the evidence and insert their own ideas and biases into the discussion.

In the following passage, for example, the writer claims that career training undermines the essential purpose of colleges and universities. As you read it, observe how the writer mounts an attack on career training with a series of opinionated statements.

The appalling statistic that 83 percent of college seniors graduate without a job has led many in the public to clamor for making "career training" a requirement for college degrees. This suggestion calls to mind the axiom about the merits of teaching a hungry man to fish, rather than giving him a fish dinner. Four-year colleges and universities are not places for students to learn specific skills required to perform a particular task. That is the purpose of vocational school or on-the-job training. Students go to college to develop the abilities of thinking, writing, analysis, and communication that will allow them to respond effectively to the innumerable, and largely unpredictable, professional and personal challenges they face in life, including landing a good job,

Dedicating classroom time to teaching students how to find and apply for jobs would undercut even further the ability of American colleges and universities to remain centers of intellectual expansion, experimentation and enrichment, rather than institutions whose merit the public (and, increasingly, the federal government) measures only in the hollow terms of "return on investment" and graduates' ability to secure the highest paying jobs possible.

(Adapted from letter to *New York Times* by Christopher Tozzi, 9/8/2014)

The passage starts with what may seem like a factual statement, but the adjective "appalling" slants it severely against career training in college. As though to justify his position, the writer then alludes to the widely known maxim that it's better to teach a hungry man to fish than to give him a fish dinner. The rest of the passage consists of the writer's opinions couched in language that sounds factual, but isn't—a tactic that writers use all the time. Arguments consisting of facts and opinions are hardly rare. Every editorial in the media, for example, combines the two.

Some ideas clearly and strongly support a claim. Others are less supportive. Writers, therefore, often include ideas that themselves may need support to be convincing. This so-called *secondary evidence* may not directly support the writer's primary claim, but it still adds to the persuasiveness of the overall argument. In a sense, such evidence works like the steel cables on a suspension bridge. Individual cables can't hold up the bridge, but working together, they keep the roadway from dropping into the river. So it is with an assortment of evidence. Each piece in concert with all the other individual pieces does the job.

TIP

Secondary evidence doesn't support a primary claim directly but reinforces evidence used in behalf of the primary claim.

Even in the most coherent sources, you may encounter an idea or two that seem irrelevant to the writer's primary claim. Perhaps the writer put it there by accident. More likely, though, it may be an interesting detail the writer thought you'd like to know, or it may have been planted there as a hint of things to come later in the passage. The following paragraph, for example, claims that electricity is the wave of the future. With one exception, every sentence more or less supports the validity of the claim. Can you locate the one that doesn't?

[Claim]: *Electricity is the wave of the future.* **[Evidence]:** Our lives are already filled with electrical gadgets from vibrating beds to toothbrushes. Soon, the faint tinkling of a broken filament will become a sound of the past. Futuristic shops in Japan are already selling electric shoes, combs, watches, glasses, even clothes. Within about fifteen years every new car sold in the United States will be electric. Tesla Motors, the world's largest electric car company, plans to sell half a million of its new mid-priced models by 2017. To prepare for an exploding demand for electric cars, the company is building the world's largest battery factory, near Reno, Nevada.

You're right, if you picked the sentence about the sound of a broken filament. Yes, it alludes to electric light bulbs, and it may sound like a claim, but it needs elaboration to make it germane to the point of the paragraph—that electricity is the wave of the future. Obviously, the writer chose not back it up, perhaps to keep readers focused on the paragraph's main topic—the future role of electricity.

4. Word Choice

Good writers take pains to use vocabulary appropriate to the tastes, habits, and reading level of their intended audience. Sixth-graders won't grasp a passage filled with so-called "SAT words." Sophisticated adults expecting to be entertained and informed won't respond favorably to cliché-ridden jargon. General readers are likely to lose their way in the technical terminology found in most professional journals. In other words, a writer's choice of words, also known as *diction*, can make or break the effectiveness of a piece of writing, and that's especially true when the writer's aim is move readers to a course of thought or action.

Hoping to persuade its freshman students not to plagiarize, for example, the English department of a Midwestern state university handed out a set of instructions that read, in part:

> To the Student:
>
> The purpose of this statement is to help and protect you by defining what sorts of aid you may and may not receive in preparing your themes for freshman English. This has proven a vexing problem for students faced for the first time with the writing of many papers, so we ask you to read this statement with care.
>
> Clearly you have come to this university to exchange ideas with others as well as to take in new ideas from your teachers, books, and other sources. But unless you make them your own by thinking them through and finally developing them in your own language— they are worthless. ...
>
> If you are to do an intellectually responsible job, you must never passively accept the ideas and work of others. Conceivably we could grade Wikipedia, if that were the source of a paper, or the graduate who left a paper behind in a fraternity or sorority file cabinet, or a sleazy online business that sells papers to insecure students. ...
>
> We do not list these many qualifications to bedevil you but to protect you, because to hand in work as your own that is not your own or to help another student improperly— according to any of the conditions detailed in this document—lays you open to charges of plagiarism or cheating. These are harsh words, but the reality is harsher still. For the disciplinary action required in such cases by *University Rules and Regulations* can include a statement on the student's permanent record and may mean dismissal from the university. The permanent record is read by all prospective employers and consulted by all graduate schools which the student might want to attend; in short, the record haunts him or her for the rest of his or her life. This may seem severe to you. In affairs of cheating and plagiarism, however, the integrity of the university, which depends on the integrity of individual students, is at stake.

As a soon-to-be college freshman, you are in a unique position to judge whether or not this statement would persuade students not to plagiarize. Some of the statement uses threats and "harsh words" (e.g., "sleazy," "cheating," "haunts") no doubt chosen to scare students into submission. Still other words may appeal to students' image of themselves as responsible but slightly insecure college freshmen (e.g., "Purpose … is to help and protect you, "vexing problem for students," "integrity of individual students"). Are there other words or phrases, or other ideas in the statement that strike you as notably persuasive? Or just the opposite, do some words turn you off?

By way of contrast, during orientation week at a small liberal arts college in New England freshmen received the following antiplagiarism statement:

ETHICS OF SCHOLARSHIP

This college is part of a broader community of scholars, a community where ideas, hypotheses, new concepts, and carefully established facts are the currency. None of us, faculty or students, is able to survive without borrowing from the work of others. Just as we expect to have our work recognized in examination reports, reappointments and promotions, or the footnotes of those who borrow from us, so must we carefully recognize those from whom we borrow.

Brief guidelines are presented in the next few pages for the proper acknowledgement of sources upon which we draw for course papers, examinations, oral presentations, artistic productions, and so on. We acknowledge the work of others not only in gratitude to them, but also to provide our readers with the opportunity to consult our sources if they wish to review the evidence, consider other interpretations, or to determine the basis for the cited passage. In the evaluation of scholarly work, the writer's creativity in locating appropriate sources and using them well can be assessed only if those sources are identified.

The failure to acknowledge one's sources is more than a failure to be properly socialized into a community of scholars. Writers who fail to note sources are, at best, ignorant, and, at worst, dishonest. Unacknowledged borrowing from the work of others in any medium is a fundamental repudiation of the deepest values of the academic community.

Not only is the tone of this statement 180 degrees from the preceding one, it uses gentle words and phrases such as "borrowing," "broader community of scholars," and "recognize those from whom we borrow."

Which of the two statements is more persuasive? The one that threatens or the one that appeals to students' ethics and sense of community?

A single well-chosen and adroitly placed word can make a huge difference to a reader. Not that the word needs to be unusual, or shocking, or emotionally potent. But in a given context a particular word may work extraordinarily well, helping writers fulfill their purpose.

In the passage below, consider the word *slaughtered*. It turns a mostly factual account of the death of African elephants into an unsettling accusation:

In 2011, about twenty-five thousand African elephants were killed for their ivory. Since then, an additional forty-five thousand elephants—perhaps ten percent of the total population—have been *slaughtered*. Just since 2012, their numbers have declined about sixty percent. If this trend continues, within a decade there might be no more elephants in Africa.

Had the writer used *destroyed, put to death, dispatched, did in*, or any other common synonym for *killed*, the reader might well have remained unmoved, but the word *slaughtered*, by suggesting brutality and a wanton spilling of blood, is apt to stir up a reader's emotions. Of course other synonyms might be equally potent: *slain, murdered, liquidated, finished off, zapped*, among others. Which word would you have chosen?

CONNOTATION OF WORDS

At the heart of word choice lie the principles of *denotation* and *connotation*. You probably know that denotation refers to the dictionary definition of a word and to a whole range of ideas and feelings and images that a word may suggest. The word *home*, for instance, denotes a place you live. But it has multiple connotations—for some a sense of comfort and safety; for others, tension and conflict; and for still others, a mixture of good, bad, and indifferent feelings. It may also bring to mind an image of a small Victorian house on a leafy street, a walk-up flat above a nail salon, a condo on the edge of town, or one of countless other places where people hang their hats at the end of a day. In brief, *home* is a word that can conjure up infinite shapes and shades of meaning and emotion.

The SAT Essay puts your sensitivity to the connotation of words on the line, both as a reader and a writer. When the author of a source uses a juicy word, ripe with connotation, you might want to explain in your essay precisely what that word contributes to the writer's argument. Hold it! Stop for a moment and go back to the word *juicy*. What do you think of it? Isn't it a surprising word to run across in a discussion of essay writing? Well, this writer chose it exactly for that reason. It's unusual in the context, and what's more, it's bursting with connotations of succulence and dripping with meaning. It's also slightly suggestive, stimulating, tantalizing. How better to illustrate that a single word can ignite a reader's imagination. *Juicy* is so much juicier than, say, *interesting, engaging, inviting, catchy*, and other synonyms.

Mini-Workout in Connotation

> **Directions:** In the context of each sentence below, mark the italicized word that has the richer connotation.

1. Considering that she is a twenty-one-year-old college senior, Martina conveyed a surprising (*innocence, naiveté*) in her belief that candidates for public office always tell the truth.

2. The ancient vases found at the excavation site must be handled with extreme care. They are very (*fragile, delicate*).

3. By proudly (*bashing, criticizing*) her opponent's argument during the debate, Ms. Hagan won a round of applause from the audience.

4. (*The data revolution, The rise of data*) will bring untold benefits to the citizens of the future.

5. Owen left Olivia in tears when he cruelly (*rebuffed, declined*) her offer to go with him to the prom.

6. The (*magnitude, amount*) of change in China since the Cultural Revolution is almost unimaginable.

7. Isn't it (*mind-blowing, surprising*) that the terrorists threw down their weapons and surrendered.

8. Julius Caesar filled his (*well-known, immortal*) account of the Gallic Wars with titillating details about the barbarian tribes he had fought.

9. Apparently, the author is (*transfixed by, drawn to*) sensational plots. This is her eighth novel about a secret love affair and a murder.

10. What the Greyhound bus driver really (*desired, longed for*) was a bowl of pasta and a beer.

Answers are on page 247.

The purpose of this Mini-Workout was to alert you to the slight but often significant implications of two words or phrases that at first glance may seem almost synonymous but are not. Because **word choice** is specifically listed as a rhetorical technique for discussion in your SAT Essay, it pays to stay alert for words and phrases that a writer uses specifically to shape readers' impressions and/or to emphasize a certain idea.

Incidentally, word choice is probably one of the more clear-cut and easy-to-explain rhetorical features to discuss in an essay. Use it if you can, but avoid choosing just any old random word. Pick one instead that contributes in a substantial way to the development of the author's claim.

5. Emotional Appeal

You can bet that the author of the source will enlist logic and reason to build a strong argument. But emotional words and ideas can sway readers in ways that reason never can. As you read the source, therefore, be on the lookout for examples of language that appeal specifically to the emotions. They'll come as single words, as phrases, and sometimes as whole sentences or paragraphs, and they're bound to stimulate a vast spectrum of feelings, ranging from disgust to disappointment, patriotism to pity, sentimentality to scorn. The possibilities are endless.

As a case in point, the writer of the passage below argues that low-income kids need more after-school supervision. In support of his cause, he uses emotionally charged language meant to tug at readers' heartstrings.

How do innocent little children feel when they walk home from school to an empty house or apartment? Lonely, deserted, resentful, angry? Some do, of course, but most of them screw up their courage and feel proud, trusted, responsible—yes, grown up at age ten or eleven, or even seven or eight. Truly these "latch-key" children are brave little heroes to remain patiently on their own, whiling away hour after lonely hour until an adult arrives home and puts an end to their isolation.

Lonely, deserted, resentful. Along with phrases like "innocent little children" and "brave little heroes" the words convey the writer's concern and affection for elementary school youngsters. Not every reader will be swayed by such sappy sentimentality, but all are likely to recognize the writer's sincerity, feel his chagrin, and agree that it's shameful and irresponsible to neglect small children after school is out.

The writer of the following excerpt takes on another social problem and uses a series of provocative images (*italicized*) to stir up readers' feelings of sadness (perhaps), or anger or contempt or guilt, or a mix of these and other emotions.

On any given night in the United States, an estimated 600,000 people are homeless. Of those, approximately 200,000 suffer from serious mental illness. Unfortunately, these are facts that no longer hold surprise for most Americans. We have grown accustomed to the sights of the *wild-eyed dirt-covered man on the corner.* We have become used to averting our gaze from the *toothless old woman who mutters to herself* at the bus stop and wears many layers of clothes even in warm weather. We are no longer shocked as we once were at the sight of *small children crouched beside their parents*, panhandling on some of our busiest streets. Although most Americans feel compassion for homeless men and women they encounter on the street, many are puzzled, not knowing how to react to this problem.

Similarly, the passage below, from the diary of Siegfried Sassoon, a poet and World War I soldier, uses powerful, emotionally charged words and images to persuade readers that war is hell—as if anyone really needs to be persuaded.

Inferno—inferno—bang smash!! Since 6:30 there has been hell let loose. The air vibrates with the incessant din—the whole earth shakes and rocks and throbs. It is one continuous roar—bullets whistling over our head—small fry quite outdone by the gangs of hooligan-shells that dash over to reach the enemy lines with their demolition parties. ...

My heart is heavy-laden now. I sit burning my dreams away beside the fire, for death has made me wise and bitter and strong. And I am rich in all I have lost.

Eric Kester, the author of an op-ed piece "What I Saw as an N.F.L. Ball Boy" describes another kind of war, the kind called a "game" that, if Kester is to be believed, resembles a battle.

On game days my pockets were always full of smelling salts, tiny ammonia stimulants that, when sniffed, can trick a brain into a state of alertness. After almost every crowd-pleasing hit, a player would stagger off the field, steady himself the best he could, sometimes vomit a little, and tilt his head to the sky. Then, with eyes squeezed shut in pain, he'd scream, "Eric!" and I'd dash over and say, "It's OK, I'm right here, got just what you need."

A sniff of my salts would revive the player in alertness only, and he would run back onto the field to once again collide with opponents with the force of a high-speed car crash. As fans high-fived and hell-yeahed and checked the progress of their fantasy teams, and as I eagerly scrambled onto the field to pick up shattered fragments from exploded helmets, researchers were discovering the rotting black splotches of brain tissue that indicate chronic traumatic encephalopathy. Known as C.T.E., this degenerative disease is the result of players' enduring head traumas again and again.

(Adapted from "What I Saw as an N.F.L. Ball Boy," *New York Times,*
October 11, 2014, p. A23)

The power of Kester's prose derives from vivid, emotionally jarring images such as "vomit a little" and "force of a high-speed car crash" and "shattered fragments from exploded helmets"—all intended to alert readers to the brutality behind the glitter of the game.

Strong emotional appeals, of course, don't all stem from the dark side of human experience. They can be inspirational, contemplative, and full of joy. Take, for example, this poignant appreciation of the centuries-old network of man-made stone walls strung throughout New England's woodlands.

There is drama in the woods of New England ... that may not be found anywhere else in the world. This is a drama that comes not just from physical beauty of this part of the world, though that is considerable: a seemingly endless repetition of narrow valleys and steep hills punctuated by enormous rock outcroppings that rise from the floor of young forests like great gray whales surfacing for air. Nor does it come from the possibility—so eagerly embraced when walking in the woods—that you are walking where no man or woman has walked before. Strangely enough, it arises instead out of this possibility's exact opposite: the sure knowledge that someone *has* walked here before, and most likely in the company of an ox or a plow.

... Hikers come across stone walls in the woods and they are surprised, puzzled until they dig back in their minds for the key that opens the lock of these mysterious works of backbreaking effort, as out of place and evocative as a shipwreck on the ocean floor. This was where the country began, in these woods, and in agriculture, not industry.

Written in these walls are eloquent reminders of the odds against which the early farmers of this area worked, tilling thinly soiled ground whose main claim to fecundity was the abundant crop of rock that heaved to the surface each winter. There are reminders too of our own mortality: that rough wall over there may be all that remains of one man's labors. And yet in this age of planned obsolescence, that shiver of a thought must be closely followed by another: "My God, how that wall endures!" There is not a sign of the house and barns that would make sense of this sprawl of rocks on rock, yet that wall is still there to say that these woods were not always so, that they once were fields, and that the walls enclosed not young birches and shaggy-bark hickories but cows and crops.

(Adapted from Susan Allport, *Sermons in Stone*," WW Norton, 1990, pp. 15ff)

Throughout the passage, the author makes references to the sea, to the "great gray whales," a "shipwreck on the ocean floor," even rocks that are "heaved to the surface." Like the sea, the stone walls evoke awe and wonder, not just because of their age, but because they remind us of our own fleeting existence on the earth, a notion fortified by references to the long-gone "house and barns" and the long-ago presence of farm families at work in once-fertile fields.

6. Features of Your Own Choice

Your own choice is a phrase that dangles a gift in front of you—one that you may accept or reject. It invites you to write about virtually any rhetorical technique you find in the passage.

But please, proceed with caution. It's a gift that may not be as generous as it seems. For one thing, don't assume that whatever you happen to find in the passage is worth writing about. Just because you happen upon a metaphor doesn't necessarily mean that figurative language is a major element in the passage. To warrant discussion in your essay, a metaphor, a simile, the author's tone, or any other rhetorical feature must contribute markedly to the overall meaning or effect of the source. In short, not every rhetorical feature deserves your attention. Write about only the most significant ones—those that help build the persuasiveness of the writer's argument.

Once you've found such a feature, be sure to explain its role in the passage. For example, does it mark a shift in the author's tone, point of view, or purpose? Does it shock or surprise the reader? Might it add an element of humor or irony to the discussion and, if so, to what purpose or effect? Does the length or structure of certain sentences have a hand in developing the writer's argument? An essay that points out and insightfully explains these or other unusual rhetorical features will be noticed, appreciated, and rewarded by SAT readers who every day find their desks piled high with scores of cookie-cutter essays. How pleased they'll be to find some that sparkle with fresh ideas and flashes of originality. Try to make sure that one of those essays is yours.

Perhaps you're wondering what makes a rhetorical feature significant enough to write about? A few examples will provide an answer or two.

REPETITION

Repetition can be a bore, that's true, but repetition thoughtfully used can add punch to an idea. Use of the same word or phrase over and over may introduce an appealing rhythm to the prose. The occasional re-use of a single word or phrase can add emphasis to a thought or idea. Compare the effect of these two sentences, each taken from an announcement about an important business meeting:

> Please come to the meeting by 8:00 o'clock.
> Please, please, come to the meeting by 8:00 o'clock.

The repetition of "please" is an astonishingly simple and effective way to heighten the sense of urgency in the writer's request.

In a far more sophisticated and complex example of repetition, notice how the recurring use of similar words and phrases helps the writer define the concept of freedom:

> [1] Freedom is not fun. [2] It is not the same as individual happiness, nor is it security or peace or progress. [3] It is not the state in which the arts and sciences flourish. [4] It is also not good, clean government or the greatest welfare of the greatest number. [5] This is not to say that freedom is inherently incompatible with all or any of these values— though it may be and sometimes will be. [6] But the essence of freedom lies elsewhere. [7] It is responsible choice. [8] Freedom is not so much a right as a duty. [9] Real freedom is not freedom from something; that would be license. [10] It is freedom to choose between doing or not doing something. [11] It is never a release and always a responsibility. [12] It is not "fun" but the heaviest burden laid on man: to decide his own individual conduct as well as the conduct of society, and to be responsible for both decisions.

The word *freedom* appears seven times. More than half the sentences describe not what freedom is but what it is not. Denying ordinary conceptions of freedom amounts to a rhetorical strategy meant to build suspense and pique readers' curiosity to know what freedom is.

"Well," readers may wonder, "if freedom is not all these things, then what is it?" The writer answers the question by naming various aspects of freedom in sentences 7–12. By saying again and again that freedom is "not fun," the writer contrasts the allegedly "fun" things that freedom represents—such as "individual happiness" and "peace"—with practical "not-fun" necessities like "duty" and "responsibility." The rhetorical use of repetition, then, has enabled the writer to build an argument that encourages readers to appreciate and accept the serious obligations that freedom entails.

REFUTING THE OPPOSITION'S VIEWS

A popular rhetorical device that can strengthen an argument is to concede that an issue has more than one side. Recognizing that reason carries more weight than stubborn close-mindedness, writers might summarize their opponents' point of view but then point out flaws in their opponents' position. In the following excerpt from a source entitled "Charter Schools vs. Public Schools," for instance, the writer calmly refutes arguments against his claim that school choice (i.e., the creation of charter schools) is a bad idea.

TIP

An argument can be strengthened with a compelling refutation of the opposition's point of view.

[Introduction of opposing arguments]: Considering the many challenges facing public schools, it's understandable that many people are eager to pursue new options. Supporters of school choice point out that under the current public school system, parents with economic means already exercise school choice by moving from areas with failing or dangerous schools to neighborhoods with better, safer schools. Their argument is that school choice allows all parents the freedom, regardless of income level, to select the school that provides the best education for their children. Schools, therefore, compete for students by offering higher academic results and greater safety. Schools unable to measure up to the standards of successful schools often fail and close. [Acknowledgment of valid parts]: Activists within the school choice movement are to be applauded for seeking to improve public education, [Start of counterargument]: but the changes they in fact support seriously damage public education as a whole.

[Continuation of counterargument]: One of the biggest flaws in school choice is the power behind large corporations specializing in opening and operating charter schools. Two notable companies are Green Dot, which is the leading public school operator in Los Angeles, and KIPP, which in 2014 operated 162 schools in 20 states. These companies represent a growing trend of privatization of public schools by large corporations, thereby threatening the loss of educational control by the public. Education policy is being put in the hands of entrepreneurial think tanks, corporate boards of directors, and lobbyists who are more interested in profit than educating students. [Start of conclusion]: Education should be left in the hands of professional educators and not business people with MBAs. To do otherwise is not only dangerous, it defies common sense.

With such phrases as "Supporters of school choice point out that …" and "Their argument is that …" the writer cues readers that he is citing the concerns of those whose views differ from his own. First, he lauds his adversaries' good intentions and their desire "to improve public education." But then he challenges their views, asserting that "the changes they in fact support seriously damage public education. …"

REACHING OUT TO READERS

Writers can sway their readers, too, by pulling them into the discussion. Rather than preaching from afar, they simply employ the first-person pronoun "we," and thereby create the illusion, however tenuous, that "we"—the writer and the reader—have something in common—that we are of one mind on the issue. As one loosely allied to the writer, we may be inclined to consider, if not accept, his views. In the following excerpt from a source that appraises nature, for example, Alan Lightman claims that, in spite of our spiritual connection to nature and all its wonders, Mother Nature really doesn't give a hoot about you and me. Unlike Mother Nature, however, the writer appears to appreciate his readers by including us in his presentation.

> After each deadly mudslide, tornado, earthquake, and hurricane, we grieve over the human lives lost, the innocent people drowned or crushed without warning as they slept in their beds, worked in their fields or sat at their office desks. We feel angry at the scientists and policy makers who didn't foresee the impending calamity or, if forewarned, failed to protect us. Beyond the grieving and anger is a more subtle emotion. We feel betrayed. We feel betrayed by nature.
>
> Aren't we part of nature, born in nature, sustained by the food brought forth by nature, warmed by the natural sun? Don't we have a deep spiritual connection with wind and the water and the land that Emerson and Wordsworth so lovingly described, that Turner and Constable painted in scenes of serenity and grandeur? How could Mother Nature do this to us, her children?
>
> Yet despite our strongly felt kinship and oneness with nature, all the evidence suggests that nature doesn't care one whit about us. Tornadoes, hurricanes, floods, earthquakes and volcanic eruptions happen without the slightest consideration for human inhabitants.

(Adapted from Alan Lightman, "Our Lonely Home in Nature," *New York Times*, **May 3, 2014, p. A17)**

Maybe you've noticed that Lightman, speaking for both himself and for us, bombards us with repetition? The word *nature* appears 7 times in 15 lines, not because he couldn't think of another word (actually he alludes to nature in several different ways, from "earthquakes" and "hurricanes" to "serenity and grandeur") but to keep us focused on the topic—another effective rhetorical device meant to bolster the persuasiveness of his argument.

STORYTELLING

Because everybody loves a good story, hardly anything beats a gripping narrative or anecdote to bring readers around to the writer's way of thinking. Take, for instance, this tale of a poverty-stricken Jessica Lopez told by Douglas Quenqua in *Columbia Magazine*, a publication for a university's alumni.

> In the summer of 2010, everything was looking up for Jessica Lopez. A thirty-year-old high-school dropout who had been working for years at a Popeyes restaurant, she landed a job as a teacher's assistant at PS 287 in downtown Brooklyn. "It was always my dream to be a teacher," she says. "I was so excited."
>
> Around the same time, Lopez and her four-year-old son, Nolan, moved into an apartment in the Bedford-Stuyvesant neighborhood of Brooklyn. It was the first home they had called their own. They needed no moving van: they had previously lived for six months in a homeless shelter, after unexpectedly getting kicked out of a room in a friend's apartment. "We moved into our new place on Nolan's fourth birthday," Lopez says, sounding happy at the memory.
>
> Then everything fell apart. In November, Nolan began having tantrums so violent he had to be hospitalized. Doctors said he had a combination of attention deficit hyperactivity disorder, oppositional defiant disorder, and mixed receptive-expressive language disorder. Lopez, with no help from Nolan's imprisoned father, was forced to quit her job to care for her son.
>
> Today, Lopez gets by on a combination of cash assistance ($138 a month), food stamps ($210 a month), Medicaid (about $300 a month for Nolan's medication), and Supplemental Security Income ($740 a month). She is still unable to work, because Nolan often can't go to school or must be retrieved early.
>
> "When I get that call—'He won't get on the bus' or 'Nolan took off his clothes'—I have to get over there as fast as I can," Lopez says. "So I'm not working. I worry about money every day. It's that kind of life."

The writer, aiming to persuade his readers that the United States is ignoring many of its neediest citizens, relates Lopez's story to an educated audience of readers unlikely themselves to have experienced the ravages of poverty—at least not recently. In terms of persuasiveness, it's a brilliant rhetorical stroke, for he puts a human face on a problem that most of his readers probably understand only in the abstract.

CHOOSING RELEVANT FEATURES

Sources chosen for the SAT Essay will invariably include a profusion of rhetorical features to analyze. Like a salad bar, they offer a little bit of this and a little bit of that—a little logical reasoning here, a little emotional language there, and so forth. But in some sources—or at least in some segments of a source, a single rhetorical feature may be "most relevant." Standing out like a lighthouse beacon, it will be so vital that its removal would drain the passage of its lifeblood.

The passage below, for example, comes from a source claiming that the island of Zanzibar off the coast of Africa is nothing less than a paradise on earth. You'll quickly see what the writer has done to persuade you to agree with him.

> On the surface, Zanzibar fills all the romantic requirements of being one of the few paradises left on earth. The markets overflow with tropical fruits—not only the usual avocados, papayas, and pineapples but guavas, jack fruit, durians, and little red balls with prickles, locally called leaches. (The Chinese dry them and call them litchi nuts.) If you want to buy

a banana, you must specify the type—*bungala, pukasa,* or "sugar." The same goes for mangoes—*boribo, dodo, muyuni, shomari, or "ordinary."* Vegetables are even more numerous, ranging from the familiar butter beans, corn, spinach, marrow, and eggplant, to the exotic cassava, breadfruit, *majimbi* root, guarri, lady's-fingers, and luffa. The only foods imported into Zanzibar are carrots and cabbage, from Kenya.

The text consists largely of a catalogue of fruits and vegetables found in Zanzibar. Rhetorically, the writer intends to impress readers with the island's bounty. Its markets "overflow" with exotic produce. Even bananas, not to speak of mangoes, come in several varieties. This paragraph by itself may not turn doubters into believers that Zanzibar is a paradise on earth but as part of a longer passage that relies on similar rhetoric, the cumulative effect may indeed be persuasive.

Another form of rhetoric, irony, dominates an excerpt adapted from a source entitled "The Principles of Poor Writing." With his tongue lodged firmly in his cheek, the author claims that essay writing can be greatly improved by following these guidelines.

Write hurriedly, preferably when tired. Have no plan; write down items as they occur to you. The essay will thus be spontaneous and poor. Hand in your essay the moment it is finished. Rereading a few days later might lead to revision—which seldom, if ever, makes the writing worse. If you submit your essay to trusted and knowledgeable readers (a bad practice), pay no attention to their criticisms or comments. Later resist firmly any editorial suggestions. Be strong and infallible; don't let anyone break down your personality. The critic may be trying to help you or he may have an ulterior motive, but the chance of his causing improvement in your writing is so great that you must be on guard.

The paragraph depends on its ironic tone from beginning to end. Were the paragraph to be taken literally, its effect would go poof!—just vanish into thin air.

SCREENING THE EVIDENCE

The authors of sources used on the SAT would like readers to embrace whatever claims they make and be swayed by whatever evidence they use to support those claims. But a thoughtful reader will maintain a degree of skepticism, knowing that not all evidence literally proves the validity of all claims. To be convincing, evidence should live up to three basic standards: *sufficiency, believability,* and *accuracy.*

1. **SUFFICIENCY.** There should be enough of it. Making a generalization or drawing a conclusion based on a single fact, example, statistic, or supporting statement is insufficient, although writers do it all the time. (Maybe you've done it, too.) Two is better, and three is better still. Additional evidence will bolster an argument still further, of course, but in a short passage, the writer risks overkill and the reader might soon begin to think, "Okay, enough already!"

   The point is that, as you write your essay, it won't be enough simply to identify rhetorical elements and describe what they contribute to the persuasiveness of the author's argument. A word or two about the sufficiency of the evidence could add considerable substance to your analysis.

2. **BELIEVABILITY.** Writers often adopt a tone meant to lull readers into believing that every word in the passage is true. They cite, among other things, facts, statistics, and

quotations from authoritative sources. As you analyze the text of the passage, watch for evidence that fails to square with your own knowledge, experience, and observation of the world. Examine sources cited by the writer. Granted, it won't always be easy to distinguish between reputable sources and pulp, but be wary of accepting every source as credible.

Common wisdom says that data from research studies, ideas generated by reputable universities, information provided by scholars and writers whose work relates to the subject being discussed—yes, all these seem to be credible sources. But common wisdom can be wrong, and some measure of skepticism on your part will help you maintain perspective on the veracity of the evidence.

3. **ACCURACY.** In your analysis of the evidence in the passage, ask yourself whether the writer is telling the truth, the whole truth, and nothing but the truth. Quotations are often taken out of context. (An excerpt taken from a movie review, for example, reads: "A film you want to see." The reviewer's entire sentence, however, read, "This is not a film you want to see.") The fact is that it's easy to lie with excerpted quotations, with statistics, half truths, and incomplete data. A statement saying that "Nine out of ten homeowners object to the mandatory switch from incandescent lighting to fluorescent lighting" sounds as though the public overwhelmingly objects to fluorescent lighting. What is unclear, however, is how the findings were determined. Were more than ten homeowners surveyed? Who conducted the poll? How was the question phrased? Where and when was the question asked?

Even after you've judged the trustworthiness of evidence presented in the source, remain wary. Express your doubts if you have any. But don't overdo it. After all, your main goal is not to assess the legitimacy of the evidence but to identify and explain the rhetorical techniques the writer has used to build an argument.

Mini-Workout in Source Analysis

> **Directions:** Carefully read the following passages, all of them far shorter than a typical source. In space A write your understanding of the major claim made by the writer and identify the sentence(s) in which the claim is articulated or implied. In space B, identify any rhetorical elements used by the writer and explain how they support the claim.
>
> Please don't limit your responses to the lines provided; add paper as needed. Sentences are numbered for your convenience.

1. [1] At the end of the eighteenth century the Omaha Indian tribe controlled the fur trade on the upper Missouri River. [2] Without the say-so of Chief Blackbird, French and Spanish fur traders could not do business with tribes farther up the Missouri.

   A. _____

   _____

   B. _____

   _____

2. [1] The government's official statistic for college tuition inflation has become somewhat infamous. [2] It appears frequently in the news media, and policy makers lament what it shows. [3] No wonder: [4] College tuition and fees have risen an astounding 107 percent since 1992, even after adjusting for economy-wide inflation. [5] No other major household budget item has increased in price nearly as much.

A. _____

_____

B. _____

_____

3. [1] Instead of widening toward its mouth, the Mississippi River grows narrower; grows narrower and deeper. [2] From the junction of the Ohio to a point half-way down to the sea, the width averages a mile in high water; thence to the sea the width steadily diminishes until at the "Passes" above its mouth, it is but a little over half a mile. [3] At the junction of the Ohio, the Mississippi's depth is eighty-seven feet; the depth increases gradually, reaching one hundred and twenty-nine just above its mouth. [4] What's more, it is the longest river in the world—four thousand three hundred miles. [5] It's safe to say that it is also the crookedest river in the world, since in one part of its journey it uses up one thousand three-hundred miles to cover the same ground that a crow would fly in over six-hundred and seventy-five. [6] Clearly, the Mississippi is not a commonplace river, but on the contrary is in all ways remarkable and well worth reading about. [7] What man or woman can deny that the river is exceptional when they learn that its drainage basin is as great as the combined areas of England, Wales, Scotland, Ireland, France, Spain, Portugal, Germany, Austria, Italy, and Turkey?

A. _____

_____

B. _____

_____

4. [1] If the English nature is cold, how is it that it has produced a great literature and a literature that is particularly great in poetry? [2] And yet the English are supposed to be so unpoetical. [3] How is this? [4] The nation that produced Shakespeare and the Lake Poets cannot be a cold unpoetical nation. [5] We can't get fire out of ice. [6] Since literature always rests upon national character, there must be in the English nature hidden springs of fire to produce the fire we see. [7] The warm sympathy, the romance, the imagination that we look for in the English whom we meet, and too often vainly look for, must exist in the nation as a whole, or we could not have this outburst of national song.

A. _____

_____

B. _____

_____

5. [1] Pressure, darkness, and—we should have added only a few years ago—silence are the conditions of life in the deep sea. [2] But we know now that the conception of the sea as a silent place is wholly false. [3] Wide experience with hydrophones and other listening devices for the detection of submarines has proved that, around the shore lines of much of the world, there is the extraordinary uproar produced by fishes, shrimps, porpoises and probably other forms not yet identified. [4] There has been little investigation as yet of sound in the deep, offshore areas, but when the crew of *Atlantis* lowered a hydrophone into deep water off Bermuda, they recorded strange mewing sounds, shrieks, and ghostly moans, the sources of which have not been traced. [5] But fish of shallower zones have been captured and confined in aquaria, where their voices have been recorded for comparison with sounds heard at sea, and in many cases satisfactory identification can be made.

A. _____

_____

B. _____

_____

6. [1] Democracies have always been subject to terrorist attacks. [2] Our constitutional rights, the restrictions set on police power, and our citizens' enjoyment of due process of the law—the very qualities of our society that terrorists despise—are the same qualities that for years made us easy prey. [3] Although many people view this as a cruel irony, we have within our free society the tools with which not only to fight and destroy terrorists but to keep them at bay. [4] Following the attacks of 9/11, America went to war against terrorism. [5] A federal Department of Homeland Security was created. [6] The citizenry was put on alert. [7] Our superbly trained law enforcement people at every level of government began to coordinate their efforts as never before. [8] The courts granted more liberal use of wiretap surveillance and search warrants, and a system of laws was introduced to fight terrorism as both a crime and a military assault instead of merely a political act. [9] Terrorists from foreign lands were put on notice that they faced prosecution in military tribunals, and American citizens who chose to terrorize their own country faced the maximum penalties allowed by criminal law.

A. _____

_____

B. _____

_____

7. [1] The telling of tales is one of he earliest forms of human pastime, and its origins are lost in the mists of antiquity. [2] From the primitive form of the fable, or example, as it was sometimes called, designed to teach some principle, it grew and took on a multitude of expressions which reflected the taste of successive epochs. [3] Before Miguel de Cervantes's day there existed all the derivations of the epic, the novels of extraordinary adventures, the romances of chivalry, the pastoral novels, the earliest of the Moorish and picaresque novels, these latter both of Spanish invention. [4] But the novel as we know it today came into being with *Don Quixote*. [5] All these preceding forms meet and fuse in a new and glorious synthesis. [6] Cervantes was so in advance of his day that, despite the instant popularity of *Don Quixote*, it had no immediate successors; and it was not until the nineteenth century, when the novel came to be the prevailing literary mode, that his invention was fully understood and utilized. [7] The realistic novel dealing with ordinary people seen against their commonplace background, had its origins in Cervantes. [8] And its finest cultivators, forerunners like Stern and Smollett in the eighteenth century, Flaubert, Dickens, and our own Mark Twain, who was never without a copy of *Don Quixote* in his pocket, William Faulkner, who is quoted as saying that he had two passions, his daughter and *Don Quixote*—in short, all novelists deserving of the name have acquired the basic canons of their art directly or indirectly from Cervantes.

A. _____

_____

B. _____

_____

8. [1] The question "Is college invariably worthwhile?" can be answered, but not with the usual claim that a college degree leads to a better-paying job, which is not always the case. [2] What justifies a college education is that it exposes students to books they might otherwise never have read, ideas they might never have had, convictions they might never have entertained, friends they might never have made, and educators they might never have encountered.

[3] College exposes them to the ideologue who preaches in the classroom, seeking converts as well as professors without an agenda and in love with their subject, which they present as if they were hosting a weekend getaway at which students are guests, not trainees.

[4] What better preparation for analyzing the news, in which interpretation is often passed off as gospel truth, and facts embellished to add drama to the mundane?

**(Adapted from a letter to the editor of *New York Times*
by Bernard F. Dick, Teaneck, NJ, 9/7/14)**

A. _____

_____

B. _____

_____

9. [1] What we love, when on a summer day we step into the coolness of a wood, is that its boughs close up behind us. [2] We are escaped, into another room of life. [3] The wood does not live as we live, restless and running, panting after flesh, and even in sleep tossing with fears. [4] It is aloof from thoughts and instincts; it responds, but only to the sun and wind, the rock and the stream—never, though you shout yourself hoarse, to propaganda, temptation, reproach, or promises. [5] You cannot mount a rock and preach to a tree how it shall attain the kingdom of heaven. [6] It is already closer to it, up there, than you will grow to be. [7] And you cannot make it see the light since in the tree's sense you are blind. [8] You have nothing to bring it, for all the forest is self-sufficient; if you burn it, cut, hack through it with a blade, it angrily repairs the swathe with thorns and weeds and fierce suckers. [9] Later there are good green leaves again, toiling, adjusting, breathing—forgetting you.

A. _____

_____

B. _____

_____

10. [1] The arguments for academic freedom are the same as those for freedom of speech, and they rest on the same foundation. [2] Here are the familiar words of John Stuart Mill:

> [3] If all mankind minus one were of one opinion, and only one person were of the contrary opinion, mankind would be no more justified in silencing that one person, than he, if he had the power, would be justified in silencing mankind. … the peculiar evil of silencing the expression of an opinion is, that it is robbing the human race; posterity as well as the existing generation; those who dissent from the opinion, still more than those who hold it. [4] If the opinion is right, they are deprived of the opportunity of exchanging error for truth: if wrong, they lose what is almost as great a benefit, the clearer perception and livelier impression of truth, produced by its collision with error.

[5] Man is a learning animal. [6] The state is an association the primary aim of which is the virtue and intelligence of the people. [7] Men learn by discussion, through the clash of opinion. [8] The best and most progressive society is that in which expression is freest. [9] Mill said, "There ought to exist the fullest liberty of professing and discussing, as a matter of ethical conviction, any doctrine, however immoral it may be considered." [10] The civilization we seek is the civilization of the dialogue, the civilization of the logos.

[11] In such a society the intelligent man and good citizen are identical. [12] The educational system does not aim at indoctrination in accepted values but at the improvement of society through the production of the intelligent man and the good citizen. [13] Education necessarily involves the critical examination of conflicting points of view; it cannot flourish in the absence of free inquiry and discussion.

A. _____

_____

B. _____

_____

Answers are on pages 248–249.

ANNOTATING: THE GOLD STANDARD OF SOURCE ANALYSIS

Get in the habit of annotating (i.e., exploring passages word by word and line by line).

Nothing—absolutely nothing—will unlock the rhetorical features of a source more efficiently than a thorough, insightful annotation. Good annotators habitually explore passages word by word, line by line, paragraph by paragraph. They mark up passages profusely, highlighting in some way all the rhetorical features they find. They take for granted that nothing in a well-written passage exists by accident, that good writers leave nothing to chance. Rather, everything is carefully chosen—the words, the sentences, the punctuation, even the footnotes, if any. Good writers labor over the order and content of paragraphs as well as the total structure of their work. Every bit of their prose has a point and purpose. In short, good writers are perfectionists who work hard to find the best words to put in the best order. And your job on the SAT Essay is to analyze what they've done.

Frankly, for some students annotating can be hard slog, at least at the beginning. But the good news is that you can train yourself to do it expeditiously, and before long find yourself reading with eye-popping awareness of the rhetoric that writers employ to build an argument, support claims, appeal to readers' emotions, and all the rest.

Under the pressure of time on SAT test day, you can't write out a complete annotation of the source before writing your essay. If you regularly write comments, underline ideas and words, and generally scrawl notes all over the things you read, however, the habit will vastly—and I mean *vastly*—improve your ability to analyze an SAT source quickly and efficiently. But, as with most skills, proficiency in annotation declines if you stop practicing. Because slipping out of the groove happens just like that, try to make annotation a part of every day from now until the SAT.

What follows is a source entitled "Our Bees, Ourselves: Bees and Colony Collapse" by Mark Winston, who makes the claim that the recent decline of the honeybee population is a catastrophe. The text on the left side of the page is accompanied by annotations on the right. As you read the source, observe that the annotations explain what Winston has done to convince readers of the seriousness of a problem that affects us all.

Around the world, honeybee colonies are dying in huge numbers: About one-third of hives collapse each year, a pattern going back a decade. [1] For bees and the plants they pollinate—as well as for beekeepers, farmers, honey lovers and everyone else who appreciates this marvelous social insect [2]—this is a catastrophe.

But in the midst of crisis can come learning. Honeybee collapse has much to teach us about how humans can avoid a similar fate, [3] brought on by the increasingly severe environmental perturbations that challenge [4] modern society.

Honeybee collapse has been particularly vexing [5] because there is no one cause,

[1] By citing a statistic as evidence to support the claim that honeybee hives are diminishing at a rapid rate, the writer begins to show that, indeed, a "catastrophe" is in progress.

[2] The writer's use of the phrase "marvelous social insect" subtly plays on the reader's emotions by suggesting that bees are not mere insects. Rather, they, like humans, are social creatures.

[3] The writer extends the parallel between bees and humans by claiming in this paragraph that by studying the decline of honeybee colonies humans can avoid a similar catastrophe.

[4] "Catastrophe," "crisis," "collapse"—this sequence of alarming words serves to evoke an emotional response in the reader by emphasizing the seriousness of the bees' plight. Additional usages such as "fate," "increasingly severe," and "challenge" add an ominous tone to the crises faced both by honeybees and ourselves.

[5] The writer's secondary claim— that the honeybee problem is "particularly vexing"—is explained and supported by a subsequent list of abuses—or mistakes—that have contributed to the crisis. That all the errors are related to man-made pesticides reinforces still more forcefully the writer's view that the fate of the honeybee and the fate of man are linked.

but rather a thousand little cuts. [6] The main elements include the compounding impact of pesticides applied to fields, as well as pesticides applied directly into hives to control mites; fungal, bacterial and viral pests and diseases; nutritional deficiencies caused by vast acreages of single-crop fields that lack diverse flowering plants; and, in the United States, commercial beekeeping itself, which disrupts colonies by moving most bees around the country multiple times each year to pollinate crops.

The real issue, [7] though, is not the volume of problems, but the interactions among them. Here we find a core lesson from the bees that we ignore at our peril: the concept of synergy, where one plus one equals three, or four, or more. A typical honeybee colony contains residue from more than 120 pesticides. Alone, each represents a benign dose. But together they form a toxic soup [8] of chemicals whose interplay can substantially reduce the effectiveness of bees' immune systems, making them more susceptible to diseases.

These findings provide the most sophisticated data set available for any species about synergies among pesticides and between pesticides and disease. The only human equivalent is research into pharmaceutical interactions with many prescription drugs showing harmful or fatal side effects when used together, particularly in patients who already are disease-compromised. Pesticides have medical impacts as potent as pharmaceuticals do, yet we know virtually nothing about their synergistic impacts on our health, or their interplay with human diseases. [9]

Observing the tumultuous demise of honeybees should alert us that our own well-being might be similarly threatened. [10] The honeybee is a remarkably resilient species that has thrived for 40 million years, and the widespread collapse of so

[6] The metaphor "a thousand little cuts" further highlights the enormity of the problem by implying that it will take more than just a Band-aid to solve.

[7] The writer abruptly changes his focus to the "real" issue. By distinguishing what the issue is not (it is "not the volume of problems") to what it is ("the interactions among them"), the writer begins to develop two earlier claims—first that we can learn a crucial lesson from the bees' experience with pesticides and, second, that it would be perilous to ignore what the bees can teach us.

[8] By joining "soup" and "toxic" into the same phrase the writer has added an alarming emotional dimension to the discussion of pesticides and their harmful effects.

[9] Continuing to develop the claim that bees' experience can be instructive to humans, the writer compares research into the disease that has decimated honeybee colonies to research on drugs for treating human diseases.

[10] By referring to the history of bees—here in the context of discussing the bees' resiliency—the writer develops his argument in two ways: He continues to develop the idea that humans must undertake studies of bees' long-term survival, and he again reminds readers of his claim that humans and bees have much in common.

many colonies presents a clear message: We must demand that our regulatory authorities require studies on how exposure to low dosages of combined chemicals may affect human health before approving compounds.

Bees also provide some clues to how we may build a more collaborative relationship with the services that ecosystems can provide. Beyond honeybees, there are thousands of wild bee species that could offer some of the pollination service needed for agriculture. [11] Yet feral bees—that is, bees not kept by beekeepers—also are threatened by factors similar to those afflicting honeybees: heavy pesticide use, destruction of nesting sites by overly intensive agriculture and a lack of diverse nectar and pollen sources thanks to highly effective weed killers, which decimate the unmanaged plants that bees depend on for nutrition.

Recently, my laboratory at Simon Fraser University conducted a study on farms that produce canola oil that illustrated the profound value of wild bees. [12] We discovered that crop yields, and thus profits, are maximized if considerable acreages of cropland are left uncultivated to support wild pollinators.

A variety of wild plants means a healthier, more diverse bee population, which will then move to the planted fields next door in larger and more active numbers. Indeed, farmers who planted their entire field would earn about $27,000 in profit per farm, whereas those who left a third unplanted for bees to nest and forage in would earn $65,000 on a farm of similar size. [13]

Such logic goes against conventional wisdom that fields and bees alike can be uniformly micromanaged. The current challenges faced by managed honeybees and wild bees remind us that we can manage too much. Excessive cultivation, chemical use and habitat destruction

[11] By expanding the discussion to include feral bees, the writer portrays the decline of bees as even more dire than stated earlier and reinforces his claim that the indiscriminate use of pesticides is the major culprit.

[12] Here the writer makes a significant stylistic switch. He concludes a relatively objective presentation of facts about bee colony decline and begins a first-person account of a research study at his university. In making this change, the writer presents evidence drawn from an authoritative source—a research lab—and abruptly refocuses the essay on certain farmers who benefit from the presence of wild bees on their land. The combination of factual material and a summary of the writer's own research provides still more compelling evidence to support his claim.

[13] The writer cites statistics as evidence to support the claim that farmers' profits grow when some of their cropland is left uncultivated. This assertion leads directly into one of the writer's major claims—that because we have overcultivated the land and overmanaged the bee population, we must bear the blame for the bees' decline.

eventually destroy the very organisms that could be our partners.

And this insight goes beyond mere agricultural economics. There is a lesson in the decline of bees about how to respond to the most fundamental challenges facing contemporary human societies. We can best meet our own needs if we maintain a balance with nature—a balance that is as important to our health and prosperity as it is to the bees. [14]

> **[14]** By referring to a claim made early in the passage that the decline of bees can teach us a lesson, the writer makes a final appeal to the reader's sense of reason, claiming that "a balance with nature" is our best course of action.

A Pep Talk from Your Coach

NOTE

If you are already a competent annotator or expect to readily become one, please skip "A Pep Talk from Your Coach."

Okay, okay. I hear you. I hear some of you sighing and muttering under your breath, "No way!" "Are you kidding?" "Zoiks, that's beyond me," "Fuggetaboutit."

If that's you, please listen up:

Lots of SAT test-takers fresh from their first brush with annotation find themselves thinking Wow! That's hard. Well, it's true that no one says that annotating a passage is a cinch. But neither is it that hard. Just think positive thoughts. Make up your mind not to get caught in a web of defeatism. Instead, believe that you can and will do it. Sure, it'll take practice, but that's exactly what this book is for—to help you overcome doubt and master this annotation stuff.

Remember, too, that you're not aiming to become a champion annotator. Annotation, after all, is only a device to help you write a better essay. Furthermore, once you've annotated a few sources, you'll discover that the content of an essay virtually takes shape right before your eyes. All you need to do is sort through your annotations to pick out which rhetorical elements the writer uses most often and then choose those that do the most to strengthen the writer's argument. Once you've done that—voila!—which rhetorical elements to discuss in your essay will be readily apparent. Then, the only major decision you're left with is to decide which element to write about first, second, third, and so on.

To illustrate how that process works, here's a thumbnail guide to writing an essay based on the annotations for the passage on honeybees:

- Six of the 14 annotations relate to reasoning techniques—that is, to evidence the writer used to support various claims.
- An essay should certainly mention the use of various kinds of data and the findings of a research study.
- Most of the other annotations point out the emotional impact made by the writer's choice of words and images. Some stress the seriousness of the honeybee crisis, and others pertain to the writer's observations about the interrelationship between honeybees and human beings.
- A major portion of the essay, therefore, should analyze the meaning, purpose, and effect of the writer's language.

PRACTICE IN ANNOTATION

While analyzing a source, you'll probably locate with ease statistics and examples the writer used to back up claims. Instances of persuasive word usage or emotional appeal may take a bit more effort to spot. Explaining their purpose and effects, though, will require thought, and until you've had practice, you may struggle a bit at first to find the right words to describe clearly and cogently how each rhetorical strategy contributes to the persuasiveness of the writer's argument.

If that's a concern of yours, the following list of sample annotations is sure to help.

Sample Annotations: The Language of Source Analysis

(A.K.A. ... shhh, "The Annotations Crib Sheet" ... shhh)

As you've already seen, the SAT Essay prompt suggests several kinds of evidence to look for, but it doesn't tell you how to put those suggestions into words.

The list below is meant to help you find the right words. Each suggestion consists of carefully worded but generic annotation that can be used verbatim or adapted for your essay. Because every source is different, references to the specific content of sources have been omitted. In their place you'll find clusters of letters such as *AAA* and *ZZZ*, each one representing an idea—one that you must draw from whatever source you happen to be annotating.

- **Evidence Such as Examples and Facts, to Back Up Claims**

    The writer uses an example of XXX as evidence to support the claim that YYY ...

    The author uses an example of ZZZ as evidence to inform a subsequent claim that AAA ...

    Providing evidence from authoritative sources (BBB) adds legitimacy to the claim that CCC ...

    The writer continues to draw evidence from authorities cited above. He reiterates this evidence to emphasize the point that DDD ...

    The presentation of facts and evidence backs up the claim at the end of the paragraph that says "EEE ..."

- **Reasoning to Connect Claims**

    The writer reasons that if FFF, then GGG is valid. HHH is also used as evidence to support her previous claim that I I I ...

    The argument concludes by recalling JJJ ...

    The writer synthesizes multiple sources of evidence (e.g., the previously mentioned KKK) as part of reasoning that concludes that the decrease in LLL has implications outside MMM ...

    The writer then connects this point to his subsequent claim that NNN. She goes on to cite another authoritative source as further evidence for OOO ...

- **Evidence to Develop Ideas**

    By first discussing PPP and then moving into a discussion of QQQ, the writer is able to build his argument about RRR ...

    This statistic is used as evidence to support the claim that SSS, which leads into the writer's point that TTT ...

The writer moves from evoking UUU to reassuring readers that VVV …

Johnson cites data commissioned from an authoritative source (WWW) to lend credibility to his subsequent point that there is XXX …

The writer cites survey data as evidence to support his point in the previous paragraph that YYY. This point and supporting evidence contribute to the writer's central claim that ZZZ …

The writer again uses data, this time from AAA to support her earlier claim that BBB. Here, her evidence links CCC to DDD and "EEE" …

By referring to this report again, this time in the context of discussing FFF, the writer further supports the point he has just made …

The writer contrasts GGG with HHH, which is intended to frame a critical choice between I I I and JJJ …

■ **Stylistic or Persuasive Elements**

The writer compares KKK to the effects of LLL, using imagery that dramatizes the MMM …

The author makes a stylistic choice here, contrasting a "NNN" with OOO. These words allow her to characterize PPP and to depict QQQ as an RRR …

To highlight the irony and gravity of SSS, the writer juxtaposes TTT to UUU …

■ **Word Choice**

The descriptive words in this sentence add visual intensity, evoking VVV …

Lichtenstein chooses her words carefully in this paragraph in order to shape readers' perception and bolster her claims. For example, she argues WWW and also suggests how XXX by using the word "YYY" to describe ZZZ …

The author uses precisely chosen, powerful words to characterize AAA as a BBB …

This juxtaposition of words underscores the writer's claim that CCC signifies DDD and thereby creates a compelling appeal to readers' emotions …

■ **Emotional Appeals Meant to Add Power to Expressed Ideas**

The suggestion of EEE and the notion of FFF are also designed to evoke an emotional reaction in the reader …

The use of rhetorical questions encourages readers to consider GGG and what HHH inspires …

By returning to the introduction's description of an III, the writer creates another emotional appeal—this one to JJJ …

That KKK happens, as evidenced over the course of the writer's argument, serves as the final appeal to the reader's emotions …

The allusion to LLL creates a compelling appeal to readers' emotions …

The writer uses the final sentences of the passage as an appeal to fear and national pride by warning that unless MMM, we will NNN. These lines serve as an emotional call to action and raise the stakes of the argument the writer is making.

These are just a few examples of how text analyses might be worded. There is no limit to the number of other ways to convey these and similar ideas. As you practice writing annotations and essays, you'll no doubt invent many variations of your own. If ever you get stuck, however, turn back to this list. It might start a flow of ideas or help you identify the rhetorical features in the source you must analyze.

Your Turn to Annotate

Now it's time for you to try your hand at annotating a source, this one about the late South African leader Nelson Mandela, adapted from "Bigger Than South Africa," *Columbia Magazine*, Winter 2013–14, pp. 29–30. The author, Mamadou Diouf, makes the claim that Mandela had earned a legacy for all humanity to honor for decades to come.

Here's a recommendation: Read the passage at least twice—first to see what it's about. Then, during the second reading, begin to jot down whatever you notice about the author's claims and the evidence used to support them. As always, look for

- evidence such as examples and facts to back up claims
- reasoning to connect claims
- evidence used to develop ideas
- stylistic or persuasive elements such as word choice and emotional appeals meant to add power to expressed ideas
- important rhetorical elements not listed here

The text of the source appears on the left. Use the adjoining blank space to write your comments. Assign each comment a number that corresponds with a number you've inserted in the passage itself. If you run out of room, please add your own paper. If you get stuck, turn back a couple of pages to "Sample Annotations" for help and inspiration.

The legacy of Nelson Mandela will be with us for decades to come. The reasons are linked to his own history, to the way he understood power, and to the way he led his long-divided country. This is a man who lived under apartheid, a man who had been locked up for twenty-seven years. Of course, he did not solve all the problems South Africa faced, but Mandela is also bigger than South Africa. He's bigger than the continent. His legacy is a legacy for all humanity to honor.

This is a man who came out of jail and was ready to talk to the people who jailed him. He was ready—because he was mostly a man of the 1960s, an era defined by radicalism, and you see this driving the charter of the African National Congress. Out of jail, he was able to adjust to a completely new moment—adjust as an individual, but also as a politician. And

Write your comments here:

while most people predicted bloodshed, Mandela single-handedly ensured that South Africa would not go through a racial civil war; that a space was open for negotiation; that a space was open for compromise; that a space was open to invent a new world.

Mandela was behind the idea that it was possible to invent a new world. That it was possible to turn enemies not into friends, but into partners. That it was possible to pull together different memories and multiple heritages to avoid the tensions and confrontations of a history of segregation, violence, and systematic spoliation. Insisting strongly on not forgetting, he advocated forgiveness. He believed that it was possible to reinvent South Africa. A new and ideal South Africa. He kept saying that South Africa was a complex country, and that reconciliation was the only appropriate response to the challenge the country was facing—the only way things should be done.

The second element, probably the most important of his legacy, is that this man decided to serve one term and leave office. This was a revolution in Africa. He could have stayed until his death. Because he was already a myth. The message he conveyed was a powerful message. By stepping down he showed that he didn't believe in the notion of the charismatic leader, a messiah destined to eternally lead his people. Even when he left power, he remained the person to go to in a moment of crisis, the person to go to when you needed advice, the person to go to when you needed voice to mobilize. Mandela's is a very powerful voice, but it's the voice of a democratic politician, of an icon who behaves like an ordinary citizen. It's the voice of a man who was able to say, at a point, "I have been too long in jail. I have done what I had to do to help the transition. Now I'm too old to remain president. I have to pass the baton to a new generation."

The third element, which seems very trivial but is very important, is that he decided to drop his suits and ties—the formal uniform of the president—and to wear his colorful shirts. It signaled a return to the state of an ordinary citizen of the world, a return home to live his life as an ordinary man. After working for the future of a nation, after setting the foundation of the future of South Africa, he decided to revisit his past and rediscover a life he hadn't lived. After the long march to freedom, he began a long march back to all he had missed because of the struggle to free South Africa—the twenty-seven years in jail and the challenges of the transition from apartheid to the rainbow nation.

Politically, of course, we can discuss some of the choices he made. But something that will remain with us, and remain with history, is not only the way he ensured a peaceful transition in a context of violence, but also the way he left power—and held himself as a powerful, wise man, universally acclaimed as the most important world leader from the mid-twentieth century to the present.

Well, you've done it. Congratulations!

Now take five. When you come back compare your annotations with those of an experienced annotator—printed below. Because your notes are not identical to hers doesn't mean yours are wrong. Different, yes, but perhaps full of perfectly valid observations. In the end, what counts is that you have accurately identified and explained important persuasive features used by the writer.

The legacy of Nelson Mandela will be with us for decades to come. [1] The reasons are linked to his own history, to the way he understood power, and to the way he led his long-divided country. This is a man who lived under apartheid, a man who had been locked up for twenty-seven years. Of course, he did not solve all the problems South Africa faced, but Mandela is also

[1] In the first sentence, the author Mamadou Diouf claims that Mandela's legacy will last for decades, and supports the claim with details about Mandela's life, including the fact that he lived under apartheid and spent twenty-seven years in jail. These, along with other biographical data support the claim that follows at the end of the paragraph that Mandela has a legacy "for all humanity to honor."

bigger than South Africa. [2] He's bigger than the continent. His legacy is a legacy for all humanity to honor.

[3] This is a man who came out of jail and was ready to talk to the people who jailed him. He was ready—because he was mostly a man of the 1960s, an era defined by radicalism, and you see this driving the charter of the African National Congress. Out of jail, he was able to adjust to a completely new moment—adjust as an individual, but also as a politician. And while most people predicted bloodshed, Mandela single-handedly ensured that South Africa would not go through a racial civil war; [4] that a space was open for negotiation; that a space was open for compromise; that a space was open to invent a new world.

[2] To suggest Mandela's stature and to dramatize the historical significance of the man, Diouf uses powerful hyperbolic language. Mandela is described as "bigger" than both the country of South Africa and the entire African continent. This emotional appeal is heightened still further by the last sentence of the paragraph in which the writer argues that Mandela deserves a legacy for "all humanity to honor."

[3] Diouf continues to provide evidence that Mandela holds an exalted place in history by citing more specific examples of his achievements and personal attributes both inside and outside of jail. To highlight Manela's extraordinary qualities still further, Diouf contrasts him with "most people"—that is the people who predicted a bloody civil war in South Africa. Not Mandela, who "single-handedly" prevented it.

[4] Using a style of writing made up of rhythmic and repetitious phrases—"that a space was open"—(used three times in succession), the writer not only emphasizes Mandela's openness but chooses a kind of poetic language that echoes biblical cadences, thereby casting Mandela in a mythical, if not quasi-divine light. Indeed, the author subsequently claims that Mandela "was already a myth." [See # 6 below] Such stylistic choices seem designed specifically to spawn readers' admiration and awe of Mandela.

[5] Mandela was behind the idea that it was possible to invent a new world. That it was possible to turn enemies not into friends, but into partners. That it was possible to pull together different memories and multiple heritages to avoid the tensions and confrontations of a history of segregation, violence, and systematic spoliation. Insisting strongly on not forgetting, he advocated forgiveness. He believed that it was possible to reinvent South Africa. A new and ideal South Africa. He kept saying that South Africa was a complex country, and that reconciliation was the only appropriate response to the challenge the country was facing—the only way things should be done.

[6] The second element, probably the most important of his legacy, is that this man decided to serve one term and leave office. This was a revolution in Africa. He could have stayed until his death. Because he was already a myth. The message he conveyed was a powerful message. By stepping down he showed that he didn't believe in the notion of the charismatic leader, a messiah destined to eternally lead his people. Even when he left power, he remained the person to go to in a moment of crisis, the person to go to when you needed advice, the person to go to when you needed voice to mobilize. Mandela's is a very powerful voice, but it's the voice of a democratic politician, of an icon who behaves like an ordinary citizen. It's the voice of a man who was able to say, at a point, "I have been too long in jail. I have done what I had to do to help the transition. Now I'm too old to remain president. I have to pass the baton to a new generation." **[7]**

[8] The third element, which seems very trivial but is very important, is that he decided to drop his suits and ties—the formal uniform of the president—and to wear his colorful shirts. It signaled a return to the state of an ordinary citizen of the

[5] With additional repetition, Diouf further enhances Mandela's reputation as a visionary leader. The recurring use of the word "possible" in the next paragraph and the repeated reference to "South Africa" are meant to suggest that Mandela and South Africa are virtually one and the same.

[6] By first showing Mandela's stature and then discussing his modesty with the claim that Mandela "didn't believe in the notion of the charismatic leader, a messiah . . . ," the writer elevates Mandela still further, to "a myth," to "an icon," virtually to the level of a secular saint. Indeed, the writer presents a list of characteristics meant to prove how accessible and generous Mandela had been to the people, or, as the writer claims repeatedly, Mandela was "the person to go to" for support and advice.

The author's regular use of repetition ultimately has the effect of portraying Mandela as larger than life, a notion introduced by the title of the piece—"Bigger than South Africa"—and amply supported by evidence throughout.

[7] The writer quotes Mandela to underscore the claim that he was a man of the people. Mandela's words create a compelling appeal to the readers' emotions, in the end revealing more about his character and values than several secondhand descriptions.

[8] The writer's choice of an inconsequential detail about

world, a return home to live his life as an ordinary man. After working for the future of a nation, after setting the foundation of the future of South Africa, he decided to revisit his past and rediscover a life he hadn't lived. After the long march to freedom, he began a long march back to all he had missed because of the struggle to free South Africa—the twenty-seven years in jail and the challenges of the transition from apartheid to the rainbow nation.

Politically, of course, we can discuss some of the choices he made. But something that will remain with us, and remain with history, is not only the way he ensured a peaceful transition in a context of violence, but also the way he left power—and held himself as a powerful, wise man, universally acclaimed as the most important world leader from the mid-twentieth century to the present.

Mandela's clothes serves to shape readers' perception of Mandela's personality. It also gives a boost to the writer's claim that Mandela, although an illustrious historical figure, was an ordinary man—like you and me—at heart.

The writer's language and ideas throughout the passage are meant to a touch readers' emotions. Yet the passage is presented in a logical, highly-structured way. Two successive paragraphs near the end, for example, begin with "The second element," and "The third element. . . ." This contradiction between content and form adds a touch of legitimacy to the author's glorification of his subject, Mandela.

ANOTHER KIND OF ANNOTATION

Here's hoping that you are satisfied with your annotation. If not, you may be feeling the uncertainty that grips many first-time annotators. But listen: You've probably learned something and you are bound to do better the next time.

In the meantime, you might try an altogether different approach to annotation, one with no right or wrong or good or bad about it. Your notes can't be evaluated in the usual way because they come directly from your natural impulses as a social being. What that means is that, instead of analyzing the rhetoric of a source, you respond to the text of the source as though the writer is sitting across the table from you at Starbucks. As he talks, you sip your high-calorie peppermint-mocha frappuccino. As you listen, the questions, comments, and feelings that course through your brain become your annotations.

Of course, this so-called "Starbucks Annotation" is not a substitute for the real thing. But it's a start, a place to familiarize yourself with a source and get warmed up for taking on the challenge of a full-fledged analysis.

Don't forget that an annotation is not an end in itself but just one step in the process of getting ready to write an SAT Essay. With that in mind, what rhetorical features might you discuss in an essay written about the passage on Nelson Mandela?

Here are a few possibilities: Analyze the writer's use of reasoning to support his claim that Nelson Mandela deserves a legacy "for all humanity to honor." Or focus on the writer's choice of biographical details—how, for instance, Mandela endured decades in prison and later prevented a civil war in South Africa. Another fertile topic is how the writer creates emotional effects to add power to his argument.

Throughout the passage the writer provides evidence that Mandela was more than just another hero. He portrays Mandela as an ordinary man who rejected the trappings of power, deciding, for instance, to wear colorful shirts instead of a suit and tie. Such fine points cause readers—presumably ordinary people themselves—to identify with the man and marvel at him.

The writer's use of sentence structure also deserves analysis. Several instances of repetition highlight Mandela's accomplishments. Consider, for instance, the rhetorical purpose of a sentence constructed this way: "Mandela single-handedly ensured that South Africa would not go through a racial civil war; that a space was open for negotiation; that a space was open for compromise; that a space was open to invent a new world." Because wordiness and repetition are usually considered stylistic flaws, why didn't the writer say more concisely, "Mandela single-handedly ensured … that a space was open for negotiation, compromise, and invention of a new world?" Presumably, the writer repeated the phrase "that a space was open" for effect—to stress the depth and breadth of Mandela's vision. Repeating the word "open" underscores an important feature of Mandela's character.

Mini-Workout in Annotating Sources

Directions: This Mini-Workout consists of two sources. Read each one carefully and consider how each author uses facts, examples, and other evidence to support his position on an issue. Note the use of reasoning to develop ideas, and take into account any significant stylistic or rhetorical features (e.g., choice of words, appeals to emotion, or any other features you choose) that serve to strengthen his point of view on the subject.

Write your annotations in the blank space on the right. Assign each comment a number that corresponds with a number you've noted in the text of the passage itself. Add your own paper, if necessary.

Source 1

In the following passage, the author Malcolm Gladwell argues that *in the 1990s greater understanding of America's homeless population helped to ease some problems associated with homelessness but did not solve them.* Note the use of reasoning to develop ideas and take into account any significant stylistic or rhetorical features (e.g., choice of words, appeals to emotion, or any other features you choose) that serve to strengthen his point of view on the subject.

Do not explain whether you agree or disagree with the author's views. Rather, explain how he builds an argument to persuade his audience.

Write your annotations in the blank space on the right. Assign each comment a number that corresponds with a number you've noted in the text of the passage itself. Add your own paper, if necessary.

(Adapted from Malcolm Gladwell, "Million Dollar Murray," in *What the Dog Saw*, Back Bay Press, 2009, pp. 183–185)

In the 1980's, when homelessness first surfaced as a national issue, the assumption was that the vast majority of the homeless were in the same state of semipermanent distress. It was an assumption that bred despair: if there were so many homeless, what could be done to help them? In the early 1990s, a young Boston College graduate student named Dennis Culhane lived in a shelter in Philadelphia for seven weeks as part of the research for his dissertation. A few months later he went back and was surprised to discover that he couldn't find any of the people he had recently spent so much time with. "It made me realize that most of these people were getting on with their own lives," he said.

Culhane then put together a database—the first of its kind—to track who was coming in and out of the shelter system. What he discovered profoundly changed the way homelessness is understood. "We found that eighty percent of the homeless were in and out really quickly," he said. "The most common length of time that someone is homeless is one day. And the second most common length is two days. And they never come back. Anyone who ever has to stay in a shelter involuntarily knows that all you think about is how to make sure you never come back."

The next 10 percent were what Culhane calls episodic users. They would come for three weeks at a time, and return periodically, particularly in the winter. They were quite young, and they were often heavy drug users. But the last 10 percent interested Culhane the most. They were chronically homeless and lived in the shelters, sometimes for years at a time. Many were older, mentally ill or physically disabled. When we think about homelessness as a social problem—people sleeping on sidewalks, aggressively panhandling, lying drunk in doorways,

Write your comments here:

huddled on subway grates and under bridges—it's this group we have in mind. Culhane's database suggested that New York City had a quarter of a million people who were homeless at some point in the previous half decade—a surprisingly high number. But only about twenty-five hundred were *chronically* homeless.

This group costs the health-care and social-services systems far more than anyone had ever anticipated. New York spent at least $62 million annually to shelter just those 2500 hard-core homeless. "It costs twenty-four thousand dollars a year for one of these shelter beds," Culhane said. "We're talking about a cot eighteen inches away from the next cot." Boston Health Care for the Homeless Program, a leading service group for the homeless in Boston, recently tracked the medical expenses of 119 chronically homeless people. Over five years, 33 people died and seven more were sent to nursing homes. The group accounted for 18,834 emergency-room visits—at a minimum of $1,000 a visit.

"If its a medical admission, it's likely to be the guys with the really complex pneumonia," James Dunford, San Diego's emergency medical director and the author of the observational study, said. "They are drunk and they get vomit in their lungs and develop a lung abscess, and they get hypothermia on top of that, because they've been out in the rain. They end up in the intensive care unit with complicated medical infections. These are the guys who typically get hit by cars and buses and trucks and are very prone to just falling down and cracking their heads open. It's the guy with a head injury who ends up costing you at least $50,000. Meanwhile, they're going through alcohol withdrawal and have devastating liver disease that only adds to their inability to fight infections. There is no end to the issues. We run up big lab fees, and the nurses want to quit, because they see the same guys come in over and over, and all we are doing is making them capable of walking down the block."

Suggested answers on pages 250–252.

Source 2

Directions: Read the following source carefully and consider how the author, Joe Nocera, uses facts, examples, and other evidence to support his claim *that for-profit colleges are essential to higher education in America.* Note the use of reasoning to develop ideas, and take into account any significant stylistic or rhetorical features— *e.g.,* choice of words, appeals to emotion (or any other features you choose)—that serve to strengthen his point of view on the subject.

Do not explain whether you agree or disagree with the author's views. Rather, explain how he builds an argument to persuade his audience.

Write your annotations in the blank space on the right. Assign each comment a number that corresponds with a number you've noted in the text of the passage itself. Add your own paper, if necessary.

(Adapted from Joe Nocera, "How to Improve on an F," *New York Times Magazine,* September 9, 2011, pp. 64–65)

The for-profit college industry makes its money by recruiting students—overwhelmingly poor and working-class students—who must draw from the federal till to pay tuition. In many cases, as much as 90 percent of the revenue of a for-profit college company comes from the federal government, in the form of Pell Grants and student loans. The more students the companies enroll, the more federal money they get—and the more profit they make.

This has led to a widespread view that the for-profits will do just about anything to get that federal money. Allegations abound that for-profit recruiters use high-pressure sales pitches and inflated claims about career placement to increase student enrollment, regardless of the applicants' qualifications. Although for-profit colleges enroll 12 percent of the nation's college students, they soak up about 25 percent of

Write your comments here:

the federal government's student-aid budget.

Many critics conclude that the only way to "fix" for-profit education is to get rid of it entirely. This approach obscures what really ought to be the most important fact about the industry: the country can't afford to put it out of business. On the contrary, America needs it—and needs it to succeed—desperately.

To start with the obvious, a college education has never been more necessary for a decent life in America. Many manufacturing jobs now demand a level of skill and education that virtually requires a college degree. A lot of white-collar employers won't even consider a job applicant who hasn't graduated from college.

And yet for the poor and working class, that education is not easy to attain. State university systems have become increasingly expensive. Community colleges are terribly overcrowded. The schools most capable of meeting the country's growing educational needs are the for-profits. In the decade beginning in 1998, enrollment in public and private universities went up less than 25 percent. Enrollment in the for-profit colleges, meanwhile, was up 236 percent.

What's more, the traditional university isn't really set up to educate a person who has a full-time job. The for-profits can offer class times that are convenient for students, rather than for professors. They can offer online classes, which many traditional universities have been reluctant—or unable—to dive into. They pay professors to teach, not conduct research. A well-run for-profit college could teach its nonprofit counterparts a thing or two about efficiency and innovation. That's the part of the profit motive that grades well.

The bad part, of course, is that capitalists will always behave more or less like greyhounds chasing a mechanical rabbit, motivated by whatever incentives are put in front of them. Just as the federal government created perverse incentives that helped bring about the subprime crisis, so have the government's rules for the for-profit industry unwittingly led to its excesses. When the industry reaps all the profit from student loans and the taxpayer has to pick up the losses, how can we be surprised when things turn out badly? What is needed now is creative, enlightened policy-making that will change the incentives so that good outcomes matter more than sheer volume.

Recently, the Department of Education issued a series of regulations that are supposed to do just that. Unfortunately, the new rules are cumbersome, complicated—and more than a little punitive. The most controversial of them, known as the gainful employment rule, is built in part on the actual earnings of all the graduates of a given for-profit college. Yet, astonishingly, the schools themselves are never allowed to see the income numbers of individual graduates because the government considers them private. Rules like that aren't likely to help fix anything.

There is an easier way. Robert Silberman, the chairman and chief executive of Strayer Education, widely regarded as one of the better for-profit companies, suggests replacing the plethora of regulations with two simple changes. First, he says, the government should force the for-profits to share in the losses when a student defaults. And second, the government should set up a national eligibility test to screen out students who lack the skills to attend college. Would there still be defaults? Of course. But plenty of students at non-profit universities default, too. Silberman's solution would help ensure that both the government and for-profit companies are taking smarter risks on the students they enroll and educate.

There is nothing inherently wrong with the idea of for-profit education. The for-profits have flaws, but so do the non-profits, with their bloated infrastructure, sky-high tuition, out-of-control athletic programs, and resistance to change. In a country where education matters so much, we need them both.

Suggested answers are on pages 253–256.

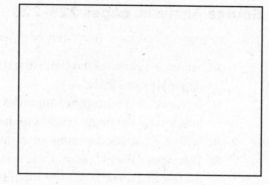

ANSWER KEY TO MINI-WORKOUTS

Connotation, pages 214–215

1. *naiveté.* To count on the veracity of politicians, Martina must be both innocent and naive. *Innocence* is the more general word, implying, among other things, a kind of childishness, immaturity, gullibility, and lack of experience. *Naiveté*, on the other hand, also suggests an inability to interpret reality, a trait that shapes Martina's view of political candidates.

2. *fragile.* The vases' fragility puts them in danger because they are old and brittle. That they are *delicate*, too, may describe their condition but might just as easily refer to their design.

3. *bashing. Bashing* rings of demolishing and destroying—just what a debater aims to do to an opponent's argument. *Criticizing* is more diffuse and, hence, far weaker.

4. *The data revolution.* A phrase containing the word *revolution*, although overused in everyday parlance, is bound to suggest a drastic change from the present. The intent of the writer is to do just that—to predict "untold benefits" to people in the future. The alternate phrase, "*The rise of data,*" lacks the vehemence of a data *revolution.*

5. *rebuffed.* To have an invitation rebuffed implies a forceful refusal or resistance. Declining to go to the prom is a far gentler and more humane way to say "Get lost!" No wonder Olivia wept.

6. *magnitude.* The ambiguity of the word *amount* leaves the reader guessing whether China has changed a little or a lot. In contrast, *magnitude* strongly implies vast, significant change.

7. *mind-blowing.* In this day and age, to hear that terrorists abandoned their cause is more than a surprise. It's mind-blowing, or unbelievable.

8. *immortal.* The word *immortal* means more than just *well-known* or famous. Fame is fleeting, immortality lasts forever.

9. *transfixed by.* To write eight novels with similar plots suggests more than an ordinary attraction to the subject. Rather, it suggests a passion for, even a fixation on, tales of love and murder.

10. *longed for.* The phrase suggests a deeper yearning than a simple *desire* or wish for pasta and beer.

Source Analysis, pages 223–228

These are suggested answers. Yours may be different but equally valid.

1. **A.** Sentence 1 contains the claim that the Omaha tribe controlled the fur trade on the upper Missouri River.

   B. Sentence 2 supports the claim with a fact: Foreign fur traders were kept from doing business on the upper reaches of the river.

2. **A.** Sentence 1 states the claim—that the statistic has become infamous.

   B. The writer calls 107 percent rise in tuition and fees "astounding." That, along with the fact that no other budget expense has risen as much explains why "infamous" is an apt description.

3. **A.** The writer's primary claim does not appear in the paragraph until sentence 6.

   B. Except for a phrase ("What man or woman can deny that …") in sentence 7, the paragraph contains nothing but facts that portray the river as "remarkable."

4. **A.** In sentence 6 the writer uses logic to make two related claims: (a) a country's literature depends on the character of its people, and (b) therefore, England's people must possess fiery qualities that are evident in English poetry.

   B. To support these claims, the writer makes a stylistic choice—to use a metaphor that associates poetry with heat, or fire. This alludes to sentence 1, which points out an apparent disconnect between the stereotypical "cold" nature of the English and the "heat" of their poetry. To explain the contradiction logically, the writer ascribes the warmth of English poetry not to the alleged reserve of stereotypical English men and women but to a quality in their "national character."

5. **A.** The primary claim in the passage—that the sea below the surface is Noisy—appears in sentence 2.

   B. The writer draws evidence from the results of studies that used listening devices such as hydrophones. The carefully chosen phrase "extraordinary uproar" allows the writer to shape the readers' perception of conditions deep beneath the waves. Additional noises vividly described with images such as "mewing sounds," "shrieks," and "moans" vividly emphasize the variety of sounds and bolsters the writer's claim.

6. **A.** The second clause in sentence 3 makes the claim that America has the ability to control terrorism.

   B. Sentences 1 and 2 argue that the values that Americans hold dear ironically make the country easy prey for terrorists. The writer juxtaposes that idea with the strongly worded claim that follows in sentence 3, and then, alluding to the attacks of 9/11—always appealing to readers' emotions—itemizes in a series of no-nonsense, precise sentences the anti-terrorist actions taken by the federal government, thereby creating a compelling appeal to readers' emotions—in particular, to patriotic feelings of pride in America. The assertion that foreign terrorists have been warned not to mess with us serves as a climactic appeal to the readers' emotions.

7. **A.** Sentence 4 comes closest to stating the writer's major claim.

  B. The claim is supported most directly by the last part of sentence 8, which says that all novelists have "acquired the basic canons of their art … from Cervantes." Historical background provided by the first three sentences provides evidence that prior to Cervantes no one wrote novels. As part of the reasoning to prove that Cervantes's work was a turning point of literary history, the writer names several novelists who followed and were influenced by him.

8. **A.** In the first clause of sentence 1 the writer claims that the question "Is college … worthwhile?" has an answer.

  B. In the remainder of the passage, the writer provides the answer, especially in sentence 2, which consists of a list of five identically structured phrases, each citing a different benefit of a college education. The cumulative effect of the list creates a compelling argument that, yes, a college education is worthwhile. Sentence 3 provides further support for the claim, and the use of a rhetorical question (sentence 4) causes the reader to consider how an informed and humane teacher or professor can indeed stimulate one's thinking.

9. **A.** The writer maintains that the natural world, represented by a "wood"—what we ordinarily call "the woods"—is alive just as humans are alive, but the style and substance of natural life differ drastically from ours. This claim is spelled out most directly in sentence 3, but it pervades the rest of the passage as well.

  B. Throughout the passage the writer uses an extended analogy to compare and contrast two kinds of life: human life and the life found in nature. This device enables the writer to depict human life as troubled and hectic, as suggested particularly by evidence in sentence 3, and natural life as just the opposite—serene and well-balanced. To highlight this difference, the writer characterizes human life with unfavorable words such as "restless," "panting," "fears," "hoarse," and "reproach" while choosing salutary words and phrases such as "coolness," "self-sufficient," "the sun and the wind," and "good green leaves" to describe nature's qualities. In sentences 5 and 6 the writer supports his claim still further by asserting that humans must strive to "attain the kingdom of heaven," while a tree, simply by being a tree, is already there in both the physical and spiritual sense.

10. **A.** The first sentence of the passage articulates the writer's claim that arguments for academic freedom are no different from arguments for free speech. Equating the two allows the writer to express his views on academic freedom by focusing on freedom of speech.

  B. Quoting the eminent philosopher, John Stewart Mill, on the harm wrought by suppressing free speech, the writer provides authoritative evidence that supports subsequent claims in sentences 7, 10, and 13 that learning cannot flourish without free inquiry and examination of conflicting points of view. The primary claim is bolstered still further by another quotation by Mill (sentence 9), stating that society is ethically bound to discuss every issue, whether moral or not. Then, echoing and also supporting his initial claim that equates free speech and academic freedom, the writer asserts in sentence 11 that in a society committed to open expression of ideas the intelligent man and the good citizen are identical, or to put it another way, academic freedom and free speech foster good citizenship.

Annotating Sources, pages 241–247

SOURCE 1

Your annotations will almost certainly be different from those you'll find here. Different, yes, but not necessarily wrong. In fact, yours may be full of perfectly valid observations that accurately identify and explain important persuasive features used by the writer. What ultimately matters is that your annotations would serve you well if you were to write an SAT Essay based on this source.

[1] In the 1980's, when homelessness first surfaced as a national issue, the assumption was that the vast majority of the homeless were in the same state of semipermanent distress. It was an assumption that bred despair: if there were so many homeless, what could be done to help them? [2] In the early 1990s, a young Boston College graduate student named Dennis Culhane lived in a shelter in Philadelphia for seven weeks as part of the research for his dissertation. A few months later he went back and was surprised to discover that he couldn't find any of the people he had recently spent so much time with. "It made me realize that most of these people were getting on with their own lives," he said. [3]

Culhane then put together a database— the first of its kind—to track who was coming in and out of the shelter system. [4] What he discovered profoundly changed

[1] Historical facts about homelessness lead directly to the claim that the public's assumptions about homelessness "bred despair." A rhetorical question (i.e., a question with no answer) makes plain why despair evolved.

[2] The writer begins to build an argument that assumptions about long-term homelessness were faulty. In short, the homelessness problem was less bleak than previously thought. The fact that the researcher Culhane lived for seven weeks in a homeless shelter adds credibility to his findings.

[3] The writer uses a direct quote taken from Culhane's research to provide additional evidence to support the claim that assumptions about the homeless were incorrect.

[4] Statistical evidence drawn from a researcher's findings enable the writer to claim that the data "profoundly changed the way homelessness is understood." (The use of "profoundly" adds a sense of drama to the claim.) Also, the author's allusion to a "database—the first of its kind" lends credence to Culhane's work and enables the writer to give the evidence a more objective slant— thereby strengthening the persuasiveness of his argument.

the way homelessness is understood. **[5]** "We found that eighty percent of the homeless were in and out really quickly," he said. "The most common length of time that someone is homeless is one day. And the second most common length is two days. And they never come back. Anyone who ever has to stay in a shelter involuntarily knows that all you think about is how to make sure you never come back." **[6]**

The next 10 percent were what Culhane calls episodic users. They would come for three weeks at a time, and return periodically, particularly in the winter. They were quite young, and they were often heavy drug users. But the last 10 percent interested Culhane the most. They were chronically homeless and lived in the shelters, sometimes for years at a time. Many were older, mentally ill or physically disabled. **[7]** When we think about homelessness as a social problem—people sleeping on sidewalks, aggressively panhandling, lying drunk in doorways, huddled on subway grates and under bridges—it's this group we have in mind. Culhane's database suggested that New York City had a quarter of a million people who were homeless at some point in the previous half decade—a surprisingly high number. But only about twenty-five hundred were *chronically* homeless.

[5] The writer enhances objectivity still further by categorizing the homeless into groups rather than lumping them all together. By citing various statistics, the writer suggests that Culhane's research was reliable and accurate, and he bolsters the basic claim that original assumptions about the homeless were erroneous.

[6] Additional details, including a quotation from the research, provide evidence to show why common conceptions of homelessness had to change.

[7] To explain why the researcher may have been drawn to study the so-called *chronically* homeless, the writer turns to highly descriptive, emotionally potent language. He uses this segment of the passage to counterbalance his earlier claim that despair over homelessness is unwarranted. Examples of dismal conditions of homelessness emphasize the seriousness of the problem, bring the notion of "despair" back into the discussion, and appeal strongly to readers' emotions.

This group costs the health-care and social-services systems far more than anyone had ever anticipated. [8] New York spent at least $62 million annually to shelter just those 2500 hard-core homeless. "It costs twenty-four thousand dollars a year for one of these shelter beds," Culhane said. "We're talking about a cot eighteen inches away from the next cot." Boston Health Care for the Homeless Program, a leading service group for the homeless in Boston, recently tracked the medical expenses of 119 chronically homeless people. Over five years, 33 people died and seven more were sent to nursing homes. The group accounted for 18,834 emergency-room visits—at a minimum of $1,000 a visit.

[9] "If its a medical admission, it's likely to be the guys with the really complex pneumonia," James Dunford, San Diego's emergency medical director and the author of an observational study, said. "They are drunk and they get vomit in their lungs and develop a lung abscess, and they get hypothermia on top of that, because they've been out in the rain. They end up in the intensive care unit with complicated medical infections. These are the guys who typically get hit by cars and buses and trucks and are very prone to just falling down and cracking their heads open. It's the guy with a head injury who ends up costing you at least $50,000. Meanwhile, they're going through alcohol withdrawal and have devastating liver disease that only adds to their inability to fight infections. There is no end to the issues. [10] We run up big lab fees, and the nurses want to quit, because they see the same guys come in over and over, and all we are doing is making them capable of walking down the block."

[8] The gravity of "hard-core" homelessness is highlighted with evidence consisting of startling figures related to the costs incurred to shelter and care for homeless people in New York and Boston. The use of the adjective "hard-core" suggests that these figures won't change very soon. Itemizing these financial burdens is meant to evoke an emotional reaction in the reader. A small detail, such as "a cot eighteen inches away from the next cot" adds a human dimension to the discussion of costs and suggests that miserable conditions persist in spite of a huge investment of funds.

[9] In the final paragraph, the writer quotes a physician whose experience observing homeless people qualfies him as an authority on the subject. The physician's words echo the "despair" discussed early in the passage and trigger a variety of emotional responses. Readers may be repulsed by details of drunkenness and hypothermia or take pity on homeless people for their mental distress and physical disabilities.

[10] By the end, the writer, using the physician as his spokesman, has shed light on the plight of the homeless and argued that recent research into homelessness reveals that the problem is far more complex than previously thought and, therefore, much harder to solve.

SOURCE 2

Your annotations will almost certainly be different from those you'll find here. Different, yes, but not necessarily wrong. In fact, yours may be full of perfectly valid observations that accurately identify and explain important persuasive features used by the writer. What ultimately matters is that your annotations would serve you well if you were to write an SAT Essay based on this source.

The for-profit college industry makes its money by recruiting students—overwhelmingly poor and working-class students—who must draw from the federal till to pay tuition. **[1]** In many cases, as much as 90 percent of the revenue of a for-profit college company comes from the federal government, in the form of Pell Grants and student loans. **[2]** The more students the companies enroll, the more federal money they get—and the more profit they make.

This has led to a widespread view that the for-profits will do just about anything to get that federal money. Allegations abound that for-profit recruiters use high-pressure sales pitches and inflated claims about career placement to increase student enrollment, regardless of the applicants' qualifications. Although for-profit colleges enroll 12 percent of the nation's college students, they soak up **[3]** about 25 percent of the federal government's student-aid budget.

[1] By using the words "industry" and "company" the writer shapes the reader's perception of for-profit colleges as businesses. That is, they are primarily money-making organizations rather than educational institutions. His assertion that they recruit "overwhelmingly poor and working-class students" is an appeal to emotions meant to induce the reader to take a dim view of such colleges.

[2] The writer reinforces his earlier claim that for-profits exist only to make money. The sentence also serves as a transition to the next paragraph in which statistical evidence of the for-profits' success is cited.

[3] The use of "soak up" adds to the negative portrayal of for-profits by implying that the for-profit industry somehow contrives to drain the government's student-aid budget. This allegation reinforces the preceding assertion that for-profit recruiters use "high-pressure sales pitches and inflated claims about career placement" to lure prospective students to enroll.

Many critics conclude that the only way to "fix" for-profit education is to get rid of it entirely. This approach obscures what really ought to be the most important fact about the industry: the country can't afford to put it out of business. On the contrary, America needs it—and needs it to succeed—desperately. [4]

To start with the obvious, a college education has never been more necessary for a decent life in America. Many manufacturing jobs now demand a level of skill and education that virtually requires a college degree. A lot of white-collar employers won't even consider a job applicant who hasn't graduated from college. [5]

And yet for the poor and working class, that education is not easy to attain. State university systems have become increasingly expensive. Community colleges are terribly overcrowded. The schools most capable of meeting the country's growing educational needs are the for-profits. [6] In the decade beginning in 1998, enrollment in public and private universities went up less than 25 percent. Enrollment in the for-profit colleges, meanwhile, was up 236 percent.

What's more, the traditional university isn't really set up to educate a person who has a full-time job. [7] The for-profits can offer class times that are convenient for students, rather than for professors. They can offer online classes, which many traditional universities have been reluctant—or unable—to dive into. They pay professors to teach, not conduct research. A well-run for-profit college could teach its nonprofit counterparts a thing or two about efficiency and innovation. That's the part of the profit motive that grades well.

The bad part, of course, is that capitalists will always behave more or less

[4] A startling tag line that ends the paragraph reverses the thrust of the passage and marks the starting point of the author's main argument—that for-profit colleges fulfill an educational need. By first discussing the unfavorable characteristics of for-profit colleges, and then moving into a discussion of their good qualities, the writer presents a more balanced—and thereby, more credible—view of the issue. The writer's forceful, emotionally laden assertion that America "desperately" needs for-profit education foretells the claim made by the last sentence of the passage, below.

[5] The paragraph is a classic example of the use of inductive reasoning. Its initial generalization is followed by specific evidence that supports the claim that living a decent life requires a college education

[6] A discussion of problems that poor and working-class people face in pursuit of a college education supports the claim that the country needs for-profit colleges. Enrollment statistics bolster the argument still further.

[7] Three paragraphs in a row begin with statements couched in negative terms: "never been more necessary," "not easy to attain," and "isn't really set up. ..." This stylistic pattern creates a subtle tension, or conflict, that helps develop the writer's argument. By starting with a negative, he adds potency to the positive evidence that follows.

like greyhounds chasing a mechanical rabbit, motivated by whatever incentives are put in front of them. **[8]** Just as the federal government created perverse incentives that helped bring about the subprime crisis, so have the government's rules for the for-profit industry unwittingly led to its excesses. When the industry reaps all the profit from student loans and the taxpayer has to pick up the losses, how can we be surprised when things turn out badly? **[9]** What is needed now is creative, enlightened policy-making that will change the incentives so that good outcomes matter more than sheer volume.

Recently, the Department of Education issued a series of regulations that are supposed to do just that. Unfortunately, the new rules are cumbersome, complicated—and more than a little punitive. The most controversial of them, known as the gainful employment rule, is built in part on the actual earnings of all the graduates of a given for-profit college. Yet, astonishingly, the schools themselves are never allowed to see the income numbers of individual graduates because the government considers them private. Rules like that aren't likely to help fix anything. **[10]**

There is an easier way. Robert Silberman, the chairman and chief executive of Strayer Education, widely regarded as one of the better for-profit companies, suggests replacing the plethora of regulations with two simple changes. First, he says, the government should force the for-profits to share in the losses when a student defaults. And second, the government should set up a national eligibility test to screen out students who lack the skills to attend college. Would

[8] A figure of speech, a simile, compares capitalists to mindless dogs, thus returning the passage to its opening disparagement of for-profit colleges. Here, however, the author focuses on emotional, money-related matters—arguing that we the taxpayers suffer when the government lends money to students who can't pay it back. This discussion leads directly to the author's pitch for "more enlightened policy-making," that in turn will allow education rather than money-making to flourish.

[9] A rhetorical question encourages readers to consider the negative consequences of permitting for-profits to get financial help from the government. Because the answer is self-evident—the question effectively buttresses the author's argument.

[10] The writer chooses forceful words—"cumbersome," "complicated," "punitive," "controversial"—to characterize the uselessness of government regulations and to support his subsequent claim that such rules "aren't likely to help fix anything."

there still be defaults? Of course. **[11]** But plenty of students at non-profit universities default, too. Silberman's solution would help ensure that both the government and for-profit companies are taking smarter risks on the students they enroll and educate.

There is nothing inherently wrong with the idea of for-profit education. The for-profits have flaws, but so do the non-profits, with their bloated infrastructure, sky-high tuition, out-of-control athletic programs, and resistance to change. In a country where education matters so much, we need them both. **[12]**

[11] Evidence drawn from Silberman, an authority from within the problematic for-profit community, adds credibility to the claim that there is "an easier way" to repair the system. By asking and answering his own question—a handy rhetorical tactic that appeals to readers' emotions by creating an aura of fairmindedness and objectivity to the discussion—the writer acknowledges that the proposed solution isn't perfect.

[12] In spite of abundant evidence meant to reveal the shortcomings of for-profits, the writer concludes with a compromise that echoes the solution proposed by the authoritative source cited in the previous paragraph. The last sentence alludes to the claim made early on that America's educational system "desperately" needs for-profit colleges.

How to Write an Analytical Essay in 3,000 Seconds

5

➜ **TACTICS FOR WRITING A 4/4/4 ESSAY**
➜ **PLANNING YOUR ESSAY**
➜ **SAT ESSAYS: WHAT TO SAY AND HOW TO SAY IT**

Don't be misled by the title of this part. It's more of a come-on than a promise. For one thing, writing an analytical essay in 3,000 seconds—more commonly known as 50 minutes—may be a contradiction in terms. An essay is basically the product of a writer's thinking, arrived at after reflection, analysis, or interpretation of a subject or issue. When you're given the subject to write about a mere 50 minutes before the essay is due, thinking deeply may be a luxury you can't afford.

One reason you can't dawdle is that, prior to writing a single word, you need several minutes to read the source from beginning to end. During that time, you may catch a glimpse or two of the writer's use of rhetorical elements, but the real hunt can't begin until you do second reading. Once you've identified rhetorical strategies, sorted them by function or category, picked those to discuss in your essay, and prepared a brief outline (highly recommended), half the 3,000 seconds may be history.

Here's another reason that the title above is illusory: You can't learn to write well by reading about how to do it. Rather, you learn to write by writing, by messing around with ideas and words, by experimenting, by practicing, and by doing what seasoned writers do when they face a sheet of blank paper or an empty computer screen: they write!

Honestly, the best this chapter can do is to lay out some basic rules, principles, and techniques for you to practice. The more writing experience you have, the more control you'll have, and the better you'll do not only on the SAT Essay but in college courses—and Wow!— maybe for the rest of your life.

With that in mind, let's begin with some analytical essay-writing tactics—steps that generations of students have relied on *en route* to producing insightful, high-scoring analytical essays.

TACTICS FOR WRITING A 4/4/4 ESSAY

A MESSAGE FROM THE AUTHOR

The next pages are full of pointers for writing a first-rate essay. Many of the guidelines apply not only to SAT Essays but to analytical writing in general. Familiarity with these principles will help to make you more adept at analyzing the source. In other words, skill in writing and skill in reading, as you'll soon see, go hand in hand.

Our favorite language, English, contains all sorts of adjectives that describe good writing: *eloquent, well-written, lively, stylish, polished, descriptive, honed, vivid, engaging,* and countless others. On the SAT you're instructed simply to "write an essay." Although the essay instructions don't tell you to write an essay that is well-organized (it should be) or carefully reasoned (it should be) or grammatically correct (yes, it should be that, too), the SAT reader will be looking for those qualities in your work. In addition, to earn the highest score, an essay should be

1. **CLEAR, OR EASY TO FOLLOW.** (Your ideas need to be clear to you before you can make them clear to others.)
2. **INTERESTING.** (Use economical, entertaining language because readers are put off by wordy, lifeless prose.)
3. **CORRECT.** (Your writing will inevitably be judged according to how well your prose follows the conventions of standard written English.)

If your ideas are expressed clearly, interestingly, and correctly, there is no reason that you can't expect to write a winning SAT Essay—one awarded gold-star status—that is, a 4/4/4, or as close to that as you can get.

Have you noticed that people deal with essay-writing in a variety of ways? Maybe you've seen some writers start with an outline, while others dive right in to the text. Some may write a sentence or two, then reread and edit it. Others go full bore from start to finish without rereading a word. Which method is best? That's an unanswerable question because what works for one person won't necessarily work for others. Nevertheless, some tactics tend to help virtually everyone regardless of their ability, approach, and essay-writing experience.

Several are described in the pages that follow. Give them an honest chance to help you raise your essay score.

1. Plan Ahead

Because you won't have time to devise an essay-writing process during the exam, it pays to have one in mind ahead of time, one that you've used multiple times, one you can count on to help you work rapidly and efficiently.

Consider, therefore, using the following three-stage process. It has a long history of helping students write essays under the pressure of time.

FIRST STAGE: PREWRITING

The planning that needs to be done before you actually commit words to paper or the computer screen

- Reading the prompt and the passage
- Finding examples of the writer's use of rhetorical strategies
- Selecting the strategies to discuss in your essay and deciding the order in which to discuss them

SECOND STAGE: COMPOSING

Converting your thoughts and ideas into written words and sentences

- Introducing the main idea of your essay
- Developing paragraphs
- Choosing the best words for expressing your ideas
- Structuring sentences for variety and coherence
- Writing a conclusion

THIRD STAGE: EDITING AND PROOFREADING

- Editing for clarity, coherence, and economy of expression
- Revising to create interest
- Checking for standard usage and mechanical errors, including spelling, punctuation, and capitalization

HOW LONG DOES EACH STAGE LAST?

The truth is that the three stages overlap and blend. Writers compose, revise, and proofread simultaneously. They jot down sentences during prewriting, and even late in the process may weave new ideas into their text. In fact, no stage really ends until the final period of the last sentence is put in place—or until the SAT proctor calls "Time!"

2. Pace Yourself

This book can't presume to tell you exactly how to divide up the 50 minutes you're given to write the essay. Everybody works at a different speed. Nevertheless, as you begin to write SAT Essays for practice, try devoting about 5 minutes to reading the passage and 10 minutes to hunting down examples of the writer's rhetoric and preparing a rough outline. During the next 25 minutes, compose your essay, and then allow 10 minutes for editing and proofreading.

Recommended time line for the SAT Essay

Reading the passage	5 minutes
Identifying the rhetoric	10 minutes
Composing the essay	25 minutes
Editing and proofreading	10 minutes

If this schedule works for you while you practice, stick with it. Otherwise, adjust the time for each step until you get the results you want.

During the weeks before the exam, or even sooner, write an essay a day for several days in a row until you get the feel of 50 minutes' writing time. Keep track of how much time you usually spend reading the source, how quickly you can find rhetorical strategies, how long it takes you to compose the essay, and how many minutes you need to proofread and edit. Once you've developed a pattern that works, use it over and over until it becomes second nature.

TIP

Don't waste time inventing a title; you don't need one.

On test day, make every second count. Don't waste time inventing a title for your essay. Don't count words, and don't expect to recopy handwritten drafts. Because SAT readers understand that the essays are first drafts, feel free to cross out, insert words using carets (^), and move blocks of text with neatly drawn arrows. If necessary, number the sentences to make their sequence clear. You won't be penalized for a sloppy-looking essay. Just be sure it's legible.

3. Know What the Prompt Says

By the time you take the SAT, the prompt should be engraved in your memory, maybe even haunt your dreams. What a waste of precious minutes it would be on test day to read it again. Instead, at the very start of the test go directly to the second section of the prompt and underline the last clause in the first sentence—the one that follows the word *that* and spells out the writer's claim, as in

> Write an essay in which you explain how [writer's name] builds an argument to persuade his audience *that e-cigarettes should be banned.*

Write the claim in your test booklet. Refer to it again and again as a constant reminder of your focus as you read the passage and write your essay.

By using the word "essay," the College Board means *essay*, not a story, poem, dialogue, one-act play, or any other genre. Therefore, expect to write an expository piece that analyzes the rhetoric in the given passage. Once you've read the source and figured out more or less what you want to say, you'll have approximately 30–35 minutes left to write and edit your essay.

CHOOSING RHETORICAL STRATEGIES TO WRITE ABOUT

The prompt lists six categories of rhetorical strategies:

1. Use of examples and facts as evidence
2. Reasoning methods
3. Stylistic/persuasive elements
4. Diction (word choice)
5. Appeals to emotion
6. Your choice

Should you discuss all of them? No! Instead, pick the most prominent ones, those the writer has used to the greatest effect.

Unless the writer has relied almost solely on one rhetorical strategy, try to incorporate a discussion of at least one, two, or three others, although a total of four could be asking for trouble because time won't permit you to discuss each one fully. In general, it's preferable to do a thorough analysis of a few strategies than to deal superficially with several.

Let's say that the writer of the passage has relied primarily on facts to support a claim. By digging deeply into the type of facts (statistics, research findings, quotations, examples, precedents, etc.), you might write a perfectly respectable essay. Likewise, the source may set out to persuade readers by appealing to their emotions, trying to arouse a range of feelings—from fear to pride to the milk of human kindness and countless others. Again, a whole essay can be devoted to the writer's use of emotion, although it's likely that diction, or word choice, will be the fuel that stirs up a stew of emotional responses. In other words, each rhetorical strategy more often than not is a hybrid—a complex blend of more than one, each contributing something to the reader's response. Think, for example, of an orchestra with several instruments playing at the same time. If you listen hard, you can hear each one individually, but the experience will leave its mark by the sound of all of them playing together.

4. Read the Source with Two Goals in Mind: Comprehension and Analysis

To write even half way intelligently about the rhetoric in a passage you must know what the passage says. As you read, therefore, keep two goals in mind: (1) to comprehend the passage and (2) to locate the author's use of rhetorical elements. Doing both simultaneously may not come easily at first, but with practice, you can make it a habit. Actually, it may be less demanding than, say, reading a passage in order to answer multiple-choice questions about it, as you've no doubt done in the past on countless standardized tests. That's because, while reading the source, you needn't zero in on every tiny detail but only on the writer's overall meaning and use of rhetorical strategies.

Ultimately, however, everything in your essay should be tied to your understanding of the passage's contents. It won't be enough simply to identify figures of speech or to say the tone is nostalgic or that the writing style is sophisticated. What counts is an insightful discussion of how rhetorical choices contributed to the meaning and persuasiveness of the author's argument.

PLANNING YOUR ESSAY

Preparing an Outline

Spend a few minutes outlining your essay before writing your opening sentence. You don't need a formal outline but just a list of ideas arranged in the order you'll use them in your essay. In general, an essay outlined in advance is likely to be clearer and more coherent than one thrown together willy-nilly. It speaks well of you as a writer when you present ideas in a thought-out sequence instead of spilling them onto the page in the order they happened to pop into your head. Since time is short, your outline need be nothing more than a handful of scrawled words or phrases arranged in some sort of sequence and indicative of each paragraph's main idea.

Abigail's Outline

As she prepared to write an analysis of the rhetoric used by Carla R. Morrisey, author of the passage entitled "The Influenza Epidemic of 1918" (see below), Abigail G, a high school senior, constructed an outline. The SAT Essay prompt gave Abigail standard instructions:

> **Write an essay in which you analyze how Carla R. Morrisey builds an argument to persuade her audience that *the negligible effect left by the devastating influenza epidemic of 1918 is difficult to explain.***

Although it now seems merely an ancient folk-memory, the Influenza epidemic of 1918 was the third greatest plague in the history of mankind. The most devastating epidemic since the Middle Ages, it took over 21 million lives and affected over half the world's population. Logically, one would think that an epidemic of this proportion would have left an indelible imprint on the American people. In the United States alone, 550,000 died within the 16-week period from October 1918 to February 1919. Yet, it never inspired awe, not in 1918 and not since.

As one searches for an explanation as to why Americans took little notice of the epidemic and then quickly forgot what they did notice, a mystery and a paradox emerge. The mystery was the complacency the American people displayed as a group toward the epidemic. The paradox was the common individual's clear acknowledgement that the epidemic was the most influential experience of his life.

To understand this lack of attention, one must look at the years preceding the outbreak. Lethal epidemics were not as unexpected and therefore not as impressive as they might be today. Most Americans remembered living through the typhoid and small pox epidemics of 1876 and 1890. Beyond complacency toward epidemics, further answers are entirely speculative.

If the "Spanish Influenza" had become a permanent fixture, then Americans might have granted this variety of the flu the notoriety it deserved. But the devastation came, scooped up victims, and all but disappeared within a few months. If the flu evoked memories of terror, Americans might have panicked, but their fear was absent, and is reflected in an announcement from the U.S. Public Health Service, saying: "The placidity by which the people have generally taken the almost sudden loss of thousands of lives is remarkable."

Perhaps the nature of the disease and its contagiousness encouraged forgetfulness. The swiftness of its spread before it had any real effect on the economy made it easier for people to accept, despite killing 3 percent of the nation's population.

World War I may explain the country's relative indifference. The *New York Times* suggested that "war had taught the people to think in terms of other than individual interest and safety, and death itself had become so familiar as to lose its grimness." Such an explanation may seem quite naive, but most of those who died were young adults of the same age as those lost in combat. The obituary columns of influenza victims became one and the same blur with the war casualty list.

Influenza seemed unimportant compared with the news on the front pages of the city's newspapers. Agitation grew as the Senate vote on the rights for women approached. Eugene V. Debs was on his way to jail for allegedly violating the Espionage Act. On 31 August 1918, Babe Ruth made headlines as he pitched a three-hitter and hit a double to win the pennant for the Boston Red Sox. It was apparently of no consequence that on the same day the first cases of flu were recognized among Navy personnel in Boston and 26 sailors died.

The interweaving of the war and pandemic seems almost to resemble a pattern of insanity. On 11 September Washington officials disclosed that the Spanish Influenza had arrived in the city. The next day 13 million men, precisely the age most likely to die of the flu, crammed city halls, post offices, and schools across the country to register for the draft. It was a gala flag-waving affair everywhere including Boston where 96,000 registered, and then sneezed and coughed on one another.

The epidemic didn't kill the ranks of the famous and powerful. Perhaps if Woodrow Wilson or someone of like stature had died, the world might have remembered. It killed the daughter of General Edwards of the 26th Division of the American Expeditionary Forces, but not the general. It killed the daughter of Samuel Gompers, president of the American Federation of Labor, but left America's most powerful labor leaders alive.

On the level of organizations and institutions, the Spanish Influenza had little impact. It did spur great activity among medical scientists and their institutions, but this was the single great exception. It did not lead to great changes in government, armies, and corporations. It had little influence on the course of political and military events because it affected all sides equally.

(Adapted from "The Influenza Epidemic of 1918," an article by Carla R. Morrisey and published by the Naval Historical Center, an agency affiliated with the U.S. Department of the Navy)

While reading the passage, Abigail concentrated not only on the meaning of the words but on how the author stated and organized her ideas. She searched particularly for examples of evidence used to support claims and for notable words and expressions intended to jolt a reader's emotions.

Just prior to starting her outline, Abigail jotted down a few general impressions of the passage and its author:*

1. The author—an historian who wants to tell readers about effects of the flu epidemic on the American people.

2. Using words like *mystery* and *paradox*, the author characterizes America's indifference to the devastating epidemic as puzzling, if not totally baffling.

3. The author claims that America's unusual response can largely be explained by the conditions and other events occurring at the same time.

4. The author acknowledges that her explanations are speculative.

*Abigail's notes and the following outline are spelled out here in complete sentences. In reality, to save time, Abigail hurriedly jotted down just a key word or phrase for each item. For example, next to note #2, she wrote two words: "mystery" and "paradox." Her note for #4 consisted of the single word "speculation." Likewise, in her outline she used a shorthand devised to record ideas as quickly as possible.

Using these notes as a springboard, Abigail prepared an outline for an essay on the author's use of rhetoric.

Abigail began her outline by choosing three important rhetorical strategies to analyze in her essay. She numbered them I, II and III, then she returned to the passage and decided which ones to discuss first, second, and third.

Abigail's Outline Based on Analysis of "The Influenza Epidemic of 1918"

I. Introduction. The writer uses three main rhetorical strategies to argue that it is a mystery and a paradox that the devastating influenza of 1918 turned out to be a relatively minor event in American history.

II. The Writer uses evidence and emotionally charged language to convince the reader that the influenza of 1918 was highly destructive and devastating.

   A. The writer repeatedly refers to the influenza as an "epidemic" and also "pandemic" and "plague."

   B. The writer calls the influenza the "third greatest plague in the history of mankind," and the "most devastating epidemic since the Middle Ages."

   C. The writer cites statistics: Influenza killed off 21 million people worldwide including 550,000 Americans.

   D. The phrase "scooped up victims" reflects both the speed and randomness of the disease.

III. Despite its deadliness, it "never inspired awe," an assertion that leads the writer to claim that America's anemic response is a "mystery and a paradox."

 Reword

   A. The mystery is characterized as America's "complacency," or general absence of fear and panic.

   B. A paradox stems from the contradiction between Americans' indifference and many individuals' "acknowledgement that the epidemic was the most influential experience" of their lives.

IV. The writer claims that reasons for America's indifference to the influenza of 1918 are "entirely speculative." Stylistic elements testify to speculative tone of writer's explanations.

   A. The "If ..., then" construction of several sentences.

   B. The Use of tentative verbs such as "may explain," "may seem," and "seemed."

   C. The Use of "perhaps" to introduce ideas.

V. Conclusion. The passage itself illustrates a paradox: Much of it is speculative, but the evidence is strong enough to be persuasive.

Abigail's Essay Based on Her Outline

Carla R. Morrisey, in "The Influenza Epidemic of 1918" takes readers back about 100 years to a puzzling event in history that should have been much more significant than it was. Morissey claims that it is difficult to explain why an epidemic that killed 21 million people all over the world plus over half a million American citizens, had very little impact on America history.

In order to persuade readers that her claim is right, Morrisey uses three main rhetorical strategies. First, she uses emotional language to show how deadly the influenza epidemic really was. Then she describes how in America the epidemic "never inspired awe," which means she believes that America's response to the epidemic is a mystery and a paradox rolled into one. Thirdly, she mentions several reasons that may explain why America was so indifferent.

At the beginning, Morrisey uses emotionally-strong language to support her claim that the spread of influenza was awesomely tragic and serious. She repeats the word "epidemic" a few times and also uses "plague" and "pandemic." In addition, Morrisey says that the outbreak of influenza was the "third greatest plague in the history of mankind," and also "the most devastating epidemic since the Middle Ages". As evidence, she uses statistics of how many people died. She says that the epidemic "scooped" the victims, a word which implies the speed and randomness of the spread of the deadly infection. Even though all these facts, statistics and use of frightening words are meant to appeal to the reader's emotions, Morrisey turns to logic to draw a conclusion, saying that it would be reasonable for an epidemic so tragic to be feared and remembered. But her conclusion did not work out, and Morrisey wonders why.

This leads to the subsequent claim discussed through the rest of the passage that America's indifference is both a "mystery and a paradox," since one would logically expect that a deadly epidemic could not be ignored. She defines the "mystery" as America's "complacency," or general absence of fear and panic, and she sees a "paradox" as growing out of the contradiction between America's indifference to the epidemic and many individual's "acknowledgment that the epidemic was the most influential experience" of their lives.

For the rest of the passage, Morrissey brings up situations and examples that might explain America's reaction to the epidemic. She admits that her explanations are "entirely speculative." Therefore, she makes constant use of language that is stated as theories and not facts. Several sentences use the "if ... then" construction. She uses tentative verbs such as "may explain," "may seem" and "seemed." She begins some sentences with "Perhaps ..." She even quotes a speculative statement from the New York Times, saying that the newspaper "suggested" that "war had taught the people to think ... death itself had become so familiar as to lose its grimness."

Reading that kind of language, a reader might reject Morrisey's theories as weak and unconvincing evidence to explain an unusual situation. But there is something like a paradox in her accumulation of theories and situations. Even though it is mostly speculation, she has built a strong persuasive argument.

(535 words)

contrary to expectation

Abigail's 535-word essay has been printed here as an example of how an outline can be turned into an essay: It begins with a brief introduction that lists the three rhetorical strategies Abigail plans to discuss in the body of her essay. This is followed by three paragraphs, each covering a different strategy, each one profusely illustrated with quotations from the passage. As the essay ends, Abigail creates a sense of closure for the reader by alluding to a key idea discussed earlier—namely, a paradox.

As an actual SAT Essay, Abigail's work would likely earn a score of 4/4/3, based on her perceptive reading of the source, her exacting analysis of the rhetoric, and her generally competent—but not error-free—writing. Abigail should also be commended for avoiding the common error of trying to say too much in a short time. In other words, she limited her focus to three important rhetorical features of the source.

ABIGAIL'S ESSAY-WRITING STORY

Thinking that readers of this book might benefit from hearing about Abigail's experience writing an SAT Essay, this author asked her to recount both what she did and what she thought during the allotted 50 minutes' writing time. Here, in her own words, is what she said:

Well, I was a little anxious at the beginning when I opened my test booklet and found a passage about a flu epidemic that I'd never even heard of before. But as I began to read it, I found it pretty interesting, specially the parts that described how intense it was— killing millions of victims—and the fact that it hardly seemed to matter to most people in the country.

When I glanced back at the prompt, I thought, "what luck"— the people's lack of concern about the epidemic really interested me the most, and that was also related to the writer's goal—to prove that the people's indifference was hard to explain.

Luckily, during the few weeks before the SAT I wrote a bunch of essays for practice, so I was very familiar with the list of rhetorical devices I could write about. So, I didn't have to bother with the list in the prompt. I read the passage slowly, hoping that the writer's use of rhetoric would sort of just strike my eye. And the first thing I noticed was the strong words the writer used to describe the epidemic—like "plague," and the huge death toll, and stuff. I think that I spent about 10 minutes reading the passage the first time and another 5 or 10 minutes the next time.

My English teacher suggested that I should do a lot of underlining or to take some very quick notes as I read, so that's what I did, and I think it helped me focus more on the ideas in the passage and also write an outline that I used to organize thoughts to put in my essay. (Thanks for the suggestion, Ms Flanagan. You get points for that. Ha!)

Anyway, I was really interested when the author said that the people's indifference was a mystery and a paradox, and I used that in my essay as the second of three rhetorical strategies because so much of the passage referred back to the mystery and the paradox.

Then the third rhetorical thing just came to me in a flash because the writer was using language that was really tentative. She called it "speculation," and that's what it was. She didn't have positive proof, so almost the whole last half of the passage is written in speculative words— "maybes" and "perhapses" and "If … thens." And that hit me as a really good rhetorical trick or paradox, really, because even though the language was speculative, it seemed like a logical explanation of why the American people reacted like they didn't really care that much about the epidemic. And that's how I came up with the conclusion. I thought that if I put that idea into the essay I'd be showing the SAT readers that I could think with insight about an issue and maybe even get extra credit.

I came to the end of essay with about three minutes left on the clock and used the time to proofread my essay and change a few words to make it sound more mature.

… I'm hoping for at least 3's on my essay, but 4's would be awesome.

As you write essays for practice, take Abigail's story to heart. Let it convince you that preparation can really help. That she had memorized the list of the rhetorical features enabled her to pick out three to write about during her initial reading of the source—a real time saver. Her approach also illustrates the importance of taking a few notes and/or sketching a brief outline. *Brief* is the key word. She didn't overdo it but just noted one or two words to remind her of an idea to use in her essay. Overloading an outline not only wastes precious minutes but is likely to burden you with more ideas than you'll have time to discuss in your essay.

DANGER: PROCEED WITH CAUTION

In case you didn't get the word, here's a head's-up about what **not** to write in your essay: Anything different from an analysis of rhetoric used in the source is off limits and is doomed to fail.

Take heed, therefore, of the following:

1. As tempting as it may be to show the reader that you understood the source, don't summarize its contents.
2. Don't evaluate the writer's views on the issue. Study them, judge them, analyze them to death, but keep to yourself your own take on the issue. In a word, your opinion is irrelevant. Sorry.

THE CASE OF JEFF S, A HIGH SCHOOL SENIOR

Jeff S, from Anytown, USA failed to pay attention to the SAT's guidelines: In a dress rehearsal for writing his essay, Jeff read a source that claimed, "*College athletic programs give students a false sense of values.*" Here is an excerpt:

Undergraduate and alumni interest in athletics cannot be overstated; nor can the harm that results from it be too vigorously condemned. The alumni—and some students, too—have so exaggerated athletic importance that the athletic tail is at this moment doing a fair job of wagging the academic dog. Sports for sport's sake, sports as a learning experience, sports as preparation for competing in the post-college world—these have become mere slogans, hypocritical masks for professionalism to hide behind. Such professionalizing of athletics, including generous jock scholarships, luxury dorms for athletes, the media's out-of-sight payments to colleges for football and basketball broadcasting rights, athletes' endorsements of commercial products from toothpaste to Teslas, and outrageous overemphasis on the value of athletics give undergraduates a false sense of values that is injurious both to them and to their college.

After reading the entire passage, Jeff began to write his essay. This is the first paragraph:

The author of the passage doesn't like college sports. He thinks that they are pretty harmful. Everything is wrong with them. As the author says, they "wag the academic dog," meaning they are more important to colleges than their academic programs. That's an interesting accusation. The author also lists abuses that harm the values of students and their colleges, including athletic scholarships and players endorsing things like toothpaste and Teslas. In my opinion, sports in high school are really just as bad, especially when a player is cut from a team for no reason except the coach doesn't like you.

Two days later, while rereading his essay, Jeff muttered, "OMG, that rots." In a flash, he knew that he'd gotten so wrapped up in the writer's views that he'd completely forgotten the purpose of his essay—to analyze the writer's rhetoric. In addition, Jeff saw that in summarizing the passage he'd relied on vague phrases such as "pretty harmful" and "interesting accusation." Not only that, but he had tossed in his own irrelevant opinion on the topic.

Vowing to stick to the guidelines for SAT Essays, Jeff decided to try again:

The first sentence makes two assertions about alumni interest in college athletics. One is intellectual—that student and alumni interest in athletics "cannot be overstated"—and the other is emotional: The writer's disapproval is made clear with the words *harm* and *condemned*, and as readers, we are meant to feel like the writer does—indignant that athletics are contrary to the educational purpose of colleges.

Evidence that student and alumni interest "cannot be overstated" is supported by an amazing list of benefits given to college athletes, including scholarships, luxury dorms, and opportunities to endorse commercial products. The author's claim that extreme interest in athletics cannot "be too vigorously condemned" leads directly to the writer's version of a cliché about the" tale wagging the dog." Normally, a good writer would not use this cliché, but this writer has added some words, saying that "the athletic tail is at this moment doing a fair job of wagging the academic dog." Stated this way, the statement has much more interest and power. Backing up that idea, the writer refers to it a number of times later in the rest of the passage. For example, in the second paragraph from the end, the writer talks about how athletic coaches at many universities are actually paid more than the president of the university.

Clearly, Jeff's revision has put him on the right track. His essay now zeroes in on the writer's use of rhetoric.

Arranging Ideas Purposefully

Unless you're blessed with a digital mind that instantly processes information and draws insightful conclusions, spend a few prewriting moments to arrange the rhetorical strategies you've picked out of the source. List them on paper—just a word or two for each. Use these jottings as a working outline of your essay. Draw circles around key words, connect related ideas with arrows, or underline the thoughts you'll definitely use in your essay.

No single technique for gathering and arranging ideas excels any other, provided it helps you nail down what you are going to discuss in your essay. While you plan, one idea may trigger another or even bring on a flood of others. Maybe you'll wind up with more brilliant insights than you can possibly use. (Everyone should have such a problem!) Your task then would be to pick out and develop only the best of the best.

With ideas assembled, decide which of them should come first in your essay, and second, and third. Logic may dictate that you discuss rhetorical strategies in the order you found them in the source, but that won't necessarily be the best order. The best order is the clearest one, the one your reader can follow with the least effort.

Another way to look at it is that the least effective order is the aimless one in which ideas are presented at random, based, say, according to how they popped into your head. To guard against such aimlessness, decide which rhetorical strategy seems the most important in the passage and then list the ones that come in second and third.

As you write, build your argument toward the best point—that is, the most persuasive technique used by the writer—the one that clinches his case.

Giving away your *pièce de résistance* at the start is self-defeating. Therefore, if you've come up with three good rhetorical strategies to discuss, save the strongest for last. Begin with the second best, and sandwich your least favorite between the other two. A solid opening draws readers into the essay and creates that all-important first impression, but a memorable ending is even more important. Coming last, it is what readers have fresh in their minds when they assign the essay a grade.

The following guideline won't apply to every essay, but a body consisting of three sections or paragraphs may be just about right. Why three? Mainly because three is a number that works. The analysis of three different rhetorical principles used in a passage creates the impression that you know what you're talking about. One is insufficient—unless you can discuss it from a variety of angles—and two is only slightly better. But three indicates thoughtfulness. Psychologically, three also creates a sense of rhetorical wholeness, like "blood, sweat, and tears," and "of the people, by the people, and for the people."

Each of the three rhetorical strategies may not demand an equal amount of emphasis, however. You might dispose of the least important strategy in just a couple of sentences, while each of the others may require a whole paragraph.

The Formula

The five-paragraph essay formula is a simple, all-purpose plan for arranging ideas into a clear, easy-to-follow order. It's a technique you can rely on any time you need to set ideas in order. It's greatest virtue is clarity. Each part has its place and purpose.

THE FORMULA

Introduction	
Body	Point 1
	Point 2
	Point 3
Conclusion	

You needn't follow the formula to the letter. In fact, a professionally written essay organized according to this five paragraph arrangement is a rarity. Yet, many essay writers, even those who take a circuitous path between the beginning and end, use some version of it. Their introduction tells readers what they plan to say. The body says it, and the conclusion may review what has been said, although to rehash the contents of a short essay is not only unnecessary but could be insulting. After all, readers don't want to be treated as airheads who can't remember the contents of a few short paragraphs. Rather, write a conclusion that gives the reader a new idea to think about. Or comment on an engaging feature of the passage, or express your opinion of how the writer built an argument—whether or not you agree with it. In the end, if you can't think of an appropriate conclusion, just stop writing. That's preferable to imposing on your readers a warmed-over review of what they already know.

TIP

Rank rhetorical techniques in order of importance.

TIP

Don't write a conclusion that summarizes all you've just said.

Mini-Workout in Gathering and Arranging Ideas

> **Directions:** Each of the claims below is arguable. For each of them write three statements in favor and three against. Think of each statement as the main idea of a separate paragraph in an essay. Then rank them in order of importance.

A. All students should be required to take a physical education class every semester.

Advantages

1. _____

2. _____

3. _____

Disadvantages

1. _____

2. _____

3. _____

B. Video games are an example of worthwhile technology.

Pros

1. _____

2. _____

3. _____

Cons

1. _____

2. _____

3. _____

C. My school should institute an honor code.

For

1. _____

2. _____

3. _____

Against

1. _____

2. _____

3. _____

D. "There never was a good war or a bad peace."—Benjamin Franklin
Agree

1. _____

2. _____

3. _____

Disagree

1. _____

2. _____

3. _____

Answers are on pages 299–300.

Composing an Introduction

Introductions let readers know what lies ahead. They also set the essay's boundaries. Because you can't cover all there is to say about a source, simply and briefly inform the reader of your plans. There are ways to do this and ways not to. Let's discuss the don'ts first.

Don't make a formal announcement of your plans. Don't do what Owen B did when he wrote the following introduction to an essay meant to analyze the rhetoric in a source entitled "Twitter Trash Talking."

> I intend to analyze "Twitter Trash Talking," a passage written by Wilma Spitzfar. In my essay I plan to write three paragraphs, each one discussing a different rhetorical method used by the author to build a persuasive case in support of her claim that the government should exert stricter control over digital communications. My first paragraph will be about Spitzfar's use of statistics. In my middle paragraph, I will discuss her use of deductive reasoning used throughout the passage, and I will end with a discussion of examples of emotional imagery that she has used in her argument.

Yes, Owen deserves kudos for planning his essay meticulously, but in announcing his intentions, he's overdone it. Using more than a hundred words of what may turn into a four-to five-hundred word essay, Owen is needlessly picky and verbose. What's more, an opening that comprises, say, more than a quarter of his essay reflects poorly on his sense of proportion.

Owen also gets credit for clearly spelling out which rhetorical strategies he'll discuss in his essay. Almost everything else in his introduction is superfluous, however, and a waste of Owen's, as well as the reader's, time.

Lilah C, writing about the same passage, introduced her essay in another way.

Wilma Spitzfar employs three rhetorical strategies in making an argument for strict government control over digital communications. Using deductive reasoning throughout the passage, she presents persuasive evidence that Twitter and other social media have polluted the digital airwaves. By citing a number of startling statistics, she shows that young children in huge numbers are being exploited by digital predators. Most significantly, though, Spitzfar uses emotionally powerful images to rouse her audience into action, more specifically, to urge their elected representatives to support legislation that will make illegal certain types of digital communication.

TIP

Use the introduction to identify rhetorical features you'll discuss in the essay.

In her introduction, Lilah, like Owen, identifies three rhetorical strategies that she'll discuss, coincidentally, the same as Owen's. But unlike Owen, she carefully explains how each one contributes to the overall purpose of the passage. In effect, Lilah's introduction gives readers a comprehensive overview of things to come. Presumably, she'll present details of each strategy in the paragraphs that follow.

Lilah's introduction is slightly shorter than Owen's. But it digs far deeper into the passage. As she identifies each rhetorical strategy, she also explains its function. In effect, Lilah has used her introduction to start analyzing the passage.

Using an altogether different approach, Jake R, whose essay is meant to analyze the rhetoric in a source claiming that school administrators must not be permitted to violate students' rights, introduced his essay this way.

On Monday morning, October 20, I arrived in school to find every locker door in my corridor standing ajar. Over the weekend, school officials had searched through students' lockers for drugs and alcohol. I believe that this illegal action was a violation of both my civil rights and civil rights of every other student in the school. I also believe that Richard Burns, the author of "Freedom Behind the Schoolhouse Gate" would agree with me.

Obviously, Jake begins his essay with a personal anecdote that relates to the content of the source. By recounting the experience, he pulls the reader into his essay—always a good thing to do. Having captured the reader, however, he must quickly change course and avoid the temptation of discussing his views on the issue of student rights. Regardless of how strongly he feels and how eloquently he can express his views, he must put his opinions aside and focus on the rhetoric used by the author of the source.

Because there's no time to dawdle during the time allotted for writing an SAT Essay, an introduction consisting of a plain statement conveying the limits of your discussion can do the job. If you can't think of a viable opening right away, don't put off writing the body of your essay. A good introduction might strike you at any time. In fact, many writers, needing time to warm up, begin with material that fits into the body of the essay. Once they hit their stride and figure out what they want to say, they work on a fitting introduction. As you write essays for practice, you might try a similar tactic.

Paragraphs: The Building Blocks of an Essay

The inventor of the paragraph devised a simple way to guide readers through a piece of writing. Each new paragraph alerts readers to get ready for a shift of some kind, just as a car's directional blinker tells other drivers that you're about to turn.

Yet, not every new paragraph signals a drastic change. The writer may simply want to nudge the discussion ahead to the next step. Some paragraphs spring directly from those that preceded them. The paragraph you are now reading, for instance, is linked to the one before by the connecting word, *Yet*. The connection was meant to alert you to a change in thought, but it was also intended to remind you that the two paragraphs are related. Abrupt starts may be useful from time to time to keep readers on their toes. But good writers avoid a string of sudden turns that can transform surprise into confusion.

In an essay, paragraphs usually play a primary role and one or more secondary roles. An *introductory paragraph*, for instance, launches the essay and makes the intent of the essay clear to the reader. The *concluding paragraph* leaves the reader with a thought to remember and provides a sense of closure. The majority of paragraphs, however, are *developmental*. They carry forward the main point of the essay by performing any number of functions, among them:

- Adding new ideas to the preceding discussion
- Continuing or explaining in more detail an idea presented earlier
- Reiterating a previously stated idea
- Citing an example of a previously stated idea
- Evaluating an opinion stated earlier
- Refuting previously stated ideas
- Providing a new or contrasting point of view
- Describing the relationship between ideas presented earlier
- Providing background material
- Raising a hypothetical or rhetorical question about the topic

Whatever its functions, a paragraph should contribute to the essay's overall growth. A paragraph that fails to amplify the main idea of the essay should be revised or deleted. Similarly, any idea within a paragraph that doesn't contribute to the development of the paragraph's topic needs to be changed or eliminated.

TOPIC AND SUPPORTING SENTENCES

Whether readers skim your paragraphs or slog doggedly through every word, they need to find sentences now and then that, like landmarks, help them to know where they are. Such guiding sentences differ from others because they define the paragraph's main topic; hence the name *topic sentence*.

Most, but not all, paragraphs contain topic sentences. The topic of some paragraphs is so obvious that to state it would be redundant. Then, too, groups of paragraphs can be so closely knit that one topic sentence states the most important idea for all of them.

Use topic sentences to guide readers through your essay.

Topic sentences come in a variety of forms. What they all have in common is their helpfulness. Consider them landmarks. To drive from your home to school, for example, you turn left at the stop sign, take a half right under the railroad trestle, and a right at the Exxon station. Each landmark tells you where to turn. Similarly, in a piece of writing, a topic sentence often marks a turning point that tells readers the direction they'll be going for a while.

Most topic sentences come first in a paragraph, but they can be located anywhere. And some paragraphs don't even need a topic sentence. Instead, the main idea can be strongly implied by an accumulation of details and ideas.

For instance, a description of people who initially signed up for a so-called MOOC, one of those Massive Open Online Courses that are taken for college credit via the Internet, might read this way:

> Three-quarters of the six thousand people from 136 countries who had enrolled in Professor Faludi's MOOC by its opening day live in North America. Most others are from Europe and Asia. The remainder come from South and Central America. Only 17 percent described themselves as students in an introductory poll. Nearly a third identified themselves as high school teachers, college instructors, or professional historians. The vast majority described themselves as "history enthusiasts."

Readers of this paragraph would certainly get the picture. To state explicitly that "Professor Faludi's MOOC attracted a wide range of people from all over the world" would serve no purpose.

PARAGRAPH DEVELOPMENT

Like an essay, a paragraph should have a discernible organization. Ideas can be arranged from general to specific, or vice versa. Logic dictates that causes precede effects, but the opposite may sometimes be preferable. As always, clarity and intent should govern the sequence of ideas.

In general, a paragraph of only one or two sentences may be too scanty. Most of the time, thorough development of an idea calls for several sentences. Journalists, however, often write paragraphs consisting of one or two sentences. But the bulk of contemporary nonfiction consists of paragraphs of four to eight sentences.

In a coherent paragraph each sentence has its place and purpose. Disjointed paragraphs, on the other hand, consist of sentences arranged in random order. Or they contain ideas vaguely related or irrelevant to the main idea. Meaning serves as the primary glue that holds a coherent paragraph together, but transitional words and phrases such as *for example, also, but,* and *on the other hand* also help. In the following paragraph, notice how the italicized words and phrases tie sentences to each other.

> [1] Philip Adams is one of the most informative writers in the world on matters of home improvement. [2] He is *also* a writer who, over many years and far too many books, has fallen deeply in love with his own prose. [3] He is notoriously wordy, and repetition has become his trademark. [4] In his latest book, *however*, his usual deficiencies stand him in good stead. [5] "When sawing lumber" he advises "measure twice and cut once." [6] Carpenters in a hurry usually skip *that very important second measurement* and end up with "Everests of wasted lumber," as Adams puts it. [7] "Maybe 'Measure twice and cut once' should be emblazoned on bumper stickers," he muses, "and engraved on hammers and saws, too. [8] *While we're at it*, imprint these words of wisdom on coffee mugs and on tool boxes." [9] Adams's prose is *indeed repetitious here*, but for a good purpose. [10] *In this book repetition* provides texture to his writing, and texture provides clarity, and clarity promotes appreciation, and maybe, just maybe, do-it-yourselfers will take his advice.

Sentence 1 expresses the paragraph's most general idea and serves as the topic sentence. The pronoun *he* throughout the paragraph ties every sentence to *Philip Adams*, the subject of the topic sentence. The word *also* ties sentence 2 to sentence 1. Then sentences 3 and 4 are tied to each other by the word *however*. In sentence 6, the phrase *that very important second measurement* refers back to sentence 5. *While we're at it* (sentence 8) refers to the suggestion he's made in sentence 7, and the allusion to repetition in sentence 9 recalls allusions made in several earlier sentences. Because of these linking elements, the ten sentences cannot be arranged in any other way without destroying the paragraph's coherence.

Mini-Workout in Developing Paragraphs

Directions: The sentences in each of the following groups make up a coherent paragraph. They are not in order, however. Rearrange sentences logically. In the blank spaces, write the number that represents the position of each sentence in the paragraph.

1. ____ a. A particular worker, for example, may lack the skill to do a certain job.
   ____ b. Another important variable is inclement weather, which can set a project back for days on end.
   ____ c. In spite of the best laid plans and preparation, building projects sometimes work out badly.
   ____ d. The main reason is that the foreman can't always predict what the workers will do.
   ____ e. Then, the project can't proceed until another worker is found.

2. ____ a. They also tend toward an unhealthy lifestyle, according to a study of 374 college undergraduates at Carleton University.
   ____ b. Here is some bad news for students who put off studying.
   ____ c. In addition, student procrastinators are more likely to eat poorly, smoke more, and sleep less than students who keep up with their schoolwork.
   ____ d. Their overall college experience, as a result, is far less satisfying than the experience of students who do their homework promptly.
   ____ e. Procrastinators get more cold and flu symptoms and have more digestive problems than their punctual classmates.

3. ____ a. College students swipe IDs to open doors, buy tickets to athletic events, operate ATMs, do their laundry, and even indicate their presence in a lecture hall.
   ____ b. It also identified students when they took books from the library.
   ____ c. Most colleges issue ID cards to students.
   ____ d. But magnetic strips and wireless chips have converted this modest piece of plastic into an essential, multiuse appendage.
   ____ e. At one time, a student ID was just a laminated card good for gaining access to campus buildings.

4. ____ a. In addition, a college official can often tell from an essay whether the applicant is eligible for a particular kind of scholarship or other type of financial aid.

____ b. At some colleges the essay counts heavily in admissions decisions and is used to place students in the proper academic programs.

____ c. College admissions officials read application essays with great care.

____ d. One reason is that the essays help colleges see each applicant more clearly and personally.

____ e. For example, an essay may explain why a bright student earned mediocre grades in high school.

5. ____ a. Soon thereafter, some colleges began to ask applicants whether they received professional help in completing their application essays.

____ b. They also found that teachers, counselors, and other adults were giving more than casual lessons in essay writing.

____ c. Wondering what caused the change, admissions officials soon discovered that many high schools had made instruction in writing an application essay a part of the curriculum.

____ d. In recent years, students from certain parts of the country started sending in polished college application essays in large numbers.

____ e. For up to $250 an hour, some "consultants" were all but composing essays for anxious students.

Answers are on page 300. For additional practice in arranging sentences, turn to page 270.

Mini-Workout in Identifying Paragraph Unity and Coherence

Directions: The following paragraphs may suffer from either lack of unity, lack of coherence, or both. Identify the problem in each, and write a comment that offers an effective remedy. Some paragraphs may not need revision.

1. [1] *Lord of the Flies* is about a group of English schoolboys stranded on a remote island after an airplane crash. [2] When they arrive, they divide into groups. [3] There are groups at this high school, too. [4] On the island, Piggy is the leader of the group consisting of the most intelligent and rational boys. [5] He is a thinker, but he gets killed by another group, the savages, led by Jack. [6] A third group on the island is led by Ralph, who wants law and order and a set of rules. [7] The different groups in the novel are amazingly similar to groups in this school, known as the nerds, the jocks, and the preps.

Comment:_____

_____

2. [1] Under the present law, doing illegal drugs can have serious consequences for young people. [2] They may find their education interrupted and the future put in doubt by having a police record. [3] An arrest or conviction for a felony can complicate their lives and plans. [4] A police record causes embarrassment to a person's family. [5] Parents like to brag about their children's accomplishments. [6] Can you imagine a mother who would be proud of her daughter's experience in the courts and in prison?

Comment:_____

_____

3. [1] Today there is general agreement that we are experiencing unprecedented change. [2] Established institutions are crumbling. [3] The majority of people no longer live in traditional families that consist of two natural parents and their children. [4] Old moralities are being questioned. [5] The United States has an increasingly diverse population. [6] At an early age, ghetto children may learn the thrills offered by drugs, crime, and gang warfare. [7] Children at all social and economic levels learn to expect that lying, cheating, and stealing are rampant in business, politics, and almost every other endeavor. [8] Even churches are not exempt from corruption.

Comment:_____

_____

4. [1] Rival political parties make elections meaningful by allowing voters to choose among candidates with contrasting views and interests. [2] Most parties try to unite divided interests within their ranks in order to appeal to the widest number of voters. [3] In the United States and Great Britain, a two-party system has long been effective in uniting various interests. [4] In dictatorships, criticism of the party in power may be regarded as treason. [5] Often, only a single, controlling party is permitted to exist. [6] Elections mean little in such countries, for the people have no real choice among the candidates. [7] Nor do they have the freedom to openly criticize their government.

Comment:_____

_____

5. [1] Department stores, unless they are like general stores that still function in some small towns, usually hire employees by the hundreds for different jobs. [2] A large number of workers engage in buying, pricing, and selling merchandise. [3] A sales staff promotes sales by advertising and by designing attractive displays of goods to be sold. [4] In recent years, mail-order buying on the Internet has forced many department stores to go out of business. [5] In addition, the store's comptroller handles financial affairs, such as billing, credit, and payroll. [6] The personnel department hires employees and deals with employment problems.

Comment:_____

_____

6. [1] The porpoise, or bottlenose dolphin, is one of the most intelligent animals. [2] It can imitate the sounds of human speech and communicate with its fellow porpoises using barks, clicks, and whistles. [3] Scientists rate their intelligence between that of the chimpanzee, long held as the most intelligent nonhuman animal, and the dog. [4] Porpoises can be trained to leap high in the air, jump through hoops, catch a ball, fetch a stick, and even to participate in underwater work by serving as messengers between divers and surface ships.

Comment:_____

_____

7. [1] *Robinson Crusoe* is a memorable adventure story about a man marooned on a desert island and was written by the British author Daniel Defoe. [2] Defoe was born in London in 1660 and started writing only after he went bankrupt in a business career. [3] He wrote about politics, religion, economics, and geography in addition to writing poetry and novels. [4] Today, he is best known for *Robinson Crusoe*, which is but a tiny fraction of his work.

Comment:_____

_____

8. [1] Aristotle made valuable contributions to the study of logic. [2] Plato, the teacher of Aristotle and Socrates' star pupil, believed that understanding the nature of perfect forms such as the circle and the square leads to understanding of ideal forms in all areas of life. [3] Socrates fought the Sophists all his life because he believed in truth, and the Sophists denied the existence of truth. [4] They said that everything was relative, including knowledge and morality. [5] The period of ancient philosophy reached its climax in Greece in 600–500 B.C.

Comment:_____

_____

9. [1] The American pioneers made simple farm implements and household tools. [2] They made pitchforks, for example, by attaching long handles to deer antlers. [3] Brooms were made by fastening together ten or twenty small tree branches. [4] They whittled wooden spoons, bowls, platters, and used gourds and the horns of sheep and other animals for drinking cups. [5] They made graters by punching holes into a piece of sheet iron. [6] Then they would rub kernels of corn across the jagged surface to make cornmeal.

Comment:_____

_____

10. [1] You can't find Potter's Field on a map. [2] It is not a real place. [3] Rather, it is the name given to any plot of land reserved for the burial of unidentified and destitute people. [4] The name was first used in the New Testament of the Bible. [5] After Judas betrayed Christ for thirty pieces of silver, the priests used the money to buy "the potter's field to bury strangers in." [6] Today, in many urban areas, potter's fields have disappeared. [7] Land is too valuable to use for burying unknown and unclaimed corpses. [8] For a fraction of the cost, bodies are cremated and ashes thrown into common graves.

Comment:_____

_____

Answers are on pages 300–301.

SAT ESSAYS: WHAT TO SAY AND HOW TO SAY IT

Stylistic Conventions

Frankly, most SAT Essays don't rank high on the list of preferred literary genres—up there, say, with an immortal poem or quality short story. Nevertheless, your essay should follow the customary practices of literary writing.

1. Use standard English prose, as error-free as you can make it.

2. Discuss the source using the "literary present." In other words, use verbs in the present tense as in "The writer *claims* that ..." or "A shift *occurs* when ...." Use other tenses only when it's necessary or logical to do so.

3. Refer to the author of the source as "author," "writer," or "speaker." You might also use the writer's last name as it appears in the prompt. To save a few seconds, you might simply use the author's initials. If the gender of the writer is unclear, use either masculine or feminine pronouns—whichever you prefer. Stay away, however, from "he or she," a pedantic and cumbersome usage.

4. Keep yourself in the background or out of the essay altogether. The SAT Essay is not a personal statement such as a college application essay. It's not about you, so avoid using "I" unless you absolutely must, and don't pass judgment on the quality of the writing or express your personal opinion on the issue being argued by the author of the source. Maintain a detached, objective tone throughout, but don't be a slave to it if another will serve you better.

5. Don't summarize the source. Essay readers know what it says. Your analysis of the source will demonstrate how well you comprehend it,

6. When quoting the text of the source, copy the words and punctuation exactly. If you must omit something, indicate the omission with an ellipsis (...). Instead of copying long quotations verbatim, save time by using an ellipsis between the first and last words, as in "Admittedly ... possible." Finally, put square brackets [ ] around any words you insert into a quotation.

7. A plain, natural style of writing is probably best. Think of your readers as everyday folks who appreciate straight, everyday language.

Using Plain and Precise Language

The SAT Essay is not a place to show off your vocabulary. To write clearly, use plain words. Use an elegant word only when it's the best and only word that expresses what you want to say. Why? Because an elegant word used merely to use an elegant word is bombastic … er … big-sounding and artificial. Besides, simple ideas dressed up in ornate words often obscure meaning. Or worse, they make writers sound phony if not foolish. For instance, under ordinary circumstances you'd never utter the words, "Let's go to our domiciles" at the end of a day at school. Nor would you call your teachers *pedagogues* or your dog a *canine*. Yet, the following overblown sentence appeared in a student's essay:

> Although his history pedagogue insisted that Finn labor in his domicile immediately upon arrival, Finn was obliged to air his canine before commencing.

How much clearer and more direct it would have been to write:

> Finn had to walk his dog before starting his history homework.

Fortunately, English is loaded with simple words that can express the most profound ideas. A sign that says STOP! conveys its message more clearly than CEASE AND DESIST. When a dentist pokes at your teeth, it *hurts*, even if dentists call it "experiencing discomfort." Simple doesn't necessarily mean short, however. It's true that plain words tend to be the short ones, but not always. The word *fid* is short, but it's not plain unless you are a sailor, in which case you'd know that a fid supports the mast on your boat or is an instrument used to pry open a tight knot in your lines. On the other hand, *spontaneously* is five syllables long. Yet it is a plain and simple word because of its frequent use.

Simple ideas dressed up in ornate words not only obscure meaning but make writers sound pretentious:

Fancy: The more I recalled her degradation of me, the more inexorable I became.
Plain: The more I thought of her insults, the more determined I grew.

Fancy: Mr. Lester has a proclivity toward prevarication.
Plain: Mr. Lester is a liar.

Fancy: The coterie of harriers gleaned the salience of synergy in competitive racing engagements.
Plain: The runners learned that teamwork pays off in races.

Ernest Hemingway called a writer's greatest gift a "built-in, shock-proof crap detector." Hemingway's own detector worked well. He produced about the leanest, plainest writing in the English language—not that you should try to emulate Hemingway. (That's already been done by countless imitators.) But an efficient crap detector of your own will encourage you to choose words only because they express exactly what you mean.

EUPHEMISMS

Of course there are occasions when the plainest words won't do. Fortunately, our language provides countless euphemisms—words and phrases that express unsavory or objectionable ideas more delicately. In some contexts—a funeral service, for instance—the verb *die* may be too coarse or painful. In its place, a euphemism such as *pass away*, *pass on, be deceased, rest, expire, meet one's maker* may be more suitable. Think also of *toilet*, a word almost never posted on a public bathroom door. Instead, you'll find such labels as *W.C., lounge, powder room, washroom, comfort station*, and, probably the most euphemistic usage of all—*ladies* and *men*.

Euphemisms unquestionably have their place and function. In essay writing, however, use them only when you have a valid reason for doing so.

Don't interpret this admonition to use plain words as a reason to use the language of blogging, IMs, or texting on the SAT Essay. Everyday language brimming with colorful words and expressions like *bulk out, cop some z's, awesome*, and *total babe* has its place, but its place is not your SAT Essay unless you definitely need the latest lingo to create an effect that you can't produce in any other way. If you insist on using slang, that's okay, but don't use quotation marks to draw attention to the fact that you can't think of standard or more original words. If, to make a point, you overload your essay with slang, be sure to demonstrate your mastery of standard English in at least part of the piece. After all, colleges want to know that you can write good, standard prose.

When writing an analytical essay, choose the style that you prefer. You can use a plain, conversational style in which the language sounds like you, but try to keep references to yourself to a minimum. Analytical essays generally focus on the subject matter rather than on the writer. That doesn't mean, though, that you need to sound stiff and artificial.

The point is, don't be phony! SAT Essay readers are old hands at spotting pretense in students' writing. Let your genuine voice ring out, although the way you speak is not necessarily the way you should write. Spoken language is often vague, clumsy, repetitive, confused, and wordy. Consider writing as the everyday speech of someone who speaks exceedingly well—grammatically correct and free of pop expressions and clichés. Think of it as the kind of mature speech expected of you in serious conversation, say, with a panel of parents concerned about your school's curriculum. Or maybe even the way this paragraph sounds. You could do a lot worse!

PRECISE LANGUAGE

Precise words are memorable, but hazy, hard-to-grasp words fade quickly away. Tell your garage mechanic vaguely, "This car is broken," and he'll ask for more information. Say precisely "My car won't start in freezing weather," and he'll raise the engine hood and go to work. If a patient in the E.R. says, "I feel pain," a surgeon might at least like to know exactly where it hurts before pulling out her scalpels. In other words, precise language is more informative, more functional, and thus more desirable.

Surely, vague, shadowy words are easier to think of. But they often cover up a lack of clear and rigorous thinking. For example, it's easy to pass judgment on a book by calling it "good" or "interesting." But what readers should be told is precisely why you think so. How simple to call someone an "old man" without bothering to show the reader a "stooped white-haired gentleman shuffling along the sidewalk." A student who describes her teacher as "ugly" sends a different image of ugliness to each reader. But if the teacher is a "shifty-eyed tyrant who spits when she talks," then say it. Or if the teacher's personality is ugly, show her ill-temper, arrogance, and cruelty as she curses her hapless students.

Good writers understand that their words must appeal to a reader's senses. To write precisely is to write with pictures, sounds, and actions that are as vivid on paper as they are in reality. Exact words leave distinct marks; abstract ones, blurry impressions. As the following pairs of sentences illustrate, precise writers turn hazy notions into vivid images:

Hazy: The announcer said that one of the players exhibited violent behavior.

Precise: The announcer reported that Carolyn yelled "Get out of my face," as she bloodied the goalie's nose.

Hazy: Everett's parents were happy when he got 1600 on the SAT.

Precise: Everett's 1600 on the SAT thrilled his parents. Their worried looks suddenly disappeared, they stopped nagging Everett about doing homework, and they never again asked him desperately, "What in the world will become of you?"

Clearly, the precisely worded sentences are richer than the hazy ones. But they are also much longer. In fact, it's not always desirable or necessary to define every abstraction with precise details. Each time *dinner* is mentoined, for instance, it's not necessary to recite the menu. When you use an abstract word in an essay, ask yourself what is more important—to give readers a more detailed account of your idea or to push on to other, more important, matters. Context determines how abstract your essay should be. Just remember that nobody likes reading an essay that fails to deal concretely with anything.

Mini-Workout in Using Precise Wording

Directions: The next ten sentences desperately need more precise wording. Please provide the verbal antidote to their vagueness.

1. The abandoned house was old and run-down.

_____

_____

2. The witness did not take it lightly when the judge accused her of perjury.

_____

_____

3. The air was terribly polluted.

_____

_____

4. She tried diligently to study physics, but one could see that it made no difference.

_____

_____

5. The atmosphere at the graduation ceremony was intense.

_____

_____

6. One must do many things to earn a place on the roster of an athletic team.

_____

_____

7. Events at the O'Malley funeral surprised Greg.

_____

_____

8. Kara met with little academic success in high school.

_____

_____

9. Teddy and Joey's family was very poor.

_____

_____

10. In a perilous situation, Rod acted bravely.

_____

_____

Answers are on page 301.

Fresh Language and Surprises

Dull language has three main qualities: (1) boring, (2) boring, and (3) boring. So, do your essay readers a favor by giving them a verbal surprise. After reading hundreds of predictable essays on the same topic, readers will do cartwheels for something fresh and new. (Ha! SAT readers doing cartwheels—that's kind of a surprise, isn't it?) It takes courage and imagination to use fresh language, but here's a guarantee: A verbal surprise may not turn SAT readers into acrobats, but it will unquestionably give your essay a boost.

What is a verbal surprise? Nothing more than an interesting image or choice of words. That doesn't mean use odd words like *twit* or *fop*. Even ordinary words, used deftly, can dazzle readers. Moreover they'll sound more natural. For example:

Ordinary: The writer claimed that city children see pigeons at an early age.
Surprising: The writer claimed that city children meet pigeons at an early age.

Because we don't ordinarily "meet" pigeons, the unanticpated change from *see* to *meet* is mildly surprising.

Ordinary: Mosquitoes bit the builders of the Panama Canal.
Surprising: Mosquitoes dined on the builders of the Panama Canal.

Changing the verb makes a common sentence surprising because *dined* suggests gentility and good manners, qualities that most mosquitoes haven't yet acquired.

Ordinary: The gunshot frightened the geese, which flew away.
Surprising: The gunshot filled the sky with frightened geese.

The ordinary sentence states literally that the sound of the gunshot scared the geese. In the revision, the shot becomes a vital force with the power to fill the sky. Both the geese and the sentence have sprung to life.

Words can also surprise readers by suggesting certain sounds. The word *bombard*, for instance, has a heavy explosive sound. *Yawn* has a wide-open sound that can be stretched out indefinitely. *Slogging* is slow, just like the action it names, and *choke* sticks in your throat. *Gurgling brooks* evokes the sound of—what else?

Readers find unexpected pleasure, too, from the repetition of sounds—both consonants and vowels, as in *the dark, dank day smelled of death; the machine sucked up sewage from the swamp;* and *the cold wind moaned over the ocean waves.* The appeal of such repetition is evidenced by the countless clichés that crowd our everyday speech and (regrettably) our writing, such as *footloose and fancy free, sink or swim,* and *blast from the past.* In short, an occasional treat for the ears will go far to captivate your readers. But don't repeat sounds too often because they might call attention to themselves and pull the reader away from the meaning of your words.

SURPRISE WITH COMPARISONS

English is filled with wonderful words to describe virtually anything. Yet, occasionally emotions and experiences seem almost beyond words. At such times, you can depend on figures of speech such as metaphors and similes to make meaning clear.

Granted, such metaphorical comparisons appear more often in so-called creative writing—stories, memoirs, personal essays. Yet, they're not out of place in analytical or expository writing such as the **SAT Essay**!

To illustrate, here is an excerpt from the text of an SAT Essay source in which the writer argues that a decline in the quality of American education is depriving our children of an opportunity to succeed in life.

Among young Americans whose parents didn't graduate from high school, 5 percent graduate from college. In other industrialized countries, the figure in 23 percent.

As recently at 2000, the United States ranked first in the percentage of college graduates. Today, according to a study by the United States Department of Education, the U.S. ranks fifth, while Russia comes in first. And among 25-to-34-year-olds, America ranks 12th, and once-impoverished South Korea tops the list.

Fixing our education system is no small challenge, but it's the only way to give all of America's children a fair start in life.

In her SAT Essay, high school senior Nora G, referring to this excerpt, wrote

The best escalator to opportunity in America is education. Providing statistics from a new study by the U.S. Department of Education, the writer underscores that the escalator is broken and needs to be fixed.

Let's hear it for Nora. By transforming the source's rather mundane presentation of facts into a metaphor, she has added an engaging flourish to her essay. Another student, Loren L, commenting on same set of statistics, wrote

The American dream seems to have emigrated to other countries.

Here, the inclusion of a single word *emigrated*, instantly gives the idea an unexpected zing.

In addition, comparisons are economical. They require fewer words than you might otherwise need to state an idea. To describe elderly residents of a nursing home, for instance, you might mention white and gray heads, pale and wrinkled faces, folds of papery skin, and wheelchairs lined up in the corridor. But if all those details are unnecessary, you could simply compare the residents to the slats on a weathered fence. Instantly your reader will see the resemblance: warped and cracked boards on a weather-beaten fence.

The limited vocabulary of young children keeps them from expressing all they want to say. By nature, therefore, they make up comparisons: "Daddy, when my foot goes to sleep it feels like ginger ale." "Mommy, this ice cream tastes like chocolate sunshine." As people grow older, they often lose this knack of making colorful comparisons and have to relearn it. But when you start consciously to seek comparisons, you'll find them sprouting like weeds in a garden—that is, everywhere.

Similes (Tim wrestles *like* a tiger) and metaphors (Tim *is* a tiger) point out likenesses between something familiar (tiger) and something unfamiliar (how Tim wrestles). To convey meaning, one side of a comparison must always be common and recognizable. Therefore, comparing the cry of the Arctic tern to the song of a tree toad won't enlighten a reader familiar with neither water birds nor tree toads. Because you can expect readers to know the sound of a fiddle, however, a more revealing comparison is *The cry of the Arctic tern sounds like a fiddler searching for a c-sharp.*

Make your comparisons fresh and original. Don't rely on old stand-bys such as "life is like a box of chocolates," or "like a bat out of hell," or "dead as a doornail." Our language is littered with countless comparisons that once may have been vibrant and fresh but have wilted from overuse. The fact is that every familiar combination of words, such as "I could care less" or "you've got to be kidding" or "what a bummer," was once new, cool, even poetic. But repetition has turned them into clichés.

TIP

Clichés belong in the clichés graveyard, not in your essay.

Let clichés rest in the cliché graveyard. Don't drag them out for your SAT Essay. That is an admonition easier to say that to follow because clichés crowd our conversations, swamp our airwaves, and deluge the media. Like the air we breathe (a cliché), we hardly notice them. In an essay, however, especially one that is supposed to demonstrate your unique cast of mind, you must avoid clichés like the plague. "Like the plague," in fact, is one you should avoid, along with other secondhand phrases and expressions like *the boom line; on the ground; how does that sit with you; touch base with; there has been a sea-change in …; off the top of my head; at the end of the day; a point well taken; two sides of the same coin; getting psyched; double-edged sword; go off the deep end; life on the edge; life in the fast lane; for openers; think outside the box; flipped out; a full plate; get a life; get real; super; chief honcho; the big cheese; so amazing; that's cool; the whole enchilada; no way; José,* and would you believe, *would you believe?* (This list of clichés is far from complete. No doubt you could add many more.)

On the SAT you won't be penalized for an essay lacking inventive and scintillating expressions, but you'll pay a price if your writing is overrun with clichés. Get into the habit, then, of purging all trite phrases from your writing vocabulary. *Half the battle,* as they say, is knowing a cliché when you meet one. The other half—expelling them—is still to be fought and won.

Mini-Workout in Writing Comparisons

PART A

> **Directions:** Untold numbers of comparisons are waiting to be born. Because you see the world differently from everyone else, you can invent memorable comparisons that no one—not Shakespeare, not Milton, not Whitman, nor any other immortal—ever thought of. Write an original comparison for each of the qualities listed below. Avoid clichés.

1. as comfortable as

_____

2. as tough as

_____

3. as gorgeous as

_____

4. as silly as

_____

5. as serious as

_____

6. as perfect as

_____

7. as wild as

_____

8. as unpredictable as

_____

9. as impetuous as

_____

10. as reliable as

_____

Answers are on pages 301–302.

PART B

> **Directions:** Try your hand at writing an extended comparison, in which you expand upon a single metaphor or simile. If you can't think of one, try one of these:
>
> In what ways is life like a river? A carousel? A hero's journey?
> How does school resemble a zoo? A shopping mall? An airport?
> How is music like a clearing in the woods? A chapel? A painting?

_____

_____

_____

_____

_____

_____

_____

_____

(Add paper, if necessary.)

Answers are on page 302.

Varying Sentence Structure

When writing an essay, it's easy to fall into a rut by using the same sentence structure over and over and over. But readers prefer a variety of sentences.

Varied sentences can bring a dull essay to life.

Variety for its own sake is hardly preferable to assembly-line writing—writing in which every sentence follows the same pattern. But variety that clarifies meaning or gives emphasis to selected ideas is something else. For one thing, it adds life to your prose.

English sentences are structured in three ways: **simple**, **compound**, and **complex**.

Simple: Terry fell asleep in math class.

The sentence is **simple** because it contains one grammatical subject (Terry) and one verb (fell). It also states a single main idea.

Compound: The competition is stiff, but it won't keep Mark from winning.

The sentence is **compound** because it is made up of two simple sentences joined by the coordinating conjunction *but*. Other coordinating conjunctions used in compound sentences are *and, yet, or, for, nor,* and *so,* as in

The competition is stiff, *and* Mark is worried about winning.
Mark is worried about winning, *for* he has a bad cold.

Notice that the structure of each of these compound sentences gives roughly equal emphasis to its two main ideas.

Complex: Although he has a bad cold, Mark will win.

The sentence is **complex** because it is made up of two parts—a simple sentence (*Mark will win*) and a clause (*Although he has a bad cold*) that is not a complete sentence in itself but depends on the simple sentence for its meaning. Because the clause begins with a subordinating conjunction (*Although*), it is called a **subordinate clause**. Subordinate clauses contain ideas related to the complete sentence (called the **independent**, or **main**, clause), but they are usually less important. Other common subordinating conjunctions include *because, after, before, though, unless, until, whenever,* and *while*.

Not every simple, compound, and complex sentence is structured in the way just described. In fact, variations abound because English is a remarkably flexible language that can be shaped in countless ways, as you'll see next.

Most simple sentences start with the grammatical subject followed by the verb, as in:

Cats (subject) *fall* (verb) asleep in about three seconds.
They (subject) *sleep* (verb) best after eating and cleaning themselves.
I (subject) *wish* (verb) to be a cat in my next life.

A string of sentences with this subject–verb pattern resembles the prose in a grade-school primer—a style that just won't do on an SAT Essay. To be sure that you write in a more mature and engaging way, analyze one of your recent essays. If several sentences begin with grammatical subjects, try shifting the subject elsewhere. Try leading off with a prepositional phrase, or with an adverb, adjective, or some other grammatical unit.

The following pairs of sentences show how a subject can be shifted from its customary position:

Before the shift: Ms. Bennett is one of the most popular teachers in the school.
After the shift: In this school, Ms. Bennett is one of the most popular teachers.

After a prepositional phrase was added, the subject (*Ms. Bennett*) has been moved further along in the sentence.

Before: She taught the novel *The Grapes of Wrath* to our eleventh-grade English class with enthusiasm.
After: Enthusiastically, she taught the novel *The Grapes of Wrath* to our eleventh-grade English class.

Obviously, the revised sentence begins with an adverb.

Before: Students were less excited about the book than she was.
After: Yet, students were less excited about the book than she was.

Well, here the subject (*students*) is stated after an opening connective.

Before: I loved the book, although it turned out to be an intolerable drag for most of my classmates.
After: Although the book turned out to be an intolerable drag for most of my class-mates, I loved it.

After introducing the sentence with a dependent clause, the writer names the subject, *I*, and then adds the rest of the sentence.

Before: Ms. Bennett pushed the class to find symbolic meaning in various characters to make the book more meaningful.
After: To make the book more meaningful, Ms. Bennett pushed the class to find sym-bolic meaning in various characters.

To revise this sentence the writer begins with a verbal, in this case "to make," the infinitive form of the verb. (Verbals look and feel much like verbs but serve a different function. Verbals, though, come from verbs, hence their name and their resemblance.)

Before: I read the book in two days, hoping that it would never end.
After: Hoping that it would never end, I read the book in two days.

Aiming to diversify sentence openings, the writer starts this sentence with another kind of verbal, known as a **participle**. The -*ing* ending often indicates that a word is a participle.

Before: I was awed by the tenacity of the Joad family and absorbed by every soul-stirring syllable of the story.
After: Awed by the tenacity of the Joad family, I was absorbed by every soul-stirring syllable of the story.

Determined to try something different, the writer begins the sentence with an adjective that happens to sound like a verb because of its -*ed* ending.

Still another variation to try now and then is the sentence constructed from matched ideas set in juxtaposition. President Kennedy used such a sentence to memorable effect in his inaugural speech:

"Ask not what your country can do for you, ask what you can do for your country."

The power of such sentences lies in the balance of parallel clauses. Each clause could stand alone, but together they express the idea more vigorously. Another famous example, from Shakespeare's *Julius Caesar*:

"Not that I loved Caesar less, but that I loved Rome more."

Emphasis can also come from a reversal of customary word order. Out of context a sentence in which the predicate precedes the subject may seem awkward. But in the right spot an inverted sentence can leave an indelible mark. "Dull the book is not" packs more wallop than "The book is not dull" or "The book is exciting." In the right context, "Perilous was the climb to the top of the cliff" sounds more ominous than "The climb to the top of the cliff was perilous." Inverted sentences should be used sparingly, however. More than once in an essay diminishes the vigor of each occurrence and may sound silly.

No rule of thumb says that a certain percentage of sentences in an essay ought to be different from the usual subject–verb structure. It really depends on the purpose and style of the essay. But if you find yourself repeating the same sentence pattern, restructure some of your sentences. SAT Essay readers are bound to reward you for the effort.

Sentence Types

Our language offers a rich menu of sentence types. Declarative sentences predominate in most essay writing. (Just to refresh your memory, a **declarative sentence**, such as the one you are now reading, simply makes a statement.) But other types of sentences can create all sorts of fascinating effects. Take interrogative sentences, for example. (Do you remember that **interrogative sentences** ask questions?) An interrogative sentence appropriately placed in an essay consisting of declarative sentences can change the pace and rhythm of the prose, underscore an idea, and promote the reader's involvement.

Don't forget about imperative sentences (Keep in mind that **imperative sentences** make requests or give commands.) and exclamatory sentences (What strong emotion an **exclamatory sentence** can express!).

Furthermore, you can write sentences interrupted at some point by a dash—although some editors and teachers claim that it's not proper to do so in formal prose. Direct and indirect quotations are useful, and on occasion you can drive home a point with a single emphatic word. Excellent!

There's peril, however, in scrambling sentence types for no other reason than to scramble sentence types, for you may end up with a mess on your hands. Be guided by what expresses your ideas most clearly and seems varied enough to interest your readers.

Repetition of Ideas

Repetition can be annoying, but adroitly used, it adds clout to an idea. When your sweetheart says, "I love you. I love you very much," the repetition intensifies the sentiment. If a coach admonishes his team, "Okay, guys, knock it off. I said knock it off," you know he really means it.

The following paragraph may suggest that the writer has a one-track mind:

> In the fall Bethany will be going to college. She is psyched to get out of high school. She is psyched to break away from her small town and live in a big city. She is psyched for meeting new people from all over the country and the world, and she is psyched to get started on a program of studies that she expects will prepare her for law school. But first, she is psyched to take the SAT.

Every sentence but the first uses the same subject–verb combination. Yet, the overall effect is anything but monotonous. What's memorable is not repetition, but relentlessness. Repeating the verb *psyched* five times emphasizes Bethany's frame of mind. The point could not have been made as emphatically using a different verb in each sentence.

Or take this passage written by an incorrigible bagel freak.

> My taste for bagels knows no bounds. I stop at the bagel shop on my way to school each morning and grab an onion bagel and coffee. Lunch consists of an olive bagel and a couple of veggie bagels smeared with cream cheese. At snack time I'm not picky. Any style bagel will do, but I hate to have dinner without a buttered poppy-seed bagel. Before bed I wash down a plain toasted bagel with a glass of milk, and in case I have insomnia, I stash two or three garlic bagels on my nightstand for a tasty middle-of the-night pick-me-up.

The writer virtually beats you over the head with bagels. But the repetition won't allow you to forget the point—that the writer has eyes not for pizza, not for burritos, not for onion rings, but only for bagels.

A word of caution: Restatements of a word or phrase can sometimes be distracting. Therefore, stay alert for accidental repetition:

> In a corner of the room stood a clock. The clock said four o'clock.
> Columbus made three ocean voyages. The voyages took him across the Atlantic Ocean.

Combining such sentences will keep you from ending one sentence and starting the next one with the same words:

> The clock in the corner of the room said four.
> Columbus made three voyages across the Atlantic.

Sentences can also be marred by words or sounds that draw attention to themselves:

> Maybe some people don't have as much freedom as others; but the freedom they do have is given to them for free. Therefore, freedom is proof enough that the best things in life are free.
> The members of the assembly remembered that November was just around the corner.

TIP

"Repetition cuts both ways: sometimes good, sometimes not."

"You can say that again!"

"Repetion cuts both ways: some ..."

"Okay, okay, you've made your point."

These writers failed to listen to the sound of their words. Had they read their sentences aloud, they may have noticed that voices were stuck in a groove. In fact, reading your words aloud allows you to step back and examine word sounds. (Hold it! Those two words—*aloud* and *allows*—sound jarring and should not be permitted to stand side by side.) Hearing your written words spoken, you're more apt to notice unwanted repetition. Whenever possible, let each of your practice essays cool for a while. Then enlist a friend to read it aloud. Hearing it in another's voice lends objectivity to the process of self-evaluation.

Short and Long Sentences

Another technique for fending off monotony in an essay is to vary the length of sentences. Long sentences (like this one) demand greater effort from readers because, while stepping from one part of the sentence to the next, they must keep track of more words, modifiers, phrases (not to speak of parenthetical asides), and clauses, without losing the writer's main thought, which may be buried amid any number of secondary, or less important, thoughts, while short sentences are usually easier to grasp. A brief sentence can make a point sharply because all its words concentrate on a single point. Take, for example, the last sentence in this passage:

> As they became more popular, more profitable, and, most important, more powerful as a means of creative expression, video games started to feel to me like the Internet had in its early days, when a technology on the verge of washing over our culture and reshaping it wholesale led millions of people of all ages to their computers to play games, and created mega-studios that produce such things like the Call of Duty series as well as small, independent developers in such profusion that art schools, which were devoted to theater and sculpture, found that the arrival of the interactive age in which video games were a most promising entertainment decided that they had better begin to teach game design. And then came GamerGate.*

A terse closing sentence following a windy, 119-word sentence produces a mild jolt. Indeed, its purpose is to startle the reader. The technique is easily mastered but should be used sparingly. Overuse dilutes its impact.

A series of short sentences can be as tiresome as a succession of long ones. A balance works best. If you have strung together four or five sentences of equal length, try to reformat them. Here, to illustrate, is an overweight sentence that needs a complete makeover:

> In the 1870s, the archaeologist Heinrich Schliemann dug in the correct spot and discovered not only one ancient city of Troy, but nine of them, one lying on top of the other, since every few centuries a new city had been built upon the ruins of the old, causing Schliemann to dig right past the layer containing the ruins of the famous city of the Trojan Horse without realizing he had done so, a mistake not corrected until almost fifty years later by Carl Blegen of the University of Cincinnati, by which time, unfortunately, it was too late for Schliemann because he had been dead for forty years.

The sentence is perfectly grammatical, but it carries a big 108-word load. Cut it down to size. Break it into pieces, rearrange it, add verbs, drop an idea or two, change the emphasis, and delete words. When you're done, the restyled sentence might sound something like this:

*A controversy centering on ethics and sexual harassment in the video game industry during 2014.

In the 1870s, the archaeologist Heinrich Schliemann dug in the correct spot and discovered not only one ancient city of Troy, but nine of them, one lying on top of the other. He figured out that every few centuries a new city had been built upon the ruins of the old. Without realizing it, he had dug right past the layer he was seeking, the layer containing the ruins of the famous city of the Trojan Horse. His mistake was corrected fifty years later by Carl Blegen of the University of Cincinnati. By then, however, it was too late for Schliemann. He had been dead for forty years.

Likewise, a string of four or five equally long (or short) sentences can be combined to create a more balanced and varied paragraph. Here, for instance, is a paragraph, also about an ancient city, made up of short, choppy sentences:

Pompeii was an ancient city. It belonged to the Roman Empire. It was near the base of Mount Vesuvius. In 79 A.D., the volcano on Vesuvius erupted. Tons of hot, wet ash fell on Pompeii. In less than a day, the city was buried. It just vanished. More than seventeen centuries later, an Italian peasant found Pompeii. His discovery was accidental. He was digging in a field. His shovel struck the top of a wall. That was two hundred years ago. Pompeii is still being excavated two hundred years later. About two-thirds of the city has been unearthed. It must have been a beautiful city.

With repetition eliminated and some ideas subordinated to others, here is what you get:

The ancient Roman city of Pompeii lay near the base of Mt. Vesuvius. In 79 A.D., Vesuvius erupted, burying the city with tons of hot, wet ash. In less than a day, the city vanished. More than seventeen centuries later, an Italian peasant digging in a field with a shovel accidentally struck the top of a wall. He had found Pompeii. Today, two hundred years later, the city is still being unearthed. The excavation reveals that Pompeii must have been a beautiful city.

For more details and practice in sentence combining, turn to Chapter 1, page 42.

VARYING SENTENCES—A SUMMARY

Use a variety of sentence types: simple, compound, and complex.
Create variety by starting sentences with a:

Prepositional phrase: *From the start, In the first place, At the outset*
Adverbs and adverbial phrases: *Orginally, At first, Initially*
Dependent clauses: *When you start with this, Because the opening is*
Conjunctions: *And, But, Not only, Either, So, Yet*
Adjectives and adjective phrases: *Fresh from, Introduced with, Headed by*
Verbal infinitives: *To launch, To take the first step, To get going*
Participles: *Leading off, Starting up, Commencing with*
Inversions: *Unique is the writer who embarks ...*

Balance long and short sentences.
Combine series of very short sentences.
Dismember very long sentences.

Mini-Workout in Varying Sentences

Directions: The following passages need greater balance. Divide some of the long sentences and combine some of the short ones. Try to preserve the original meaning of each passage.

1. Mr. Finn is the teacher. He's a good teacher. He runs the class like a dictatorship, however. He has no use for "democracy." He knows nothing about freedom. He announced his rules on the first day. He doesn't allow talking. He forbids gum chewing. He won't permit the wearing of hats. At the bell, he locks the classroom door. After-school detention is a consequence of lateness to class. His homework is compulsory. A girl once came without homework. Mr. Finn lowered the boom. The girl turned colors and almost wept. No one dares to come unprepared to class.

   _____

   _____

   _____

   _____

2. I have taken numerous science classes. In science classes we mostly talked about experiments. We didn't do experiments. The equipment was too costly. We had to make do with obsolete equipment. Scientific theories were taught. The theories were not practiced in labs. They were not demonstrated. The science department needs $1 million. With a million dollars it could give students a better education in science.

   _____

   _____

   _____

   _____

3. By dumping garbage, sewage, and other hazardous waste products into the sea, many nations are polluting the world's oceans, and in doing so are making beaches and swimming dangerous, poisoning fish with toxic materials that end up in fish, lobsters, clams, and other sea life that we humans eat, causing the toxins to enter our bodies.

   _____

   _____

   _____

   _____

   _____

4. The earth has experienced a sharp increase in natural disasters, from about 100 per year in the 1960s to five times that number in the early part of the twenty-first century, the reason being not that earthquakes, droughts, huge storms, and floods are happening more frequently and with greater intensity but that the population of the world has increased and people in greater numbers now occupy areas that are prone to natural disasters, such as flood plains, coastal lands, and cities built on subterranean fault lines. The planet has not changed. Humans have.

_____

_____

_____

_____

_____

5. The American Dream is a popular concept in American life. It has different meanings for different people. It commonly means finding a good job. It also means getting married. Dreams also consist of having a couple of kids and owning a home. The home has a white picket fence and a two-car garage. Some people think that such a dream is shallow. They say that the dream should also include a good education, friends, a feeling of well-being, good health, and above all, the blessings of liberty. By that they mean freedom of speech and freedom of religion. The dream must also have the freedom to choose to be part of an untraditional family made up of same-sex partners or any other combination of adults and children.

_____

_____

_____

_____

_____

Suggested answers are on pages 302–303.

Ending Your Essay

Because it comes last, the final sentences of your essay should be written with care. Don't resort to that old stand-by, a summary ending. When an essay is short to begin with, it's insulting to review for readers what is evident on the page in front of them. Readers are intelligent people. Trust them to remember what your essay says.

Rather than rehash what you've already written, comment on something in the passage that left an impression on you.

An effective conclusion should fit the style and mood of the essay and spring naturally from its contents. A good essay can easily be spoiled by a grating conclusion. A serious essay, for example, shouldn't end with a joke. Also stay away from endings that are too common or cutesy, such as: *that's it; so long for now; happy reading; well, I can't think of anything else; sorry, I've run out of time; good-bye and God bless you.* Such trite endings say in effect that you and your imagination have run out of gas.

TIP

Avoid summary endings.

Above all, avoid the desperate ending, the one that pleads with the SAT reader to be kind:

I worked like a dog on my essay. Please give it a high grade.
I hope you'll like this essay.
My father is making me apply to Princeton, so I need at least a score of 4/4/4. Thank you.

A short ending is preferable to none at all. A carefully written ending leaves readers satisfied that they have arrived somewhere and may sway them to judge your essay more favorably than otherwise. There are no guarantees, of course, but readers are bound to be touched by a memento of your thinking, your sense of humor, or your vision. Even an ordinary thought, uniquely expressed, will leave an agreeable afterglow.

Here are some common techniques for writing conclusions.

If you focused your essay on two or three major rhetorical elements, you might single out the one that's most compelling. Or you might add an insightful idea that occurred to you while reading the text:

Conclusion: The writer clearly has a wonderful way with words. The portrait he paints of Native American tribes would not be as persuasive without his deeply felt admiration for the now-vanished people who lived in what is now California's Silicon Valley. How odd that the land they once worshipped is now occupied mainly by computer geeks, to whom the land means little more than the area they pass through going to and from work.

Or, if the writer has built an argument with indisputable evidence and has piled up enough facts to convince even the most skeptical readers that his position is valid, you might compliment the writer for his work:

Conclusion: In making a case for openness, Nelson has compiled a vast array of facts about the NSA and the FBI's secrecy. His evidence in support of full public disclosure is so convincing that, were I ever in need of a lawyer to represent me in court, I'd phone Nelson first. Beyond the shadow of a doubt, he'd win my case for me.

Another option is to review something in the essay that might make your reader smile. For example, the source might argue that in spite of its popularity in some quarters, the sport of boxing ought to be banned in the United States. As your essay ends, you might show your sense of humor:

Conclusion: With his heavy-hitting style and tons of knock-out evidence, the writer Brendan Kahn has struck avid boxing fans a mighty blow below the belt.

Or if the source has convinced you that livestock being raised for meat should be fed grass rather than corn products, you might say what you plan to do about it:

Conclusion: You can bet that the next time I go to McDonald's I'll think twice about ordering a Big Mac.

Lets' say the source reminded you of an anecdote germane to the writer's argument. The writer, for instance, may have claimed that older people seem to be younger than ever—that today's 70-year-olds are like 50-year-olds in days gone by.

Conclusion: Standing on a crowded city bus a seventy-ish-looking grey-haired gentleman carrying a bunch of packages almost fell down as the bus lurched to a stop. At one point a young, gum-chewing woman stood up and pointed to the unoccupied seat. "Here, Pops, take this."

He looked at her in amazement. "Cool it, girlie," he said, "I still run marathons," and stood all the way to his stop.

An apt quotation might also serve the purpose. Here's an ending of an essay on a source claiming that because many consumers are ill-informed, they waste lots of money when purchasing the latest digital devices.

Conclusion: To paraphrase an old saying, "What you don't know can hurt you."

Reiterating the essay's main point in different words might also work. You might, for example, add a short tag line, a brief statement that creates a dramatic effect. Here's such an ending on a source claiming that sexual harassment of employees in many businesses decreases profits.

Conclusion: Businesses lose in every way when positions of authority are held by sexists and lechers.

Writing on a source that discussed benefits that teenagers derive from texting, a student ended her essay appropriately punctuated with a popular texting emoticon:

Conclusion: A day without texting is a day I should have stayed in bed :-(.

Another approach is to bring your readers up to date or project them into the future. In an essay on a passage that claimed vandalism in schools reflects the values of society at large, a student wrote:

Conclusion: How long can this go on? How can we turn away meekly? How much longer can we let vandals make us their victims? The writer, sadly, ignores these crucial questions.

If a passage argues that it is imperative to save the world from global warming, an appropriate ending to the essay might be:

Conclusion: When the history of the twenty-first century is ready to be written, let us hope that the globe hasn't already warmed us to death.

So, what happens if you can't think of a satisfactory ending or time is called before you finish? For one thing, don't despair. Although an effective conclusion adds luster to an essay, don't feel obliged to provide one at all costs. SAT readers will know how well you write long before reaching your essay's last sentence. Be confident that a good but incomplete piece of writing will be graded according to what you've done well, not what you haven't done at all.

Mini-Workout in Writing Conclusions

> **Directions:** Try your hand at writing an appealing ending for each of the essays described here.

1. *Topic:* Language taboos

    Our society prohibits or frowns on the use of certain categories of words. The writer is alarmed by the trend in recent years that has made many language taboos obsolete.

    _____

    _____

    _____

    _____

2. *Topic:* The value of school sports

    The writer, in comparing athletics in school to life, makes the point that in both endeavors a winning mental strategy is what makes a big difference.

    _____

    _____

    _____

    _____

3. *Topic:* High school vs. junior high

    The writer of the passage argues that, although high school is not perfect, it is far better than junior high, where students are often treated like inmates instead of human beings.

    _____

    _____

    _____

    _____

Suggested answers are on page 303.

Editing and Proofreading: The Final Touches

Once you've ended your essay, spend whatever time is left editing and proofreading. You can't do a complete makeover, but you can do a great deal to improve communication between you and your readers.

EDITING FOR CLARITY

Check your essay for clarity by asking yourself whether a reader could misconstrue anything you've written. Penny T. wrote her SAT Essay about runaway teenagers—those desperate kids who leave home in search of a different life. One of her sentences read "The last thing parents should do is talk to their kids." Coming to that sentence, a reader might well wonder whether Penny meant that parents should talk to their kids as a last resort, or, that in a list of what parents ought to do, the final step is talking to their kids.

Later citing an excerpt from the source, in the essay Penny wrote, "Ellen told her friend Delilah that she had made a serious mistake by running away from home." Penny certainly understood what she intended to say, but a reader can't tell whether Ellen took a dim view of Delilah's actions or whether Ellen herself had second thoughts about her own flight. Granted, these sentences have been quoted out of context, but the point remains: What may seem perfectly clear to a writer may send a puzzling message to the reader.

That's why you must arrange your words in the clearest order. Watch for grammatical perils that interfere with meaning, especially (1) misplaced modifiers, (2) dangling participles, and (3) lack of parallelism.

ANSWER KEY TO MINI-WORKOUTS
Gathering and Arranging Ideas, page 270

Answers will vary. The order of ideas is strictly a matter of personal preference.

A. Advantages:

1. Many more students would become physically fit.

2. Regular exercise reduces stress and promotes feelings of well-being.

3. Students learn lifelong physical/recreational skills.
Disadvantages:

1. Opportunity to take important elective courses is reduced.

2. Students lose time that can be used to study for tests and quizzes.

3. Tiring physical activity weakens ability to concentrate/focus on academics.

B. Pros:

1. Video games provide pleasure and entertainment.

2. Many interactive games stimulate the mind and foster problem-solving skills.

3. They improve hand-eye coordination.
Cons:

1. Video games tend to be addictive.

2. They glorify violence and destructive behaviors.

3. Their high cost diverts family funds from more worthwhile pursuits.

C. For:

1. Cheating is rampant and something should be done about it.

2. A code will improve the moral climate in the school.

3. Students must learn that there are consequences for cheating.

Against:

1. A code creates an atmosphere of fear and apprehension, like a police state.

2. Students will be reluctant to rat on each other.

3. It discourages students from helping each other learn.

D. Agree:

1. War causes people and nations to abandon the qualities that make them human.

2. Wars cause death, suffering, and destruction.

3. Wars cost money that can and should be used for improving lives, not destroying them.

Disagree:

1. War against terrorism provides security for the people.

2. War to depose tyrants is of benefit to mankind.

3. Wars on poverty, drugs, and other social evils improve the quality of life.

Developing Paragraphs, pages 275–276

1. a. 3	2. a. 3	3. a. 5	4. a. 5	5. a. 5
b. 5	b. 1	b. 3	b. 4	b. 3
c. 1	c. 4	c. 1	c. 1	c. 2
d. 2	d. 5	d. 4	d. 2	d. 1
e. 4	e. 2	e. 2	e. 3	e. 4

Identifying Paragraph Unity and Coherence, pages 276–279

1. Sentence 3 destroys the coherence of the paragraph. Delete it. There's no reason to save it, because the idea is reiterated in sentence 7.

2. The paragraph lacks unity. It starts by discussing consequences on young people of smoking marijuana and ends by explaining parents' problems. One way to overcome the paragraph's lack of unity is to divide it into two parts. Another is to expand the topic sentence to include parents, *e.g., Under present law, smoking marijuana can have serious consequences for both young people and their parents.* If this were done, however, the paragraph would need further development.

3. The paragraph is coherent except for sentence 5, which should be deleted. Sentence 2 strongly supports the topic sentence (1). The remaining sentences, except 5, support sentence 2, which is the major supporting sentence in the paragraph.

4. Although the entire paragraph discusses political parties, the discussion is not unified. Sentences 1–3 deal with the two-party system, while sentences 4–7 are about dictatorships. Either divide the paragraph, or add a topic sentence that justifies discussing both topics within a single paragraph.

5. Sentence 1 is the topic sentence. Sentence 4 is unrelated to the topic sentence. Delete it.

6. The paragraph is mostly unified and coherent, although the topic sentence would be more accurate if it mentioned the human qualities of porpoises.

7. Although the opening sentence leads the reader to think that what follows will be all about *Robinson Crusoe*, the paragraph is really about the author Daniel Defoe. To improve the coherence of the paragraph, delete or revise the misleading topic sentence.

8. Although the entire paragraph is about Greek philosophy, it is terribly disjointed. Only sentences 3 and 4 connect with each other. The others are independent thoughts, related in subject matter but not in style. For coherence, add a topic sentence, possibly using material in sentence 5. The fact that Socrates taught Plato, who taught Aristotle might serve as a starting point in revising the paragraph.

9. The paragraph is coherent and unified until the last sentence. Delete sentence 6, but if the idea is too good to discard, save it for another place in the essay or revise sentence 1, the topic sentence.

10. The paragraph is unified and coherent. No revision needed.

Using Precise Wording, pages 282–283

Answers will vary. The words in your sentences may be as precise as or even more precise than the words in these samples.

1. The barn's rotted walls bulged, its windows wouldn't open, and moss covered the sagging roof.

2. When accused of lying to the jury, the witness turned beet red, burst into tears, and, with eyes turned to heaven, asked, "What in the world is happening to me?"

3. My Air Quality Index app showed that Springfield was the most polluted city in the country. You could see and smell the fog. In the park, a game of basketball was in progress. In the yellow haze, the players seemed to float across the court.

4. Molly's reward for six hours at her desk studying physics was a big fat F on the quiz.

5. The seniors celebrated their graduation but wept inside, realizing that tonight was the last time they would ever be together.

6. To make it on the swim team, the bowling team, or any other team, there are but three things to do: practice, practice, practice.

7. At the wake, Greg was startled by the joviality of the mourners, who rejoiced over Mr. O'Malley's life instead of lamenting his death.

8. In high school Linda rarely went to class, flunked English and math in summer school, and finally dropped out altogether.

9. Teddy and Joey, the family's twins, never went out at the same time because they shared the same pair of shoes.

10. Although the current had smashed the canoe against the rocks, Rod unhesitatingly leaped into the water to save the drowning child.

Writing Comparisons, pages 286–287

The comparisons that you wrote may be as good as or even better than these examples.

PART A

1. as comfortable as a baby in its mother's arms
2. as tough as a wrecking ball
3. as gorgeous as gold
4. as silly as putty
5. as serious as 9/11
6. as perfect as a circle
7. as wild as a leaping salmon

8. as unpredictable as the lottery
9. as impetuous as a flash of lightning
10. as reliable as a sheepdog

PART B

School is like an airport, a place one passes through for the sole purpose of going somewhere else. Just as no one goes to the airport just to be at the airport, who would go to school in order to go to school. Instead, school is a step one takes while preparing for college and for life. One spends a certain amount of time there, follows the rules, does the work, and then escapes like a traveler en route to Aruba, or Italy, or the Far East. Similarly, at the airport, you must obey the rules: check in at the counter, have your photo ID ready, go through security checks, stand in lines. If you fail to follow the prescribed procedure, trouble can follow, delaying your departure. In that sense, it's no different from school, where one must do what is expected in order to graduate on time.

Varying Sentences, pages 294–295

These are illustrative answers only, Many other variations are possible.

1. Mr. Finn is a good teacher but he runs the class like a dictatorship. Democracy and freedom have no place in his class. On the first day he announced his rules, among them no talking, no gum chewing, no hats in class, no lateness. If you arrive late, you should expect to find the door locked and to go to detention after school. All homework is compulsory. No one dares to come to class unprepared because a girl who once came to class without her homework turned colors and almost wept after Mr. Finn lowered the boom on her.

2. In the numerous science classes that I have taken, we talked about experiments instead of doing them because the equipment was obsolete and too costly to replace. We learned scientific theories but could not practice them in labs or see them demonstrated. To give students a better education, the science department needs money. About a million dollars would do.

3. By dumping garbage, sewage, and other hazardous waste products into the sea, many nations are polluting the world's oceans. They are making beaches and swimming dangerous. Toxic pollutants also taint all forms of sea life with materials that humans ingest when eating fish, lobsters, clams, and other seafood.

4. The earth has experienced a sharp increase in natural disasters, from about 100 per year in the 1960s to five times that number in the early part of the twenty-first century. Earthquakes, droughts, huge storms, and floods are not happening more frequently, however. Nor are they occurring with greater intensity. Rather, the population of the world has increased. People in greater numbers now occupy areas that are prone to natural disasters, such as flood plains, coastal lands, and cities built on subterranean fault lines. The planet has not changed but humans have.

5. Although the American Dream is a popular concept, it means different things for different people. Most commonly, it means finding a good job, getting married, having a couple of kids and owning a home with a white picket fence and a two-car garage. Some people, thinking that dream shallow, say that the dream won't be complete without a good education, friends, a feeling of well-being, good health, and above all, the blessings of liberty, including the freedom of speech and religion and the freedom to choose

to be part of an untraditional family made up of same-sex partners or any other combination of adults and children.

Writing Conclusions, page 298

Because every writer is different from every other, these answers are no more than possibilities for concluding three different essays.

1. In a generation or less, today's profanity may be no different from the everyday language in newspapers, on television, and even in essays like this one.
2. Some people succeed because they are lucky. Others succeed because they are more talented or smarter than the competition. But success comes to the vast majority because they have planned how to succeed. When a split second determines the winner in a race, is it fair to say that the second-place finisher is not as good as the winner? No, but it's a certainty that the winner planned his racing strategy better than the person who lost.
3. If by magic I happened to find myself in junior high again, I wouldn't rest until I'd made my escape.

You Be the Ump: Essays for Evaluation

6

→ **SAT ESSAY READERS: WHAT THEY DO AND HOW THEY DO IT**

→ **ESSAY SCORING GUIDE**

→ **ESSAYS FOR EVALUATION**

SAT ESSAY READERS: WHAT THEY DO AND HOW THEY DO IT

How SAT Essays Are Read

SAT evaluators are expected to read essays quickly and to avoid the "Gotcha! Syndrome" (*i.e.,* hunting down every little error). To determine your essay's score, they'll look for evidence that you've understood the reading passage, that you've analyzed the rhetoric used by its author, and that your essay reflects a degree of writing competency.

> **TIP**
>
> **SAT Essay readers don't deduct points for every little mistake.**

Knowing that you wrote the essay in roughly 30–35 minutes, they'll approach it with a positive mind set, prepared to reward you for what you've done well. When reading your essay, they'll compare it to other essays written about the same passage at the same time. Your essay, in other words, won't be competing with an ideal essay written by a pro or even with essays by students who took the SAT at some other time.

Like other readers, they're bound to enjoy and reward you for good, fresh writing, and a thoughtful, well-focused discussion of the source. And like other readers, too, they'll be bored by essays full of lifeless prose, empty platitudes, bull-throwing, sentences that confuse, vagueness, pointless repetition, organization so chaotic that they can't follow it, and all the rest.

How Essays Are Scored

Two different readers will score your essay on a scale of 1 to 4 in three different categories: Reading, Analysis, and Writing. An outstanding essay will earn 4 in each category, and the score will be designated 4/4/4. On the other end of the scale, a poor essay will be graded 1/1/1. Ultimately, the two readers' scores will be combined and reported as a total of 2 to 8 points in each of the three categories.

Readers use the following adjectives to describe performance in each category.

Performance	Score
Advanced	4
Proficient	3
Partial	2
Inadequate	1

Essay readers try to be as objective as possible. Because they are human, however, judgments may vary. An essay assigned a score of, say, 3/2/3 by one reader may not be conspicuously superior to an essay scored 2/3/2 by another reader.

> Before looking in detail at what the numbers mean, here's a little diversion for all you math whizzes out there:
>
> Essay scores consist of three numbers from 1 to 4, as in 4/2/3, 3/3/2, and so on.
>
> What is the total number of different scores available to an essay reader?
>
> To find the exact figure, look on the page in this book that bears the same number as the correct answer.

No list of standards can include everything that readers take into account when they evaluate essays, but the following descriptions include the main criteria.

ESSAY SCORING GUIDE

Reading

4 Demonstrable and thorough understanding of text, central ideas, important details, and the author's overall purpose; use of apt direct quotes, paraphrases, and accurate summaries to support general claims; no errors or misinterpretation of facts or ideas

3 Appreciable comprehension of text; use of appropriate textual evidence—quotes, facts, other data—to demonstrate an understanding of the main ideas, important details, and interrelationships of ideas

2 Limited comprehension of the overall text; some evidence of awareness of important details or major ideas but without substantial elaboration or significant development

1 Little or no evidence of understanding of the purpose or content of the passage

Analysis

4 Clearly stated or insightful understanding of the analytical task; specific identification of analytical elements with textual examples quoted or described; insightful explanations of why elements were chosen and what they achieved; thorough evaluations of the effectiveness of each element

3 A sufficient awareness of the analytical task; generally articulate analysis of some important rhetorical elements; mostly adequate explanations of how some elements add persuasiveness to the author's argument; proficient but not distinguished evaluation of rhetorical elements

2 Limited understanding of analytical task; few or passing references to important rhetorical elements; emphasis on minor rhetorical elements; little analysis of how the author builds an argument; little or incomplete assessment of each identified element

1 Demonstrable lack of understanding of analytical task; next to no discernible effort to analyze text; absence of any explanation of author's use of language, evidence, reasoning, or any other significant rhetorical elements

Writing

4 Extremely well organized and focused on a precisely stated main idea; fully developed with convincing, appropriate, and insightful supporting material; varied and engaging sentence structure, effective use of language; few, if any, errors in standard written English

3 Generally effective and reasonably consistent in clarity and competence; basically insightful and developed with coherent and apt supporting material; some evidence of critical thinking and insight; reasonably varied sentence structure and appropriate use of language; few, if any, significant errors in standard English

2 Somewhat weak or confusing organization and expression of ideas; partial development of a main idea; barely adequate evidence of critical thinking and supporting material; little variation in sentence structure; some sentence errors; occasional misuse of words; inclusion of material that wanders from topic

1 Significant weakness in quality; generally unclear or incoherent; notably undeveloped or confusing; insufficient evidence of a main idea or critical thinking; frequent errors in expression; limited vocabulary; sentence errors that distort or obscure meaning; inclusion of material not relevant to the topic

ESSAYS FOR EVALUATION

You are about to meet a set of student-written SAT Essays. Using the Essay Scoring Guide, rate each one on a scale of 1 (low) to 4 (high) in each of three categories: Reading, Analysis, and Writing. The highest cumulative score you can give is 4/4/4, the lowest is 1/1/1.

All the essays were completed during a 50-minute period—the same amount of time that you'll be given when you take the SAT. All are unedited and typed exactly as submitted. Read each essay quickly, spending no more than about four or five minutes. Look for strengths and weaknesses. Mark them up freely, as though you were grading a paper. Then write a summary of your findings in the space set aside for your comments. Finally, compare your evaluation with that of an experienced SAT Essay reader.

If you've never before evaluated an essay, get ready for a demanding, but exhilarating experience. Be prepared to devote a good deal of time to it. The more essays you evaluate, the less time each one will take, and the more skillful you'll become.

The first and most general thing to look for in evaluating SAT Essays is how well the writer has followed the instructions given by the prompt. This is determined in part by answers to these basic questions:

1. Does the essay contain evidence that the writer has read the source with understanding?
2. Has the writer analyzed the persuasive rhetoric used by the author of the source?
3. Does the essay contain a well-developed main idea, varied sentence structure, precise choice of words, and an appropriate, consistent writing style that adheres to the conventions of standard written English?

To evaluate each essay you must, of course, familiarize yourself with the passage on which it's based. Because no two people are likely to agree on every detail, your evaluations will probably differ from those of the SAT reader. Nevertheless, your observations may be equally valid and perceptive. If your evaluation differs greatly from that of the experienced reader, be sure to review the criteria the reader used to evaluate the essay, and keep those criteria in mind as you plan and write essays of your own.

After you've read a few essays, you're likely to start comparing one to the other and maybe return to some of the earlier ones for a second, more perceptive, look.

Prompt for SAT Essay #1

P.241-244

> Read the following passage carefully. Consider how the author
>
> - uses evidence such as examples and facts to back up claims
> - provides reasoning to connect claims and evidence to develop ideas
> - uses stylistic or persuasive elements, such as word choice or emotional appeals meant to add power to expressed ideas
>
> *Note*: Ordinarily, the source would be printed here. For this essay, however, the source by Malcolm Gladwell can be found on pages 241–244. If you've read it before, please reread it to refresh your memory.
>
> Write an essay in which you explain how Malcolm Gladwell builds an argument to persuade his audience that *in the 1990s greater understanding of America's homeless population helped to ease but not solve problems related to homelessness.*
>
> In your essay, analyze how Gladwell uses one or more of the features listed in the set of instructions for this essay above (or features of your own choice) to strengthen the logic and persuasiveness of his argument. Be sure that your analysis focuses on the most relevant features of the passage.
>
> Do not explain whether you agree or disagree with Gladwell's views. Rather, explain how Gladwell builds an argument to persuade his audience.

RAY P'S ESSAY

The topic of the source is there was a problem in knowing all about homelessness. The author says that when homeless became a problem in the 1980's most people didn't know what to do. There was "despair" about it. That word is an emotional one. It makes readers feel really bad for homeless people.

The author is Gladwell, he thinks they should not feel that way because homeless people are not always homeless forever and it's a mistake to say they are based on research by a graduate student named Culhane in Boston College. He discovered that homeless people are homeless for shorter times, so despair is not the right feeling. Most of them are homeless for one day or two days. The reason being shelters are scuzzy and they try to escape from them as fast as possible. Some people stay in shelters for a few weeks, mostly in winter when it is cold. Chronic homeless people stay even for years. The word "chronic" is a good choice because it usually describe sick people and when they are chronic they are homeless because of drugs or mental illness or some disabled. Gladwell says a quarter of a million people are like that sleeping on sidewalks and panhandling in the streets, and other things.

Gladwell puts up many numbers about how much the homeless cost. Homeless men 1 stay out in the rain and get sick or fall down drunk a crack their heads open and end up in the ER which charges $1000 a visit. They also get liver diseases and hypothermia. They can't afford their doctor bills so someone else like society has to pay for a head injury at a price of $50,000.

YOUR COMMENTS ABOUT THE ESSAY

Reading

_____

_____

_____

_____

Analysis

_____

_____

_____

_____

Writing

_____

_____

_____

_____

COMMENTS TO RAY P FROM AN SAT ESSAY READER

Reading

Your essay suggests that you read the source earnestly and with some degree of comprehension. You mention a few important details, such as the fact that homelessness is largely a temporary condition and you allude to the writer's use of a few well-chosen words. Yet you provide little evidence that you grasped Gladwell's overall purpose—to prove that research into homelessness mitigated but did not erase faulty perception and misunderstanding of the homeless population. Overall, your response demonstrates marginal reading comprehension.

Analysis

Your essay contains only slight evidence that you grasped the purpose of the essay—to analyze the writer's use of facts, statistics, reasoning and other rhetorical elements to support Gladwell's claim that "in the 1990s a greater understanding of America's homeless population helped to ease some problems associated with homelessness but did not solve them." While discussing research done by Culhane, for example, you might have explained that Gladwell reviews Culhane's findings in order to support his claim that the homeless should not be regarded as a single homogeneous group. Also, an analysis of the last paragraph of the passage, in which facts about specific costs of sheltering and caring for the homeless are cited, you might have explained how the writer uses numbers as evidence to show that the "chronically" homeless differ from homeless people in other categories. Sad to say, you fell short of drawing these or *any other equally worthy conclusions. Overall, your response demonstrates insufficient analysis.*

Writing

Perhaps your essay's most redeeming quality is its use of language. Your expression of ideas is generally clear, but on the whole, your work lacks a sense of organization, a comprehensible progression of thought, and a central idea around which the essay is built. In short, you jump randomly from topic without focusing specifically on the author's use of rhetoric. For example, your last paragraph about the costs of homelessness, although accurate in its content, seems like a gratuitous add-on rather than an integral part of a unified essay. Overall, your response demonstrates inadequate control of writing and language skills.

Score: 2/1/1

MELINDA'S ESSAY

The writer has said that views on homelessness have been changed since homelessness originally was an issue for the first time back around in the 1980's. To prove this claim, the writer describes the feelings of despair over what to do to solve the problem of the large numbers of homeless people who were in the "same state of semipermanent distress."

The writer claims that the despair actually existed because of the public did not understand the homeless population. To support the claim he tells about a graduate student with the name of Dennis Culhane, who did research in a homeless shelter and learned that most homeless people don't stay homeless for long. Culhane actually lived in a shelter for seven weeks, a fact Gladwell uses to show to readers that Culhane actually had plenty of time to observe the place and know what he was talking about. The writer treats Culhane as an authority on the subject and that is why his research is important. What happened is that Culhane left the shelter and actually returned months later to find that none of the homeless people he knew were still there, which lead to the conclusion that assumptions about the homeless were wrong and change was needed.

Data taken from Culhane's database that tracked who was actually "coming in and out" of the shelter system. Based on that information, he claims that Culhane's discoveries "profoundly changed the way homelessness is understood," with the stress on "profoundly" inferring that few of the old beliefs about homelessness were accurate any more.

The writer breaks down homeless people into categories, using such terms as "episodic users" and the "chronically homeless." Dividing homeless people into categories is an approach serving Gladwell's claim that each group of homeless can be characterized by distinctive and discreet features.

We now understand the conditions of homelessness better, but the problem is still very grave. As evidence, Gladwell lists some financial costs of social-service systems needed by the homeless, like $62 million per year being spent for shelters in New York, $25,000 per bed in Boston. It could sound like Gladwell's argument is made up of cold-hearted facts and figures about homeless people. Nothing could be more far from the truth. All through the passage, he talks about the suffering and the awful conditions of the lives of homeless people. In one place uses very descriptive and emotional language, telling about "people sleeping on sidewalks, ... lying drunk in doorways, huddled on subway grates and under bridges...." Only someone very cold and heartless would not have emotions affected by such descriptions.

The writer says the cots in a homeless shelter as being "18 inches apart." Gladwell presents a basic picture of homelessness in America. Although his claim seems accurate that homelessness has many aspects to it, the author doesn't actually propose any ideas to show that society really knows what to do make the problem go away.

YOUR COMMENTS ABOUT THE ESSAY

Reading

_____

_____

_____

_____

Analysis

_____

_____

_____

_____

Writing

_____

_____

_____

_____

COMMENTS TO MELINDA FROM AN SAT ESSAY READER

Reading

This response demonstrates your understanding of the Gladwell's text. You summarize its central point early in the essay and include several significant details from the text, using a mixture of paraphrases and direct quotations. Then, detailing the research work by Culhane, you further demonstrate your comprehension of the source by accurately pointing out that, as a consequence of Culhane's work, the public's perception of homelessness began to change. The last paragraphs of the essay cite several pertinent facts about homelessness that echo Gladwell's description—still more evidence that you have a firm grasp of the point and purpose of the entire source. Overall, your response demonstrates very good reading comprehension.

Analysis

You show a commendable understanding of the analytical task by identifying several of the writer's claims and citing the specific evidence used to support them. The account of Culhane's research and the effect of his findings is perhaps the most coherent, well-developed part of your analysis. Your explanations of Gladwell's categories of homeless people and the financial costs of social-service systems admirably exemplify how close a relationship between a claim and the evidence meant to support it can be. An insightful comment about the entire passage brings your essay to a satisfying conclusion. Well done!

Writing

Your response demonstrates some clarity of thought and some awareness of the conventions of standard written English. In spite of these and other strengths, however, your essay has a monotonous and repetitive structure, consisting of a series of paragraphs, each starting with one of Gladwell's claims and followed by a description of the evidence used to support it. Also, five of your essay's six paragraphs begin with the same words "The writer," indicating that you're unaware of the need to vary sentence structure and the use of transitional words and phrases for improved cohesiveness. In addition, your essay loses some of its effectiveness because of occasional awkwardness ("The writer says the cots … as being '18 inches apart.'"), redundancy, ("originally became an issue for the first time"), repetition, ("… breaks down homeless people into categories," … "Dividing homeless people into categories") as well as some odd quirks such as the repeated use of "actually," a word that adds little or nothing to the meaning of your essay.

Score: 4/4/2

CARITA'S ESSAY

The author, Malcolm Gladwell ("MG" from now on) discusses homelessness from the time it surfaced as an issue in the 1980s until today. His aim is to convince readers that the problem of homelessness isn't solved, but we've come a long way since the beginning when it "bred despair," because it was misunderstood and nobody knew how to deal with it. Throughout the passage MG backs up his claims with evidence made up of facts, statistics, and quotations taken from research. He also describes the homeless in language that leaves an impact on a reader's emotions.

Early in the passage, America's deep despair is forcefully illustrated by the rhetorical question: "if there were so many homeless, what could be done to help them?" An answer of sorts comes from research by Dennis Culhane a graduate student whose qualifications as an expert on the plight of the homeless is derived in part from his residency in a homeless shelter for seven weeks. Based on Culhane's observations and on a database, MG claims that Culhane's work "profoundly changed the way homelessness is understood." To illustrate the change, formerly the homeless people were viewed as one giant clump of people, but Culhane showed that they are made up of various subgroups. 10 percent were "episodic users" who come to shelters "three weeks at time," and returned "periodically, particularly in the winter." Another 10 percent were "chronically homeless." Even though some live in shelters for a long time, most stay a day or two. A quote from Culhane explains why: "Anyone who ever has to stay in a shelter involuntarily knows that all you think about is how to make sure you never come back." Later in the passage, when he says that residents' cots are just eighteen inches apart, Culhane is adding another detail to account for movement in and out of shelters.

Breaking down the homeless population into groups supports MG's claim that Culhane's work "profoundly" changed the way homelessness was understood. MG also claims that because of Culhane, the chronically homeless needed and got the most help. To show why, he describes some of their characteristics in emotion-stirring language, such as "people sleeping on sidewalks ... lying drunk in doorways," etc. By describing this group as "hard-core" homeless, Gladwell reinforces the depth of their misery.

In contrast to the despair he mentioned at the start, MG adds facts to prove that changed perceptions led to greater funding for care and shelter of the hard-core homeless. That may create the impression that money alone offers a promising solution to the problem. But he adds a long quote from James Dunford, an authority in San Diego to show that there's still a long way to go. Dunford's choice of words evokes many of the same emotions stirred by Gladwell, but with a more negative slant. Repeatedly calling them "guys" and emphasizing their most disagreeable characteristics: "They are drunk and they get vomit in their lungs ... ," and they are very "prone to falling down and cracking their heads open ...," etc.) Dunford's tone resonates with the "despair" discussed early in the passage and adds strong support to Gladwell's claim that the homeless problem is still far from over.

YOUR COMMENTS ABOUT THE ESSAY

Reading

_____

_____

_____

_____

Analysis

_____

_____

_____

_____

Writing

_____

_____

_____

_____

COMMENTS TO CARITA FROM AN SAT ESSAY READER

Reading

Your response demonstrates thorough comprehension of the source text. In the introductory paragraph, you briefly summarize the purpose of Gladwell's passage ("His aim is to convince readers that the problem of homelessness isn't solved"... etc.) and consistently add throughout your essay an abundance of important details from the text through a mixture of appropriate *quotations and paraphrases. You also show your understanding of how various details and quotations contribute to the overall impact of the passage on readers. Your response, free from errors of fact or interpretation, deserves a top score.*

Analysis

Your response offers a thorough and effective analysis of Gladwell's argument and demonstrates a laudable understanding of the analytical task. Implementing the plan you articulated in the introductory paragraph, you cite facts (e.g., "the homeless ... are made up of various subgroups"), statistics ("10 percent were 'episodic users'"), and quotations ("Anyone who ever has to stay in a shelter ... [makes sure they] never come back"). But even more to the point, you cogently explain the effect of each piece of evidence on the overall persuasiveness of Gladwell's argument (e.g., "By describing this group as 'hard-core' homeless, Gladwell reinforces the depth of their misery."). Your analysis of the source is enhanced, too, by abundant examples of emotionally charged language ("people sleeping on sidewalks ... lying drunk in doorways") invariably followed by a brief analysis of the probable effect of those words on readers. Your unwavering attention to the evidence and its effect on readers demonstrates a high level of analytical thinking.

Writing

Your opening paragraph is exemplary. It introduces the topic of the source, spells out its central idea, and provides a preview of the rhetorical elements ("facts, statistics, and quotations and emotional language") that you plan to discuss in your essay. The body of the essay contains precisely what you promise in the introduction. Each paragraph remains on topic, and your ideas progress clearly within and between paragraphs. Throughout the essay you maintain an objective, relatively formal style befitting its topic and purpose. Especially noteworthy is the unity you achieve with an ending that brings the reader back full circle to the opening discussion of despair. Although not totally free of flaws, your essay demonstrates ample writing gifts and merits a top rating.

Score: 4/4/4

Time for a Break

Okay, now that you've evaluated a set of essays, it's time for a well-earned break. Take 5, 10, 20, or whatever. But before you return to work, broaden your perspective on essay evaluation with an alternate set of scoring guidelines.

A 4/4/4 ESSAY

Essays deserving three 4s are like WOW! They demonstrate an almost God-like mastery of writing techniques, skill in source analysis, and a high degree of insightfulness. They examine the source with laser-like precision and make frequent, accurate, and convincing references to the writer's use of rhetorical techniques and to the potential reader's good looks and brilliance. They take into account how such matters as the use of evidence, reasoning, word choice, tone, and emotional appeals contribute to the purpose, meaning, and effect of the source.

Occasional or minor lapses in diction, grammar, or mechanics hardly matter. Ordinarily, writers of such essays insert between the pages a blank check made out to the reader.

AN ESSAY SCORED WITH PAIR OF 4S AND A 3

Essays earning a 3 and two 4s are very, very good—WORTH A HIGH FIVE. They are insightful and they demonstrate considerable mastery of written English. They meet all the criteria for essays earning all 4s but somewhere fall just slightly short of distinction. Sorry, no blank check, but maybe a gift card to the local Shake Shack will be stapled to page 2.

AN ESSAY WITH A PAIR OF 3S AND A 4

These deserve a PAT ON THE BACK because they've competently analyzed the source and cited specific examples from the text to explain the writer's use of rhetorical strategies. They've also discussed, directly or indirectly, such matters as use of evidence, tone, word choice, appeals to emotion, and how desperately the writer needs all 4s. They are reasonably well-developed and coherent. A few errors in sentence structure and English usage may exist, but not to worry. The writer's family plans to endow a new building wherever the writer goes to college, and besides, no error is serious enough to interfere with the clear expression of ideas.

AN ESSAY SCORED 3/3/3

Symbolically THUMBS UP, this essay may be the equivalent of another receiving some combination of 3s and a 4. The prose may be less developed or the analysis slightly less astute than those earning a 4. Or they may contain a number of lapses in word choice, syntax, and grammar and usage, but who's counting?

ESSAY SCORED WITH TWO 3S AND A 2

This one gets a SMILEY FACE STICKER. It adequately analyzes the source but may lack full development. Ideas may be presented clearly but remain relatively unsupported. The essay may be reasonably well organized and convey the writer's ideas, but errors in word choice, sentence structure, or standard English weaken the overall impact of the essay and suggest that the writer, probably a freshman with plenty of opportunities to retake the test, lacks the status of a junior or senior.

A 2/2/2 RATING

This one gets an ENCOURAGING NOD and a SEMI-SMILE because it responds marginally to the assignment. Its analysis of the source may be limited, inconsistent, or uncertain. The writer may have discussed secondary stylistic or rhetorical strategies superficially, or without reference to the purpose, meaning, or effect of the source. Although there's an outside chance that the writer grasps the point of his or her own essay, the prose is immature and reveals weak control of organization, word choice, or sentence structure. On second thought, scratch the nod.

AN ESSAY WITH A 1 IN ITS SCORE

Such an essay gets an ANEMIC SMILE. In some ways it may be close to an essay without any 1's, but the analysis of the source may be significantly flawed. Or the prose reveals the writer's loss of sleep during the preceding days, along with difficulty in controlling organization, choosing the correct words, or using standard English. Overall, the essay may demonstrate only marginal wakefulness and comprehension of the source.

AN ESSAY EARNING TWO 1S AND A 2

This one gets a SHOULDER SHRUG because its analysis of the source may be weak or garbled or unfocused or all three. It also may wander off the topic or substitute a simpler task than the one assigned by the prompt. The prose may reveal problems in organizing material, in expressing ideas clearly, in writing grammatically, and in just getting it all together.

A 1/1/1 ESSAY

An essay deserving three 1's gets an EMOTICON WITH A DOWNTURNED MOUTH. (Sorry about that.) It may be similar to an essay scored with 2's, but the ideas may be more simplistic or harder to follow. Analysis is close to nil. The writing is flawed, perhaps bordering on the incomprehensible.

A SCORE OF ZERO

Oh, boy! This gets a DISBELIEVING SHAKE OF THE HEAD, meaning that the writer, having taken to heart the old saying that "Less is more," submitted a blank paper or one filled with 50 minutes' worth of doodling.

You've no doubt noticed that these descriptions lack precision. It's no secret that grading essays is far from an exact science. But the readers do try to be objective and weigh every essay's strengths more than its weaknesses.

Okay, it's time to go back to work.

Prompt for SAT Essay #2

Read the following passage carefully. Consider how the author David Frum

- uses evidence such as examples and facts to back up claims
- provides reasoning to connect claims and evidence to develop ideas
- uses stylistic or persuasive elements, such as word choice or emotional appeals meant to add power to expressed ideas

(Adapted from David Frum, "The Harm That Casinos Do," *CNN Opinion*, 9/24/2013)

Until the late 1980s, casino gambling was illegal almost everywhere in the country. Today, casinos are allowed in 23 states. These newly authorized casinos are not Las Vegas-style grand hotels. Their customers come from nearby. They don't stay overnight. They don't watch a show or eat in a fine restaurant. Perhaps most surprisingly, they don't play cards.

Modern casino gambling is computer gambling. The typical casino gambler sits at a computer screen, inserts a credit card and enters a digital environment carefully constructed to keep them playing until all their available money has been extracted.

Small "wins" are administered at the most psychologically effective intervals, but the math is remorseless: the longer you play, the more you lose. The industry as a whole targets precisely those who can least afford to lose and earns most of its living from people for whom gambling has become an addiction. Studies show that 75% of casino customers who play only occasionally provide only 4% of casino revenues. It's the problem gambler who keeps the casino in business.

When New Jersey allowed casinos into Atlantic City back in 1977, casino advocates promised that gambling would revive the town's fading economy. The casinos did create jobs as promised. But merchants who expected foot traffic to return to the city's main street, were disappointed. Money that comes to the casinos, stays in the casinos. Liquor stores and cash-for-gold outlets now line the city's once-premier retail strip.

The impact of casinos on local property values is "unambiguously" negative, according to the National Association of Realtors. Casinos do not revive local economies. They act as parasites upon them. Communities located within 10 miles of a casino exhibit double the rate of problem gambling. Unsurprisingly, such communities also suffer higher rates of home foreclosure and other forms of economic distress and domestic violence.

Before the spread of casino gambling, the typical gambler was more affluent than average: it cost money to travel to Las Vegas. That's no longer true. Low-income workers and retirees provide the bulk of the customers for the modern casino industry. And because that industry becomes an important source of government revenue, the decision to allow casino gambling is a decision to shift the cost of government from the richer to the poorer, and, within the poor, to a subset of vulnerable people with addiction problems.

Research by the Institute for American Values, a think tank, found that "Modern slot machines are highly addictive because they get into people's heads as well as their wallets. They engineer the psychological experience of being in the 'zone'—a trance-like state that numbs feeling and blots out time/space. For some heavy players, the goal is not winning money. It's staying in the zone. To maintain this intensely desirable state, players prolong their time on the machine until they run out of money—a phenomenon that people in the industry call 'playing to extinction.'"

How heavily gambling weighs upon the poor, the elderly, the less educated, and the psychologically vulnerable is difficult to answer exactly, because government has shirked the job of studying the effects of gambling. Most research on the public health effects of gambling in the United States is funded by the industry itself, with a careful eye to exonerating itself from blame.

But here's what we can conclude: State-sponsored casino gambling parallels the separate and unequal life patterns in education, marriage, work, and play that increasingly divide America into haves and have-nots. Those in the upper ranks of the income distribution rarely, if ever, make it a weekly habit to gamble at the local casino. Those in the lower ranks of the income distribution often do. Those in the upper ranks rarely, if ever, contribute a large share of their income to the state's take of casino revenues. Those in the lower ranks do.

Is this really OK? Are Americans content to allow the growth of an industry that consciously exploits the predictable weakness of the most vulnerable people? Twenty-seven states still say "no." If yours is one such state, fight to keep it that way. If not, it's never too late to find a better way.

Write an essay in which you explain how David Frum builds an argument to persuade his audience that *casino gambling harms the people who can least afford to lose—the poor.*

In your essay, analyze how Frum uses one or more of the features listed in the set of instructions for this essay (or features of your own choice) to strengthen the logic and persuasiveness of his argument. Be sure that your analysis focuses on the most relevant features of the passage.

Do not explain whether you agree or disagree with Frum's views. Rather, explain how Frum builds an argument to persuade his audience.

BOBBY'S ESSAY

This argument can be seen as an argument against casino gambling and their ability to harm especially the poorest, most disadvantaged people. The author named Frum at first describes the way customers gamble using computers that are programmed to cheat customers out of their money, but it makes them think that they just were unlucky. Frum makes a powerful claim backed up statistics saying that gambling addicts are the customers who keep casinos in business. Further along in the source, he tells the reader that an addict of slot machines with low incomes are like hypnitized or in the "zone" when playing the slots and they keep playing till they run out of money. One reason for this is that Frum explains that gambling was illegal almost every where the USA until the 1980s but now it's legal in 23 states and poor people can afford to go to casinos without spending lots of money to get there, a fact Frum uses to make the argument claiming that the poor suffer the most from gambling.

While he continues to build his argument, Frum writes about Atlantic City. They were promised to have gambling build up their economy. Instead of doing that, the city has high rates of home forclosures and other woes like "domestic violence" that Frum names to get an emotional rise out of the readers and convince them that gambling totally wrecked the whole community. He adds another statement to explain the reason, quoting The National Association of Realtors. They say that casinos make property values go down.

Frum also claims that casinos make the gap between rich and poor even bigger. To prove that he says that poor people lose a larger percent of their income on gambling than rich people. That makes sense since the "have nots" gamble more often and a small loss is much bigger in relation to their total income

Near the end, Frum asks the question, is this OK? It's supposed to be a rhetorical question that the reader can't really answer, but Frum basicly answers it. No, it's not OK, telling them to fight against gambling in their states if permitted, and prevent it from entering into their states if they don't have it.

YOUR COMMENTS ABOUT THE ESSAY

Reading

_____
_____
_____
_____

Analysis

_____
_____
_____
_____

Writing

_____
_____
_____
_____

COMMENT TO BOBBY FROM AN SAT ESSAY READER

Reading

Your response demonstrates an understanding of Frum's text and a grasp of its central idea ("against casino gambling and [its] ability to harm ... the poorest, most disadvantaged people"). There are no substantial errors of fact or interpretation in your essay, although more

specific references to the text using direct and indirect quotations as well as paraphrases of important details would provide evidence of deeper, more substantial comprehension.

Analysis

It's obvious that you understood the purpose of the assignment—to analyze the writer's use of rhetoric to support the claim that casino gambling is most harmful to those who are poor and vulnerable. The reference to slot machine addicts "with low incomes" becoming "hypnotized," for instance, clearly exemplifies a rhetorical element in the passage. Likewise, your insightful description of how Frum supports his claim that casinos enlarge the gap between rich and poor illustrates a high level of analytical thinking. On the other hand, an undeveloped reference to "statistics ... that gambling addicts are the customers who keep casinos in business" carries little weight if left unsupported by specific data or other details. Overall, your essay demonstrates a moderate grasp of text analysis.

Writing

Although you accurately explain how the author of the source text develops some of his claims, basic grammatical errors sometimes interfere with clarity. Take, for example, your opening sentence in which you use the phrase "their ability to harm...." To whom does the pronoun "their" refer? Presumably, you meant casino owners, but the reference is faulty because no such plural noun appears in the sentence. One slip-up in pronoun reference is not a serious error, but your essay contains several. This, along with an overall awkwardness of expression, diminishes the effectiveness of the essay. On the other hand, your ideas are well organized into coherent paragraphs, and your use of transitional words and phrases at the start of the second, third, and fourth paragraphs help to unify the essay.

Score: 3/2/2

AURORA'S ESSAY

In this passage Frum describes changes in the casino gambling industry since the 1980s. Gamblers now sit in front of computer screens in modern casinos instead of "Las Vegas-style grand hotels." He states that more poor people are now gamblers and says that the industry purposely creates gambling addicts. In addition, he describes the adverse effects of casino openings on surrounding communities. His main concern, though, is the harm it causes to the most vulnerable people in society, the poor.

As he discusses each of these issues, he uses a variety of evidence to support his claims and prove to readers that his argument is right on target. The evidence consists of examples such as the negative consequences to Atlantic City after gambling returned in 1977, including such things as "higher rates of home foreclosures and other forms of economic distress and domestic violence." Using such loaded words as "foreclosures," "distress," "violence" and others throughout the passage like "remorseless," "parasites," and "exploit" Frum is trying to arouse in readers' the same anger and disgust he apparently feels about the way the gambling casinos take advantage of poor, vulnerable people.

Another form of evidence that Frum likes to use is statistics. Right at the start, he says that 23 states allow gambling casinos. Then he writes that "75% of casino customers who play only occasionally provide only 4% of casino revenues," a statistic he uses to show that its the addict, the people who are the "problem gambler," and who are mostly poor, who keep the casinos in business. Illustrating how casinos achieve that, Frum quotes a shocking statement from research done by the think tank Institute for American Values, which describes how very addictive slot machines are engineered to "get into people's head" by putting them in a trance-like state that numbs feeling and blots out time/space." It's called a "zone," that people remain in until they run out of money, a condition the industry calls "playing to extinction." A reader reading that description is bound to have an emotional reaction about this cruel and inhumane treatment shown by casinos toward innocent customers.

How can casinos can get away with this policy of taking advantage of addicts and targeting those people that Frum describes as "those who can least afford to lose?" The answer is startling because he says that research on the health effects of gambling is paid for by the gambling industry itself – an obvious conflict of interest and another piece of evidence that supports Frum's goal of revealing the abuses of casino gambling. To make an ugly picture even more ugly, Frum brings up the idea that gambling "parallels the separate and unequal life patterns in education, marriage, work, and play that increasingly divide America into haves and have-nots." One interpretation to be made by readers of this comparison is that the horrors that gambling imposes on many Americans won't be abolished until all aspects American society are cleaned up. That probably won't happen soon, so what can be done to speed it up?

He ends the passage with a feeble answer, encouraging readers to take action to drive gambling out of their states or to keep it out in the future. Considering the gravity of the problem, that is a weak and unpersuasive conclusion.

YOUR COMMENTS ABOUT THE ESSAY

Reading

_____
_____
_____
_____

Analysis

_____
_____
_____
_____

Writing

_____
_____
_____
_____

COMMENT TO AURORA FROM AN SAT ESSAY READER

Reading

Your response demonstrates a thorough comprehension of the source text. The opening paragraph immediately reveals an ability to get right to the heart of the matter. In the rest of your essay, using several appropriate quotations and paraphrases from the text you show an understanding of how details in the passage support and contribute to the development of a central idea. You cite statistics, for example, indicating that casinos earn 96% of their revenue from "mostly poor" addicts and discuss Frum's assertion that gambling "parallels the separate and unequal life patterns … that increasingly divide America into haves and have-nots." Your response, free of errors of fact or interpretation, demonstrates advanced reading comprehension.

Analysis

Your skill in synthesizing several disparate ideas becomes increasingly apparent as you explain the forms of evidence Frum has used to build his critique of casino gambling. One feature that distinguishes your essay from most others is that it views the source holistically rather than piece by piece. That is, it discusses matters not in the order they appear in the passage but rather from a broader perspective, an approach that has enabled you to write a comprehensive and readable analysis of the passage. Overall, your essay demonstrates superior analytical skills.

Writing

This is an exemplary essay, not totally free of flaws but close enough to rank as a first-rate piece of work. It is well focused on rhetorical issues, admirably organized, and very clearly presented. You use a rational tone with a slight edge of disapproval, an appropriate choice for analyzing a source that discusses an unsavory side of the casino gambling industry. Your essay also contains examples of sophisticated sentence structure, seamless transitions from one subject to another, and precise word choice. Of particular note is the pair of sentences at the beginning of the fourth paragraph, where first you ask a probing question about how casinos can get away with predatory practices and then proceed to provide a "startling" answer.

Score: 4/4/4

THAD'S ESSAY

This source by Frum blew me away. I could of written it. I had the unbelievable opportunity to spend the summer after 11th grade with Hank, my cousin that works in a casino in Las Vegas. I am too youthful to gamble but I could and did devote undescribeable hours to scrutinize from the sidelines. I witnessed first hand the ineffable vision of sorry looking chain smoking men and women totally and miserably "zoned" on the slots hour following hour 24/7 until their hollowed out wallets and purses stood empty and they evacuated the area with sanguine blood shot eyes and shoulders that angled obliquely to the grungy ground. Where they went I am handicapped to speculate but they lacked the appearance of the rich and famous. No Porsches and Maseratis sat waiting for them outside in superheated sunny furnace parking lots and garages of Las Vegas summer. Mostly they trundled themselves onto A/C buses bound for the boonies and transported them to hopeless paint peeling trailers in weedy lots and bleached out threadbare laundry droopily draped on rusted wires strung from telephone pole to telephone pole.

Frum the writer is "write" on (ha!), nailing the situation in gambling casinos. The message is poverty driven unfortunates soaked by cheating casino owners is a reality. I didn't need Frum to tell me that.

I credit him to open eyes to Atlantic City's downward plunge due to casinos. That was news to me to hear that casinos act like cancer spreading outward into homes that foreclose where gambling junked husbands and wives beat each other up. If that scene is true I don't know from personal experience in Vegas. I'll haftoo tweet cousin Hank and ask.

YOUR COMMENTS ABOUT THE ESSAY

Reading

_____

_____

_____

_____

Analysis

_____

_____

_____

_____

Writing

_____

_____

_____

_____

COMMENT TO THAD FROM AN SAT ESSAY READER

Reading

Your piece demonstrates that you have at least a partial understanding of the source, particularly of Frum's account of the miseries endured by addicted slot machine gamblers. Apparently, Frum's review of Atlantic City's woes also left its mark on you. Whether your reading of the source went very much deeper than that is difficult to tell. Giving you a benefit of the doubt, and based on the absence of any errors of fact or interpretation, this reader thinks you have demonstrated a more than adequate comprehension of the source.

Analysis

This reader wishes that the prompt had instructed you to write something other than an analytical essay of the source writer's use of rhetorical elements. Why? Because you failed to write anything that comes close. Indeed, your essay, except perhaps for your recognition that Frum's portrait of casino gamblers resembles what you yourself perceived in Las Vegas ignores analysis in favor of an account of your own observations and thoughts about the plight of gambling addicts.

Writing

This reader again wishes that the assignment had been different because you write joyfully. Your off-beat prose style, unusual diction, and rich imagination show that you've got a rare but evolving gift for writing attention-grabbing prose. At present the gift is raw and unpolished, but in the future it can doubtlessly be shaped and shined. That said, this reader is obliged to assign a low score to your work because it fails to respond to the question, and the usual criteria for evaluating SAT essays don't apply.

PS. Recommendation: Take the SAT again and use your innate talent in order to write a crackerjack essay that responds to the assignment.

Score: 3/1/1

Prompt for SAT Essay #3

Read the following passage carefully. Consider how the author David Bell

- uses evidence such as examples and facts to back up claims
- provides reasoning to connect claims and evidence to develop ideas
- uses stylistic or persuasive elements, such as word choice or emotional appeals meant to add power to expressed ideas

(Adapted from David Bell, In Defense of Drones: A Historical Argument,
www.newrepublic.com, 1/27/2012)

Once upon a time, American military might was symbolized by the heavy boots of the Marine Corps, stomping ashore to reestablish order in unruly parts of the world. Today, it is symbolized by unmanned drone aircraft, controlled from thousands of miles away, dropping bombs on terrorists. Drone use aims to cut troops, ships and planes while concentrating our military energies on spy technology, cyber warfare, jammers, and special operations forces.

The embrace of technology over traditional methods of combat has provoked critics who doubt the morality and political implications of "remote control warfare." Notre Dame law professor Mary Ellen O'Connell, argues that "to accept killing far from battlefields where there is an understanding of necessity is ethically troubling." "The Economist" similarly asked: "If war can be waged by one side without risk to the life and limb of its combatants, has a vital form of restraint been removed?"

Other critics tend to present this new frontier of warfare as something largely novel—one that radically changes the political dynamics of warfare. But if our current technology is new, the desire to take out one's enemies from a safe distance is anything but. From the beginnings of warfare, combatants have sought technological advantages allowing them to kill enemies with minimum risk to themselves. And, these advances have always provoked criticism. We don't know if anyone excoriated the inventor of the bow and arrow as a dishonorable coward who refused to risk death in a hand to hand fight. Not surprisingly, after gunpowder weapons appeared, critics unloosed torrents of chivalric outrage. As late as the 1500's, the Italian poet Ariosto raged at this "wicked and terrible discovery" which had "destroyed martial glory and reduced valor and virtue to nought."

Over the centuries, advances in military technology added to the anonymity of killing. By 1918, the Germans had developed guns that could fire 200 pound shells a distance of 80 miles, over a trajectory that took them to an altitude of over 130,000 feet. This and other developments provoked criticism similar to that now heard against drone warfare.

It is crucial to note that since 1975 the sort of mass warfare characterized by anonymous killing and massive conscript armies has been quite strikingly reversed. Except for two campaigns in Iraq, the U.S. has largely fought against irregular, insurgent forces and terrorists, and actual combat has mostly taken place at much closer range than it did for the average infantryman of either world war. This development ought to console critics who worry about the moral and political implications of anonymous, long-distance killing: Soldiers remaining on the battlefield—and none more than the special operations forces that the administration relies on so heavily—are more likely to see their enemies up close than their grandfathers did, and to run very great risks indeed.

Of course, drone warfare aims to safeguard American lives and also put a premium on other lives for very practical, political reasons. The critics of drone warfare argue that without Americans running the risk of death, a vital restraint upon murderously aggressive military action will disappear, and countless innocent civilians will die. But in combating insurgents and terrorists, an action's political effects matter just as much, if not more, than their purely military ones, and high civilian death tolls are not just moral outrages, but political disasters.

What the history of war makes clear is that "remote control warfare" does not signal an abolition of restraints on war's destructive power. Using technology to strike safely at an opponent is as old as war itself. It has been seen in eras of highly-controlled and restrained warfare, and in eras of unrestrained total war—and the present day, thankfully, belongs to the first category. Ultimately, restraints upon war are more a matter of politics than of technology. If you are concerned about American aggression, it is not the drones you should fear, but the politicians who order them into battle.

Write an essay in which you explain how David Bell builds an argument to persuade his audience that *in spite of opinions to the contrary, the military use of drones does not eliminate restraints on carrying out deadly destruction of an enemy's land and people.*

In your essay, analyze how Bell uses one or more of the features listed in the set of instructions for this essay (or features of your own choice) to strengthen the logic and persuasiveness of his argument. Be sure that your analysis focuses on the most relevant features of the passage.

Do not explain whether you agree or disagree with Bell's views. Rather, explain how Bell builds an argument to persuade his audience.

BRANDON'S ESSAY

Everybody agrees that drone warfare is much safer than fighting in the usual way. However, not everybody agrees that fighting a war from thousands of miles away is the right thing to do. Opponents of using drones say that fighting from a long distance away is immoral. They say that bombing from a distance takes away restraints on performing deadly acts of destruction and replacing it with an attitude saying "Anything goes." The writer David Bell disagrees with that, and he claims that bombing from drones does not remove restraints.

How he supports that claim is with evidence from history. It's interesting that he began his passage with "Once upon a time," a phrase that is often found at the beginning of fairy tales or a children's story. Maybe he began that way to be ironic because readers will think an innocent little story is coming, but then he shocks them by talking about "dropping bombs on terrorists," and "cyber warfare, jammers, and special operations forces," So, in the opening paragraph Bell makes a shocking contrast on purpose playing with reader's emotions.

Another contrast he makes in the first paragraph is he describes the Marine Corp with "heavy boots … stomping ashore, etc.," the purpose is being to give readers a picture of brave warriors charging into battle. That is compared to today's "remote control warfare" where soldiers sit in front of a computer and make drones shoot rockets at the enemy. Some people say that's alright to do, it is safer than fighting directly with people who want to kill you as much as you want to kill them.

But there is also opposition to drones and Bell gives quotations by a college professor and the "Economist" to tell the reasons why they dislike them. One says they are "ethically troubling," meaning immoral and the other one says it removes the restraints on one side and lets them do whatever they want to blast the enemy to their doom.

Bell doesn't disagree with the morality accusation, but he does say that restraints are not eliminated when one side fights a war using a computer. He backs that up by saying since 1975 anonymous killing has "been quite strikingly reversed, which he supports by presenting facts about U.S. troops fighting insurgents and terrorists at closer range than the soldiers in World War II. He says restraints remain for "very practical, political reasons," which Bell says they "matter just as much, if not more," than military ones.

He says that people feel "moral outrage' about things like immoral killing of innocent civilians. That's one reason for the restraints to still be used. The other one is more complicated. It has to do with the history of wars since the old days. When a new invention was made like gun powder and the bow and arrow, it helped soldiers stay a farther distance from the enemy, complaints were made that the invention eliminated restraint to keep troops from performing mass slaughter against the enemy, so drones do the same thing because they are a recent invention.

YOUR COMMENTS ABOUT THE ESSAY

Reading

_____

_____

_____

_____

Analysis

_____

_____

_____

_____

Writing

_____

_____

_____

_____

COMMENTS TO BRANDON FROM AN SAT ESSAY READER

Reading

Your response demonstrates a thorough comprehension of the source. The first paragraph consists of clear background information leading to an accurate statement of Bell's claim—that drones do not remove restraints in waging war. Throughout the essay, you quote and paraphrase key ideas that capture both the main idea of the passage and details that develop and support it, especially those discussing the history and effect of innovative weapons in warfare since "the old days." There are no misstatements of fact or erroneous interpretations of the source.

Analysis

The insightfulness of your essay's first half is commendable. After expertly summarizing the main point and purpose of the source, in the next paragraph you provide a unique explanation of the effects achieved by juxtaposing "Once upon a time," a traditional literary usage against terminology of ultra-modern warfare. The second half of your essay, however, drifts away from its original purpose—to analyze how the writer uses rhetoric to argue the validity of his claim— and becomes more of a paraphrase of the author's views. Yet, you do comment on Bell's use of authorities on the subject of drones to argue that moral restraints are no less effective than they have always been.

Writing

Early on you articulate the essay's main central idea but omit any mention of the rhetorical elements you plan to discuss. Overall, you express ideas clearly, although not without awkwardness ("but there is also opposition and Bell gives quotations") and repetition. Note, also, how often you use the word "says" instead of varying your prose with synonyms that our language offers, such as claims, argues, remarks, states, and so on. Occasional errors in sentence structure also take a toll on the general effectiveness of the writing ("Another contrast he makes in the first paragraph is he describes the Marine Corp …"). Overall, the essay reflects that you need further development of your writing skills.

Score: 3/3/2

DELILAH'S ESSAY

In the beginning, David Bell describes a change in the way war is being fought. He dramatizes the change with contrasting symbols. The old style of war, which he labels "traditional methods of combat," is represented by the "heavy boots" of the Marines "stomping ashore...." This image may stir up a kind of "gung-ho" feeling that appeals to militants and fans of war movies. The new style is symbolized by impersonal technology represented by "unmanned drone aircraft, controlled from thousands of miles away," and "cyber warfare" and "jammers." These symbols may reflect Bell's bias toward traditional style warfare. He is not advocating that soldiers should meet face to face on battlefields, but he claims that when fighting involves real people risking lives, a "vital restraint upon murderously aggressive military action" goes into effect.

   Starting with that premise, Bell, claims that the need for "vital restraint" is behind many critic's disapproval of drone warfare. As evidence Bell quotes "The Economist," (obviously not a person but a publication I think) which asks that question—has technology removed "a vital form of restraint?" Bell doesn't think so. He knows that drone warfare is new, but his claim is that it is not novel, and he backs up this claim by giving examples of other inventions in history that have allowed combatants kill the enemy with little risk to themselves, such as the bow and arrow and gunpowder, which Bell claims led to the same kind of criticism that drones have inspired. To emphasize the point, Bell quotes Ariosto, a 16th century poet, who raged against some "wicked and terrible discovery … that destroyed martial glory and reduced valor and virtue to nought." Adding to his argument that the critics of drones are mistaken, Bell states that since 1975 anonymous warfare has been reduced. He again uses historical events to support his idea, saying that the U.S. war on terrorism has taken place "at much closer range than it did for the average infantryman in either world war." And he adds an emotional punch to his argument by making a reference to our "grandfathers" who fought back then.

The other thing that Bell wants to prove is that critics of drones are overly-concerned about the moral implications of drone warfare. As evidence of the critics' concern, he quotes a Notre Dame law professor who says that remote control warfare is "ethically troubling." He agrees that killing civilians is a moral outrage, but it's also a "political disaster." Based on his argument that "an action's political effects matter just as much, if not more, than purely military ones," Bell reasons that *"the military use of drones does not eliminate restraints on carrying out deadly destruction of an enemy's land and people."*

That claim leads him to answer the objections by the critics discussed earlier in the passage. By using examples from the long history of war, from bows and arrows to the German's use of guns that could be fired from 80 miles away, he makes the claim that every new weapon has led to accusations that technology has abolished restraints against all-out destruction. That claim leads directly to the conclusion of the passage, where Bell tells the reader that if you are concerned about America's aggressiveness, it's not the drones that are at fault but the politicians who decide to use them.

YOUR COMMENTS ABOUT THE ESSAY

Reading

_____

_____

_____

_____

Analysis

_____

_____

_____

_____

Writing

_____

_____

_____

_____

COMMENTS TO DELILAH FROM AN SAT ESSAY READER

Reading

Your response demonstrates thorough comprehension of Bell's passage. In your first paragraph you quickly summarize the issue and conclude with a combined quotation-paraphrase of Bell's claim about drones and their effect on "vital restraint" exercised by troops in battle. Throughout the essay, you display a keen awareness of how Bell builds his argument. You make reference to Bell's use of examples and to an assortment of quotations meant to advance the idea that technological innovation is not a new or unusual phenomenon in the history of warfare. You also discuss Bell's advocacy of the position that drones don't eliminate moral and other restraints on combatants. In all, your essay's accurate and wide-ranging review of the source is impressive.

Analysis

Your essay begins with a particularly fresh and insightful analysis of Bell's choice of words. After that your analysis of the text for the most part moves beyond the identification of rhetorical elements and into discussions of how various elements contribute to Bell's argument. For instance, you point out that Bell bolsters his claim that new weapons of war have always met the same sort of criticism now being leveled against drones by citing numerous historical examples, such as gunpowder and the bow and arrow. You also explain Bell's use of reasoning, quotations by authoritative sources, and emotional language to support claims, in particular his assertion that "military use of drones does not eliminate restraints on carrying out deadly destruction of an enemy's land and people." Overall, your essay often demonstrates good understanding of the analytical task

Writing

Most of your essay demonstrates highly effective use and command of language. Although the ending of your essay accurately reports Bell's claim regarding politicians' decisions to use drones, it seems like a last-minute add-on to the essay. Because it deals with the effect of innovations in weapons or war, much of the material is more suited to the essay's second paragraph, where you discuss similar innovations. Let's attribute that misstep to a fast-approaching time limit. Besides, it is a rather minor glitch in the coherence of an essay that otherwise has a great many virtues, including the use of interesting words and phrases ("gung-ho feeling, premise, combatants, raged against," etc.) and a deliberate and highly effective progression of ideas, both within paragraphs and throughout the essay as a whole.

Score: 4/3/4

ROBBIE'S ESSAY

Throughout history, various countries have been accused of being extremely violent in the wars they fought. In WW II Japan was one of the most extreme when they tried to colonize or take over other parts of Asia. Now, the United States is being singled out as a very brutal country. It is using drones to bomb terrorists in the middle east like Pakistan and also in Africa including Yemen and other Islam countries, and very often innocent civilians are killed.

In many religions, religious laws and practices pertain not only to special events and holidays but to everyday lives of the people who follow that religion. In the Christian religion, the primary belief is in Jesus Christ, the son of God. Christians are instructed to follow Christ's teachings through the bible. However another great belief pertains to the ten commandments of God and is about neighborly love and the rule which instructs "Thou shall not kill."

The U.S. has Jews and Muslims but it is mostly a Christian country. Even so, the government is bombing with drones and killing many innocent men, women and children. This action violates Christ's teachings and therefore, it should be stopped. It is wrong to do it. It also makes others hate the United States. Killing innocent people turns more people into terrorists who aim to plant bombs and perform destruction in our country or in American embassies in other countries.

The article by author David Bell talks about the negative effects of bombing with drones especially since they are fired by remote control from far away. From there the violence grows even more violent since there are no restraints on it. The more violent it becomes, the more freedom they use to kill and destroy the enemy.

One of the people quoted in Bell's passage talks about how drone strikes are ethically troubling. I think that is true and as simple as that. Killing is wrong and it turns people into anti-Americans just at a time when we need more friends around the world.

One of D. Bell's ideas is that technology has let wars be fought from a distance. And people criticized every time a new inventions was brought into battle like the bow and arrow and gunpowder. Now, the same kind of "outrage" exists against drones. Wars did not stop after those inventions, and so it probably won't stop after the inventions of drones unless Bell's idea at the end of the passage is followed, where he says that drones should not be feared "but the politicians who order them into battle."

YOUR COMMENTS ABOUT THE ESSAY

Reading

_____

_____

_____

_____

Analysis

_____

_____

_____

_____

Writing

_____

_____

_____

_____

COMMENTS TO ROBBIE FROM AN SAT ESSAY READER

Reading

Passing references to the text of the source suggest that you have read the source with a consid-erable degree of understanding and insight ("… the United States is being singled out as a very brutal country," "… drone strikes are ethically troubling"). A fair assessment of your reading of the source, however, is compromised because so much of your essay discusses matters, such as the precepts of Christianity, only marginally related to Bell's concerns. Insofar as possible, this reader has chosen to ignore the irrelevancies in your essay and to reward you for material that attests to your reading comprehension.

Analysis

Throughout the essay, your anti-violence and anti-war passions come through loud and clear. With but one exception—where you discuss the invention of new weapons and how such advances have invariably provoked criticism—the essay fails to analyze Bell's rhetoric. Instead, you've written an opinion piece against killing. Without question there are times and places appropriate for stating your views on war and violence. Unfortunately, the SAT Essay is not one of them.

Writing

Everything from word choice to your essay's overall organization demonstrates a respectable level of writing competence. However, your essay's main shortcoming—its disregard of the assigned purpose—cannot be overlooked.

Score: 3/1/1

Prompt for SAT Essay #4

Read the following passage carefully. Consider how the author

- uses evidence such as examples and facts to back up claims
- provides reasoning to connect claims and evidence to develop ideas
- uses stylistic or persuasive elements, such as word choice or emotional appeals meant to add power to expressed ideas

(Adapted from Anonymous, "The Virtue of Business: How Markets Encourage Ethical Behavior," Institute for Faith, Work, and Economics)

The notion that virtue leads to long-term business success is not a new idea. In his 1999 book *Capitalism, Democracy and Ralph's Pretty Good Grocery*, political scientist John Mueller traces how the relationship between ethical behavior and business success became commonplace in the U.S. over a century ago. According to Mueller, a policy of treating customers and employees ethically gave businesses a competitive advantage, and was often adopted by other companies. His primary example of ethical entrepreneurial innovation is the Barnum & Bailey Circus.

Prior to the founding of the Barnum & Bailey, billed as the "Greatest Show on Earth," circuses functioned dishonestly. From the moment customers entered until they returned home, they ran a high risk of being cheated. Ticket takers would short-change them at ticket windows; pickpockets were paid commissions to roam the grounds and victimize visitors. Circus sideshows were tacky; and games were impossible to win. So-called Monday Men stole from nearby clotheslines and houses while homeowners attended the circus shows and parades. Longtime Hollywood columnist Jim Tully relates from firsthand experience how circuses pretended to be honest while exploiting innocent rubes:

When a large group of rustics assembled, the circus spokesman would say, "Now Ladies and Gentlemen, we aim to run an honest show—but as you perhaps know there are thieves in high and low places all around. In fact, you may have a band of thieves right here in your own fair city. Hence, I warn you: Protect your valuables." Immediately rustic hands would feel for wallets and purses. The pickpockets would watch where the hands went and would follow soon after.

Circuses that practiced deception often earned quick profits, but their success was short-lived. Disappointed and suspicious, customers soon stopped attending. But in 1880 Barnum & Bailey Circus set in motion a variety of changes in the circus industry. Unlike earlier circuses, Barnum & Bailey created value for customers. They worked hard to change negative impressions of circuses and to attract new customers. They marketed the circus as an honest entertainment for families, vouched for the honesty of ticket takers, and monitored the behavior of workers, punishing those who lied and cheated. They also hired private detectives to catch and scare off the pickpockets.

Barnum & Bailey made their business ethical and honest because it was the right thing to do and not coincidentally, made it *profitable.* Whether they actually produced the "greatest show on earth" is debatable, but they convinced crowds to value and enjoy a visit to the circus.

By 1910, Barnum & Bailey, as well as other "clean" circuses such as the Ringling Brothers, had moved to the top of the industry and consistently profited from their honest business methods. A few circuses continued to take advantage of the rubes, but the dominant business model became Barnum & Bailey's so-called Sunday-School approach.

The experience of Barnum & Bailey illustrates the point that markets reward firms that try to do the right thing. Some customers flocked to Barnum & Bailey because they wanted to reward a company for being honest in a dishonest industry. Others didn't know or care about the company's business strategy. They came because their enjoyment was worth the money paid for admission, food, and souvenirs. The reputations of ethical circuses continued to rise and so, too, did their profits. Typically, consumers don't consciously reward companies because of their ethics and virtues. Instead, companies that focus on creating long-term relationships with customers are more likely than others to behave honestly and ethically.

P.T. Barnum and James Bailey didn't set out to reform the circus industry or get all circuses to adopt a Sunday-School approach. Their goal was to be profitable in the long term. To reach that goal, they created value for the customer. The unintended beneficial result of their action was that many other circus owners replicated their behavior in order to succeed. What we learn from the evolution in the treatment of circus customers is that unethical behavior in the free market causes companies to fail. Unethical businesses trying to prosper in a market where good ethics are the norm, are doomed to fail.

Write an essay in which you explain how the unnamed writer builds an argument to persuade his audience that *businesses gain a competitive advantage when they treat their customers and employees ethically.*

In your essay, analyze how the writer uses one or more of the features listed in the set of instructions for this essay (or features of your own choice) to strengthen the logic and persuasiveness of his argument. Be sure that your analysis focuses on the most relevant features of the passage.

Do not explain whether you agree or disagree with the writer's views. Rather, explain how the writer builds an argument to persuade his audience.

DARREN'S ESSAY

Companies are always running their business to earn money. When they have earned income and pay workers a good salary they are usually successful. The author who is named Anonymous by the passage he says that a business succeeds when it has virtue. This means they treat their customers and workers honestly and which gives them a "competitive advantage," He got this idea by reading a book by the political scientist John Mueller who said over a century ago it was common that the relationship of ethical behavior helped businesses success.

Proving that honest behavior made a difference for the famous Barney and Bailey Circus, which he uses as an example. Before Barney and Bailey, the circus business was dishonest. For evidence, he states a number of kinds of cheating and criminal acts done at the circus. Hiring pickpockets to steal from customers and they gave the wrong amount of change when they bought tickets of admission.

People discovered what was going on and they didn't attend the circus any more. This fact is used to lead in to what happened in 1880. The Barney and Bailey Circus changed to make value for customers. This means they grew honest to attract new people as customers. They also advertised telling everybody that the circus was honest and any worker who cheated customers is going to have a punishment.

All those changes lead the writer to talk about what happened when the circus discovered that the crowds started coming back and valued and enjoyed the time at the circus and they made it profitable again. This goes back to repeat what the writer has said at the beginning, businesses gain from showing virtue. They did the right thing so the public rewarded them. It is called the Sunday school approach and as the writer said "unethical behavior in the free market causes companies to fail.

In my opinion, the writer should of told how much money the circus made in profits after they decided to be honest and compare it to how much they made when they cheated, and then it would proves that it pays to be honest.

YOUR COMMENTS ABOUT DARREN'S ESSAY

Reading

_____

_____

_____

_____

Analysis

_____

_____

_____

_____

Writing

_____

_____

_____

_____

COMMENTS TO DARREN FROM AN SAT ESSAY READER

Reading

Aside from the questionable assertion that businesses are "usually successful" when they pay their workers well, this essay demonstrates a reasonably accurate comprehension of the source's text by summarizing several of its key ideas and providing appropriate textual evidence ("... businesses gain from showing virtue") and important details ("Hiring pickpockets to steal from customers..."). Frequent references to the central idea—that honesty leads to businesses success—contribute to the impression that you read the source with understanding.

Analysis

Your essay also reveals occasional awareness of its basic intent—to analyze how the author uses rhetorical techniques to support the general claim that businesses tend to make money when they treat their customers and employees ethically. For instance, you point out a few specific relationships between claims and evidence—such as citing the book from which the writer drew the idea that virtuous businesses tend to make profit. On the whole, however, your essay summarizes more than it analyzes the text.

Writing

Your essay displays weaknesses in basic writing skills. A number of sentence errors such as fragments and run-ons and several ambiguous pronoun references detract from the essay's effect and often obscure its meaning ("This means that they treat their customers..."). In all, your response indicates that you would stand to benefit from a remedial writing program.

Score: 2/2/2

ALYS'S ESSAY

The basic message of the source is a cliché: "Honesty is the best policy," at least as it applies to business. The anonymous writer believes that virtuous business practices lead to a profitable bottom line. The origin of this claim comes mostly from a book published in 1999 by Mueller, about the "relationship between ethical behavior and business success." Mueller is a political scientist but probably a historian also because his theory is based on his knowledge of the history of the "greatest show on earth," the Barnum & Bailey Circus.

The passage from the beginning until the end is basically a summary of Mueller's book. Every claim and piece of evidence seems to be taken from him except a quote from a Hollywood columnist's experience which describes how circuses hoodwinked audiences into being victimized by pickpockets. It's not clear whether the source of the quote was the book or if it came from Jim Tully's column. Either way, the quote is used to support the claim made near the beginning that circuses "functioned dishonestly" for a long time before Barnum & Bailey was founded.

The writer supplies a long list of unethical actions in order support the claim about the dishonesty of circuses. For example, he says that customers would be short-changed by ticket takers and that pickpockets were hired by the circus and were paid commissions to steal from the customers. Maybe even more insidious were the "Monday Men" who stole clothes from the outdoor laundry lines of homeowners who were at the circus.

After a while the public realized that they were being cheated. So they stopped going to the circus. The writer uses this fact to explain the reason behind Barnum & Bailey's attempt to change the negative image of the circus industry. To highlight the dramatic shift from dishonest to ethical values, the writer provides details that are the exact opposite of earlier circuses, such as vouching for the honesty of ticket takers, and hiring detectives to prevent pickpockets from victimizing customers.

The writer gives the experience of Barnum & Bailey a happy ending by including evidence that by doing the "right thing," their company brought the crowds back to the circus and started making a profit again. As a way to emphasize the strength of Barnum & Bailey's new approach, the writer claims that other circus companies followed suit and modeled themselves after Barnum & Bailey and as a result began to make more money, too.

In the end, the writer draws a broad conclusion from the experiences of ethically-run circuses like Barnum & Bailey that all businesses in a free market stand to profit from making ethical behavior a norm. He also claims that unethical businesses are doomed to fail. Whether that principle is true or not remains unclear, but it is probably worth thinking about if you own or run a business.

YOUR COMMENTS ABOUT THE ESSAY

Reading

_____

_____

_____

_____

Analysis

_____

_____

_____

_____

Writing

_____

_____

_____

_____

COMMENTS TO ALYS FROM AN SAT ESSAY READER

Reading

Your response demonstrates a complete comprehension of the text. References and quotations, both direct and indirect, attest to your understanding of details related to the author's main idea. For example, you point out how well a lengthy quote from a Hollywood columnist not only illustrates the author's claim that circuses for a long time "functioned dishonestly" but provides a contrast to what circuses—or at least the Barnum & Bailey Circus—ultimately became. Also, your essay perceptively captures the essence of the source by relating the history of the circus as though it were a narrative with a beginning, a middle, and, as you put it, "a happy ending."

Analysis

Your astute observation that the source is essentially a summary of Mueller's book provides a solid framework for analyzing the rhetoric in the passage. Putting aside that few, if any, of the writer's claims come from his own reflection, research, or experience, you have shown how some claims reasonably lead to others, among them that Barnum & Bailey's commitment to doing the "right thing" ultimately led to reforms that revitalized the whole circus industry. Using specific evidence drawn from the history of the circus you also show how the writer validates the claim that in the past circuses functioned dishonestly.

Writing

In all respects, your response demonstrates a substantial ability to express your ideas in standard written English. Your essay begins by specifying the origins of the source, in effect giving readers some perspective on the reliability of the source as an accurate historical account of the circus industry. The insinuation that the source is not altogether reliable serves as a kind of sub-text or secondary theme throughout your essay. You also demonstrate a command of precise, potent word choice ("hoodwinked," "victimized," "insidious," "vouching for," "followed suit"). Paragraphs in the body of the essay are tightly focused and along with transitions ("After a while … ." "In the end…") contribute to the essay's overall cohesiveness. A thoughtful concluding sentence brings the essay to a satisfying close.

Score: 4/4/4

TRAVIS'S ESSAY

In my AP American class we recently learned about faulty ignition switches installed in many General Motors cars a few years ago and how the company deliberately kept it a secret and did nothing to fix or replace them until more than 15 people were killed when their engines shut down by accident and the drivers could not steer or put on the brakes. The scandal shocked the public and outraged members of Congress. You might expect that people would stop buying GM cars after that, but just the opposite happened. A few months after the scandal made headlines, GM had the most profitable period in its history.

This story is relevant because of the passage about the circus. The writer claimed that unethical acts by circus owners kept people from going to the circus, and that is the exact opposite of what happened at GM. In the circus, business declined and at GM it improved, although the improvement could not have resulted from GM's bad ethics but for other unrelated reasons. Yet, what happened at GM raises doubts about the accuracy of the argument made by the author of the source about the circus. He claimed that unethical businesses are "doomed to fail" and ethical businesses are likely to attract customers and earn bigger profits. Obviously, that did not happen with GM.

In telling about the circus, the writer goes over the background of circuses and claims that they were dishonest and they took advantage of customers by cheating them, stealing their money and fixing the circus games so that no one could win. All these facts come from a book about capitalism where the author claims that for a long time there has been a relationship between ethical behavior and business success, and he uses the circus as an example.

Back in 1880, the Barnum and Bailey circus decided to try to convince customers to come back by creating an image of the circus as a fun place for the whole family. They worked hard to spread the word about their honesty. Circus workers who were caught cheating people were punished. They hired detectives to catch and scare off pickpockets, etc. The result was an increase in attendance and also an increase in profits. This so-named "Sunday-school" approach led to the author's claim that by doing the right thing, businesses are rewarded with satisfied customers and bigger profits. On the other hand, businesses that cheat and lie will soon lose customers, close up shop and disappear. Maybe that's a good theory but as the General Motors experience shows, it doesn't always work.

YOUR COMMENTS ABOUT THE ESSAY

Reading

_____

_____

_____

_____

Analysis

_____

_____

_____

_____

Writing

_____

_____

_____

_____

COMMENTS TO TRAVIS FROM AN SAT ESSAY READER

Reading

Your essay demonstrates effective comprehension of the source text in terms of both its central idea and the details of circus history. Because a substantial portion of your essay is devoted to the General Motors scandal, however, you give short shrift to the source itself, omitting specific references to the text, quotations, paraphrases, and other evidence that might have shown the depth and insightfulness of your understanding.

Analysis

Your observations about General Motors prevent you from paying full attention to the main purpose of the essay—to analyze the use of textual evidence to support and develop the writer's claim that ethical businesses are more apt to be profitable than those whose practices lack integrity. Instead, you pass judgment on the writer's claim and find it wanting. To be sure, you make a reasonable case against the credibility of the claim, but in the process pay almost no attention to analyzing of the source text. The last two paragraphs of your essay, the logical place for such an analysis, show few signs that you understand the nature of the analytical task.

Writing

In the first paragraph you make an eye-opening comparison between a contemporary phenomenon—the General Motors debacle—and the development of the circus as described by the source. A shorter introduction to your essay, however, might have been better because yours comprises about a quarter of your essay. Nevertheless, you deserve credit for pointing out a fascinating parallel.

In some other context, such as your AP American class, the essay might be considered relevant and illuminating. Here on the SAT, unfortunately, it misses the mark. To your credit, however, the writing demonstrates a moderately effective use of language and an awareness of the rules of standard written English.

Score: 2/1/3

Practice, Practice, Practice 7

Well, you've arrived. Congratulations! Having patiently trudged through the pages of this book, you should now to be ready to write an SAT Essay on your own.

For each essay, allow yourself exactly 50 minutes to read the source, plan what to say about it, and put your words on paper. If possible, stick to whatever schedule you've devised for prewriting, composing, and editing your essay. If, on your first try, you finish early or run out of time, adjust your use of time for the second essay, and the third and the fourth, until it's finely tuned and produces the results you want.

To write each essay, use either the lined pages provided or a few sheets of standard 8-1/2" × 11" composition paper, the size of the SAT answer booklet you'll receive on test day.

To evaluate and rate each essay, refer first to the Essay Scoring Guide on pages 306–307. Then fill out the Self-Scoring Guide for each essay.

PRACTICE ESSAY #1

Climate change is not an event in your children's future. It is bearing down upon you now. And there is nothing you—or anyone else—can do to prevent the hit.

Over the next quarter century, heat-related death rates will probably double in the southeastern states. Crop losses that used to happen only once every 20 years because of cataclysmic weather will occur five times as often.

This is our future even if every person on the planet abruptly stopped burning coal, gas, oil, wood or anything else containing carbon today and we hooked the world economy onto the wind and the sun tomorrow. The change is baked in, caused by CO_2 spewed into the air long ago.

This stark future is rendered vividly in a comprehensive report recently by the Risky Business Project, a coalition of political and business luminaries representing widely different political views that is intended to raise awareness about the impending perils of a changing climate. . . . The picture is not pretty. It punctures the hopes held by some of the most uncompromising environmentalists and the most compromising politicians that humanity can still prevent climatic upheaval if we only start replacing fossil fuels today.

For starters, it seems clear by now that the world's temperature will almost certainly rise more than two degrees Celsius—or 3.6 degrees Fahrenheit—above the average of the late 19th century, a ceiling that the world's leaders have repeatedly promised never to breach and a point at which climate-related risks rise even more sharply.

Second, despite the rising awareness of the risks caused by our unrestrained consumption of fossil fuels, there is no evidence that we plan to break the habit and leave a substantial portion of the Earth's oil, gas and coal in the ground.

"We are swinging to fossil fuels in ways that couldn't have been imagined a few years ago," said Michael Greenstone of the Massachusetts Institute of Technology. "We've made substantial progress in renewables, but there's been even more innovation in fossil fuels. Incentives to invest in low-carbon energy are going down."

By 2100, up to $507 billion worth of coastal property will be underwater if we continue emitting CO_2 at the same pace as we have over recent decades, New York will face a one-in-100 chance of seeing the sea rise almost seven feet. Crop yields in the Southwest, Midwest and lower Great Plains could fall up to 70 percent as extreme heat spreads throughout the country. By the final decade of the century, Nebraska will face a one-in-20 chance that climate change will reduce its agricultural production by almost $2,000 for each man, woman and child in the state. North Dakota will face a one-in-20 chance that declining productivity will cost the state $1,600 per person, as workers stay indoors out of the sun. Arizona will face one-in-20 odds that energy costs will rise by $800 per person.

The question, for corporate chieftains, business leaders, and voters remains: What is it worth to prevent these costs?

Perhaps our new understanding—detailed and specific—of their magnitude and timing will compel us to act. Professor Greenstone supports a tax coupled with a major expansion of investment in research to develop cost-competitive technologies, which the U.S. could also make available to the big polluters of the future: China and India.

But don't hold your breath.

Write an essay in which you explain how Eduardo Porter builds an argument to persuade his audience that *dire consequences of climate change are virtually inevitable*. In your essay, analyze how Porter uses one or more of the features listed in the set of instructions for this essay (or use features of your own choice) to strengthen the logic and persuasiveness of his argument. Be sure to focus your analysis on the most relevant features of the passage.

Do not explain whether you agree or disagree with Porter's views. Rather, explain how Porter builds an argument to persuade his audience.

Self-Scoring Guide for Practice Essay #1

Before scoring your essay, let it sit for a day—or more, if possible. The passage of time will prepare you to read your essay with an open mind and a fresh pair of eyes.

After referring to "How Essays Are Scored" on page 305, use the chart below to help you evaluate your performance in each category: Reading, Analysis, and Writing.

Because a totally unbiased perspective on one's own writing requires amazing objectivity, you may get a more accurate evaluation of your essay by enlisting a trusted, well-informed friend or an experienced teacher to do it for you.

	Definitely!	Pretty Much	Only a Little	No
Reading				
Did you fully comprehend the source?	☐	☐	☐	☐
Is the author's central idea or claim accurately reported or summarized in your essay?	☐	☐	☐	☐
Have you discussed or alluded to the relationship between the central idea and various forms of evidence in the source?	☐	☐	☐	☐
Have you made reference to important details in the text using paraphrases, appropriate quotations, and/or your own words?	☐	☐	☐	☐
As far as you know, is your essay free from errors of fact and interpretation of the source?	☐	☐	☐	☐
Analysis				
Does your essay include an effective analysis of the source text?	☐	☐	☐	☐
Can you point out a place in your essay where you discuss the important claim made by the author of the source?	☐	☐	☐	☐
Can you identify a place where you point out facts, statistics, or the reports of experts that the author uses to support a claim?	☐	☐	☐	☐
Can you point to a place where you discuss the author's use of potent language or some other stylistic feature to build an argument?	☐	☐	☐	☐
Can you point to a place where you describe the author's use of reason to build an argument?	☐	☐	☐	☐
Can you point to a place where you identify an important rhetorical element of your own choice that the author uses to build an argument?	☐	☐	☐	☐
Can you point to one or more places where you have discussed the effect of a rhetorical element on a reader?	☐	☐	☐	☐

	Definitely!	Pretty Much	Only a Little	No
Writing				
Can you point to the place or places in your essay that states your essay's main idea?	☐	☐	☐	☐
Can you explain how you've arranged your ideas?	☐	☐	☐	☐
Does your essay include an introduction?	☐	☐	☐	☐
Is each paragraph related to the essay's main idea?	☐	☐	☐	☐
Are sentences varied in length and structure?	☐	☐	☐	☐
Have you used plain and precise words?	☐	☐	☐	☐
Do transitions tie paragraphs together and link sentences to each other?	☐	☐	☐	☐
Have you maintained a consistent style or tone throughout your essay?	☐	☐	☐	☐
As far as you know, does your essay adhere to the conventions of standard written English?	☐	☐	☐	☐
Total of checks in each column:				

Ratings skewed to the left mean your essay has earned scores in the 3–4 range, and vice-versa, right-leaning scores put you in the 1–2 range. Read the Self-Scoring Summary below for another way to interpret the numbers.

Self-Scoring Summary

READING

4 Thorough and perceptive comprehension of the source

3 Basically correct and adequate comprehension of the source

2 Partial or somewhat uncertain comprehension of the source

1 Minimal, confused, or absent comprehension of the source

ANALYSIS

4 Extremely thorough and insightful analysis and discussion of major and minor rhetorical elements

3 Basically sound and relatively insightful analysis and discussion of important rhetorical elements

2 Fairly unfocused or shallow analysis of rhetorical elements with little discussion of each

1 Generally insufficient, erroneous, or nonexistent analysis of rhetorical elements

WRITING

4 Well-planned and fully developed; varied and engaging sentence structure; effective word choice; no consequential errors in grammar and usage

3 Reasonably well-organized and sufficiently developed; sufficiently varied sentence structure to create interest; minor sentence errors; ranges from competent to conventional word choice; mostly correct grammar and usage

2 Slightly disorganized; weak development with some relevant material; little sentence variety; sentence errors that may obscure meaning; essentially correct but with some errors in diction or idiom; basically correct grammar and usage but occasional major errors

1 Poor or no discernible organization; little or no development; serious sentence errors interfere with or obscure meaning; inappropriate word choices; meaning obscured or blocked by grammar and usage errors

PRACTICE ESSAY #2

Read the following passage carefully. Consider how the author Benedict Cary

- uses evidence such as examples and facts, to back up claims.
- provides reasoning to connect claims and evidence to develop ideas.
- uses stylistic or persuasive elements, such as word choice or emotional appeals meant to add power to expressed ideas

The 8-year-old juggling a soccer ball and the 48-year-old jogging have something fundamental in common: At some level, both are wondering whether their investment of time and effort is worth it.

How good can I get? How much time will it take? Is it possible I'm a natural at this? What's the percentage in this, exactly?

Scientists have long argued over the relative contributions of practice and native talent to the development of elite performance. This debate swings back and forth. In a landmark 1993 study of musicians, a research team led by K. Anders Ericsson, a psychologist now at Florida State University, found that practice time explained almost all the difference (about 80 percent) between elite performers and committed amateurs.

A new paper, a comprehensive review of relevant research to date by Zach Hambrick, a Michigan State University psychologist, and others, comes to a different conclusion. Compiling results from 88 studies across a wide range of skills, it estimates that practice time explains about 20 percent to 25 percent of the difference in performance in music, sports and games like chess. In academics, the number is much lower—4 percent—in part because it's hard to assess the effect of previous knowledge, the authors wrote.

"We found that, yes, practice is important, and of course it's absolutely necessary to achieve expertise," said Hambrick. "But it's not as important as many people have been saying" compared to inborn gifts.

One of those people, Dr. Ericsson, points out that the paper uses a definition of practice that includes a variety of related activities, including playing music or sports for fun or playing in a group.

But his own studies focused on what he calls deliberate practice: one-on-one lessons in which an instructor pushes a student continually, gives immediate feedback and focuses on weak spots.

Like most branches of the nature-nurture debate, this one has produced multiple camps, whose estimates of the effects of practice vary by as much as 50 percentage points. And because truly elite performance takes many years to achieve, he said, the exact contribution of practice may never be known precisely.

Yet the range of findings and level of disagreement are themselves hints that there are likely to be factors involved in building expertise that are neither genetic nor related to the amount of practice time.

One is the age at which a person picks up a violin, or a basketball, or a language. People who grow up in bilingual households fully integrate both languages at the same time that language-specialized areas in their brains are developing. The same may be true of many other skills—there may exist a critical window of learning in childhood that primes the brain to pick up skills quickly later on.

Other factors are much easier to control. For instance, scientists have shown that performance itself—that is, testing oneself, from memory—is a particularly strong form of practice. One of the studies that the new review paper includes found that chess masters with similar abilities varied widely in the amount of hours they reported practicing, from 3,000 to more than 25,000.

"We may find when looking more closely that playing in tournaments, under pressure, is an important factor," Dr. Hambrick said.

The content of isolated practice is another. In dozens of experiments, scientists have shown that mixing related skills in a single practice session—new material and old, scales and improvisation, crawl and backstroke—seems to sharpen each skill more quickly than if practiced repeatedly on its own. Varying the place and timing of practice can help as well, for certain skills, studies suggest.

"The question is: What is the optimal kind of practice in the area you wish to achieve expertise?" Dr. Ericsson said. "These are things we are now beginning to study, in areas like medical training."

Practice time is critical indeed, and its contribution to accumulated expertise is likely to vary from one field to the next as the new paper found, experts said. Personality is an enormous variable, too, (although partly genetic). Things like grit, motivation, and inspiration—that ability to imagine achieving this high level, to fantasize about it—these are largely unknown things that need to be studied.

But in the end, the most important factor over which people have control—whether juggling, jogging or memorizing a script—may be not how much they practice, but how effectively they use that time.

Write an essay in which you explain how Benedict Carey builds an argument to persuade his audience that *in the development of certain skills, uncertainty remains whether practice or native talent is more important*. In your essay, analyze how Carey uses one or more of the features listed in the set of instructions for this essay (or use features of your own choice) to strengthen the logic and persuasiveness of his argument. Be sure to focus your analysis on the most relevant features of the passage.

Do not explain whether you agree or disagree with Carey's views. Rather, explain how Carey builds an argument to persuade his audience.

Self-Scoring Guide for Practice Essay #2

Before scoring your essay, let it sit for a day—or more, if possible. The passage of time will prepare you to read your essay with an open mind and a fresh pair of eyes.

After referring to "How Essays Are Scored" on page 305, use the chart below to help you evaluate your performance in each category: Reading, Analysis, and Writing.

Because a totally unbiased perspective on one's own writing requires amazing objectivity, you may get a more accurate evaluation of your essay by enlisting a trusted, well-informed friend or an experienced teacher to do it for you.

	Definitely!	Pretty Much	Only a Little	No
Reading				
Did you fully comprehend the source?	☐	☐	☐	☐
Is the author's central idea or claim accurately reported or summarized in your essay?	☐	☐	☐	☐
Have you discussed or alluded to the relationship between the central idea and various forms of evidence in the source?	☐	☐	☐	☐
Have you made reference to important details in the text using paraphrases, appropriate quotations, and/or your own words?	☐	☐	☐	☐
As far as you know, is your essay free from errors of fact and interpretation of the source?	☐	☐	☐	☐
Analysis				
Does your essay include an effective analysis of the source text?	☐	☐	☐	☐
Can you point out a place in your essay where you discuss the important claim made by the author of the source?	☐	☐	☐	☐
Can you identify a place where you point out facts, statistics, or the reports of experts that the author uses to support a claim?	☐	☐	☐	☐
Can you point to a place where you discuss the author's use of potent language or some other stylistic feature to build an argument?	☐	☐	☐	☐
Can you point to a place where you describe the author's use of reason to build an argument?	☐	☐	☐	☐
Can you point to a place where you identify an important rhetorical element of your own choice that the author uses to build an argument?	☐	☐	☐	☐
Can you point to one or more places where you have discussed the effect of a rhetorical element on a reader?	☐	☐	☐	☐

	Definitely!	Pretty Much	Only a Little	No
Writing				
Can you point to the place or places in your essay that states your essay's main idea?	☐	☐	☐	☐
Can you explain how you've arranged your ideas?	☐	☐	☐	☐
Does your essay include an introduction?	☐	☐	☐	☐
Is each paragraph related to the essay's main idea?	☐	☐	☐	☐
Are sentences varied in length and structure?	☐	☐	☐	☐
Have you used plain and precise words?	☐	☐	☐	☐
Do transitions tie paragraphs together and link sentences to each other?	☐	☐	☐	☐
Have you maintained a consistent style or tone throughout your essay?	☐	☐	☐	☐
As far as you know, does your essay adhere to the conventions of standard written English?	☐	☐	☐	☐
Total of checks in each column:				

Ratings skewed to the left mean your essay has earned scores in the 3–4 range, and vice-versa, right-leaning scores put you in the 1–2 range. Read the Self-Scoring Summary below for another way to interpret the numbers.

Self-Scoring Summary

READING

4 Thorough and perceptive comprehension of the source

3 Basically correct and adequate comprehension of the source

2 Partial or somewhat uncertain comprehension of the source

1 Minimal, confused, or absent comprehension of the source

ANALYSIS

4 Extremely thorough and insightful analysis and discussion of major and minor rhetorical elements

3 Basically sound and relatively insightful analysis and discussion of important rhetorical elements

2 Fairly unfocused or shallow analysis of rhetorical elements with little discussion of each

1 Generally insufficient, erroneous, or nonexistent analysis of rhetorical elements

WRITING

4 Well-planned and fully developed; varied and engaging sentence structure; effective word choice; no consequential errors in grammar and usage

3 Reasonably well-organized and sufficiently developed; sufficiently varied sentence structure to create interest; minor sentence errors; ranges from competent to conventional word choice; mostly correct grammar and usage

2 Slightly disorganized; weak development with some relevant material; little sentence variety; sentence errors that may obscure meaning; essentially correct but with some errors in diction or idiom; basically correct grammar and usage but occasional major errors

1 Poor or no discernible organization; little or no development; serious sentence errors interfere with or obscure meaning; inappropriate word choices; meaning obscured or blocked by grammar and usage errors

PRACTICE ESSAY #3

Security and privacy are a shared responsibility between companies, users and the institutions around us. Companies like Google, Apple, Amazon and Facebook are expected to safeguard data, prevent their systems from being hacked into and provide the most effective tools for users to maximize control of their privacy and security. But it is up to us, their customers, to use these tools. Each day you choose not to utilize them you will experience some loss of privacy and security as the data keeps piling up. And you cannot assume there is a simple delete button. The option to "delete" data is largely an illusion—lost files, deleted e-mails and erased text messages can be recovered with minimal effort. Data is rarely erased on computers; operating systems tend to remove only a file's listing from the internal directory, keeping the file's contents in place until the space is needed for other things. (And even after a file has been overwritten, it's still occasionally possible to recover parts of the original content due to the magnetic properties of disc storage. This problem is known as "data remanence" by computer experts.)

The potential for someone else to access, share or manipulate parts of our data will increase particularly due to our reliance on cloud-based storage. (In nontechnical language, cloud computing refers to software hosted on the Internet that the user does not need to closely manage. Storing documents or content "in the cloud" means that the data is stored on remote servers rather than on local ones or on a person's own computer, and it can be accessed by multiple networks and users.) Cloud computing only reinforces the permanence of information, adding another layer of remote protection for users and their information.

Such mechanisms of retention were designed to save us from our own carelessness when operating computers. In the future, people will increasingly trust cloud storage—like ATMs in banks—over physical machinery, placing their faith in companies to store some of their most sensitive information, avoiding the risks of hard-drive crashes, computer thefts or document loss. This multilayer backup system will make online interactions more efficient and productive, not to mention less emotionally fraught.

Near-permanent data storage will have a big impact on how citizens operate in virtual space. There will be a record of all activity associations online, and everything added to the Internet will become part of a repository of information. The possibility that one's personal content will be published and become known one day—either by mistake or through criminal interference—will always exist. People will be held responsible for their virtual associations, past and present, which raises the risk for nearly everyone since people's online networks tend to be larger and more diffuse than their physical ones. The good and bad behavior of those they know will affect them positively or negatively. (And no, stricter privacy settings on social-networking sites will not suffice.)

This will be the first generation of humans to have an indelible record. Colleagues of President Nixon may have erased sections of audio tapes containing his conversations about the Watergate scandal, but today's president faces a permanent record of every e-mail sent from his BlackBerry, accessible to the public under the Presidential Records Act.

Since information wants to be free, don't write anything down you don't want read back to you in court or printed on the front page of a newspaper, as the saying goes. In the future this adage will broaden to include not just what you say and write, but the websites you visit, who you include in your online network, what you "like" and what others who are connected to you do, say, and share.

Never before will so much data be available to so many people. Citizens will draw conclusions about one another from accurate and inaccurate sources, from "legitimate" sources like LinkedIn profiles and "illegitimate" ones like errant YouTube comments long forgotten. Public acceptance for youthful indiscretions documented on the Internet will move a few paces forward, but probably not before a painful period of time passes. The fallibility of humans over a lifetime will provide an endless stream of details online, and some of us will spend our entire lives acutely aware of the potentially volatile parts of our lives, wondering what might surface online today or tomorrow.

Write an essay in which you explain how Eric Schmidt and Jared Cohen build an argument to persuade their audience that *the electronic age compels us to exercise extreme vigilance in order to maintain our privacy in the future.* In your essay, analyze how Schmidt and Cohen use one or more of the features listed in the set of instructions for this essay (or use features of your own choice) to strengthen the logic and persuasiveness of their argument. Be sure to focus your analysis on the most relevant features of the passage.

Do not explain whether you agree or disagree with Schmidt and Cohen's views. Rather, explain how Schmidt and Cohen build an argument to persuade their audience.

Self-Scoring Guide for Practice Essay #3

Before scoring your essay, let it sit for a day—or more, if possible. The passage of time will prepare you to read your essay with an open mind and a fresh pair of eyes.

After referring to "How Essays Are Scored" on page 305, use the chart below to help you evaluate your performance in each category: Reading, Analysis, and Writing.

Because a totally unbiased perspective on one's own writing requires amazing objectivity, you may get a more accurate evaluation of your essay by enlisting a trusted, well-informed friend or an experienced teacher to do it for you.

	Definitely!	Pretty Much	Only a Little	No
Reading				
Did you fully comprehend the source?	☐	☐	☐	☐
Is the author's central idea or claim accurately reported or summarized in your essay?	☐	☐	☐	☐
Have you discussed or alluded to the relationship between the central idea and various forms of evidence in the source?	☐	☐	☐	☐
Have you made reference to important details in the text using paraphrases, appropriate quotations, and/or your own words?	☐	☐	☐	☐
As far as you know, is your essay free from errors of fact and interpretation of the source?	☐	☐	☐	☐
Analysis				
Does your essay include an effective analysis of the source text?	☐	☐	☐	☐
Can you point out a place in your essay where you discuss the important claim made by the author of the source?	☐	☐	☐	☐
Can you identify a place where you point out facts, statistics, or the reports of experts that the author uses to support a claim?	☐	☐	☐	☐
Can you point to a place where you discuss the author's use of potent language or some other stylistic feature to build an argument?	☐	☐	☐	☐
Can you point to a place where you describe the author's use of reason to build an argument?	☐	☐	☐	☐
Can you point to a place where you identify an important rhetorical element of your own choice that the author uses to build an argument?	☐	☐	☐	☐

	Definitely!	Pretty Much	Only a Little	No
Can you point to one or more places where you have discussed the effect of a rhetorical element on a reader?	☐	☐	☐	☐
Writing				
Can you point to the place or places in your essay that states your essay's main idea?	☐	☐	☐	☐
Can you explain how you've arranged your ideas?	☐	☐	☐	☐
Does your essay include an introduction?	☐	☐	☐	☐
Is each paragraph related to the essay's main idea?	☐	☐	☐	☐
Are sentences varied in length and structure?	☐	☐	☐	☐
Have you used plain and precise words?	☐	☐	☐	☐
Do transitions tie paragraphs together and link sentences to each other?	☐	☐	☐	☐
Have you maintained a consistent style or tone throughout your essay?	☐	☐	☐	☐
As far as you know, does your essay adhere to the conventions of standard written English?	☐	☐	☐	☐
Total of checks in each column:				

Ratings skewed to the left mean your essay has earned scores in the 3–4 range, and vice-versa, right-leaning scores put you in the 1–2 range. Read the Self-Scoring Summary below for another way to interpret the numbers.

Self-Scoring Summary

READING

4 Thorough and perceptive comprehension of the source

3 Basically correct and adequate comprehension of the source

2 Partial or somewhat uncertain comprehension of the source

1 Minimal, confused, or absent comprehension of the source

ANALYSIS

4 Extremely thorough and insightful analysis and discussion of major and minor rhetorical elements

3 Basically sound and relatively insightful analysis and discussion of important rhetorical elements

2 Fairly unfocused or shallow analysis of rhetorical elements with little discussion of each

1 Generally insufficient, erroneous, or nonexistent analysis of rhetorical elements

WRITING

4 Well-planned and fully developed; varied and engaging sentence structure; effective word choice; no consequential errors in grammar and usage

3 Reasonably well-organized and sufficiently developed; sufficiently varied sentence structure to create interest; minor sentence errors; ranges from competent to conventional word choice; mostly correct grammar and usage

2 Slightly disorganized; weak development with some relevant material; little sentence variety; sentence errors that may obscure meaning; essentially correct but with some errors in diction or idiom; basically correct grammar and usage but occasional major errors

1 Poor or no discernible organization; little or no development; serious sentence errors interfere with or obscure meaning; inappropriate word choices; meaning obscured or blocked by grammar and usage errors

PRACTICE ESSAY #4

Read the following passage carefully. Consider how the author Fareed Zakaria

- uses evidence such as examples and facts to back up claims
- provides reasoning to connect claims and evidence to develop ideas
- uses stylistic or persuasive elements, such as word choice or emotional appeals meant to add power to expressed ideas

In 1492, as everybody knows, Christopher Columbus set sail on one of the most ambitious expeditions in human history, What is less well known is that eighty-seven years earlier a Chinese admiral name Zheng He began the first of seven equally ambitious expeditions. Zheng's ships were much bigger and better constructed than those of Columbus, or Vasco da Gama, or any of Europe's other great fifteenth- and sixteenth-century seafarers. On his first trip, in 1405, he took 317 vessels and 28,000 men, compared with Columbus' four boats and 150 sailors. The largest vessels in the Chinese fleets, the "treasure ships," were over four hundred feet—more than four times the length of Columbus' flagship, *Santa Maria*—and had nine masts. Each required so much wood that three hundred acres of forest were felled to build a single one. There were ships designed to carry horses, supplies, food, water, and, of course, troops. The smallest vessel in Zheng's flotilla, a highly maneuverable five-masted warship, was still twice as large as the legendary Spanish galleon.

The Chinese ships were constructed of special woods, intricate joints, sophisticated waterproofing techniques, and an adjustable centerboard keel. The treasure ships had large, luxurious cabins, silk sails, and windowed halls. All were constructed on dry docks in Nanjing, the world's largest and most advanced shipbuilding port. In the three years after 1405, 1,681 ships were built or refitted at Nanjing. Nothing remotely comparable could have happened in Europe at the time.

Size mattered. These massive fleets were meant to "shock and awe" the inhabitants of the surrounding area, making clear the power and reach of the Ming dynasty. On his seven voyages between 1405 and 1433, Zheng traveled widely through the waters of the Indian Ocean and around Southeast Asia. He gave gifts to the natives and accepted tributes. When encountering opposition, he did not hesitate to use military might. On one voyage, he brought back a captured Sumatran pirate; on another, a rebellions chief from Ceylon. He returned from all of them with flowers, fruits, precious stones, and exotic animals, including giraffes and zebras for the imperial zoo.

But Zheng's story ends oddly. By the 1430s, a new emperor had come to power. He abruptly ended the imperial expeditions and turned his back on trade and exploration. Some officials tried to keep the tradition going, but to no avail. In 1500, the court decreed that anyone who built a ship with more than two masts (the size required to go any distance at sea) would be executed. In 1525, coastal authorities were ordered to destroy any oceangoing vessels they encountered and throw the owners in prison. In 1551, it became a crime to go to sea on a multimast ship for any purpose. When the Qing dynasty came to power in 1644, it continued this basic policy, but it had less faith in decrees: instead, it simply scorched a 700-mile-long strip of China's southern coast, rendering it uninhabitable. These measures had the desired effect: China's shipping industry collapsed. In the decades after Zheng's last voyage, dozens of Western explorers traveled the waters around India and China. But it took three hundred years for a Chinese vessel to make its way to Europe—on a visit to London for the Great Exhibition of 1851.

What explains this remarkable turnaround? Beijing's new rulers considered the naval expeditions failures. They were extremely expensive, forced higher taxes on the people, and provided very little in return. Only traders and pirates benefited from the trade produced. Also, by the mid-fifteenth century, Mongols and other raiders threatened the empire's frontiers, demanding attention and consuming resources. Seafaring seemed like a costly distraction.

It was a fateful decision. Just as China chose to turn away from the outside world, Europe was venturing abroad, and it was Europe's navel expeditions that allowed it to energize itself and spread its power and influence across the globe. If China had kept its navy afloat, would the course of modern history have been different? Probably not. China's decision to turn inward was not simply one bad strategic call. It was an expression of a civilization's stagnation. Behind the decision to end the expeditions lay a whole complex of reasons why China and most of the non-Western world lagged behind the Western world for so many centuries. And lag they did. For hundreds of years after the fifteenth century, while Europe and the United States industrialized, urbanized, and modernized, the rest of the world remained poor and agricultural.

Write an essay in which you explain how Fareed Zakaria builds an argument to persuade his audience that *in the 15th century a regressive regime put an end to China's robust exploration of the world, thereby opening the way to centuries of Europe's leadership during the Age of Discovery.*

In your essay, analyze how Zakaria uses one or more of the features listed in the set of instructions for this essay (or features of your own choice) to strengthen the logic and persuasiveness of his argument. Be sure that your analysis focuses on the most relevant features of the passage.

Do not explain whether you agree or disagree with Zacaria's views. Rather, explain how Zacaria builds an argument to persuade his audience.

Self-Scoring Guide for Practice Essay #4

Before scoring your essay, let it sit for a day—or more, if possible. The passage of time will prepare you to read your essay with an open mind and a fresh pair of eyes.

After referring to "How Essays Are Scored" on page 305, use the chart below to help you evaluate your performance in each category: Reading, Analysis, and Writing.

Because a totally unbiased perspective on one's own writing requires amazing objectivity, you may get a more accurate evaluation of your essay by enlisting a trusted, well-informed friend or an experienced teacher to do it for you.

	Definitely!	Pretty Much	Only a Little	No
Reading				
Did you fully comprehend the source?	☐	☐	☐	☐
Is the author's central idea or claim accurately reported or summarized in your essay?	☐	☐	☐	☐
Have you discussed or alluded to the relationship between the central idea and various forms of evidence in the source?	☐	☐	☐	☐
Have you made reference to important details in the text using paraphrases, appropriate quotations, and/or your own words?	☐	☐	☐	☐
As far as you know, is your essay free from errors of fact and interpretation of the source?	☐	☐	☐	☐
Analysis				
Does your essay include an effective analysis of the source text?	☐	☐	☐	☐
Can you point out a place in your essay where you discuss the important claim made by the author of the source?	☐	☐	☐	☐
Can you identify a place where you point out facts, statistics, or the reports of experts that the author uses to support a claim?	☐	☐	☐	☐
Can you point to a place where you discuss the author's use of potent language or some other stylistic feature to build an argument?	☐	☐	☐	☐
Can you point to a place where you describe the author's use of reason to build an argument?	☐	☐	☐	☐
Can you point to a place where you identify an important rhetorical element of your own choice that the author uses to build an argument?	☐	☐	☐	☐

	Definitely!	Pretty Much	Only a Little	No
Can you point to one or more places where you have discussed the effect of a rhetorical element on a reader?	☐	☐	☐	☐
Writing				
Can you point to the place or places in your essay that states your essay's main idea?	☐	☐	☐	☐
Can you explain how you've arranged your ideas?	☐	☐	☐	☐
Does your essay include an introduction?	☐	☐	☐	☐
Is each paragraph related to the essay's main idea?	☐	☐	☐	☐
Are sentences varied in length and structure?	☐	☐	☐	☐
Have you used plain and precise words?	☐	☐	☐	☐
Do transitions tie paragraphs together and link sentences to each other?	☐	☐	☐	☐
Have you maintained a consistent style or tone throughout your essay?	☐	☐	☐	☐
As far as you know, does your essay adhere to the conventions of standard written English?	☐	☐	☐	☐
Total of checks in each column:				

Ratings skewed to the left mean your essay has earned scores in the 3–4 range, and vice-versa, right-leaning scores put you in the 1–2 range. Read the Self-Scoring Summary below for another way to interpret the numbers.

Self-Scoring Summary

READING

4 Thorough and perceptive comprehension of the source

3 Basically correct and adequate comprehension of the source

2 Partial or somewhat uncertain comprehension of the source

1 Minimal, confused, or absent comprehension of the source

ANALYSIS

4 Extremely thorough and insightful analysis and discussion of major and minor rhetorical elements.

3 Basically sound and relatively insightful analysis and discussion of important rhetorical elements

2 Fairly unfocused or shallow analysis of rhetorical elements with little discussion of each

1 Generally insufficient, erroneous, or nonexistent analysis of rhetorical elements

WRITING

4 Well-planned and fully developed; varied and engaging sentence structure; effective word choice; no consequential errors in grammar and usage

3 Reasonably well-organized and sufficiently developed; sufficiently varied sentence structure to create interest; minor sentence errors; ranges from competent to conventional word choice; mostly correct grammar and usage

2 Slightly disorganized; weak development with some relevant material; little sentence variety; sentence errors that may obscure meaning; essentially correct but with some errors in diction or idiom; basically correct grammar and usage but occasional major errors

1 Poor or no discernible organization; little or no development; serious sentence errors interfere with or obscure meaning; inappropriate word choices; meaning obscured or blocked by grammar and usage errors

PRACTICE ESSAY #5

Read the following passage carefully. Consider how the author Peter Singer

- uses evidence such as examples and facts to back up claims
- provides reasoning to connect claims and evidence to develop ideas
- uses stylistic or persuasive elements, such as word choice or emotional appeals meant to add power to expressed ideas

Do animals other than humans feel pain? How do we know? Well, how do we know if anyone, human or nonhuman, feels pain? We know that we ourselves can feel pain. We know this from the direct experience of pain that we have when, for instance, somebody presses a lighted cigarette against the back of our hand. But how do we know that anyone else feels pain? We cannot directly experience anyone else's pain. Behavior like writhing, screaming, or drawing one's hand away from the lighted cigarette is not pain itself. Pain is something that we feel, and we can only infer that others are feeling it from various external indications.

If it is justifiable to assume that other human beings feel pain, is there any reason why a similar inference should not be justifiable in the case of other animals?

Nearly all the external signs that lead us to infer pain in other humans can be seen in other species, especially the species most closely related to us—mammals and birds. The behavioral signs include writhing, facial contortions, moaning, yelping or other forms of calling, attempts to avoid the source of the pain, appearance of fear at the prospect of its repetition, and so on. In addition, we know that these animals have nervous systems very like ours, which respond physiologically like ours do to painful stimuli: an initial rise of blood pressure, dilated pupils, perspiration, an increased pulse rate, and, if the stimulus continues, a fall in blood pressure.

We also know that the nervous systems of other animals were not artificially constructed—as a robot might be artificially constructed—to mimic the pain behavior of humans. The nervous systems of animals evolved as our own did, and in fact the evolutionary history of human beings and other animals, especially mammals, did not diverge until the central features of our nervous systems were already in existence. A capacity to feel pain obviously enhances a species' prospects for survival, since it causes members of the species to avoid sources of injury. It is surely unreasonable to suppose that nervous systems that are virtually identical physiologically, have a common origin and a common evolutionary function, and result in similar forms of behavior in similar circumstances should actually operate in an entirely different manner on the level of subjective feelings.

The overwhelming majority of scientists who have addressed themselves to this question agree. Lord Brain, one of the most eminent neurologists of our time, has said:

> I personally can see no reason for conceding mind to my fellow men and denying it to animals. I at least cannot doubt that the interests and activities of animals are correlated with awareness and feeling in the same way as my own, and which may be, for aught I know, just as vivid.

The author of a book on pain writes:

Every particle of factual evidence supports the contention that the higher mammalian vertebrates experience pain sensations at least as acute as our own. To say that they feel less because they are lower animals is an absurdity; it can easily be shown that many of their senses are far more acute than ours—visual acuity in certain birds, hearing in most wild animals, and touch in others. Their nervous systems are almost identical to ours and their reactions to pain remarkably similar, though lacking (so far as we know) the philosophical and moral overtones. The emotional element is all too evident, mainly in the form of fear and anger.

That may well be thought enough to settle the matter; but one more objection needs to be considered.

There is a hazy line of philosophical thought, deriving perhaps from some doctrines associated with the influential philosopher Ludwig Wittgenstein, which maintains that we cannot meaningfully attribute states of consciousness to beings without language. This position seems to me very implausible. Language may be necessary for abstract thought, at some level anyway; but states like pain are more primitive, and have nothing to do with language. Human infants and young children are unable to use language. Are we to deny that a year-old child can suffer? If not, language cannot be crucial. [...]

So to conclude: there are no good reasons, scientific or philosophical, for denying that animals feel pain. If we do not doubt that other humans feel pain we should not doubt that other animals do so too.

Write an essay in which you explain how Peter Singer builds an argument to persuade his audience that *animals feel pain*. In your essay, analyze how Singer uses one or more of the features listed in the set of instructions for this essay (or use features of your own choice) to strengthen the logic and persuasiveness of his argument. Be sure to focus your analysis on the most relevant features of the passage.

Do not explain whether you agree or disagree with Singer's views. Rather, explain how Singer builds an argument to persuade his audience.

Self-Scoring Guide for Practice Essay #5

Before scoring your essay, let it sit for a day—or more, if possible. The passage of time will prepare you to read your essay with an open mind and a fresh pair of eyes.

After referring to "How Essays Are Scored" on page 305, use the chart below to help you evaluate your performance in each category: Reading, Analysis, and Writing.

Because a totally unbiased perspective on one's own writing requires amazing objectivity, you may get a more accurate evaluation of your essay by enlisting a trusted, well-informed friend or an experienced teacher to do it for you.

	Definitely!	Pretty Much	Only a Little	No
Reading				
Did you fully comprehend the source?	☐	☐	☐	☐
Is the author's central idea or claim accurately reported or summarized in your essay?	☐	☐	☐	☐
Have you discussed or alluded to the relationship between the central idea and various forms of evidence in the source?	☐	☐	☐	☐
Have you made reference to important details in the text using paraphrases, appropriate quotations, and/or your own words?	☐	☐	☐	☐
As far as you know, is your essay free from errors of fact and interpretation of the source?	☐	☐	☐	☐
Analysis				
Does your essay include an effective analysis of the source text?	☐	☐	☐	☐
Can you point out a place in your essay where you discuss the important claim made by the author of the source?	☐	☐	☐	☐
Can you identify a place where you point out facts, statistics, or the reports of experts that the author uses to support a claim?	☐	☐	☐	☐
Can you point to a place where you discuss the author's use of potent language or some other stylistic feature to build an argument?	☐	☐	☐	☐
Can you point to a place where you describe the author's use of reason to build an argument?	☐	☐	☐	☐
Can you point to a place where you identify an important rhetorical element of your own choice that the author uses to build an argument?	☐	☐	☐	☐

	Definitely!	Pretty Much	Only a Little	No
Can you point to one or more places where you have discussed the effect of a rhetorical element on a reader?	☐	☐	☐	☐
Writing				
Can you point to the place or places in your essay that states your essay's main idea?	☐	☐	☐	☐
Can you explain how you've arranged your ideas?	☐	☐	☐	☐
Does your essay include an introduction?	☐	☐	☐	☐
Is each paragraph related to the essay's main idea?	☐	☐	☐	☐
Are sentences varied in length and structure?	☐	☐	☐	☐
Have you used plain and precise words?	☐	☐	☐	☐
Do transitions tie paragraphs together and link sentences to each other?	☐	☐	☐	☐
Have you maintained a consistent style or tone throughout your essay?	☐	☐	☐	☐
As far as you know, does your essay adhere to the conventions of standard written English?	☐	☐	☐	☐
Total of checks in each column:				

Ratings skewed to the left mean your essay has earned scores in the 3–4 range, and vice-versa, right-leaning scores put you in the 1–2 range. Read the Self-Scoring Summary below for another way to interpret the numbers.

Self-Scoring Summary

READING

4 Thorough and perceptive comprehension of the source

3 Basically correct and adequate comprehension of the source

2 Partial or somewhat uncertain comprehension of the source

1 Minimal, confused, or absent comprehension of the source

ANALYSIS

4 Extremely thorough and insightful analysis and discussion of major and minor rhetorical elements

3 Basically sound and relatively insightful analysis and discussion of important rhetorical elements

2 Fairly unfocused or shallow analysis of rhetorical elements with little discussion of each

1 Generally insufficient, erroneous, or nonexistent analysis of rhetorical elements

WRITING

4 Well-planned and fully developed; varied and engaging sentence structure; effective word choice; no consequential errors in grammar and usage

3 Reasonably well-organized and sufficiently developed; sufficiently varied sentence structure to create interest; minor sentence errors; ranges from competent to conventional word choice; mostly correct grammar and usage

2 Slightly disorganized; weak development with some relevant material; little sentence variety; sentence errors that may obscure meaning; essentially correct but with some errors in diction or idiom; basically correct grammar and usage but occasional major errors

1 Poor or no discernible organization; little or no development; serious sentence errors interfere with or obscure meaning; inappropriate word choices; meaning obscured or blocked by grammar and usage errors

Index

A

Accuracy of evidence, 223
Active sentences, 54–56
Active verbs, 54
Addresses, 61
Adjective clauses, 35
Adjective phrases, 293
Adjectives, 293
Adverbial clauses, 35
Adverbial phrases, 293
Adverbs, 293
Anecdote, 206
Annotation
   description of, 228–229, 232
   examples of, 229–232
   practice in, 233–256
   sample, 233–235, 373–376
   source analysis, 233–235
Antecedents, 81–84
Apostrophes, 59
Appositives, 61
Argument, refuting of opposition's views to strengthen, 219
Augmenting, of sentences, 41–44
Awkwardness, 30–31

B

Believability of evidence, 222–223
Brief story, 206

C

Capitalization, 64–66
Chart, data interpretation from, 23–24
Claims
   description of, 204–205
   evidence and, 209–210
   facts to support, 261
   reasoning to connect, 207–210
   secondary, 207
   subclaims, 207
Clauses, 34–37, 288
   adjective, 35
   adverbial, 35
   dependent, 34–35, 47–48, 289, 293
   independent, 34, 288

   main, 288
   noun, 35
   parallel, 290
   subordinate, 288
Clichés, 286
Coherence of sentences, 9–12
Collective nouns, 68
Commas, 59–64
Comma splices, 33, 38–39
Comparative degree, of comparisons, 88
Comparisons
   comparative degree of, 88
   degrees of, 87–88
   illogical, 89–92
   incomplete, 88–89
   positive degree of, 88
   superlative degree of, 88
   writing of, 284–287
Complex sentence, 288
Compound sentence, 61, 288
Compound subjects, 66
Conclusion of essay, 295, 297
Conjunctions, 37, 47, 293
Connotation of words, 214–215
Contractions, 59
Coordination, in sentences, 47–50
Counterclaims, 209
Creative writing, 284

D

Dangling modifiers, 57–59
Data interpretation, 23–24
Dates, 61
Declarative sentences, 290
Denotation of words, 214
Dependent clauses, 34–35, 47–48, 289, 293
Dialogue, 61–62
Diction, 212
Disjointed paragraphs, 20

E

Editing, 298–299
Ellipsis, 279
Emotional appeal, 215–217

Essay. *See* SAT Essay
Euphemisms, 281
Evidence
    accuracy of, 223
    anecdote as, 206
    believability of, 222–223
    brief story as, 206
    claims and, 209–210
    development of ideas using, 210–212
    emotional appeal, 215–217
    examples as, 204–206
    facts as, 204–206
    features of your choice, 217–222
    finding of, 204–222
    reaching out to readers, 220
    reasoning to connect claims, 207–210
    refuting of opposition's views, 219
    relevant features, 221–222
    repetition, 218–219
    screening of, 222–228
    secondary, 211
    storytelling, 220–221
    sufficiency of, 222
    word choice, 212–215
Examples, 204–206
Exclamatory sentence, 290
Expression questions, 24–33

F
Facts, 204–206
First-person pronouns, 81
4/4/4 essay, 258–261
Fragments, sentence, 33–36, 75

G
Gerund, 79
Grammar, 5
Graph, data interpretation from, 23–24

H
Helping verbs, 75

I
Ideas
    evidence used to develop, 210–212
    main, 6–9
    purposeful arrangement of, 268–271
    repetition of, 291–292
Idiom, standard, 25–28
Illogical comparisons, 89–92
Imperative sentences, 290
Incomplete comparisons, 88–89
Indefinite pronouns, 68, 81
Independent clauses, 34, 288

Infinitives, 289, 293
Interrogative sentences, 290
Introduction, 271–272
Inversions, 293
Irony, 222
Irregular verbs, 75

L
Language, 280–287
Long sentences, 292–293

M
Main clause, 288
Main idea, 6–9
Metaphors, 284–285
Misplaced modifiers, 56–59
Mixed construction, 44–47
Modifiers
    dangling, 57–59
    definition of, 56
    misplaced, 56–59

N
Nominative case pronouns, 78
Nonfiction narratives, 3
Noun(s), 34
    collective, 68
    possessive, 59
    proper, 64
    singular, 67, 82
    verb and, agreement between, 66–72
Noun clauses, 35

O
Objective case pronouns, 78–79
Organization
    data interpretation, 23–24
    evidence to support claims, 12–21
    main idea, 6–9
    questions on, 6–24
    sequence/coherence, 9–12
    supporting sentences, 12–13
    topic sentences, 12–21, 273–274
    transitions, 21–23
Outline, for essay, 261–268

P
Paragraphs
    closing of, 203
    coherence of, 276–279
    development of, 274–276
    disjointed, 20, 274
    opening of, 203

sentences in, 20
   supporting sentences of, 273–274
   topic sentence of, 12–21, 273–274
   unity of, 276–279
Parallel clauses, 290
Parallelism, 45
Parallel structure, 50–53
Participles, 289, 293
Passive sentences, 54–56
Passive verbs, 54
Past perfect progressive verb, 73
Place names, 61, 64
Plural verbs, 68
Positive degree, of comparisons, 88
Possessive nouns, 59
Possessive pronouns, 77–78
Predicate, 33–34, 290
Prepositional phrases, 289, 293
Prewriting, 259
Prompt, 260
Pronoun(s)
   antecedents and, 81–84
   case of, 77–82
   choice of, 77–82
   description of, 34
   first-person, 81
   indefinite, 68, 81
   nominative case, 78
   objective case, 78–79
   possessive, 77–78
   second-person, 81
   in subject, 67
   third-person, 81
Pronoun reference, 84–87
Proofreading, 298–299
Proper nouns, 64
Punctuation, 59–64
Purpose, 6–9

Q

Questions
   answering of, 4–5
   awkwardness, 30–31
   main idea, 6–9
   organization-specific, 6–24
   redundancy, 31–33
   repetition, 31–33
   sample, 5
   sentences-related, 33–66
   sequence/coherence, 9–12
   style- and expression-specific, 24–33
   transitions, 21–23
   wordiness, 28–30
   words-in-context, 24–28
Quotation marks, 62

R

Reaching out to readers, 220
Reading power, 202–204
Reading the source, 201–204
Redundancy, 31–33
Refuting of opposition's views, 219
Repetition, 218–219
   of ideas, 291–292
   questions about, 31–33
   of sounds, 284
Rhetorical strategies, 260–261
Run-on sentences, 33, 37–38

S

SAT, vii
SAT Essay
   conclusion of, 295, 297
   description of, vii
   editing of, 298–299
   ending of, 295–298
   formula for, 269
   ideas, 268–271
   introduction of, 271–272
   language used in, 280–287
   outline for, 261–268
   paragraphs. *See* Paragraphs
   practice, 342–371
   proofreading of, 298–299
   reading of, 305
   samples, 307–340
   scoring of, 305–307
   sentences. *See* Sentence(s)
   stylistic conventions of, 279
SAT Writing and Language Test
   overview of, vii–viii
   questions on. *See* Questions
Scoring, of essays, 305–307
Secondary claim, 207
Secondary evidence, 211
Second-person pronouns, 81
Semicolons, 37, 63–64
Sentence(s)
   active, 54–56
   augmenting of, 41–44
   "bare bones" of, 36
   capitalization in, 64–66
   clauses, 34–37, 288
   coherence of, 9–12
   combining of, 41–43
   commas in, 59–64
   comma splices in, 33, 38–39
   complex, 288
   compound, 61, 288
   coordination in, 47–50
   dangling modifiers in, 57–59

declarative, 290
definition of, 33
exclamatory, 290
imperative, 290
interrogative, 290
long, 292–293
misplaced modifiers in, 56–59
mixed construction in, 44–47
parallel structure in, 50–53
passive, 54–56
predicate of, 33–34, 290
punctuation, 59–64
questions on, 33–66
run-on, 33, 37–38
sequencing of, 9–12
short, 292–293
simple, 288
structure of, 288–290
subject of, 33–34
subordination in, 47, 49–50
supporting, 12–13, 273–274
topic, 12–21, 273–274
types of, 290
varying of, 293–295
Sentence fragments, 33–36, 75
Sequencing of sentences, 9–12
Series, 61
Short sentences, 292–293
Similes, 285
Simple sentence, 288
Singular nouns, 67, 82
Sounds, repetition of, 284
Standard idiom, 25–28
Storytelling, 220–221
Style questions, 24–33
Stylistic conventions, 279
Subclaims, 207
Subject
    compound, 66
    description of, 33–34
    verb and, agreement between, 66–72, 291
Subordinate clause, 288

Subordinating conjunction, 49
Subordination, in sentences, 47, 49–50
Sufficiency of evidence, 222
Superlative degree, of comparisons, 88
Supporting sentences, 12–13, 273–274

T
Table, data interpretation from, 23–24
Tenses, verb, 72–75
Third-person pronouns, 81
Topic sentences, 12–21, 273–274
Transitions, 21–23

V
Verb(s)
    active, 54
    forms of, 75–77
    helping, 75
    irregular, 75
    noun and, agreement between, 66–72, 291
    passive, 54
    past perfect progressive tense of, 73
    past tense of, 72
    plural, 68
    progressive tense of, 72
    singular, 67–68
    tenses of, 72–75
Verbal infinitives, 293
Verbals, 289
Verbal surprise, 284

W
Word(s)
    choice of, 212–215
    connotation of, 214–215
    denotation of, 214
    precise, 281–283
Wordiness, 28–30
Words-in-context questions, 24–28
Writing preparation
    evidence. *See* Evidence
    reading the source, 201–204